K5

BIBLE TRUTHS

for Christian Schools™

Tea

MW00605733

BJU PRESS

GREENVILLE, SOUTH CAROLINA

Consultants
from the administration, faculty, and staff of Bob Jones University
  Philip D. Smith, Ed.D., Provost
  Dorothy Buckley, Elementary Authors Coordinator, BJU Press
  Bryan Smith, Ph.D., Secondary Authors, BJU Press

NOTE:
The fact that materials produced by other publishers may be referred to in this volume does not constitute an endorsement by BJU Press of the content or theological position of materials produced by such publishers. The position of BJU Press, and of the University itself, is well known. Any references and ancillary materials are listed as an aid to the student or the teacher and in an attempt to maintain the accepted academic standards of the publishing industry.

BIBLE TRUTHS K5 for Christian Schools™ Teacher's Edition

Second Edition

Coordinating Author Susan J. Lehman	**Project Manager** Vic Ludlum	**Illustrators** Matt Bjerk	**Photo Acquisition** Joyce Landis
Author Lucille Fisher	**Project Editor** Debbie L. Parker	Douglas Chaffee Paula Cheadle Johanna Ehnis	
Contributing Authors Kathleen Hynicka Susan J. Lehman	**Computer Formatting** Carol Larson	Preston Gravely Jim Hargis Nathan Kirsop	
Student Packet Authors Lucille Fisher Kathleen Hynicka	**Graphics Coordinator and Designer** Wendy Searles	Mary Ann Lumm Keith Neeley Lynda Slattery	
	Contributing Designer John Bjerk	Del Thompson Dan Van Leeuwen	

Acknowledgments:
Alice M. Knight, *1,001 Stories for Children and Children's Workers,* © 1952, 1980
Wm. B. Eerdmans Publishing Co., Grand Rapids, MI. Used by permission.

Photo credits for cover and title page: Comstock Images

Jeep is a registered trademark of DaimlerChrysler.
Jell-O is a registered trademark of Kraft Food service.
Kleenex is a registered trademark of Kimberly-Clark Worldwide, Inc.

Produced in cooperation with the Bob Jones University School of Education and Bob Jones Elementary School.

© 1989, 2004 BJU Press
Greenville, South Carolina 29614

First Edition © 1987 BJU Press

for Christian Schools is a registered trademark of BJU Press.

Printed in the United States of America

ISBN 1-59166-239-7

15 14 13 12 11 10 9 8 7 6 5 4 3 2

We asked customers what they were looking for in their teaching materials.

You told us.

I AM Looking For TEACHER's EdiTioNs

☑ THAT ARE EASY TO USE
☑ AIM AT TEACHING Comprehension
☑ Improve TEST Scores
☑ HAVE loTs of TEACHING IDEAS
☑ HELP ME REACH DiffeRent learning styles
☑ HAVE four-color throughout
☑ ARE Reasonably Priced

I WANT STUDENT BOOKS

☑ THAT HAVE On-grade activities
☑ Challenging Information
☑ engaging presentations
☑ photographs
☑ lots of color everywhere

We listened.

And we did as you asked. We think you will like what you see in this book. Enjoy your teaching. We're still listening; contact us any time.

BJU PRESS

1.800.845.5731
www.bjup.com

Contents

Introduction

Teaching Children to Live the Bible as Well as Know the Bible

Success has been defined as finding God's will and doing it. At what other time can you more effectively teach children how to be successful, productive servants of their Heavenly Father than during your Bible lesson?

As you use these materials, ask the Lord to help you successfully present the doctrines, principles, and basic Bible knowledge contained in them. Above all, seek to instill into the heart and mind of each child a desire to know Christ as his personal Savior and to obey and serve Him faithfully—to know, to do, and to love God's way.

Bible Truths K5 for Christian Schools . . .

⬤ **Teaches that the Bible is God's Word**

- Students are taught that Bible accounts are fact.

- The Bible is used as the final authority in all guided discussions.

⬤ **Aids students in recognizing their need of Christ as personal Savior**

- Lessons emphasize God's dealing with His people and the need of every individual to be saved.

- Students learn how to share the plan of salvation with others.

⬤ **Encourages Christlikeness in students**

- Application stories teach students by example which behaviors please and displease God.

- Students learn which steps of Christian obedience follow salvation.

⬤ **Instills a desire in students to know more about God**

- As students learn about the Word of God, they also learn about the God of the Word.

- Discussion questions after each Bible account focus on what the account teaches.

⬤ **Encourages students to apply Bible knowledge to their daily lives**

- Students study the principles found in the memory verses.

- Students learn that God's Word has relevance to every part of their lives.

Instructional Materials

Student Materials

Student Packet

The Student Packet contains a colorful variety of activity pages designed to reinforce the Bible lessons and review memory verses. Cutouts for cutting and gluing activities are located at the back of the Student Packet. Other activities include completing dot-to-dot pictures and making picture books. Four student booklets are included for teaching about Samuel, Creation, Thanksgiving, and the person of God. The memory verse reminders may be sent home as a reference for parents.

Miscellaneous school supplies

Each student will need standard school supplies: a Bible (optional at K5 level), crayons, pencils, scissors, and glue.

Teacher Materials

Teacher's Edition

Recognizing God's Word as our primary source and guide in preparing and teaching Bible lessons, the Teacher's Edition is the heart of this Bible program. The 160 daily lessons are organized into fifteen units. Thanksgiving, Christmas, and Easter units are included and should be taught at the appropriate times of the year.

Each lesson begins with a Bible text for the teacher to read and study in preparation for teaching the lesson. Also listed are the doctrinal truths taught, character traits emphasized, verses memorized, catechism introduced and reviewed, and materials needed to teach the lesson. Character stories and application questions and discussions help students understand who God is and the importance of living His way.

The Appendix includes the Bible Action Truths with key Scripture verses. This section provides the teacher with a useful reference tool for identifying and applying principles of behavior. Lists of the twenty-five memory verse references and fifty catechism questions and answers are also provided as useful reference tools.

The Songs section and the Index of Poetry aid the teacher in locating the hymns, songs, action rhymes, and poems used in the lessons. These are also useful in program planning. Music is provided for the hymns and songs included in the lessons.

The Teaching Materials (reproducible pages for making visuals) aid the teacher in presenting lessons. A bulletin board for each unit provides the teacher with an optional teaching aid that emphasizes the unit theme.

CD

The recording includes the hymns and songs, with accompaniment, to be sung during the Bible lessons.

Visual Packets

The *Bible Truths K5 Picture Packet* contains colorful Bible-story pictures to be used as visuals while teaching many of the lessons. The visuals may also be used for classroom display

The *Days of Creation* packet colorfully illustrates each day of Creation. An illustration of a church is included to represent the seventh day and emphasize the importance of worshiping our Creator. These visuals are designed for use in teaching the lessons and for classroom display. The cover provides miniatures of the visuals for use in review activities.

Teaching Tips

⬤ Use of Lessons

Everything that occurs during the twenty- to thirty-minute Bible lesson each day should point to your objectives for that lesson, the unit, and the entire year—repeating, reinforcing, and extending your immediate and long-range goals. The 160 lessons of this teacher's edition are organized into fifteen units designed for this purpose. The number of lessons you will be able to use depends upon the number of times each week you have a Bible lesson.

The following units may be inserted into your schedule before each vacation period. After each vacation, return to your regular lesson order.

Thanksgiving, Unit 7, Lessons 70–73 (four lessons)
Christmas, Unit 8, Lessons 74–81 (eight lessons)
Easter, Unit 11, Lessons 124–129 (six lessons)

Consider this teacher's edition a guide to your teaching. You must adapt the lessons to your time schedule. To shorten a particular lesson, you may occasionally omit some of the suggested songs and a review activity or use the student activity page as a separate lesson. You may also combine elements of two lessons or omit an entire review lesson from time to time. For example, if your class meets with the entire school for chapel once or twice a week, you will certainly not have enough time to include all the review lessons. You could, however, use the character stories contained in many of these review lessons for a quiet listening time after recess or for a story time at the end of the day. Acquainting yourself with all the material in this teacher's edition before the school year begins will assist you in effectively tailoring it to your class needs.

⬤ Use of Student Pages

The purpose of the activity pages from the Student Packet is to reinforce the Bible lessons and to review the memory verses in the lessons. These activities will also carry home a gospel testimony to the unsaved parent and an opportunity for parent and child to review the lessons together.

The text on these pages is included primarily to assist the teacher and parent in review. You may, however, encourage the children to "read" the text along with you.

Completed student activity pages are suggested as teaching visuals for some lessons.

Overview of a Lesson Plan

Bible text
Each lesson provides Scripture references to study in preparation for teaching the lesson.
- Teach the lesson with your Bible open to the Scripture reference.
- Remind the children that the Bible is our main source and guide.
- Use words from the Bible whenever possible.

Doctrinal truths
Bible doctrines are emphasized as they correlate with the lessons.
- Provide a strong foundation in the basic beliefs of Christian faith.
- Introduce basic truths and principles of the doctrines: the Bible, God, Man, Salvation, the Church, Angels and Satan, and the End Times.

Character traits
Qualities of Christian character are developed through the application of Bible knowledge.
- Establish Christian character through the use of Bible Action Truths (BATs).
- Teach the children that ultimate truth comes from God's Word, its standards, and its authority.

Memory verses
The twenty-five Scripture passages help make God's Word meaningful in the children's everyday experiences.
- Relate the verses to doctrines, Bible accounts, and character stories.
- Use the verses in conversation, in song, and in review as the occasion arises.
- Adjust the amount of required memorization to meet the needs and abilities of individual students.
- Send home the verse reminder, as a reference for the parent, after the verse has been introduced and reviewed.

Catechism
The fifty questions and answers provide a strong foundation for what a person believes and why he believes it.
- Relate each catechism question to the Bible lesson.
- Apply the catechism questions to everyday life.
- Recite catechism in a variety of appropriate situations, such as in the context of the Bible lesson, character story, verse memorization, and song.

Songs
The song selections teach the application of Bible truths.
- Introduce songs and hymns that encourage worship, inspiration, and growth in the Christian life.
- Reinforce Bible lesson objectives.
- Teach words from Scripture.

Prayer
Prayer is an integral part of each lesson.
- Teach what prayer is.
- Emphasize that God answers prayer.
- Allow children to share prayer requests occasionally.

Leading a Child to the Lord

One of the greatest desires of Christian teachers is to lead their students to the Savior. To instill in each child a desire to know Christ as his personal Savior is a great responsibility and joy.

Take advantage of opportunities that arise during lessons for presenting the plan of salvation, relying on the Holy Spirit to reach the conscience of each child. Encourage students to talk with you individually about accepting Christ and be alert to their individual needs. You may find the following outline (based on the Romans Road) helpful.

1. I have sinned. (Romans 3:23)

- I disobey God's Word (e.g., disobeying my parents, taking things that do not belong to me, saying unkind words to others).

- My sin must be punished. (Romans 6:23)

- I cannot get rid of my sin by myself.

2. Christ died for my sin. (Romans 5:8)

- God is holy and cannot sin.

- God loves me and sent Jesus Christ to die on the cross for my sins.

- I may decide to ask Jesus to forgive me of my sins and to be my Savior. It is my choice. (Romans 10:9–10)

3. I receive God's gift of salvation. (Romans 10:13)

- If I turn from my sin and believe Jesus died for me, I become a child of God.

- As God's child, I will live forever in heaven.

- Salvation is a gift of God. (Romans 6:23)

When talking individually with a child, ask questions to discern sincerity or any misunderstanding. (What is sin? Have you sinned? Why did God send Jesus?) Read the Scripture from your Bible. Ask the child, "Do you choose to accept Jesus as your Savior from sin?" If that is the child's desire, read John 1:12 to him.

When a child shows genuine readiness, ask him to pray. Sometimes children are unsure how to pray. When you ask a child whether he would like to repeat after you, be sure he understands and agrees with your words.

> Dear God, I know you love me. I know You sent Your Son Jesus to die for me. I know I am a sinner. I believe Jesus died for my sins. I ask Jesus to be my Savior from sin today. In Jesus' name I pray. Amen.

Show the child how to know from God's Word that he is in God's family (I John 5:12–13). Encourage him to obey God's Word. Point out that he can have God's forgiveness when he sins again (I John 1:9).

Table of Lesson Plans

Lesson Title	Lesson Number	Lesson Pages	Student Pages	Doctrinal Truths	Memory Verses
UNIT 1 GOD'S WORD *The Bible: God Speaks to Me*					
God Talked to a Boy Long Ago *I Samuel 3:1–18*	1	1–2		Bible	
Samuel Listened to God's Word *I Samuel 3*	2	2–4		Bible	Psalm 25:4
God Talked to Others Long Ago *II Peter 1:21; I Peter 1:24–25; Psalm 119:11*	3	4–5		Bible (inspiration)	
God Talks to Us Today in the Bible *Review*	4	5–7		Bible	
The Bible Is the Best Book *Review; Jeremiah 33:3*	5	7–8	1	Bible	
UNIT 2 GOD'S WORLD *Creation: God Made Me*					
First Day of Creation—Day and Night *Genesis 1:1–5*	6	9–10		God (existence, omnipotence)	Genesis 1:1
Second Day of Creation—Sky, Air, and Waters *Genesis 1:6–8*	7	10–11		God (existence, omnipotence)	Psalm 95:6
Third Day of Creation—Land and Seas *Genesis 1:9–13*	8	11–12		God (omnipotence, omniscience)	
Review—First Through Third Days of Creation *Genesis 1:1–13*	9	12	2	God (omnipotence, omniscience)	
Fourth Day of Creation—Sun, Moon, and Stars *Genesis 1:14–19*	10	13–14		God (omniscience)	
Fifth Day of Creation—Fish and Birds *Genesis 1:20–23*	11	14–15		God (omniscience, omnipotence)	
Sixth Day of Creation—Animals and Man *Genesis 1:24–31; Psalm 31:14*	12	15–16		God (omniscience, omnipotence)	
We Know God Is *Exodus 20:1–5; I Timothy 2:5*	13	16–17		God (existence)	
For His Glory *Psalm 69:34; Psalm 19:1; Psalms 148, 150*	14	17–18		God (His works)	
Review—Days of Creation *Genesis 1–2*	15	18	3	God	
God Rested *Genesis 1:31–2:3*	16	18–19		God Church	
We Worship God *Psalm 122:1*	17	19–20	4	God Church	
Kate Learns from a Squirrel *Review*	18	20–21		God	

Lesson Title	Lesson Number	Lesson Pages	Student Pages	Doctrinal Truths	Memory Verses
UNIT 3 **GOD'S LOVE** *Sin and Salvation: God Sees My Sin*					
Adam and Eve *Genesis 2:7–25*	19	23–24		Man Salvation	Romans 3:23
Adam and Eve Disobeyed God *Genesis 3:1–13*	20	24–25		Fall of man Satan	
The Children of Adam and Eve *Genesis 4:1–2*	21	25–26		Man	
The Children of Adam and Eve Disobeyed *Genesis 4:3–16*	22	26–27	5	Man	
What Sin Is *Genesis 4:3–16; I John 3:4*	23	27–28	6	Salvation	
Kate's Special Memory *Review*	24	29–30		Salvation	
Noah's Family Obeyed *Genesis 6:1–9, 17*	25	30–32	7	Salvation	
Sin Must Be Punished *Review*	26	32–33		Sin and salvation	Psalm 37:27
UNIT 4 **GOD'S FRIEND** *Abraham: I Love God*					
Abram's Call *Genesis 12; II Chronicles 20:7; James 2:23*	27	35–36		God	
Abram's Kindness *Genesis 13:1–12*	28	36–37		God (attributes of)	
Abram's Courage *Genesis 14:1–2, 11–24*	29	37–38		God	Proverbs 3:5–6
Abraham's Trust *Genesis 15-17*	30	39–40		God	
Abraham's Friend *Genesis 18*	31	40–41		God (faithfulness)	
Abraham and Sarah *Review*	32	41	8	God (faithfulness)	
Abraham's Prayer *Genesis 18–19*	33	42–43		Sin	
Abraham's Obedience *Genesis 22:1–19*	34	43–44	9	God	
A Servant's Prayer *Genesis 24:1–28*	35	44–45		Salvation (prayer)	
Isaac's Wife *Genesis 24:29–67*	36	45–46		God (attributes of)	
Jacob's Dream *Genesis 28:1–5, 10–22*	37	46–47		God Angels Satan	
God Is My Friend *Review*	38	47–48		God	
Review—Abraham *Review*	39	48–49	10	God (faithfulness)	

Lesson Title	Lesson Number	Lesson Pages	Student Pages	Doctrinal Truths	Memory Verses
UNIT 5 GOD'S CARE *Joseph: I Trust God*					
Joseph Obeyed *Genesis 37:1–11*	40	51–52		God (sovereignty)	I Thessalonians 5:18
Joseph's Brothers Disobeyed *Genesis 37:12–35*	41	52–53		God (sovereignty)	
God's Enemy *Isaiah 14:12–17*	42	53–54		Satan	
Joseph Trusted God *Genesis 39*	43	54–55		Satan	
Joseph in Jail *Genesis 40–41*	44	55–57	11	God (sovereignty)	
Joseph in the King's Palace *Genesis 41–42*	45	57–58		God (sovereignty)	
Joseph's Family United *Genesis 42–46*	46	58–59		God (sovereignty)	
God Cared for Joseph *Review*	47	60	12	God (sovereignty)	
God Cares for Me *Review*	48	61	13	God (omnipresence)	
God Cared for Sam *Review*	49	61–62		God (sovereignty)	
UNIT 6 GOD'S LEADER *Moses: I Obey God's Word*					
A New King *Exodus 1:8–22*	50	63–64		Man Salvation (repentance)	
A Baby in the Bulrushes *Exodus 1:22–2:10*	51	64–65	14	God (sovereignty)	Ecclesiastes 12:13b
A Burning Bush *Exodus 3–4*	52	65–67		God (omnipotence, faithfulness)	
A Stubborn Pharaoh *Exodus 5–7*	53	67–68		God (omnipotence, omniscience)	
God's Miracles in Egypt *Exodus 8–10*	54	68–70		God (omnipotence)	
God's Final Plague *Exodus 11–13:19*	55	70–71		God (omnipotence)	
The Red Sea *Exodus 13:17–14:31*	56	71–72	15	God (omnipotence)	
Review—Moses (Birth to Red Sea) *Exodus 1–15*	57	73	16	God	
Review—Moses (Birth to Red Sea) *Exodus 1–15*	58	73–74		God	
Trust and Obey *Exodus 15:22–27*	59	74–75		God (faithfulness, omnipotence)	
Manna from Heaven *Exodus 16*	60	75–76		God (faithfulness) Salvation (repentance)	Psalm 38:18

Lesson Title	Lesson Number	Lesson Pages	Student Pages	Doctrinal Truths	Memory Verses
Mount Sinai *Exodus 19–20*	61	76–77	17	God Bible	
The Golden Calf *Exodus 24–34*	62	77–78		Bible Salvation (repentance)	
The Tabernacle *Exodus 25–31; Leviticus 1–9*	63	78–79		Church	
Spies in the Land *Numbers 13–14*	64	80–81		God	
Moses' and Aaron's Sin *Numbers 20:1–13*	65	81–82		Salvation (repentance)	
God Took Moses *Numbers 27:12–14; Deuteronomy 31–34*	66	82–83		God	
Review—Moses' Life *Exodus 1–40; Numbers 13–14, 20, 27*	67	83	18	God	
Josh Is Sorry for His Sin *Review*	68	83–85		Salvation (repentance)	
Review—God's Law *Review*	69	85–86	19	God Bible Salvation	
UNIT 7 GOD'S GIFTS *Thanksgiving: I Praise God*					
O Give Thanks unto the Lord *Psalm 105*	70	88–89	20–21	God (sovereignty)	Psalm 100
Our Great Provider *James 1:17; Psalm 107:8*	71	89–90		God	
Turkey for Thanksgiving *Jeremiah 33:3; Philippians 4:19*	72	90–91	22	God	
Our Thanksgiving Psalm *Psalm 100*	73	91–92		God	
UNIT 8 GOD'S BEST GIFT *Christmas: I Thank God*					
God Planned for Our Saviour *Luke 1:26–38*	74	93–94		God the Son Salvation	John 3:16
God Sent His Messenger *Luke 1:26–38; Psalm 106:1; I John 4:9b*	75	94–95		Salvation Angels	Luke 2:11
God Sent His Son *Matthew 1:20–21; Luke 2:1–7*	76	95–96	23	God the Son Salvation	
Angel Messengers Told of the Way *Luke 2:8–20*	77	96–97		God the Son Angels Church	
Wise Men Brought Gifts *Matthew 2:1–23*	78	97–98		Salvation (sanctification)	
Christmas Brings Joy *Matthew 1:20, 21; 2:1–11; Luke 1:26–28; 2:1–20*	79	98–99		God the Son Salvation	
The Best Birthday *Review*	80	99–100	24	God the Son	
Review—Christmas *Review*	81	101	25	God the Son	

Lesson Title	Lesson Number	Lesson Pages	Student Pages	Doctrinal Truths	Memory Verses
UNIT 9 GOD'S HELPERS *Joshua to Jonah: I Will Help*					
Captain Joshua *Joshua 1–4*	82	103–4		God (omnipotence)	Joshua 1:9
Battle of Jericho *Joshua 5:13–6:20*	83	104–5		God	
Joshua and the Battle of Jericho *Joshua 1–6*	84	105–6	26	God	
David, the Shepherd *I Samuel 16:11; 17:34–36; Psalm 23; John 10:3–5*	85	106–7		God (faithfulness)	Psalm 23:1
David Anointed *I Samuel 16:1–13*	86	107–8		God (sovereignty)	Psalm 23:2
Brave David *I Samuel 17*	87	109–10	27	God	Psalm 23:3
David's Friend *I Samuel 18:1–9, 28–30; 19:10, 20; II Samuel 1:4*	88	110–11		God	Psalm 23:4
The Twenty-Third Psalm *Psalm 23*	89	111–12	28–30	Salvation	Psalm 23:5–6
Review—Our Loving Shepherd *Psalm 23; John 10:3–5; Luke 15:4–6*	90	112–13		Salvation	
God's Word Was Found *II Kings 22:1–20; 23:1–3; II Chronicles 34:1–33*	91	114–15		Bible	
The Lost Book Was Found *II Kings 22:1–20; 23:1–3; II Chronicles 34:1–33*	92	115		Bible	
God Delivered Three Men *Daniel 1; 3:1–28*	93	115–16		God (omnipotence)	
God Delivered Daniel *Daniel 6:1–23*	94	116–17		Angels	
Review—Delivered from Lions *Daniel 6:1–23*	95	117–19	31	Angels	
God Sent a Big Fish *Jonah 1–3*	96	119–20		God Salvation (repentance)	
Kate Is Sorry *Review*	97	120–22	32	God Salvation (repentance)	
UNIT 10 GOD'S SON *Life of Christ: I Believe Jesus Is God*					
Who God Is *Genesis 1:1; John 1:14; Psalm 19:1*	98	123		Bible God the Son Salvation	
The Boy Jesus Listened *Luke 2:40–52*	99	124–25		God Salvation	John 10:30
Jesus Was Baptized *Matthew 3:1–17; Mark 1:9–11; John 1:19–34*	100	125–26		God the Son	
Jesus Is God *Genesis 1:1; John 1:14; Psalm 19:1*	101	126–27		God the Son	
Jesus Obeyed the Father *Matthew 4:11; Mark 1:12–13; Luke 4:1–13; I John 2:16*	102	127–28		Angels Satan	
The Tempter *Matthew 13:39; John 8:44; I Peter 5:8; I John 3:8; 4:4; Ephesians 6:11–12, 16*	103	128		Satan	

Lesson Title	Lesson Number	Lesson Pages	Student Pages	Doctrinal Truths	Memory Verses
Jesus Called His Disciples *Matthew 4:18–22; Mark 1:16–20; John 1:35–51*	104	128–29		God the Son Church (service)	
Review—Jesus Is God *Review*	105	129–30	33	God the Son	
The Wedding at Cana *John 2:1–11*	106	130–31		God (omnipotence)	Hebrews 13:6
Jesus Healed a Nobleman's Son *John 4:46–54*	107	131–32		Bible God the Son Salvation	
Jesus Helped Some Fishermen *Luke 5:1–11*	108	132–34		God the Son Salvation	
Jesus Healed a Sick Man *Matthew 9:2–8; Mark 2:1–12; Luke 5:16–26*	109	134–35		God the Son Salvation	
Jesus Calmed the Storm *Matthew 8:23–27; Mark 4:35–41; Luke 8:22–25*	110	135–36	34	God the Son (omnipotence) Salvation (faith)	
Jesus Showed That He Is God *Review*	111	137	35	God the Son	
Many Believed *Matthew 14:13–21; Mark 6:30–44; Luke 9:10–17; John 6:1–14*	112	137–39		God the Son (omnipotence)	
Jesus Made a Girl Live Again *Matthew 9:18–26; Mark 5:22–43; Luke 8:41–56*	113	139–40		God the Son	John 14:6
Jesus Walked on the Waves *Matthew 14:22–23; Mark 6:45–52; John 6:16–21*	114	140–41		God the Son (omnipotence)	
A Son Was Sorry *Luke 15:11–32*	115	141–43	36	Salvation (repentance, faith)	I John 1:9
One Man Thanked God *Luke 17:11–19*	116	143–44		God the Son (omnipotence)	
A Kind Neighbor *Luke 10:30–37*	117	144–45		Salvation	I John 4:19
Mary and Martha Believed *John 11:1–45*	118	145–46		God the Son (omnipotence)	
The Lost Sheep *Psalm 23; John 10:3–5; Luke 15:4–6*	119	146–48		Salvation	
Jesus Loves Children *Matthew 19:13–15; Mark 10:13–16; Luke 18:15–17*	120	148–49	37	God (His love)	
Jesus Healed a Blind Man *Luke 18:35–43*	121	149–50		God the Son (omnipotence) Salvation (faith)	
Jesus Helped Zacchaeus *Luke 19:1–10*	122	150–52	38	God the Son Salvation	
Review—Life of Christ *Review*	123	152	39	God the Son	

Lesson Plans

God's Word

The Bible: God Speaks to Me

Lesson 1: God Talked to a Boy Long Ago

Bible text: I Samuel 3:1–18

Doctrinal truth: Bible

Character traits: Wisdom; Obedience

> Cutouts for the Student activity pages, booklets, and memory verse reminders are located at the back of the Student Packet.

Materials
- A completed copy of Student page 1 (for use as a visual)
- "Samuel Listened" booklet (One copy for the teacher from the Student Packet—cut on dashed line, fold on solid line, and staple to make booklet.)
- A copy of the memory verse list to be sent home with each child during the first week of school (See the Appendix.)
- "God Spoke to Samuel" (Picture Packet)
- *BIBLE TRUTHS for Christian Schools*® K5 CD (optional)

Opening chorus: "Our Bible Time's Begun"
Sing this chorus once for the children. Repeat it, asking the class to sing along with you.

Prayer

> When you lead in prayer, make your prayers short and use children's vocabulary. Include in your prayer each day thoughts pertaining to the overall objective and lesson theme.

➤ Our dear heavenly Father, we ask You to be with us in our Bible time. Help us to be good listeners. Help us to listen and obey Your Word, the Bible. We pray in Jesus' name. Amen.

Song: "God's Word"

Bible lesson

> Hold your Bible in your hand during the Bible lesson to convey that the lesson is from the Word of God. Refer to the Bible throughout the lesson.

Introduction

➤ Boys and girls, each day we will have a Bible time in our class. Each day we will have a story from God's Word, the Bible. Do you know what book this is that I am holding? *(Allow discussion.)* Yes, God's Word, the Holy Bible. (Point to the words *Holy Bible* on the outside cover or inside on the title page.)

The Bible tells us that God made all things. God made everything in the world, but He made mommies and daddies and boys and girls in a very special way. God made each of us to have fellowship with Him. That means we can talk to God and God can talk to us. God talks to us through His Word. The Bible tells us many stories about how God talked to people many, many years ago. Today our lesson is about one of these people. He was only a child when God spoke to him the first time. This little boy heard not only God's words but also God's own voice speak those words.

> To aid the teacher in locating the stories to tell within a lesson, the Bible accounts and character stories are in yellow shaded boxes.

Lesson
Display "God Spoke to Samuel" picture and your copy of the booklet "Samuel Listened." Read the title of the booklet and turn to page 2. (You are using the booklet today only as a lesson visual. The children will use their booklets in Lesson 2.)

Long, long ago a little boy named Samuel lived in the temple. Eli was the leader in God's house. Samuel was a helper in God's house. Samuel ran errands, swept the floor, and did many other things to help Eli. Samuel was a good and obedient helper for Eli.

(Display page 3.) One night after Samuel had gone to bed, he heard a voice calling him, "Samuel." Samuel jumped out of bed and ran to Eli. He said, "Here I am—you called me."

"No," Eli said, "I didn't call you, Samuel; go on back to bed and go to sleep." So Samuel did. (Display page 4.)

Samuel lay down in his bed again. He pulled the covers up and was all ready to go to sleep. Suddenly he heard a voice again. He lay very still and listened. "Samuel." He was sure he had heard someone call his name this time. So he got out of his bed again and ran into Eli's room. He said, "Here I am—you called me."

"No," Eli said, "I did not call you, Samuel; now you get back in your bed."

So Samuel went back and slowly got into bed. As he lay on his bed, he thought, "Who could be calling me? I am sure I heard a voice calling my name." While he lay there wondering about all that had happened, he heard the voice call again, "Samuel." He did hear a voice. He did hear his name. He ran in to see Eli again. "Here I am; I heard you call me."

Then Eli knew that it must be the Lord who had been calling Samuel. Eli told Samuel just what to do. "Go lie down, and if the voice calls again, you say, 'Speak, Lord; for thy servant heareth.' "

This time when the voice called his name, "Samuel, Samuel," Samuel answered, "Speak, Lord; for thy servant heareth." (Display page 5.)

Then God spoke to Samuel. God told Samuel many things that were going to happen. God told him that He must punish Eli and his sons because they had disobeyed. Samuel listened carefully while God spoke. Samuel was sad that Eli and his sons had not obeyed God, but he knew that God must punish sin.

Samuel listened to God when He spoke to him. He listened and obeyed. (Display the cover picture again.)

When Samuel grew up, he became a preacher who told many people about the Word of God. He told God's people to live God's way and serve the Lord with all their hearts. Two books of the Bible are named after Samuel—I Samuel and II Samuel. (Open your Bible to I and II Samuel and show them to the class.)

Application
➤ Does God talk to us like He did to Samuel many, many years ago? Do we hear His voice speak our names? No, but God still talks to us. God speaks to us in His written Word, the Bible. When we listen to Bible words, God is talking to us. (Display page 6 of the booklet.) God wants us to be good listeners; like Samuel we can say, "Speak, Lord; for thy servant heareth." (BAT: 6a Bible Study)

Song: "Holy Bible, Book Divine," stanza 1
Use a completed copy of Student page 1 to introduce this hymn.

➤ We are going to learn a special hymn about the Bible. Listen while I sing it for you. (Sing the first stanza in its entirety, or play the *BIBLE TRUTHS for Christian Schools*® K5 CD.)

Why do we call the Bible holy? (*Allow discussion.*) Because it is God's Word and God is holy—that means God cannot do anything wrong—God is perfect, without sin, and holy. (Point to the first illustration.) So His Word is holy. That's why we sing "Holy Bible."

Then we sing "book divine." That means the same thing—that the Bible is a special book from God. "Divine" means from God. "Perfect Bible—Book from God." Now you sing the first part with me this time. (Sing the first stanza again.)

The Bible is a special book—that is why we sing "precious treasure." (Point to the second illustration.) The Bible is the best book in the whole world—and it is for you and for me—"thou art mine." When we love something very much, it is precious to us. (Allow the children to take turns pointing to the illustrations in sequence on the student page as they all sing the song with you.)

The second part of the song says, "Mine to tell me whence I came." (Point to the third illustration.) The Bible tells us that God made the world, the first man and woman, and each one of us. "Mine to teach me what I am." The Bible tells us everything we need to know about ourselves. (Point to the last illustration.) We will be learning about this each day in our Bible time.

Sing the song together one more time.

> When teaching a new chorus or hymn, do not think that the children do not like the song if they do not participate at once. Give them time to become familiar with it.

Lesson 2: Samuel Listened to God's Word

Bible text: I Samuel 3 (review)
Doctrinal truth: Bible
Character traits: Wisdom; Obedience
Memory verse: Introduce Psalm 25:4.
Materials
• "Samuel Listened" booklet for each student and the teacher (Student Packet—cut on dashed line, fold on solid line, and staple to make booklet.)
• A completed copy of Student page 1 (for use as a visual; used in Lesson 1)
• Story-play props: two mats or towels for beds, chair, table, model of a scroll, candlestick, and cloth
• A copy of the Memory Verse List (See the Appendix.)

Opening chorus: "Our Bible Time's Begun"

Song: "Holy Bible, Book Divine," stanza 1
Use the completed copy of Student page 1 as a visual. Review the meaning of the words of the hymn discussed in Lesson 1.

> Children will benefit from repetition, especially in Bible truths.

Prayer
Ask God to help us be good listeners like Samuel when He speaks to us in His Word.

Memory verse
Read Psalm 25:4 from the Bible.

> Reading memory verses directly from God's Word reinforces the concept that the verse being taught is the Word of God.

➤ How does God show us His ways? How does God show us what He wants us to do? *(Allow discussion.)* He shows us in His Book, the Bible. The Bible is our guide-book. God shows us His ways are right. His ways are best for us.

We should ask the Lord each day to help us do the right thing. A "path" is like a walkway. If we love God and have asked Jesus to be our Savior from sin, we are walking on God's walkway or path, which is the way to heaven. In His Book, God shows us that we are sinners. He shows us that Christ died to save us from our sin. He shows us the way to become a child of God. He tells us how to obey Him and how to be faithful to Him each day.

Direct the children to repeat the verse and reference several times with you. You may want to use this as a theme verse for the year, reciting it together each day to begin your Bible time.

Song: "Show Me Thy Ways"

Song: "My Bible Book"

Student Packet: "Samuel Listened" booklet
Distribute a booklet to each child. Read the title. Encourage the children to "read" it with you. Lead a discussion about the cover of the booklet. (Samuel was a man of God, preaching to the people of God.) Read and discuss the verse. Encourage the children to read the pictures and text as you proceed through the book.

Guide the picture reading on page 2 by asking the following questions.

➤ Whom do you see in the picture? *(Samuel)*

Where is Samuel? *(in God's house)*

What is he doing? *(sweeping the floor)*

Do you think he is doing a good job? *(yes)* I'm sure he wants to do his best. God tells us to work hard and well at the jobs we have to do. (BAT: 2e Work)

Read the sentence at the bottom of the page. Encourage the children to "read" it with you.

Guide the picture reading on page 3 by asking the following questions.

➤ Whom do you see in this picture? *(Samuel)*

Where is Samuel? *(in his bed)*

What do you think is happening? *(He is listening to a voice.)*

Read the sentence at the bottom of the page and have the children "read" it with you.

Guide the picture reading on page 4 by asking the following questions.

➤ What is happening in this picture? *(Samuel went to Eli because he thought Eli had called him.)*

Who was Eli? *(the temple leader)*

What did Eli tell him to do? *(Go back to bed.)*

What happened when he went back to bed? *(The same thing happened again.)*

What did Eli tell Samuel to do after he heard the voice the third time? *(Go back to bed and answer, "Speak, Lord, for thy servant hears.")*

Read the sentence at the bottom of the page and have the children "read" it with you.

Guide the picture reading on page 5 by asking the following questions.

➤ What do you think Samuel is doing in this picture? *(listening)*

To whom is he listening? *(God)*

Does God speak to you like he spoke to Samuel? *(no)*

Can you see God? *(no)*

Read the sentence at the bottom of the page and have the children "read" it with you.

Guide the picture reading on page 6 by asking the following questions.

➤ Whom do you see on this page? *(a teacher and children in class)*

What do you think the children are doing? *(listening to a Bible lesson)*

Do the children look like good listeners? *(yes)* How do you know? *(They are sitting up straight and looking at the teacher.)*

How is God speaking to these children? *(through His words that are written down in the Bible)*

Read the sentence at the bottom of the page and have the children "read" it with you.

> You may let the children take their booklets home today, along with their Memory Verse Lists. (See the Appendix.)

Song: "God's Word"

Story play
Choose one child to be Samuel and one to be Eli. Provide Samuel with a cloth to polish a candlestick while Eli sits at a table pretending to read his Bible scroll. Explain that Bible words were written on scrolls many, many years ago.

Provide mats or towels for Samuel and Eli to rest on when the narration suggests that action.

Allow the children to dramatize the actions as you read them. Do not be afraid to prompt when necessary. Where there is dialogue for Samuel or Eli, have the children repeat the words after you.

➤ Narrator: The child Samuel worked in God's house where Eli served God. *(Have Samuel polish candlestick and Eli sit at a table pretending to read the scroll.)* One night after Samuel had gone to bed, something very special happened.

Samuel: *(Lying down on mat)*

Narrator: The Lord called, "Samuel."

Samuel: *(Sitting up in bed)* Here I am. *(Running over to Eli's bed)* Here I am. I heard you call me.

Eli: I did not call; lie down again. *(Samuel goes back to bed.)*

Narrator: The Lord called Samuel again. "Samuel."

Samuel: *(Running over to Eli's bed)* Here I am; for you *did* call me.

Eli: I did not call you, my son; lie down again. *(Samuel goes back to bed.)*

Narrator: The Lord called Samuel again the third time, and he arose and went to Eli.

Samuel: Here I am; for you did call me.

Narrator: Then Eli knew that the *Lord* had called the child.

Eli: Samuel, go, lie down; and if He calls again, say, "Speak, Lord; for your servant hears."

Narrator: So Samuel went and lay down in his bed again. And the Lord came and called, "Samuel, Samuel."

Samuel: Speak; for your servant hears.

Narrator: We must listen when we hear God's Word and obey as Samuel did. (BATs: 2a Authority; 2b Servanthood)

Class: *(Recite Psalm 25:4.)*

Song: "I Obey"
After you sing the song, you may substitute the names of children in the class for Samuel. Encourage them to sing in response to the question, and then have them tell one way they can obey God's Word.

Lesson 3: God Talked to Others Long Ago

Bible texts: II Peter 1:21; I Peter 1:24–25; Psalm 119:11
Doctrinal truth: Bible (inspiration)
Character trait: Wisdom
Memory verse: Review Psalm 25:4.
Materials
• A completed copy of Student page 1 (for use as a visual)
• "God Spoke to Samuel," "Noah's Ark," and "Moses" (Picture Packet)
• Pictures or flannel-graph figures of Adam and Eve and Abraham (optional)

Opening chorus: "Our Bible Time's Begun"
Sing the chorus, asking the children to sing along with you.

➤ Let us close our eyes and sing this as a prayer song now.

Song: "Holy Bible, Book Divine," stanza 1
Use the completed copy of student page 1 as a visual.

Prayer
Either the teacher or a child may pray and thank God for the Bible.

Remind the children why we bow our heads (to show how great our God is), close our eyes (to keep us from seeing other things and to help us to think only of God), and place our hands in our laps (so that we will not touch anything or anyone) during prayer.

Song: "My Bible Book," stanzas 1–3

Doctrinal emphasis: Inspiration of the Bible
Display pictures or figures of Bible characters as they are mentioned in the lesson.

➤ In our Bible time we have been learning how God spoke to a boy long ago. Who remembers the boy's name? Yes, Samuel. Samuel heard God's voice with his own ears. He listened to God speak, and he obeyed God's words.

Long, long ago, God spoke to other men and women with His voice so that they could hear His words with their ears also. After God created the first man and woman, Adam and Eve, He talked to them in their garden home.

Later God also spoke to his servant Noah and told him to build an ark. This ark saved Noah and his family from a terrible flood of water that covered the whole earth. Another time, God spoke to his friend Abraham. He told Abraham that he was to be the father of a great people—God's special chosen people.

One time when Moses was taking care of his sheep in the field, he saw a burning bush. As Moses came closer to see the bush, he saw that, even though the bush kept on burning, it did not burn up. Then Moses heard a voice coming from the bush. God spoke to Moses and told him that he had a special job for him to do. Moses listened and obeyed. He became a great servant of God. Later we will be learning more about this great leader for God during our Bible-time lessons.

God spoke directly to these and many other men with His voice because there was no written Bible book long ago.

Then God told some of these men like Moses and Samuel and others to write down exactly what He told them. They wrote God's Word—not their own. (Read II Peter 1:21.)

These holy men who loved and served God listened to God and wrote down what *He* said—not what they wanted to write. We call this the *inspiration* of the Bible. God's Spirit inspired them, telling them what to write. Since God is true (cannot tell a lie) and holy (without sin), His Word is true and holy. Since God is always the same, His Word never changes but is always the same. Always remember that the Bible is God's Word and will never change. God's Word tells us what we need to know to live lives that will make God happy. We should learn as much of God's Word as we can. (BAT: 6a Bible study)

Memory verse

Lead the class in reciting Psalm 25:4 together several times and then as a choral reading. Divide the class into two groups (by rows, tables, or girls and boys) and have them recite the verse antiphonally.

Group 1: "Show me thy ways, O Lord; . . ."
Group 2: ". . . teach me thy paths."

Song: "Show Me Thy Ways"

Action rhyme: "God's Word"

➤ God's Word tells me what to love.
  (Place thumbs and pointer fingers of both hands together in heart shape.)
  God's Word tells us what to say.
  (Touch lips with finger.)
  God's Word tells me what to do.
  (Step in place and hold out hands.)
  And how to live God's holy way.
  (Open hands together to form an open Bible.)

When introducing a new action rhyme, know it well or have it written on a prompt (chalkboard or card). Repeat the rhyme several times. Young children enjoy this type of activity, but your enthusiasm is the best motivator for their participation.

Lesson 4: God Talks to Us Today in the Bible

Bible text: Review.
Doctrinal truth: Bible
Character traits: Wisdom; Obedience
Memory verse: Review Psalm 25:4.
Catechism: Introduce Catechism 1–3.
Materials
• A Bible and a New Testament
• Vick family stick puppets (See the Appendix; cut out, mount on lightweight cardboard, and attach to craft sticks.)

Opening chorus: "Our Bible Time's Begun"

Song: "My Bible Book," stanzas 1–3
Choose a child to stand and hold the Bible as the class sings together. Repeat two or three times with different children.

Prayer
Select a child to stand, hold the Bible, and thank God for His Word.

Song: "Holy Bible, Book Divine," stanza 1

Memory verse
Recite Psalm 25:4 together and as a choral reading. (See Lesson 3.)

Song: "Show Me Thy Ways"

Song: "God's Word"

Doctrinal emphasis: The Bible

➤ The Bible is one book. It has two big parts—the Old Testament and the New Testament. (Show the children the two parts of the Bible.) Sometimes we see just the New Testament part of the Bible printed in a smaller book all by itself. But that is just part of the Bible. (Show them the New Testament.)

Sing "Books of the New Testament." Repeat this chorus from time to time throughout the school year.

➤ The Bible tells us about the one true and living God, who created all things. It tells us that God has always been—that nobody made God. (Quote Genesis 1:1.) It tells us why God made each one of us. (Call each of the children's names; e.g., "He made Emily, Sarah, Joshua, Kevin," and include your own name also.) The Bible tells us about ourselves—why we are sinners and why we need a Savior to forgive our sin. It tells us how God the Father sent His only Son, Jesus Christ, who is the very God Himself, to be our Savior from sin.

It tells us the stories of Jesus—how God the Father planned and prepared to send His Son, Jesus, into this world. Jesus had always lived in heaven with God and the Holy Spirit. But He left His heavenly home to come to Earth.

The Bible tells *when* God's Son came and *where* He came—that He was born in the little town of Bethlehem and lived with His family in the little town of Nazareth. It tells us, most importantly, *why* He came—to die for our sins. He grew up to obey and preach God's Word and to do many miracles that only God can do to show us who God is and what God is like.

The Bible tells us the most wonderful story about God's love. God's Son loved us so much that He died on the cross so that we could have our sins forgiven. But He did not stay dead. He arose from the grave and lives in heaven.

If we believe that we are sinners and that Jesus died for our sins, we can tell God we are sorry for our sin and ask Him to forgive our sin. When we do that, we believe and trust Jesus, God's Son, and He is our Savior from sin. When we ask Jesus to be our Savior, He promises to plan and prepare a special home in heaven for us.

The Bible even tells us about heaven where God lives and where He wants us to live someday with Him. These are all some of the important things we will be hearing about in our Bible-time lessons each day in kindergarten.

Catechism

Introduce Catechism 1–3.

- Who made you? (*God made me.*)

- What else did God make? (*God made all things.*)

- Why did God make you and all things? (*God made me and all things for His own glory.*)

Lead the children in singing "God Made Me."

Character story: "Josh Remembered God's Word"

Tell the children that they will be hearing stories about the Vick family—Mom and Dad Vick, Sam (age 9), Kate (age 5), and Josh (age 3), and the Hunter family—Mom and Dad Hunter, Grant (age 8), Dave (age 5), and Abby (age 2) during Bible time. You may hold up each puppet as you introduce the Vick family today.

➤ We will sometimes have the Vick family introduce a Bible lesson, or sometimes we will have a whole story about them to help us better understand our Bible lessons.

Display Mom, Kate, and Josh puppets as you tell the following story.

Josh and Kate were going grocery shopping with their mother. It was a big store and there was much to see. Kate had been there before, but it was a new experience for Josh.

"Stay close to Kate and me, Josh, so you'll know where we are," Mom said, as they started walking down the first aisle.

They both helped Mom. In the first aisle Kate put two bunches of carrots in the grocery cart, and in the next aisle Josh put in three boxes of Jell-O. "Yum," he said as he licked his lips. He liked Jell-O, especially with whipped cream on top.

As Mom and Kate turned to go down the next aisle, Josh caught sight of the candy shelves. He forgot to keep up with Mom and Kate. He looked at all the shelves of candy. There were lollipops and bubble gum and marshmallows and every kind of candy bar he could imagine . . . and in all different shapes and sizes. Josh's mouth began to water. It all looked so good.

"I'll ask Mom to buy Kate and me a piece of candy," he thought. But when he looked around, he didn't see them. He looked up and down the aisle. He ran back to the Jell-O aisle, but he didn't see them there. He ran to the carrot aisle, but no mother or sister were to be found there either.

He saw other mothers and daddies, and other big sisters and brothers, but not *his* mother or *his* Kate. Josh was very unhappy. A tear began to trickle down his cheek. He began to be afraid. He thought he was lost. Then he remembered two Bible verses he had learned in Sunday school. "I am with thee and will keep thee in all places," and "I will trust and not be afraid." That made him feel better. He knew that God was always with him to take care of him; but he still wanted to find his mother.

A young store clerk wearing a uniform saw Josh's sad face. He walked over to Josh and asked if he had a problem.

"I can't find my mother and sister," Josh whispered sadly.

"Come with me; I'll help you. What's your name?" the young man asked.

Josh followed the store clerk to where the people paid for their groceries at the check-out counter. The young man spoke into a microphone. The sound of his voice boomed out over the loudspeaker as he said, "Josh Vick is waiting for his mother and sister at check-out counter number six."

It didn't take long for Mom and Kate to hurry over to check-out counter number six where they found Josh waiting. Josh's sad face quickly turned into a smiling one when he saw them.

Mom thanked the young man for helping Josh. Josh thanked him too. As they walked away, Josh told his mother about remembering the Bible verses that he had learned in Sunday school.

She smiled and said, "Remember the story about how God spoke to Samuel with His voice many years ago? Well, God spoke to you today from His written Word the Bible to remind you not to be afraid. Aren't you glad you were a good listener and learned God's Word?"

Lesson 5: The Bible Is the Best Book

Bible text: Review; Jeremiah 33:3

Doctrinal truth: Bible

Character trait: Wisdom

Memory verse: Review Psalm 25:4.

Catechism: Review Catechism 1–3.

Materials
- Student page 1 and cutouts
- Scissors
- Glue
- Sketch of two large scrolls for display (for review activity)

> Pencils and crayons are not usually listed in the Materials list. Crayons are listed only when specific colors are needed.

Opening chorus: "Our Bible Time's Begun"

Song: "Holy Bible, Book Divine," stanza 1

Prayer

> Once a week lead the children in praying together the Lord's Prayer. This weekly practice will help children in two ways:
> - understanding the importance of prayer
> - understanding Catechism 44 when introduced in Lesson 138.

➤ We are going to pray together a prayer from the Bible each week in our class. It is called the Lord's Prayer. When the Lord Jesus lived on earth, He prayed this prayer to God the Father. You may know it already. If you do not, just close your eyes and listen and pray silently in your heart while we pray together. It will not be long until you will know it too.

Lead the children in praying the Lord's Prayer. Direct them to stand when you pray it each week.

Song: "My Bible Book"
Replace "He loves me, He loves me." with "He hears me, He hears me."

➤ God hears us when we pray. He tells us that, if we call to Him, He will answer our prayers. (Read Jeremiah 33:3.)

Catechism
Review Catechism 1–3.

■ Who made you? (*God made me.*)

■ What else did God make? (*God made all things.*)

■ Why did God make you and all things? (*God made me and all things for His own glory.*)

Lead the children in singing the following three-note pattern for Catechism 1.

Who made you? God made me.

Lead the children in singing the following five-note pattern for Catechism 2.

What else did God make?

God____ made all things.

Character story: "Missionary to Brazil"

Mr. Tom Mylar was a Bible teacher in a Christian school when he realized that the Lord was calling him to be a missionary. Wanting to obey God, Mr. Mylar began to pray, asking the Lord, "Where do you want me to go?" God quickly answered his prayers. God wanted Mr. Mylar to go into the jungles of Brazil to tell the natives there that Jesus loves them and wants to be their Savior.

It was a very hot day when Mr. Mylar arrived in Brazil. He didn't mind the heat. He was excitedly thinking about a native village deep in the jungle. This village was where Mr. Mylar was to serve the Lord. Mr. Mylar had been praying for the people of the village for many months, but there were still so many questions. . . . What were the people like? Could he speak their language? Would they be able to read the Bibles he was bringing? Did they worship any god at all? His questions would soon be answered.

The ride to the trail that led to the village was hot and dusty. Dust and stones flew into the air as the Jeep bounced along roads that were nothing more than wide dirt paths surrounded by many trees, bushes, and tall grass. After three days, a very tired Mr. Mylar arrived at the end of the road. It then took another full day for Mr. Mylar to walk the narrow, hilly path to the village.

As he walked into the village, Mr. Mylar was surrounded by the natives. It was very unusual for a stranger to come to their village. Imagine Mr. Mylar's surprise as the natives warmly welcomed him in English, his own language! Then, as the natives showed him around the village, they led him to a special hut. It was larger than the rest, and, when he stepped inside, Mr. Mylar realized that this special hut was a church. There were many seats, and on the table in the front of the church was an old Bible! Where had this precious Book come from? he wondered.

That evening, the natives held a special feast in honor of Mr. Mylar's arrival. They told Mr. Mylar that, many years before, a missionary had come to their village. The missionary had lived in the village several years. He had taught the natives how to speak English. He had taught them hymns and Bible verses. Most importantly, the missionary had taught them that the gods they worshiped were false gods. He taught them about the true God of Heaven and His Son, the Lord Jesus Christ. He taught them how to be saved. Sadly, the missionary became ill and died before he could teach the natives how to read. They still had the missionary's well-worn Bible, but there was no one to read it to them. Many of the natives had accepted the Lord Jesus as their Savior from sin, but there was no longer anyone to preach to them, no one to help them learn verses from God's Word. From the day the missionary died, the natives had faithfully prayed, asking God to send someone who would be able to teach them God's Word. Mr. Mylar promised the natives that he would teach them how to read. Soon they would be able to read their very own Bibles.

Application
➤ God's Word is precious, as we have learned in our song. It is a special book—the best book in the whole world. We should always love God's Word and tell others about it. (BAT: 6a Bible study)

Student page 1
Distribute Student page 1 and the cutouts for the page. Have scissors and glue available. Instruct the children to cut out the illustrations for the hymn. Refer to the small Bible symbols in each section on the scroll while guiding the children in gluing each picture in the appropriate section. Read the page and sing the hymn together.

> You may wish to provide damp paper towels for easy cleanup after a cut-and-glue activity.

➤ We learned that the first book in the Old Testament is Genesis. *Genesis* means "book of beginnings." It tells us how the world began. Who made the world? *(God)* Who made *you*? *(Catechism 1: God made me.)* What else did God make? *(Catechism 2: God made all things.)*

The first book in the New Testament is Matthew. One of Jesus' special helpers, Matthew, wrote down what God told him to in this book. That is why it is called *Matthew*.

If you open your Bible in the middle, you will find the book of Psalms. David, whom we will learn about later, wrote many of these psalms. You may have heard "the Lord is my shepherd." These words are in a psalm David wrote. We will be learning the Twenty-third Psalm this year in our class. The Psalms are like songs of praise that tell how great and good God is.

Now, the last book of the whole Bible is called *Revelation*. Open your Bible to the book of Revelation. It tells us about heaven, where God lives and where He wants us to live someday.

God is so good to give us the Bible, His Book! God wants to talk to us. The great God of heaven and earth wants to speak to you and you and you—(Point to each child in your class.) to each one of us. Let's always be good listeners when we hear God's Word read. (BAT: 6a Bible study)

Song: "Holy Bible, Book Divine," stanza 1

Review activity
Display the two large scroll sketches. Explain that many years ago the Bible was written on a scroll.

Divide the class into two teams. Choose a scorekeeper for each team. When a scorekeeper's side answers a question, he can add a mark to his scroll. Tell the class that you are going to play a game to find out what they have learned about the Bible. (Make this a positive learning experience. It should be considered an additional activity to reinforce Bible content and concepts.)

1. In what book does God talk to us? *(the Bible)*
2. Who wrote this book? *(God or God's Spirit)*
3. Why do we call the Bible holy? *(because God is holy)*
4. What does *holy* mean? *(without sin—perfect)*
5. What does "inspiration" mean? *(God told special men what to write down in the Bible.)*
6. Will God's Word ever change? *(No, it is eternal—the same forever and ever.)*
7. What is the name of the first book in the Bible? *(Genesis)*
8. What does *Genesis* mean? *(book of beginnings)*
9. What are the two parts to the Bible? *(the Old Testament and the New Testament)*
10. What is the name of the first book of the New Testament? *(Matthew)*
11. When we open our Bible to about the middle, what book do we find? *(Psalms)*
12. What is the name of the last book in the Bible? *(Revelation)*
13. Quote Psalm 25:4.

Other possible questions could be asked about the catechism or the songs and choruses taught. For example, say a line and have a child say the next line. You may also repeat the questions in a different order.

Song: "Show Me Thy Ways"

God's World
Creation: God Made Me

Lesson 6: First Day of Creation—Day and Night

Bible text: Genesis 1:1–5

Doctrinal truth: God (existence and omnipotence)

Character trait: Wisdom

Memory verse: Introduce Genesis 1:1.

Catechism: Review Catechism 1–3.

Materials
- "Father, We Thank Thee for the Night" visuals (See the Appendix; copy, color, mount on cardboard, and laminate.)
- Kate and Josh Vick puppets (See the Appendix.)
- *Days of Creation* visual, Day 1

Opening chorus: "Our Bible Time's Begun"

Song: "God's Word"

Hymn: "Father, We Thank Thee for the Night," stanza 1
Use the hymn visuals prepared from the Appendix.

Prayer
Thank God for night and day.

Call on two children to hold the first two visuals of the hymn, "Father, We Thank Thee for the Night." Ask each child to tell what is pictured on his visual and to thank the Lord for either day or night, whichever corresponds to the visual he is holding.

Song: "My Bible Book"
Replace "He loves me, He loves me" with "God made me, God made me."

Catechism
Review Catechism 1–2 with the three- and five-note patterns suggested in Lesson 5.

- Who made you? *(God made me.)*
- What else did God make? *(God made all things.)*

Review Catechism 3.

- Why did God make you and all things? *(God made me and all things for His own glory.)*

Memory verse
Read Genesis 1:1 from the Bible.

➤ Do you know that the Bible tells us God made our world from nothing?

Contrast this concept to that of a mother baking a cake with flour, eggs, sugar, milk, and butter, or to the activity of children drawing a picture of a tree with paper and crayons.

➤ When God created—that means "made"—this world, He did it just by speaking, and there it was! Our God can do anything. He is omnipotent—that means "all-powerful." God spoke to create. We should believe that God can do anything and that He will do what His Word says He will do. (BATs: 8a Faith in God's promises; 8b Faith in the power of the Word of God)

Sing "In the Beginning."

Song: "All Things Were Made by God"

Bible lesson

Introduction

> Move the various family member puppets as they sing or speak in story introductions such as the following.

➤ Today Kate and Josh are playing Sunday school. Kate is pretending to be the teacher, and Josh is her class. They are singing right now. Let's listen.

Show the puppets singing "All Things Were Made by God."

➤ Kate: Who can recite the first verse in the Bible for us today?

Josh: I can . . . well, I think I can . . . if you'll help me, Kate . . . I mean, Teacher. (Recite Genesis 1:1.)

Kate: Very good, Josh. You did a good job.

Lesson

Do you know that long, long ago there was no day and night? There was no light in our world at all. Everything was all darkness. There was no sun to shine in the day and no moon or stars to shine their lights at night. What a dark, dark place it was!

In the beginning there was only God. God has always been. No one made God. God is eternal. God has always lived, and God will never die.

God had a plan. He planned to make people to love and obey Him. So He made a world, a big, big world for people to live in. (Quote Genesis 1:1.)

We just learned how God made the world. Did He need wood or cement? *(no)* Did He need hammer and nails? *(no)* There wasn't even wood or cement, or hammers and nails to make a world, was there? No, only darkness.

What did God need? *(Nothing!)* God didn't need anything to make His world. (Open your Bible and read Genesis 1:3–5.) The Bible tells us that God just spoke when He made the light for the day. (Display *Days of Creation* visual, Day 1.) That was the first day—and our God created it.

Application

➤ God spoke, and it was done. The heaven and the earth came into being by the power of His Word.

God said, "Let there be light." And there was light. Our God can do anything. He is all-powerful. (BAT: 8b Faith in the power of the Word of God)

Song: "Creation Song," stanzas 1–2

Lesson 7: Second Day of Creation— Sky, Air, and Waters

Bible text: Genesis 1:6–8

Doctrinal truth: God (existence and omnipotence)

Character trait: Wisdom

Memory verses: Review Genesis 1:1 and introduce Psalm 95:6.

Catechism: Review Catechism 1–3 and introduce Catechism 4.

Materials
• "Father, We Thank Thee for the Night" visuals (See the Appendix.)
• Vick family puppets
• *Days of Creation* visual, Day 2

Opening chorus: "Our Bible Time's Begun"

Song: "My Bible Book"
Replace "He loves me, He loves me" with "God made me, God made me" and "God made you, God made you."

Song: "Holy Bible, Book Divine," stanza 1

Memory verses and catechism
Repeat Genesis 1:1 together and then lead in the following catechism discussion.

1. What does *create* mean? *(make)*

2. How did God create the world? *(He spoke.)*

3. What did God make the world from? *(nothing)*

4. Where did God come from? *(God always was—He has no beginning. God is eternal.)*

5. Who made God? *(Catechism 4: Nobody made God.)*

6. Who made you? *(Catechism 1: God made me.)*

7. What else did God make? *(Catechism 2: God made all things.)*

8. Why did God make you and all things? *(Catechism 3: God made me and all things for His own glory.)*

Read Psalm 95:6 to the children.

➤ When we worship God, we tell Him that we love Him and thank Him for what He does for us. We can do this any time or any place, but when we kneel we are showing Him in a very special way that He is a great God. He is the great God in heaven who created the world and all things.

Prayer

➤ Let's do what our memory verse says and kneel as we show God how great He is and thank Him for His love.

Thank God for His power and His love in making all things.

Tell the children to kneel in front of their chairs, placing their hands on their chairs.

Hymn: "Father, We Thank Thee for the Night," stanza 1
Use the hymn visuals.

Bible lesson

Introduction
Show the puppets looking up at the sky at appropriate times.

➤ Grandma Brown is flying in on an airplane. Dad has taken the family to the airport to meet their grandmother. She is coming to visit them for a few days. The children are excitedly looking for her airplane to appear.

Mom: The sky is especially beautiful today, isn't it?

Kate: Yes, the clouds are so soft and fluffy looking.

Josh: Let's see if we can find any shapes the clouds are making—ooh, I see one that looks like a dog.

Kate: And I see one that looks like a camel—see its hump?

Sam: And guess what I see? Grandma's plane is just flying in right now.

Dad: Yes, we can thank God for Grandma's safe trip through the beautiful blue sky He created.

Lesson

Did you know that before God created the world there was no sky? There were no clouds. There was not even air to breathe. (Tell the children to take a deep breath.) We need to breathe air to live. God made us that way.

Remember, we said that God had a plan. He planned to make fathers and mothers and boys and girls who would love and obey Him. He was preparing a place for them to live.

On the first day of creation what did God create? *(light, day, and night)* The second day God created the sky for birds to fly and waters below for fish to swim, and He created air for us to breathe. (Display *Days of Creation* visual, Day 2.)

Application

➤ Can anyone tell how God made the water below and the sky with its clouds above? Did He need anything to make it with? No, He made it the same way that He made light and day and night on the first day. He just spoke and it was so. Our God is a great God. His Word is all-powerful. He can do anything He wants to do. (BAT: 8b Faith in the power of the Word of God)

Action rhyme

Lead the children in the action rhyme, "Little Children, Do You Know?"

➤ Little children,
  (Point finger toward someone else.)
Do you know?
  (Shake finger.)
God just spoke,
  (Point toward heaven.)
And it was so.
  (Shake head "yes" and spread arms out wide.)

Song: "Creation Song," stanzas 1–3

Lesson 8: Third Day of Creation— Land and Seas

Bible text: Genesis 1:9–13

Doctrinal truth: God (omnipotence and omniscience)

Character trait: Wisdom

Memory verses: Review Psalm 95:6 and Genesis 1:1.

Catechism: Review Catechism 1–4.

Materials
• *Days of Creation* visuals, Days 1–3
• Dave and Dad Hunter puppets (See the Appendix.)
• Apple and peeling knife (optional)

Opening chorus: "Our Bible Time's Begun"

Song: "God Made the World," stanza 1

Prayer

Thank God for His great plan and power in His creation.

Guide the children in reciting Psalm 95:6 before prayer time each day throughout this unit.

Memory verse

Read Genesis 1:1 from your Bible. Remind the children that Genesis is the first book of the Bible.

➤ The first book of the Bible is called *Genesis*—that means "the book of beginnings." This is God's written Word that tells us all that we need to know about God, His world, and ourselves.

Repeat the verse several times, encouraging the children to try to say it with you. Divide the class into three groups, assigning each group one phrase of the verse and having them recite their appropriate phrase in answer to the following questions.

➤ When? *(In the beginning)*

  Who? *(God)*

  What? *(created the heaven and the earth)*

Lead the children in singing "God's Word."

Read Psalm 119:11 to the children from the Bible.

➤ That is what we are singing about. God's Word helps us to do good. Let's recite our memory verse about God's Word in Psalm 25:4 and then sing our chorus again.

Bible lesson

Introduction

Use the Dad Hunter and Dave puppets for the following story.

➤ Narrator: Dad is eating an apple as he sits on the front porch.

  Dad: Help yourself to an apple, Dave.

  Dave: No, thank you, Dad. I don't like apples with seeds in them.

  Dad: Well, come here and I'll cut open an apple for you and even take the seeds out. How's that? You know, God put these seeds in this apple for a reason, Dave. God put seeds in all plants so that they could grow more plants. When we plant an apple seed, an apple tree will grow and have more apples with more seeds to make more trees.

(You may want to cut an apple vertically and have Dad show Dave the star-shaped seed formation.)

Lesson

We learned that, when God began to create the world, there was only darkness all around. The first day God created light. (Display *Days of Creation* visual, Day 1.) So we have day and night. The second day He created the water below and the sky above with clouds and air. (Display *Days of Creation* visual, Day 2.) Was God's world ready for people to live in it yet? No, there was still water everywhere. There was no dry land anywhere.

Listen to what God said on day three. (Read Genesis 1:9–10 aloud.) So God created dry land called earth, big oceans and seas, and lakes and rivers.

(Display *Days of Creation* visual, Day 3.) What else do you see in this picture that God created on the third day? *(Allow discussion.)* Yes, God made beautiful green grass and other growing things, such as flowers and fruit trees. All these growing things are called plants. God made plants for animals and people to eat. God was still getting the world ready for people to live in.

The Bible tells us that God spoke again. (Read Genesis 1:11–13 to the children.)

Application

➤ God had a plan for His world. God knows all things. He knew what fathers and mothers and boys and girls would need to help them live in His world. He created everything the best way. Again on the third day God had only to speak and all the waters obeyed Him: the dry land and all growing things appeared. Our God can do anything. (BAT: 8b Faith in the power of the Word of God)

Song: "God Made the World," stanza 1

Catechism
Review Catechism 1–4.

■ Who made you? *(God made me.)*

■ What else did God make? *(God made all things.)*

■ Why did God make you and all things? *(God made me and all things for His own glory.)*

■ Who made God? *(Nobody made God.)*

Lesson 9: Review—First Through Third Days of Creation

Bible text: Genesis 1:1–13 (review)

Doctrinal truth: God (omnipotence and omniscience)

Character trait: Wisdom

Memory verses: Review Psalm 25:4 and Genesis 1:1.

Materials
• "Father, We Thank Thee for the Night" visuals (See the Appendix.)
• *Days of Creation* visuals, Days 1–3, and the miniatures of these visuals from the packet cover
• Student page 2 and cutouts
• Scissors
• Glue

Opening chorus: "Our Bible Time's Begun"

Song: "God Made the World," stanza 1

Prayer
Thank God for His world.

Call on three children to hold one of the *Days of Creation* visuals, Days 1–3, and have each thank God for what is pictured on his visual.

Hymn: "Father, We Thank Thee for the Night"
Use the hymn visuals.

Memory verses
Review Psalm 25:4 and Genesis 1:1.

Review activity: *Days of Creation* miniatures
Use the *Days of Creation* visual miniatures, Days 1–3. Place them in any order on a desk or stand them up on the chalkboard tray. Choose one child to close his eyes and another child to remove one visual and hide it behind his back. Tell the child whose eyes were closed to look at the remaining visuals and guess which one is missing. Repeat the game with various children taking turns.

Student page 2
Instruct the children to cut out the creation pictures for Days 1–3 and to glue them in the appropriate spaces on the page. Direct the children to cut out the half of the Bible and to write their names on the back. Collect the pages, keeping them for the completion of the activity in Lesson 15. Remind the children that God is all-powerful and all-knowing.

Action rhyme: "Little Children, Do You Know?"
(See Index of Poetry.)

Song: "All Things Were Made by God"

Lesson 10: Fourth Day of Creation— Sun, Moon, and Stars

Bible text: Genesis 1:14–19

Doctrinal truth: God (omniscience)

Character traits: Wisdom; Thankfulness

Memory verses: Review Psalm 95:6 and Genesis 1:1.

Catechism: Review Catechism 1–4.

Materials
• "The Wonder Song" visuals (See the Appendix; copy, color, mount on cardboard, and laminate.)
• Seasonal activity pictures (See the Appendix; copy, color, mount on cardboard, and laminate.)
• Sam and Kate Vick puppets
• *Days of Creation* visuals, Days 1 and 4

Opening chorus: "Our Bible Time's Begun"

Song: "The Wonder Song"
Use the visuals to introduce the song.

Prayer
Thank God for His creation.

Give one each of the five "The Wonder Song" visuals to five children. Encourage each child to thank God for what is pictured on his visual and to recite Psalm 95:6.

Catechism
Review Catechism 1–4.

■ Who made you? *(God made me.)*

■ What else did God make? *(God made all things.)*

■ Why did God make you and all things? *(God made me and all things for His own glory.)*

■ Who made God? *(Nobody made God.)*

Song: "All Things Were Made by God"

Memory verse
Guide the children in reciting Genesis 1:1 together and in singing "In the Beginning."

Poem
Divide the class into two groups and have them recite the following in choral response.

➤ O Sun! What makes you shine so bright?
The God who said, "Let there be light."

Bible lesson

Introduction
Use Kate and Sam puppets for the following puppet dialogue.

➤ Narrator: Kate and Sam are sitting on the front porch of their house. Supper is over, and their family has already read the Bible and prayed together.

Kate: It's dark now. Mom will be calling us soon to come inside and get ready for bed, but I'd like to just sit here and look at the stars all night.

Sam: I'd like to be on a space ship, flying right up there with those stars . . . maybe someday.

Narrator: Sam's eyes searched the sky carefully . . . a bright light suddenly streaked down through the sky toward the ground.

Sam: Wow, did you see that!

Kate: What was it, Sam? It looked like a falling star.

Sam: Well, my teacher at school says that those are called meteors. They really aren't stars, even though we call them that because that's what they look like as they streak through the sky. Do you know the sun is really a star that is much, much larger than our earth? The reason it is so big and bright is that it is closer to us than the other stars. But even the sun is millions and millions of miles away from the earth.

Kate: *(sighing)* God has made so many beautiful things in His heaven and earth.

Lesson

Our God is omniscient. Can you say *omniscient?* (Direct the children to repeat the word with you several times.) Remember, that's a big word that means "God knows all things." Only God knew how to create the world in the very best way.

God knew that we would need light to see, so He created two great big lights in the sky. He made the warm, bright sun for the day and a shiny, silvery moon for the night.

God knew that the grass, the flowers, and the trees that He created on the third day needed to be warm to grow. So He created the sun. The big, warm sun helps plants to grow. The sun helps keep us warm too.

(Display *Days of Creation* visuals, Days 1 and 4, side by side.) God created light and made day and night on the first day. Then, on the fourth day, He created a special light for the day and a special light for the night. What do we call the big light for our day? *(the sun)* What do we call the big light for our night? *(the moon)* What other lights do you see in the nighttime picture? *(the stars)* Yes, God made the stars also. The smaller lights that we see are faraway stars that make the sky so pretty at night. The Bible tells us that God has made everything beautiful. Have you ever tried to count the stars at night? You couldn't do that, could you? The Bible tells us that God can count them. God knows how many stars there are. The Bible tells us that God even knows the name of each star (Isaiah 40:26). Our God knows all things. Our God is omniscient.

When God created the lights for the sky, He said these lights in the sky would help us count the days and years. He also gave us our seasons. Seasons are special times of the year. The four seasons are summer, fall, winter, and spring. (Display the corresponding seasonal activity picture as you discuss each season.) In the summer we like to go fishing and play in the water. In the fall we like to play in pretty colored leaves. In the winter we put on our heavy coats and play outside in the snow. And in the spring we like to pick pretty flowers and watch all the green leaves begin to grow on the trees as we have fun playing and swinging. Every year, just as God promised, we have summer, fall, winter, and spring. Isn't God good to give us so many wonderful seasons?

Application

➤ All of God's creation shows how great God is. We should always thank Him for our wonderful world. (BAT: 7c Praise)

Action rhyme

➤ God's warm sun
   (Make large circle with arms above head.)
See, up high.
   (Shade eyes and look up.)
God's sun shining,
Up in the sky.
   (Reach high on tiptoes.)

God's silvery moon
See, up high.
   (Cup hands around eyes.)
God's moon shining,
Up in the sky.
   (Reach high on tiptoes.)

God's twinkling stars
See, up high.
   (Cup hands around eyes.)
God's stars shining,
Up in the sky.
   (Reach high on tiptoes.)

Lesson 11: Fifth Day of Creation— Fish and Birds

Bible text: Genesis 1:20–23
Doctrinal truth: God (omniscience and omnipotence)
Character traits: Wisdom; Thankfulness
Memory verses: Review Genesis 1:1 and Psalm 95:6.
Materials
• "The Wonder Song" visuals (See the Appendix.)
• "Father, We Thank Thee for the Night" visuals (See the Appendix.)
• A bird's nest (optional)
• *Days of Creation* visuals, Days 1–5

Opening chorus: "Our Bible Time's Begun"

Song: "The Wonder Song"
Use the song visuals.

Prayer
Thank God for His creation.

Give one each of the five "The Wonder Song" visuals to five children. Encourage each child to thank God for what is pictured on his visual and recite Psalm 95:6.

Hymn: "Father, We Thank Thee for the Night," stanza 1

Bible lesson

Introduction
➤ Sam was visiting Grandmother and Grandfather Vick. He was helping Grandfather clean up the field next to the garden in back of the farm house. Grandfather walked over to a pile of leaves and limbs in the corner of the field.

"Come here, Sam, and see what I've found in this pile of brush," Grandfather called.

Sam ran over quickly to where his grandfather stood and looked down at the pile of leaves and tree limbs. "Oh, a bird's nest," Sam whispered. "Only it isn't quite all there, is it?"

"Yes, this is a nest that a bird is just beginning to build. Look, here comes the bird right now," Grandfather said as he pointed to a bird who was fluttering around above them with a piece of string in her mouth. "She won't like what I'm going to do, I'm afraid."

Sam watched as his grandfather began to tear the nest apart.

"Grandfather," Sam cried, "what are you doing? The bird is scolding you. Listen."

They both looked up at the excited bird as she fluttered back and forth above their heads, chirping as if to say, "Let my house alone."

"Well," Grandfather told Sam, "I am really helping the bird. She just doesn't know it. Tomorrow I have to burn this pile of brush. So the bird really will be much better off building her nest in a safe place before she lays her eggs."

The next day, when Sam went out in the field with his grandfather to burn the pile of brush, he was happy to see the mother bird busily building another nest in a rose bush nearer the house.

Lesson

Grandfather Vick knew what would be best for that bird, didn't he? And that reminds us of how God knew what was best for us when He created His world.

What did God create on the second day of His creation? (Display *Days of Creation* visual, Day 2 to prompt the children.) God made the sky above and the waters below.

When we look up at the sky that God made, what do we see? Yes, all kinds of birds. When we look in the lakes, rivers, and oceans that God made, what do we see? All kinds of fish.

(Display *Days of Creation* visual, Day 5.) Who made the birds that fly in the sky above? Who made the fish that swim in the waters below? Our great God created them all. Do you know what God made the birds and fish from? Nothing! God just spoke. His Word is so powerful that the birds and fish were created. "And God saw that it was good." This was the fifth day.

Application

➤ God had a plan for His world. Does God know all things? *(Catechism 15: Yes, nothing can be hidden from God.)* What is the big word that tells us that God is all-knowing? *(omniscient)* He created the sky above and water below before He created the birds and the fish. Then they all had their special places to live. Our God does everything well.

> Sometimes catechism truths are discussed within a Bible lesson before they are formally taught. Because the students are not yet familiar with the questions and answers, you may need to provide the answers.

Do you know why God created the birds and fish? God made all things for His own glory. God had a plan. He was going to create people like us to love and serve Him. God created birds and fish to help us.

Birds help us in many ways. Big birds kill snakes and mice. Small birds kill insects that could hurt the plants that we grow for food to eat. Birds carry seeds from plants and drop them on the ground to grow more plants

to give us food. We eat some birds, such as chickens and turkeys. We eat many kinds of fish too. God knew we would need birds and fish, so He created them to help us. God planned the world that way. God's way is always best. God created many beautiful fish and birds to show us how great and powerful He is. We should thank Him for all His good gifts. (BAT: 7c Praise)

Song: "Creation Song," stanzas 1–7
Use the *Days of Creation* visuals, Days 1–5. Lead the children in singing the first stanza and in reciting Psalm 95:6.

For stanzas 2–7, divide the class into six groups and have each group sing one stanza, or divide them into three groups and sing two stanzas each. Then have all the class recite Genesis 1:1.

Lesson 12: Sixth Day of Creation— Animals and Man

Bible texts: Genesis 1:24–31; Psalm 31:14
Doctrinal truth: God (omniscience and omnipotence)
Character traits: Wisdom; Thankfulness
Memory verse: Review Genesis 1:1.
Catechism: Review Catechism 1–4.
Materials
• *Days of Creation* visuals, Days 1–6, and the miniatures of these visuals from the packet cover
• Vick family puppets (optional)
• Container—box, basket, or bag decorated with a picture of the world or a nature scene (optional)

Opening chorus: "Our Bible Time's Begun"

Song: "God Made the World," stanzas 1–5

Prayer
Thank God for making a world for us to live in.

Song: "All Things Were Made by God"

Bible lesson

Introduction
Put the *Days of Creation* visual miniatures in a container. Select a few children to come one at a time to choose a picture from the container, name the creation, and tell the day that God made it. Allow a child or a group of children to recite Genesis 1:1 after each picture is chosen. This activity may be repeated in later lessons to give more children an opportunity to participate. This could also be done by letting the children hold a Vick family puppet to choose the visual and say the verse.

Lesson

God was still doing His work of creation. He was preparing a world for people to live in. So on the sixth day God created all kinds of animals to live on the dry earth.

He created horses and cows, lambs and pigs. He created lions and tigers. He created tiny mice and great big elephants. God made every kind of animal for people to use and enjoy.

Animals help us in many ways. We ride on some animals, such as horses and camels, to get from one place to another. We use some animals to carry heavy things for us. We eat some animals for food. We use the skin of some animals to make our clothes. (Point out an example of something in your room, e.g., shoes, coats, sweater.) God's plan was perfect. He always knows what is best.

(Display *Days of Creation* visual, Day 6.) But that is not all God created on the sixth day. This was to be His special day of creation. Now God was ready to create a man—someone to love and obey Him.

God made man in a special way. He made man's body out of the dust of the earth, and He gave him life. God made man to be different from all the other things He had created. God made man with a soul—a part of him that would live forever. He made man with a mind to choose between good and evil. Do you know the name of the first man God created? *(Adam)*

Did God create anything else on that day? Look at our picture. Whom do you see? Yes, God created a woman, Eve, to help Adam serve God. God made Eve from the body of Adam. He created Adam and Eve to love each other. God created a man and a woman to love and obey Him. God gave them a beautiful home in the Garden of Eden. He gave them work to do. He told them to take care of their garden home. He told Adam to name all the animals that God had created.

Application

➤ Our Lord is a great God. We can trust in Him. We can believe His promises. The great God of heaven who created all things made and loves each one of you. I am going to read a verse from God's Word, and then you may say it with me.

Read Psalm 31:14. Repeat the verse in two phrases, having the children repeat each phrase after you. Divide the children into two groups, having one group recite the first section of the verse and the other group recite the second section. (BAT: 8a Faith in God's promises)

Song: "Creation Song," stanzas 1–7

Catechism

Review Catechism 1–4.

■ Who made you? *(God made me.)*

■ What else did God make? *(God made all things.)*

■ Why did God make you and all things? *(God made me and all things for His own glory.)*

■ Who made God? *(Nobody made God.)*

Lesson 13: We Know God Is

Bible texts: Exodus 20:1–5; I Timothy 2:5
Doctrinal truth: God (existence)
Character trait: Wisdom
Catechism: Review Catechism 4 and introduce Catechism 5 and 6.
Materials
• Large cardboard question mark visual, approximately 12 inches wide and 18 inches high. Spray-paint or decorate it attractively; attach the dot to the base of the upper part with a heavy thread.

Opening chorus: "Our Bible Time's Begun"

Song: "One God"

Doctrinal emphasis: Existence of God

➤ Have you ever seen God? *(No, we cannot see God.)* God is a spirit. He does not have a body as we have. God lives in heaven. We cannot see Him, but He sees us.

Who made God? *(Catechism 4: Nobody made God.)* Has God ever had a beginning? *(Catechism 5: No, God has always been.)* God is eternal.

There is only one God. How do we know this? *(The Bible tells us "there is one God," I Tim. 2:5.)* Some people think there are many gods. Some people worship the sun. The sun is their god. Can the sun answer their prayers? The Bible tells us that God made the sun. Some people worship animals—such as cows. Can animals take care of us or answer our prayers? The Bible tells us that God made the animals. God made many wonderful things for His world, but we are not to worship these things. We are to worship only the God who created them. We know there is a God because the Bible tells us so.

Will God ever die? *(Catechism 6: No, God lives forever.)* Remember, God was not born like you and me. He did not have to grow up. He has always been the same and always will be. Our great God of heaven never changes.

This is a difficult concept for young children since it relates to the concept of the Trinity. We tell children that Jesus Christ is God's Son and that He is God. We tell them Jesus died; yet we say God will never die. Remind the children that when God the Son came to earth, He lived in a body like ours so that He could die for us, but He rose again and lives forever because He is God. Do not expect the children to comprehend this fully.

Catechism

Review Catechism 4.

- Who made God? (*Nobody made God.*)

Introduce Catechism 5 and 6.

- Has God ever had a beginning? (*No, God has always been.*)

- Will God ever die? (*No, God lives forever.*)

> Catechism instruction should be a natural outgrowth and extension of the Bible lesson. Although several catechism questions may be introduced within a lesson, they will be repeated and reviewed at appropriate times throughout the year.
>
> Rather than present the catechism questions as a meaningless drill, recite them as a natural part of the Bible lesson, with a song or in connection with a Bible verse. As you enthusiastically use this question-and-answer method of teaching Bible truths during the Bible time and throughout the day, the children will hear the questions and answers many times, thus enabling them to memorize the answers effortlessly.

Song: "One God"

Song: "God Is with Me"

Prayer

Thank God that He is always with us.

Review activity: Question Mark visual

Display the large cardboard question mark. Tell the class that you are going to play a Question Mark game. Explain that when we use a question mark after words, it shows that we are asking a question. Demonstrate this by writing the question for Catechism 1 on the chalkboard.

Instruct the children to pass the question mark around from child to child as you sing the following to the tune, "Did You Ever See a Lassie?" Whoever is holding the question mark at the end of the song gets to answer the catechism question you ask.

> Let's listen for a question, a question, a question.
> Let's listen for a question when one comes our way.

> The idea above may be used to review memory verses and other Bible content review questions.

Lesson 14: For His Glory

Bible texts: Psalm 69:34; Psalm 19:1; Psalms 148 and 150

Doctrinal truth: God (His works)

Character traits: Wisdom; Thankfulness

Catechism: Review Catechism 3 and introduce Catechism 7 and 8.

Materials
- For God's Glory visual (See the Appendix for the visual and instructions.)

Opening chorus: "Our Bible Time's Begun"

Hymn: "Holy, Holy, Holy," stanza 1

Choral reading: "Praise Ye the Lord"
Tell the class that you are going to read two verses from God's Word, Psalm 69:34 and Psalm 150:6, and they can join in on the last phrase, "Praise ye the Lord." Repeat and have the children respond as you point to their row or table.

> Teacher: (Read Psalm 150:6a.)
> Class: Praise ye the Lord.
> Teacher: (Read Psalm 69:34.)
> Class: Praise ye the Lord.

Doctrinal emphasis: God—His Works
> Remember our lessons about God creating the world? We read from the Bible that God looked at what He had made and "saw that it was good" (Gen. 1:31).

> God's work of creation *was* good—"He hath made everything beautiful." And the Bible says that all His works were made to praise Him. Listen as I read Psalm 148.

Read Psalm 148 from the Bible.

> When we praise God, we tell Him how great He is. When we love God and obey Him, we show to others how great He is. But how can stars, and flowers, and mountains, and animals show praise to the God who created them? When we feel the warm, bright sun and see the twinkling stars and the beautiful shining moon, they all remind us of our great God; so they are praising God, or showing glory to God.

> All the animals that God made—great and small— show us what a wise God we have. The beautiful mountains, the snow and rain, the wind and storms, and the oceans of water remind us of our great and powerful God; so they bring glory to God. (BAT: 7c Praise)

Prayer

Thank God for His wonderful works.

Song: "Who God Is," stanzas 1 and 3

Review activity: For God's Glory visual
Place the flower center of the For God's Glory visual on a magnetic board or flannelboard and have the children take turns identifying and placing the correct petal (picture of creation day) next to the corresponding numeral (sequence of creation days) on the flower center.

Catechism

Review Catechism 3.

- Why did God make you and all things? (*God made me and all things for His own glory.*)

Introduce Catechism 7 and 8.

- How can you glorify God? (*I can glorify God by loving Him and doing what He commands.*)

- Why ought you to glorify God? (*I ought to glorify God because He made me and takes care of me.*)

Repeat this activity several times, allowing as many children as possible to participate.

Song: "Praise Him, Praise Him"
Replace "all ye little children" with "all of God's creation."

Lesson 15: Review—Days of Creation

Bible text: Genesis 1–2 (review)

Doctrinal truth: God

Character trait: Wisdom

Memory verses: Review Psalm 25:4 and Genesis 1:1.

Materials
- *Days of Creation* visuals and miniatures
- "Father, We Thank Thee for the Night" visuals (See the Appendix.)
- Student page 3 and cutouts
- Scissors
- Glue
- Each student's completed Student page 2 (from Lesson 9)
- Large sheet of construction paper (12"× 18" or two 9"× 12" sheets glued or taped together) for each student
- For God's Glory visual (See the Appendix.)

Opening chorus: "Our Bible Time's Begun"

Song: "Creation Song"
Use the *Days of Creation* visuals.

Prayer
Stand and pray together the Lord's Prayer.

Hymn: "Father, We Thank Thee for the Night"
Use the hymn visuals.

Memory verses
Review Psalm 25:4 and Genesis 1:1.

Review activity: *Days of Creation* miniatures
Use the *Days of Creation* visual miniatures. Place them in any order on a desk, or stand them up on the chalkboard. Choose one child to close his eyes and another child to remove one visual and hide it behind his back. Tell the child whose eyes were closed to look at the remaining visuals and guess which one is missing. Repeat the game with various children taking turns.

Student page 3
Instruct the children to cut out the creation pictures for Days 4–6 and to glue them in the appropriate spaces on the page. Direct the children to cut out the half of the Bible. Give the

children their Bible halves from Lesson 9 and a large sheet of construction paper. Demonstrate how to glue the left half of the Bible on the left side of the construction paper, with the middle of the Bible placed in the middle of the construction paper. Instruct the children to glue their left Bible half. Follow the same procedure for the right side of the Bible, having both halves come together in the middle. Review what God created on each day.

Song: "All Things Were Made by God"

Review activity: For God's Glory visual
Repeat the activity from Lesson 14 as time permits.

Song: "Holy, Holy, Holy," stanza 1

Lesson 16: God Rested

Bible text: Genesis 1:31–2:3

Doctrinal truths: God; Church

Character traits: Wisdom; Thankfulness

Memory verses: Review Genesis 1:1 and Psalm 95:6.

Materials
- A completed copy of Student page 4 (for use as a visual)
- "And God Said" booklet for each student and the teacher (Student Packet—cut on dashed line, fold on solid line, and staple to make booklet.)
- *Days of Creation* visuals, Days 1–7

Opening chorus: "Our Bible Time's Begun"

Prayer
Thank God for our church.

- ➤ There are many churches that we can go to where pastors preach the Bible and tell mothers and fathers and boys and girls about the God of heaven.

Song: "Creation Song"
Use the *Days of Creation* visuals, Days 1–7, as you sing this song, repeating Genesis 1:1 between stanzas.

Bible lesson

Introduction
Display *Days of Creation* visual, Day 7. Ask the children what they see in the picture. Direct them to stand and repeat the following action rhyme with you.

- ➤ Here is the church.
    (*Interlock fingers and fold them into a fist.*)
    Here is the steeple.
    (*Make steeple with pointer fingers.*)
    Open the door and see all the people.
    (*Open thumbs out; wiggle fingers.*)

Lesson

God looked at everything that He had made and saw that it was good. (Read Genesis 1:31 from your Bible.) It was very good because God's plans are always perfect. That means they cannot be wrong in any way. God was not tired after all His work of creation. God is never tired because He is all-powerful. Our God can do anything. He is *omnipotent*. That's a big word. Let's say it together.

God's work of creation took six days. Then God was done. God stopped His work. The Bible tells us that God rested on the seventh day. Do you know why?

God planned for us to have a special day in each week to worship and serve Him. God tells us that we should get our work done in six days, and He tells us to have one special day to rest and worship. Can you say the days of the week with me? (Guide the children in repeating them with you.) Christians worship God on the first day of the week, Sunday, because this was the day the Lord Jesus rose from the dead.

What should we do on Sunday? (*Allow discussion.*) We should go to church and worship God. Do you know what *worship* means? (Show the completed copy of student page 4.) Worship is singing songs about God, praying to God, giving money for God's work, and listening to teachers and preachers teach us God's Word. (BATs: 6a Bible study; 6b Prayer; 7c Praise)

Remember, God created us to love and obey Him. He tells us in His Word to meet together on Sundays with others who love Him so as to worship and thank Him.

(Read Psalm 95:6 aloud.) We worship God because He alone is worthy—He is holy and without sin.

Application
➤ Let's worship God with a song as we sing "Praise Him, Praise Him." (BAT: 7c Praise)

Song: "God's Special Day"
Display the completed copy of student page 4 as you sing appropriate stanzas.

> The following activity may be used as part of this lesson or as an additional lesson.

Student Packet: "And God Said" booklet
Distribute a booklet to each child and guide a discussion of the cover.

➤ What do you see on the cover of the booklet? (*the world, children*)

What are the children doing? (*praying*)

What does our verse tell us that we should (*worship our Maker*)

Encourage the children to "read" the verse together with you. Guide the children in reading the day numerals, the pictures, and the text as you proceed through the book. Call attention to each page numeral as you direct them to turn the pages. Discuss the first day of creation on page 2 and read the text. Continue with each of the other pages as you review the days of creation.

Review the catechism on the back cover. Encourage the children to take their booklets home and "read" them to their parents.

Lesson 17: We Worship God

Bible text: Psalm 122:1

Doctrinal truths: God; Church

Character traits: Wisdom; Thankfulness

Memory verses: Review.

Materials
- *Days of Creation* visual, Day 7, and miniatures, Days 1–7
- Student page 4 and cutouts
- Scissors
- Glue

Opening chorus: "Our Bible Time's Begun"

Song: "God's Word"

Prayer
Occasionally throughout the year, recite the following rhyme before you pray.

➤ God is listening to the words I say;
  (*Cup hand to ear and point to heaven.*)
  He will hear me when I bow to pray.
  (*Bow head and fold hands.*)
Thank God for our pastors and our Bible teachers.

Song: "My Bible Book"
Replace "He loves me, He loves me" with "He hears me, He hears me."

Student page 4
Instruct the children to cut out the four church-window scenes depicting worship activities. Discuss the scenes and instruct the children to glue them in the appropriate spaces, referring to the letters in the spaces if necessary. Read the page and lead the children in reciting Psalm 95:6.

Song: "God's Special Day"
Review the various aspects of worship as you sing this song.

Song: "Holy, Holy, Holy," stanza 1

Review activity: *Days of Creation* miniatures

Place the *Days of Creation* visual miniatures out of order on a desk or chalkboard tray. Let the children take turns placing them in order. If time allows, intersperse creation memory verses and catechism questions.

Lesson 18: Kate Learns from a Squirrel

Bible text: Review.

Doctrinal truth: God

Character traits: Wisdom; Thankfulness

Memory verses: Review.

Catechism: Review Catechism 1–8.

Materials
• Squirrel visual (See the Appendix for the visual and instructions.)

Opening chorus: "Our Bible Time's Begun"

Hymn: "Father, We Thank Thee for the Night"

Prayer

Thank God for making a world for us to live in.

➤ We know that God is with us wherever we are. There is a big word that means this: omnipresent. God is present everywhere. We can pray to Him when we are *walking* along the sidewalk or *playing* outdoors. Sometimes you might start to say or do something unkind to a friend. You can stop and softly whisper a prayer right then: "Dear God, help me to be kind and obey Thy Word." We can *sit* at the dinner table and thank God for our food. We can pray when we are *lying* in our beds at night and ask the Lord to forgive us for the bad things we did during the day. Anytime, anywhere—we can talk to our God.

Song: "All Things Were Made by God"

Character story: "Kate Learns from a Squirrel"

Mr. and Mrs. Vick had gone to a Christian camp retreat for the weekend. Kate was so excited! Mom and Dad had brought her, along with Sam and Josh, to visit Grandma and Grandpa Vick's home in the country.

While Josh and Sam were helping Grandpa clean up the barn, Kate was baking cookies with Grandma in the big country kitchen. Kate worked happily at rolling the peanut butter cookie dough into small, round balls and placing them in neat rows on the cookie sheet. Grandma showed her how to take a fork, dip it into some flour, place it on top of each ball, and then press lightly to flatten it on the cookie sheet.

They sang together as they worked, "Father, we thank Thee for the night." (Sing this hymn as part of your story narration.)

Suddenly Grandma hurried over to the window and called, "Come here quickly, Kate."

Kate joined her by the window and looked out at the big farmyard where Grandma was pointing. There she saw a brown bushy-tailed squirrel with a large, black walnut in its mouth. The nut was so big that it stuck out all around the squirrel's mouth. The little fellow was jumping first one way and then another—back and forth, back and forth—stopping briefly here and there as if to look and listen and smell.

"What is he doing, Grandma?" Kate asked.

"He is looking for a place to hide his nut in the ground. He will hide many more nuts and fruits and seeds. Then when winter comes, he will dig them up and eat them," Grandma answered.

They stood together quietly as the squirrel began digging into the ground with his front paws. Soon he dropped the nut from his mouth into the hole and quickly pushed the dirt and leaves back over it.

Kate looked very serious and thoughtful. Finally she said, "But how will he ever know where to look for his nuts? The yard is so big, and if he hides even more, I just don't see how he can find them all."

"God made squirrels in a very special way," Grandma told her. "He gave them an instinct that causes them to do things the way they do even though they do not have the kind of brain that people have to help them think." God has a special plan and purpose for all of His creation and for His world. "He hath made every thing beautiful in his time" (Ecclesiastes 3:11). "All things were made by him; and without him was not any thing made that was made" (John 1:3).

Review activity: Squirrel visual

Display the squirrel and his tree-trunk home. Tell the children that every time they answer a question or recite a verse, they may feed an acorn to the squirrel (put it in the hole of the tree trunk).

1. Who made you? *(Catechism 1: God made me.)* (Sing "God Made Me.")

2. What else did God make? *(Catechism 2: God made all things.)*

3. Why did God make you and all things? *(Catechism 3: God made me and all things for His own glory.)*

4. Who made God? (*Catechism 4: Nobody made God.*)

5. Has God ever had a beginning? (*Catechism 5: No, God has always been.*)

6. Will God ever die? (*Catechism 6: No, God lives forever.*)

7. How can you glorify God? (*Catechism 7: I can glorify God by loving Him and doing what He commands.*)

8. Why ought you to glorify God? (*Catechism 8: I ought to glorify God because He made me and takes care of me.*)

9. What did God create on the first day? (*light, day, and night*)

10. What did God create on the second day? (*sky, air, and water*)

11. What did God create on the third day? (*land, seas, and plants*)

12. What did God create on the fourth day? (*sun, moon, and stars*)

13. What did God create on the fifth day? (*birds and fish*)

14. What did God create on the sixth day? (*animals and man*)

Allow the children to take turns reciting memory verses.

Song: "Holy, Holy, Holy," stanza 1

God's Love
Sin and Salvation: God Sees My Sin

Lesson 19: Adam and Eve

Bible texts: Genesis 2:7–25; Romans 3:12b

Doctrinal truths: Man; Salvation

Character trait: Wisdom

Memory verse: Introduce Romans 3:23.

Catechism: Introduce Catechism 9–11.

Materials
• *Days of Creation* visual, Day 6

Opening chorus: "God's Way"

Song: "Jesus Loves Me," stanzas 1 and 4

Prayer
Ask God to help us to do the things we should.

Song: "There Is None That Doeth Good"
Read Romans 3:12b to the children. Then sing "There Is None That Doeth Good."

Memory verse
Read Romans 3:23 from your Bible. After several repetitions, encourage the children to join you in saying the verse.

Bible lesson

Introduction
➤ Do you remember what God made on the sixth day of His creation work? *(Allow discussion.)* He made animals to walk on the dry ground. What did God make next? *(He created a man.)* God named this first man *Adam.* And then He created a helper for Adam. Adam named the first woman *Eve.* Now God had made people who could love Him, talk to Him, and obey Him.

Display *Days of Creation* visual, Day 6, and sing stanza 5 of "God Made the World."

➤ Adam and Eve were the first parents God made. We call them our first parents because they were the first parents God created. Who were our first parents? *(Catechism 19: Adam and Eve were our first parents.)*

As you teach this lesson, you will use several catechism truths that will be taught in later lessons. Because the students are not yet familiar with the questions and answers, you may need to provide the answers during this lesson.

Lesson

God created Adam and Eve different from anything else that He made—different from all the plants and all the animals in His world. God made Adam out of the dust of the earth. God made Eve from a rib—a bone from Adam's body. Of what were our first parents made? *(Catechism 20: God made the body of Adam out of the dust of the ground and formed Eve from the body of Adam.)*

The Bible tells us that God made Adam and Eve like Himself. God gave them minds so that they could learn and think. (Point to your head.) Each one of you has a mind. Your mind helps you learn. You can use your mind to listen (Point to your ears.) and learn to think (Point to your head.) God's way. (Point to heaven.) You can use your mind to choose to obey God.

God also gave Adam and Eve souls. Each of you has a soul. A soul is the part of you that no one but God can see. Your soul will live forever. If you believe in God, your soul will live forever with Him in heaven, and you will want to do what He says in His Word. What did God give Adam and Eve besides bodies? *(Catechism 21: God gave them souls that could never die.)* Do you have a soul as well as a body? *(Catechism 22: Yes, I have a soul that can never die.)*

God made Adam and Eve like Himself in another way too. He made them without sin. Who can tell me what sin is? *(Answers may vary.)* Sin is doing what God tells us not to do, and sin is also not doing what God tells us to do. The first man and woman were created holy, like God, without sin. They were kind and helpful. They never did anything wrong. They did not steal or tell lies. They knew God, and they lived God's way. In what condition did God make Adam and Eve? *(Catechism 23: God made them holy and happy.)*

These first people whom God made were very happy. God had given them a beautiful garden home to live in. They could walk in their garden home and even talk to God. They could hear God talk to them. They had everything they needed. God was so good to them.

God created Adam and Eve to love Him. He wanted them to show Him how much they loved

Him by obeying Him. So He told Adam and Eve that they could use everything in their beautiful garden home. They could eat the fruit from all the trees—except for one. God said, "You may not eat the fruit of the tree of the knowledge of good and evil."

Why did God make Adam and Eve? *(to love and obey Him)* Remember, God made Adam and Eve just like Himself—perfect, without sin, with minds to think, and with souls that would live forever. He gave them a perfect garden home where they could know and live God's way. Do you know what happened? Do you think Adam and Eve obeyed God? *(Allow discussion.)* We will finish this story in our next lesson.

Application
➤ God made you and all things for His own glory. He made you to love and obey Him because He is the one true God. In the Bible, you can learn how to love and obey God. (BAT: 6a Bible study)

Song: "Jesus Loves Me," stanza 4

Catechism
Introduce Catechism 9–11.

- ■ Are there more gods than one? *(No, there is only one God.)*

- ■ In how many persons does this one God exist? *(God exists in three persons.)*

- ■ Who are the three persons of God? *(The three persons of God are the Father, the Son, and the Holy Spirit.)*

Song: "The Trinity"

Lesson 20: Adam and Eve Disobeyed God

Bible text: Genesis 3:1–13
Doctrinal truths: Fall of man; Satan
Character trait: Wisdom
Memory verse: Review Romans 3:23.
Catechism: Review Catechism 9–11.

Opening chorus: "God's Way"

Song: "Jesus Loves Me," stanzas 1 and 4

Prayer
Ask God to help us always to be sorry for our sin.

Memory verse
Review Romans 3:23.

Catechism
Review Catechism 9-11.

- ■ Are there more gods than one? *(No, there is only one God.)*

- ■ In how many persons does this one God exist? *(God exists in three persons.)*

- ■ Who are the three persons of God? *(The three persons of God are the Father, the Son, and the Holy Spirit.)*

Song: "Oh, Be Careful"

Bible lesson

Introduction
Review Lesson 19 briefly.

Lesson

God has an enemy called Satan. Satan does not love and serve God. Satan does not want anybody to love and serve God. Satan had been watching God. He saw God create the world. He saw God create Adam and Eve. He heard God tell Adam and Eve about the fruit tree in the garden.

One day Satan made himself look like a beautiful snake, and he came to Eve in her garden home. Satan said, "Did God say you could eat of all the trees in the garden?"

Eve said, "We may eat of all the trees in the garden except one. God said we could not eat fruit from the tree that grows in the middle of the garden. If we do not obey God, He will punish us."

"Well," Satan said, "God won't really punish you if you eat fruit from that tree. God doesn't want you to eat the fruit of that tree because it will make you as great as He." Satan told Eve, "Don't listen to God. Don't believe what He says. Do what you want to do."

Did Eve listen to Satan? Yes, she did. She believed Satan. Eve looked at the tree. "Hmm! That does look good," she thought. "I will see what really happens if I do eat some of the fruit. I will do what I want to do—not what God tells me to do." Eve did an awful thing. She disobeyed God. She did what God told her not to do. She picked some fruit and ate it. She gave some to Adam, and he ate it. They both did what they wanted to do. Adam and Eve both disobeyed God. They both did what God told them not to do. They both sinned.

Now Adam and Eve knew that they were sinners. They knew that God would have to punish them. They had thought and acted in their own way instead of God's way. They were so unhappy and so sad. They could not talk to God or walk with God in their garden home. Do you think God was sad? Yes, God was very sad.

What did God say would happen to Adam and Eve if they ate the fruit from that one tree in the middle of the garden? *(They would be punished.)* Now, instead of being holy and happy, they became sinful and sad. God told them they would have to leave their beautiful garden home. Now, they would have to work hard to find food to eat. They would have sickness and sadness. They would have to die someday. Adam and Eve, our first parents, had sinned. They had disobeyed God. They had done what God told them not to do. They needed a Savior from sin.

Application

➤ Does Satan want you to love and obey God? *(no)* What teaches us to love and obey God? *(the Bible)* You should listen carefully to God's Word whenever and wherever you hear it—at home, at church, or here in Bible time. (BAT: 6a Bible study)

Song: "God's Word"

Lesson 21: The Children of Adam and Eve

Bible text: Genesis 4:1–2
Doctrinal truth: Man
Character traits: Wisdom; Thankfulness
Catechism: Review Catechism 9–11 and introduce Catechism 12.
Materials
• Vick family puppets
• Baby doll (optional)
• A dog stick-puppet (optional)

Opening chorus: "God's Way"

Song: "Father, We Thank Thee for the Night"

Action rhyme: "Finger Family"

➤ God made mothers.
  (Point to thumb.)
God made fathers.
  (Point to pointer finger.)
God made brothers too.
  (Point to tall finger.)
God made sisters.
  (Point to ring finger.)
God made babies.
  (Point to little finger.)
God made both me and you.
  (Point toward self and others.)

You may repeat this, having five children hold the Vick family puppets and recite the corresponding line of the rhyme, (father for first line, etc.) with the entire class joining in on the last line.

Prayer
Thank God for our families.

Bible lesson

Introduction

➤ God is so good to plan for mothers and fathers, isn't He?

Remember in our last lesson we learned how God gave Adam and Eve the very first home in the beautiful Garden of Eden. Why did they have to leave their home? *(Allow discussion.)* Yes, because they sinned—they did not obey God. God told them they would have to leave this special home in the Garden of Eden. But God still loved them and gave them another home. God told them (Genesis 3:15) that He would send a Savior someday. It was God's plan for us to have a home with a mother and father and family. God is so good to us! (BATs: 4a Sowing and reaping; 5a Love)

Lesson

Hold a doll behind your back and make a sound like a crying baby. If you don't have a doll, just mimic a crying baby.

What did that sound like? How do you know? (Show the doll.) Yes, we have all seen a baby with our eyes and heard a baby's crying with our ears. Babies are so sweet, so soft, and so cuddly. You were each a tiny baby once. (Name children one by one as you say, "Sally was a baby," etc.) But do you know that there were not always babies in the world? No, after God made His world and all the animals and Adam and Eve, God still had another special plan for His world.

God made Adam and Eve to love and help each other. Then He gave them a baby boy. It was the first baby they had ever seen. It was the very first baby born into this world. Eve held her baby very close. (Dramatize with the doll.) I am sure she must have sung him a song. Maybe she sang: (Sing a stanza of "Creation Song" or "One God" as you rock the doll.)

Adam and Eve named their baby son Cain because they had gotten him from the Lord. God had given a baby to the first parents. Cain grew up to be a farmer. He liked to plant seeds and pull weeds and help make things grow.

Then God sent Adam and Eve another baby son, whom they called Abel. As a boy, Abel helped his father take care of the sheep and the little lambs. When Abel grew up, he became a shepherd. A shepherd is a keeper of sheep.

God's Love

And then God sent even more children into the home of the first parents.

God planned for Adam and Eve to take care of their children. God planned for Adam and Eve to tell their children about God and His ways. Adam and Eve told their children how God had created the world. They told them how God made all things. They told their children how God had created people to love and obey Him.

Then they sadly told their children about God's enemy, Satan. They told how they had disobeyed God. They reminded their children that no one is good. We all disobey God and displease Him. They told them that God must punish sin.

Then they happily told them that God had promised to send a Savior who would take the punishment for sin.

Application

➤ God is so good to us. He gives us our homes, our mommies and daddies to love and to take care of us and teach us, and our brothers and sisters to love and to play with.

God is so good. Our great God not only made us but also loves us so much that He sent His Son to die on the cross for our sins. (BAT: 1a Understanding Jesus Christ)

Let's thank God again for our families. (BAT: 7c Praise)

Lead the children in prayer.

Catechism

Review Catechism 9–11.

■ Are there more gods than one? *(No, there is only one God.)*

■ In how many persons does this one God exist? *(God exists in three persons.)*

■ Who are the three persons of God? *(The three persons of God are the Father, the Son, and the Holy Spirit.)*

Introduce Catechism 12.

■ Who is God? *(God is a spirit and does not have a body like man.)*

➤ We cannot see God, but He sees us. God is our maker, our keeper, and our Savior.

Song: "The Trinity"

Lesson 22: The Children of Adam and Eve Disobeyed

Bible text: Genesis 4:3–16

Doctrinal truth: Man

Character trait: Obedience

Memory verse: Review Romans 3:23.

Catechism: Review Catechism 12 and introduce Catechism 13.

Materials
• A completed copy of Student page 5 (for use as a visual)
• Student page 5 and cutouts
• Scissors
• Glue
• *BIBLE TRUTHS for Christian Schools K5* CD, "Even a Child Is Known" (optional)

Opening chorus: "God's Way"

Song: "Father, We Thank Thee for the Night"

Action rhyme: "Finger Family"
(See Index of Poetry.)

Prayer
Ask God to help us to be kind to our families—parents, brothers, and sisters.

Bible lesson

Introduction

➤ We learned in our last lesson that Adam and Eve, the first father and mother in God's world, had two sons. What were their names? *(Cain and Abel)* Cain was a farmer, and Abel was a shepherd. Today we are going to learn what happened to these boys as they grew up.

Lead the children in singing "Even a Child Is Known," or play the selection on the *BIBLE TRUTHS for Christian Schools K5* CD. This will be taught as a memory verse later. Use it only as an introduction to the lesson now.

Lesson
Use the completed copy of Student page 5 as a visual.

Adam and Eve taught Cain and Abel that they should obey God. They told them that God had a plan to forgive their sin. They were to bring a blood sacrifice to God, tell Him that they loved Him, and ask Him to forgive their sin. It was called a sin offering.

One day Cain, the farmer, brought some fruit that he had grown in his field for an offering to God. Cain did not bring a blood sacrifice. Instead he brought an offering of fruit—something he had grown and had done with his own hands. Cain did not come to God with a heart that loved Him and was sorry for his sin. So God did not accept the sacrifice that he laid on his altar.

Abel also brought his sacrifice—a lamb from his flock of sheep. When he laid his lamb on his altar, he told God he loved Him and was really sorry for his sin. God accepted Abel's offering because He saw Abel's sorrow for his sin. Abel trusted God to forgive him. Abel's lamb on the altar reminds us that God's Son is called the Lamb of God because He died on the cross to forgive us of our sin. He was the special gift offering for sin.

When Cain saw how happy Abel was because God had accepted his offering and forgiven his sin, he was angry and jealous. God saw Cain's sin. God knew what Cain was thinking. God knows all things. God told Cain that if he would bring a sin offering with a loving and trusting heart, his offering also would be accepted.

But Cain did not listen to God. He was so angry and jealous that later when he found Abel in the field, he killed him. To take away the life of someone is a terrible sin!

Do you think God saw what Cain did? Yes, God sees all that we do, doesn't He? God is a spirit and does not have a body like man. We cannot see God, but He sees us. God is everywhere. God sees and knows everything. God spoke to Cain. God told him that he would have to be punished. He told Cain that he would have trouble growing good food and that he would have to take his family and go far away to another land.

Application
➤ How unhappy Adam and Eve were. They had lost two sons. Abel was dead; because Cain had disobeyed, he had to be sent away. They remembered how God had punished them and sent them away from their beautiful garden home because of their sin. Sin had to be punished again.

Cain did not obey God, so he had to be punished. Because we sin, God must punish us. We must confess our sin and ask Him to forgive us. Abel obeyed. We should obey because we love God and want to please Him. (BATs: 1b Repentance and faith; 2b Servanthood)

Memory verse
Review Romans 3:23 and sing "There Is None That Doeth Good."

Student page 5
Instruct the children to cut out the illustrations of the offerings. Remind them that God forgave Abel's sin because Abel cheerfully obeyed God and that Cain chose not to obey God, so Cain's sin was not forgiven. Instruct the children to glue the offerings in the appropriate spaces. Read the page and lead the children in reciting Romans 3:23.

Song: "God Is with Me"

Catechism
Review Catechism 12.

➤ Who is God? *(God is a spirit and does not have a body like man.)*

Introduce Catechism 13.

➤ Where is God? *(God is everywhere.)*

Lesson 23: What Sin Is

Bible texts: Genesis 4:3–16 (review); I John 3:4; John 3:16; Rom. 3:23; Rom. 6:23; John 1:12; I Cor. 15:3–4

Doctrinal truth: Salvation

Character traits: Obedience; Trust

Memory verse: Review Romans 3:23.

Catechism: Review Catechism 12–13 and introduce Catechism 14.

Materials
- A completed copy of Student page 5 (for use as a visual; used in Lesson 22)
- Student page 6 and cutouts
- Scissors
- Glue

Opening chorus: "God's Way"

Song: "My Bible Book"
Replace "He loves me, He loves me" with "All have sinned, All have sinned" and "I have sinned, I have sinned."

Prayer
Thank God for sending Jesus to be our Savior from sin.

Bible lesson

Introduction
Lead the children in the "Finger Family" action rhyme. (See Index of Poetry.)

Lead the children in singing "There Is None That Doeth Good."

Lesson

Using the fingers of one hand, emphasize the five points below.

God planned for families to live in His world. He planned for fathers to be the leaders in their families. He planned for mothers to help fathers. God planned for parents to work together to take care of their children and teach them God's Word and God's way.

God wants all mothers and fathers and boys and girls to know:

1. *God made and loves us—you and me.* (Read John 3:16 to the children.) God made us to love and serve Him. God is holy and cannot sin. He lives in heaven. He wants us to live in heaven with Him for ever and ever.

2. *We have sinned.* (Read Romans 3:23 aloud.) What is sin? *(Catechism 26: Sin is the transgression of the law of God.)* Sin is not obeying God's Word. We all have disobeyed God's Word (Give examples: disobeying parents, taking things that do not belong to us, doing and saying unkind things to others). God cannot let sin into heaven. Our sin must be punished. (Read Romans 6:23a.) We cannot get rid of our sin by ourselves. (Lead the children in singing "There Is None That Doeth Good" and reciting Romans 3:23.)

3. *Christ died for our sin. He lives again.* (Read I Corinthians 15:3–4 to the children.) God wants us to live with Him in heaven someday. That is why God sent His Son to die for our sin. But Jesus is not dead now. He lives in heaven.

4. *We must believe that Jesus died for our sin and lives again.* (Read John 1:12 aloud.) We are sinners, and Jesus died to save us. We may ask Jesus to forgive us and be our Savior. It is our choice.

5. *We can live forever with God in heaven someday.* (Read Romans 6:23 aloud.) When we believe Jesus died for us and ask Him to be our Savior, we become children of God. Then we are in God's family, and we can live forever in heaven with God. Salvation is a gift of God. I am so glad God did not write just the first part of that verse (Quote Romans 6:23a.) but added the last part. (Quote Romans 6:23b.) (BATs: 1a Understanding Jesus Christ; 1b Repentance and faith)

> Not all five-year-olds are ready to make a personal decision to accept the Son of God as their Savior from sin; however, some are. It is your responsibility to go over the simple plan of salvation from time to time, building a foundation of biblical knowledge to prepare each child to make his own choice in this most important decision of his life. Rely on the Spirit of God to do the convicting work in the conscience of each child. Then their decisions will be genuine and eternal. See "Leading a Child to the Lord" in the Introduction to this teacher's edition.

Song: "Jesus Loves Me"

➤ Many boys and girls and mothers and fathers like this song because it reminds us that God loves us even though we are sinners.

Doctrinal emphasis: Sin

➤ What is sin? *(Allow discussion.)* Does God want us to sin? *(Allow discussion.)* When we disobey mommy or daddy, is that sin? *(Yes, it is sin.)* God's Word tells us to obey our parents. When we are unkind to someone, is that sin? *(Yes, it is sin.)* God's Word tells us to be kind to each other. When we do not do what God tells us to do, we sin or transgress God's law. When we do something that God tells us not to do, we sin or transgress God's law. *Transgression* is another word for sin.

Catechism

Review Catechism 12–13.

■ Who is God? *(God is a spirit and does not have a body like man.)*

■ Where is God? *(God is everywhere.)*

Introduce Catechism 14.

■ Can you see God? *(No, I cannot see God, but He always sees me.)*

Student page 6

Instruct the children to cut out the illustrations and glue them in the appropriate spaces.

Show them the completed copy of Student page 5. Remind the children that Abel believed and obeyed God by confessing his sin and bringing a sin offering to God, but Cain tried to come to God in his own way.

Instruct the children to put their pointer fingers on the Bible on page 6. Read the sentences above the picture and lead the children in reciting Romans 3:23.

Direct the children to put their pointer fingers on the cross. Explain that the cross is a symbol; it reminds us of the Lamb of God, the Lord Jesus, whom God sent to die for our sins. Tell the children that God tells us in the Bible that Jesus is the only way for us to come to God and have our sins forgiven.

Instruct the children to put their pointer fingers on the picture of the children. Read the sentence above the picture. Ask the children to "read" the sentence together.

Song: "God Is with Me"

➤ Does God see us when we sin? *(yes)* Does God see us when we obey? *(yes)* God sees all that we do. Can you see God? *(no)*

Lesson 24: Kate's Special Memory

Bible text: Review.

Doctrinal truth: Salvation

Character trait: Trust

Memory verse: Review.

Catechism: Review Catechism 1–14.

Materials
- Vick family puppets (optional)
- "Thy Word have I hid in mine heart" visual (See the Appendix for the visual and instructions.)
- Four 3½" × 4" cards, labeled with verse references Psalm 25:4; Genesis 1:1; Psalm 95:6; and Romans 3:23; with a hole punched in the top of each
- Fourteen 3½" × 4" cards, labeled with the numerals 1–14 (to represent Catechism 1–14) and with a hole punched in the top of each
- Bag, box, or basket, labeled with a large heart
- A Wordless Book (Fold sheets of construction paper width-wise— one each of 4½" × 3¼" in green, black, red, white, and yellow or gold. Layer folded black, red, white, and yellow paper in order from top to bottom and place inside the folded green [cover] paper to form a booklet. Glue the pages together.)

Opening chorus: "God's Way"

Song: "My Bible Book"
Replace "He loves me, He loves me" with "All have sinned, All have sinned" and "I have sinned, I have sinned."

Prayer
Pray that, if any child has never asked Jesus to be his Savior, he might want to do it very soon.

Review activity: "Thy Word have I hid in mine heart" visual
Review memory verses and catechism by hanging verse reference cards and numeral cards on the visual one or more at a time. Allow the children to take turns removing a card, reciting the corresponding verse or the catechism answer (after you have asked the question corresponding with the numeral picked), and then placing it in the heart container.

Character story: "Kate's Special Memory"

Kate was sitting in her kindergarten class when her teacher asked the boys and girls to think about the most exciting thing they had done during the past summer before they came to kindergarten. Kate sat quietly and thought . . . and this is what she remembered.

During the summer before Kate went to kindergarten, the whole family had gone to Grandma and Grandpa Vick's home in the country for a week of vacation.

Each day they did many interesting things. The children enjoyed going fishing with their dad and grandpa in the river nearby. They learned how to feed the animals as they helped do the chores each day. And every afternoon Grandpa would hitch the pony to a small wagon so they could all take a ride.

It had been the best vacation ever, especially for Kate; and she knew why. She remembered the most important thing that happened that week had been after one of the special tent evangelistic services they were going to each night.

The reason they were going to church in a tent was that Grandpa and Grandma's church building was being remodeled to make it larger and to have more Sunday school classrooms. They had even moved the church benches into the tent for the week of special services.

The children thought it was fun to go to church in a tent. Besides that, every night before the sermon the visiting preacher told special Bible stories just for the children.

As Kate thought back about that week, she remembered where she had sat—between her mommy and daddy on the long bench where the whole family sat together each night as they listened to God's Word.

On the very first night, during the children's story time, the preacher showed them a Wordless Book. (Illustrate the following with a Wordless Book.) It was a book without any words in it, and every time he turned a page you could see a new color that told a story. And the preacher did a strange thing: he began on the last two pages inside the green cover of the book instead of the pages at the front of the book. These last two were the gold pages to remind them of heaven. He talked about the wonderful home that God was preparing for all those who love Him and have asked His Son, Jesus Christ, to be their Savior from sin. As Kate listened, she remembered that Mom and Dad had talked to her about the very same things.

Kate knew her older brother Sam had trusted the Lord Jesus. So she sat quietly and thought very seriously about the lesson. On the way home after church that night, she listened as the grown-ups talked about what the preacher had said and how good it was to be reminded of God's promises.

The next day, when her dad came into lunch after helping Grandpa fix a fence, she ran to meet him and said, "You know, I've been thinking about what Preacher Davis said, and I think I'll be saved when I'm six . . . before I go to first grade."

Her father smiled at her and said, "That's good, Kate, but you don't have to wait that long if you understand that you are a sinner and that Jesus wants to be your Savior from sin."

Kate walked away quietly thinking as she began helping Grandma set the table for lunch.

And that night in the big tent, the preacher showed them the black pages in the Wordless Book—the ones that remind us of sin. He spoke about the holy God who is without sin . . . that we cannot go to live with a holy God in His heavenly home because we are sinners. He told the story of Adam and Eve and how they disobeyed God.

As Kate listened, she thought about the many times she had disobeyed her parents and had been unkind to Sam and Josh and sometimes even to her best friends. "Oh, I am a sinner," she thought sadly.

The next morning, before Mom and Dad got out of bed, she tiptoed quietly into their room. She heard them talking, so she knew they were awake.

"May I get in bed with you?" she whispered.

"Sure thing," her daddy answered as he gave her a hug and lifted her into the bed. She snuggled up between her parents and said, "You know, I've decided I can't wait until I go to first grade to be saved from my sin. I know I need the Savior now; so tonight when we have family notions, I will ask Jesus to be my Savior."

Kate's mother smiled, "You mean family devotions, don't you? Well, that's wonderful, Kate, but you don't even have to wait until tonight. Whenever you are ready, you know Dad and I will be happy to take the Bible and show you how to trust Jesus."

"Tonight," Kate whispered; ". . . tonight," she repeated softly.

The Vick family spent another happy day on the farm. They packed a picnic and ate their lunch down by the river.

That night as they sat around the living room, when Dad asked Sam to bring the family Bible, Kate ran over and jumped up onto her mother's lap.

She whispered into her mother's ear, "Mom, do you remember what I want to do now?"

Kate's mother smiled as she hugged her little girl. Of course she remembered. She had prayed for her little girl to ask God's Son to be her Savior from sin even before Kate was born. She whispered back, "I surely do!"

So her daddy and mommy took Kate into their bedroom and knelt down beside the bed. Right there, they showed Kate how to trust the Savior. After Kate had asked Jesus to save her from her sins, she thought of her little brother Josh and she prayed, ". . . and, dear Jesus, help Josh to be

saved too . . . when he is big enough to understand. Amen."

That is what Kate remembered as the most important thing that had happened during her summer vacation in the country. And that is what she told her class when it was her turn to share.

Application
➤ The most important thing that can ever happen to you is to ask God's Son, the Lord Jesus Christ, to be your Savior from sin. (BAT: lb Repentance and faith)

Song: "Jesus Loves the Little Children"

Lesson 25: Noah's Family Obeyed

Bible text: Genesis 6:1–9, 17
Doctrinal truth: Salvation
Character trait: Obedience
Memory verse: Review Romans 3:23.
Materials
• Toy ark (or picture of ark)
• "Noah's Ark" (Picture Packet)
• Student page 7 and cutouts
• Scissors
• Glue

Opening chorus: "God's Way"

Song: "Jesus Loves Me," stanzas 1 and 4

Prayer
Thank God for His love and care.

Song: "There Is None That Doeth Good"

Bible lesson

Introduction
Display an ark and ask the children if they know what it is. Allow a few to share their experiences of riding in a boat. Then tell them they are going to hear the story about the special ark, or boat, that God told Noah to build.

Lesson

One day God looked all around the world that He had created. He saw many, many people who did not love and obey Him. God was very sad. God knew that He would have to punish those who did not love and obey Him.

When God looked around His world, He saw one man who did love and obey Him. That man's name was Noah. God told Noah what He planned to do. He said, "Noah, these people do not listen to me. They do not love and obey me. They have sinned. I must punish them. I am going to send a big flood to punish them."

Noah did not know what a flood was. Noah had never seen a flood before. But Noah listened to God. He believed what God said. He did what God told him to do.

God said, "Noah, build a big, big ark." God told Noah just how to make the ark. He told him how big to make it and how many windows to put in it. He told Noah that the ark must have just one door. God told Noah everything that he should do. Noah listened and obeyed.

Pretty soon, "Bang, bang, bang," went the hammers. "Zzz, zzz, zzz," went the saws. Noah and his three sons were busy building an ark. (Display "Noah's Ark" picture.)

Noah knew he must obey God, so he kept on building. He was working hard to obey God. Noah's three sons were also working hard to obey.

When the work was done and the ark was built, God told Noah to take his wife and his three sons and their wives into the ark. Then God brought some of every kind of animal that lived in the world to the door of the ark. And God told Noah to let them in the ark. There were two giraffes with their long necks—a mother giraffe and a daddy giraffe. There were two elephants with their long trunks—a mother elephant and a daddy elephant. There were two rabbits with their long ears—a mother rabbit and a daddy rabbit. Two of every animal came to the ark, but God sent seven of the kinds of animals Noah used for sin offerings. So for some animals God brought seven of their kind. Noah took every kind of animal into the ark because God told him to. Then the Bible tells us that the Lord God shut the door of the ark.

They were all in the ark, but there was still no water on the earth. Soon the sky was dark all around, and raindrops began to fall from the clouds in the sky. Drip, drip, drip, drop, drop, drop—harder and harder the rain fell. It rained, and it rained, and it rained. The water that fell on the earth rose higher and higher (Raise hands higher and higher.) until it covered the grass, the bushes, the tall trees, the high hills, and the mountains. The water covered and flooded all the earth.

The ark floated on the water. Noah and his family were safe in the ark. The animals in the ark were safe. God had promised to take care of Noah if he obeyed. And He did take care of Noah. God always keeps His promises.

After many, many days the rain stopped. After many, many more days the water finally dried up. Then God told Noah that he and his family could come out of the ark. So they did. They brought all

of the animals out with them. God promised Noah that He would never again send a flood to destroy all the living things on Earth. God put a rainbow in the sky as a sign to remind Noah and us of this promise. Noah, his wife, his three sons, and their wives all thanked the Lord God who had kept them safe.

Application

➤ Did Noah love and obey God? *(Yes, he did.)*

Did all the people living around Noah love and obey God? *(No, they did not.)*

Why did God have to punish these people? *(because they had sinned)* Remember that, when Adam and Eve sinned in their garden home, God had to punish them. Sin must be punished. God must punish sin because God is holy and without sin. The Bible tells us that we all have sinned. (Recite Romans 3:23.) God promised to punish sin, but He also promised to send a Savior to take our punishment for us. He will forgive our sin when we ask Him. We must tell God we are sorry for our sin, and He will keep His promise to forgive us. (BAT: 1b Repentance and faith)

What did God promise Noah after the Flood? *(There would never again be a flood to destroy the whole earth.)*

What did God put in the sky to remind Noah of His promise? *(a rainbow)* Every time we see a rainbow we can think, "God keeps His promises." His Word never changes. God is faithful. We can thank God for taking care of us, too. (BATs: 7c Praise; 8b Faith in the power of the Word of God)

Poem: "God of Noah"

➤ God of Noah
  (Point to heaven.)
Looked down from above,
  (Cup hand above eyes and look down.)
Saw man's sin
  (Shake head "no" sadly.)
And Noah's love.
  (Make heart shape with thumb and pointer fingers of both hands.)

God told Noah,
  (Point to heaven.)
"Build the ark."
  (Cup hand to mouth.)
The ark was built.
  (Pretend to hammer.)
The sky grew dark.
  (Make cloud shape with arm overhead.)

(continued on next page)

Two by two
  (Hold up two fingers of each hand.)
In they came.
  (Walk fingers in air.)
God shut the door.
  (Pretend to shut door.)
He sent the rain.
  (Keep hands high and dangle wiggling fingers.)

The rains came down.
  (Raise hands high and gradually lower, wiggling fingers.)
The floods prevailed.
  (Hold out hands, palms up, and raise slowly.)
Over the hilltops
  (Curve right hand up and down from left to right.)
Noah's ark sailed.

Student page 7

Read and discuss the page.

➤ Noah obeyed God. What did Noah build? *(the ark)*

Guide the children in connecting the dots. Instruct them to cut out the picture of Noah giving thanks to God, to glue the picture in place, and then to color the page.

Review activity: Pantomime

Construct an outline of the ark on the floor with blocks or with the children's chairs. Select some children to pretend to be Noah and his sons building the ark; some, wives bringing their husbands water to drink; and some, different animals entering the ark. Assign definite roles to specific children.

Song: "The Rain Was Coming Down"

Let the children sit in the "ark" as they sing the song.

Lesson 26: Sin Must Be Punished

Bible text: Review; John 14:2
Doctrinal truths: Sin and salvation
Character traits: Trust; Obedience
Memory verse: Introduce Psalm 37:27.
Materials
• Rainbow Salvation Reminder (Make five strips of construction paper into rainbow shapes and connect with a brad. Use the following colors from front to back: yellow, black, red, white, and green.)

Opening chorus: "God's Way"

Song: "The Rain Was Coming Down"

Memory verse

Read Psalm 37:27 from your Bible.

➤ What does "evil" mean? *(disobeying parents, disobeying God, and not being kind)*

Ask the children to sit quietly and watch what you do. Go to the door, open it, and step outside your room for just a moment. Come back and ask the children what you did. You may get a variety of responses.

➤ *I left* the room. I *went away* from the room. That is what God wants us to do from evil things—to go away from sin. God tells us to go away, to turn away, to *depart* from evil.

Encourage the children to repeat the verse with you. Then explain that God wants us to live with Him forever.

➤ God had prepared a place—a home in heaven—for those who ask Jesus to be their Savior from sin. (Read John 14:2 to the children.) And there in heaven we can dwell or live forever and ever with God someday.

Lead the children in reciting Psalm 37:27 again.

Prayer

Ask God to help us to believe the Bible and obey it: to depart from sinful things and do good.

Bible lesson

Introduction

➤ When Mother or Father or a teacher punishes us for disobeying, he or she is reminding us that God's Word tells us to obey our parents and teachers. They are reminding us to turn away from sin and to do what is right.

When they punish us, they are doing what God tells them to do in the Bible. Remember that it is God's plan for families that fathers and mothers tell their children about God and help them to obey His Word.

Lesson

God must punish sin. God is a holy God. That means He is without sin. He is perfect and good. He wants us to be like Him. He wants us to live with Him forever in heaven someday.

Remember that when He made Adam and Eve, He made them without sin. God told them that, if they did not obey Him, they would have to be punished. How sad . . . they sinned. They chose to disobey God. What is sin? *(Allow discussion.)* Sin is disobeying or transgressing God's law.

How did God punish Adam and Eve? *(He made them leave their garden home. They had to work hard to find food; they would have sickness and sadness in their lives; now they would die. They needed a Savior from sin.)*

How did God punish the sinful people who lived in Noah's time? *(He sent a flood to destroy the earth.)*

God promised Noah that He would never again send another flood to destroy all the living things on earth. God put a rainbow in the sky as a sign to remind Noah and us of this promise. Noah thanked God. Every time we see a rainbow, we can think, "God always keeps His promises. His Word never changes. God is faithful." We can thank God for taking care of us too. (BATs: 7c Praise; 8a Faith in God's Promises; 8b Faith in the power of the Word of God.)

Application
Review the plan of salvation with the Rainbow Salvation Reminder.

➤ The colors of this make-believe rainbow remind us of God's promise to save us from our sin. (BAT: 1a Understanding Jesus Christ)

 1. Yellow (heaven)—God loves.
 2. Black (sin)—I sinned.
 3. Red (blood)—Christ died and rose again.
 4. White (cleansing)—I believe.
 5. Green (growing as a Christian)—I live.

Fan out the rainbow as you review the plan of salvation. At the conclusion, repeat that yellow (or gold) reminds us of heaven and God's love. Refer to "Leading a Child to the Lord" in the Introduction to this teacher's edition.

Song: "Jesus Loves Me"

Song: "God Is with Me"

➤ Did God see Noah obey? *(Yes, God sees all things. Nothing can be hidden from Him.)*

God's Friend

Abraham: I Love God

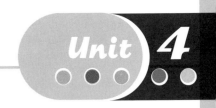

Lesson 27: Abram's Call

Bible texts: Genesis 12; II Chronicles 20:7; James 2:23

Doctrinal truth: God

Character traits: Trust; Love

Memory verse: Review Psalm 25:4.

Catechism: Review Catechism 7–11.

Materials
• Abram and Sarai visuals (See the Appendix for visuals and instructions.)

Opening song: "The Children's Friend," stanza 1

➤ Jesus is God. He is the Son of God, but He is also God. This is hard to understand, but we know it is true because God's Word tells us so.

Catechism

Review Catechism 9–11.

▪ Are there more gods than one? *(No, there is only one God.)*

▪ In how many persons does this one God exist? *(God exists in three persons.)*

▪ Who are the three persons of God? *(The three persons of God are the Father, the Son, and the Holy Spirit.)*

Song: "Jesus Loves the Little Children"

Prayer

Thank God for loving us and for being our Friend.

Song: "Trust and Obey," stanza 1

Begin by singing the entire first stanza. As you repeat it throughout this unit, the children will begin to chime in on the stanza as well as the chorus. If you feel your class is ready for an additional stanza, teach it also.

➤ When we walk with the Lord, we trust and obey God. We have faith in God. That means we believe that God will do what He says. God never fails us. He will always be our best Friend and take care of us and show us what to do. (BAT: 8a Faith in God's promises)

Bible lesson

Introduction

➤ Many years went by after God sent the Flood to punish those who did not love and obey Him. After the Flood, Noah's sons had children, and their children had children until there were many people living on the earth again. Most of these people had forgotten the one true God, and instead of worshiping Him they worshiped things that God had made. Some people worshiped the sun and the moon or the stars. They even made idols carved out of wood or stone to look like animals so that they could worship them. Are there more gods than one? *(Catechism 9: No, there is only one God.)* The people on the earth were very sinful just as the people were who lived when Noah did.

Lesson

Use the Abram and Sarai visuals.

As God looked down from heaven, he saw a man named Abram. One day God spoke to Abram. God told Abram to leave his uncles, aunts, and cousins and move to a new home. God told Abram that He would show him the place to go and the way to get there and even take care of him on the long, long trip. He told Abram that He would give him many, many children who would be a blessing to all the world. The promised Savior from sin would someday be born to Abram's children's children. God said that he would make Abram's name great—that everyone would remember who Abram was.

Abram believed God. He trusted God and believed that God would do what was best for him. He wanted God to know that he trusted Him. So he obeyed God. He did what God told him to do. He took his wife Sarai, and his nephew Lot and their servants and left his home to begin the long trip to a new land called Canaan.

There were no airplanes, buses, trains, or even cars many, many years ago. Abram and his family had to walk or ride camels or donkeys. Because Abram was a shepherd and a herder, he also took his flocks of sheep and herds of cattle along the way. It was a long, hard journey over hills and across rivers, but each day Abram and his family came closer and closer to the land that God had promised them.

Finally they came to the special place called Canaan that God had called them to. Again God spoke to Abram. God said, "This is the land that I will give to you and your children." Abram was happy to be in the place God wanted him. He built an altar to God and worshiped Him. Abram thanked God for taking care of him and his family on the long journey.

God had blessed Abram and given him many sheep and cattle. He had gold and silver, and nice tents to live in, and many servants who worked for him. Abram had become a rich man. But Abram was not happy just because he had a nice tent home and lots of animals and servants. He was happy because he loved the one true God of heaven. God was His friend, and he could talk to God and tell Him that He loved Him. He could ask God to help him obey His Word.

Application

➤ Are you happy this morning because you trust God and believe His Word? Do you want God to be your best friend? He wants you to love Him and obey His Word, the Holy Bible, and be a friend to Him. When we have friends we want to be with them, make them happy, and show them that we love them. We want to talk to our friends and have them talk to us, don't we? How can we be with God, talk to Him, and have Him talk to us? *(Allow discussion.)* Yes, we can talk to God when we pray, and let God talk to us when we listen to His words from the Bible. Let's try harder each day to show God that we love Him, and remember to ask Him to help us obey His Word. (BATs: 8a Faith in God's promises; 6a Bible study; 6b Prayer)

Song: "Trust and Obey"

➤ Remember that when we have faith in God, we trust Him. That means we believe what He tells us in His Word. If we really believe God, we will want to obey Him.

Memory verse

Review Psalm 25:4.

➤ Do you think Abram believed what our memory verse tells us? (Recite Psalm 25:4.) He surely did. He believed God would show him where to go and what to do. He had faith in God's promises. He trusted God. He believed God would do what was best for him.

Abram believed what God said. And that's what God wants us to do each day. We can't hear God speak to us today with His voice and with our ears like Abram did long ago. But we can listen when our parents and teachers and preachers tell us what God's Word says in the Bible. Then we will know what God wants us to do.

Lead the class in reciting the verse together several times and then as a choral reading.

Action rhyme: "God's Word"
(See Index of Poetry.)

Catechism

Review Catechism 7–8.

■ How can you glorify God? *(I can glorify God by loving Him and doing what He commands.)*

■ Why ought you to glorify God? *(I ought to glorify God because He made me and takes care of me.)*

➤ Did Abram glorify God? How? *(Yes, Abram loved God and did what God commanded.)*

Song: "Show Me Thy Ways"

Lesson 28: Abram's Kindness

Bible text: Genesis 13:1–12
Doctrinal truth: God (attributes of)
Character trait: Love
Catechism: Review Catechism 7.
Materials
• Grant, Dave, and Dad Hunter puppets
• "Abram and Lot" (Picture Packet)

Opening song: "The Children's Friend," stanza 1

Song: "Politeness Is"

Prayer

Ask God to help us to be polite and kind in all that we do and say.

Song: "Be Ye Doers of the Word," stanzas 1 and 4

Bible lesson

Introduction

➤ Everyone was excited at the Hunters' home. They were planning a weekend camping trip.

"I found them," Grant yelled from the garage.

"Good boy," said Dad. "Bring them here, and we'll get started."

"Oooh, I can hardly wait until Friday," squealed Dave as he brought the box and hammer from Dad's toolbox.

Dad was busy unfolding the tent. He always set up their tent in the yard to air it out just before they used it. But Dad had a problem this time. He couldn't find the tent pegs. He usually kept them in the bag with the tent. But they weren't there. Then Grant remembered. When Dad had lent the tent to some friends, they had returned the pegs in a box.

"I don't know what I'd do without such a good helper," he said as Grant laid the box down beside him on the ground.

➤ Have you ever slept in a tent? It's fun to go camping, isn't it? Some people live in tent homes all the time. Tents are easy to carry along with you when you have to move from one place to another. They are especially nice in places where it doesn't get cold. Our Bible lesson today is about some families who lived in tents because they moved their home from one place to another.

Lesson

Abram was a friend of God. He loved and obeyed God. God gave Abram many gifts. Abram had many animals and many servants to do his work. Abram lived in a tent-home. He also had many tents for his family and servants. He had much silver and gold. He was a very rich man.

God had told Abram to bring his family to this special land where they could all live and serve God. God told Abram that someday He would send His Son, Jesus Christ, down from heaven to be the Savior from sin. God's Son was to be born in Abram's family after many, many years.

We heard in our last lesson that Abram had a nephew named Lot. Abram was Lot's uncle. Abram had taken Lot with him on his long journey. Lot also had many animals and tents and servants.

One day some of Lot's servants were taking care of his animals out near the same fields where Abram's servants were taking care of Abram's animals. The servants began to argue and quarrel. Lot's servants were afraid that Abram's servants would find more grass for his animals. Each group of servants was afraid that the others would find the nicest place to pitch their tents. The servants were selfish. They all wanted the biggest and best for themselves and their masters—Abram and Lot.

When Abram heard about the servants' quarreling, he talked to Lot. (Display "Abram and Lot" picture.) He said, "Let's not have this fighting. It doesn't please God for our servants to act that way. Let's separate. Let's not live in the same place. You go to one place, and I'll go to the other. You may choose which way you want to go, and I will go the other way."

Now Abram could have chosen first. He was older. And God had already promised him that He would give all this land to Abram and his family. But Abram was a kind man. He let Lot have the first choice.

Abram and Lot climbed up to the top of a hill. (Pretend to climb.) Lot looked all around. (Shade eyes with hands.) On one side he saw the beauti-

ful, green, grassy land around the Jordan River. He knew his servants could find plenty of grass and water for his animals there. That would be the nicest place to put his tent. He saw the city of Sodom nearby. He thought he would become rich living close to Sodom. So he chose the best for himself, and Abram went the other way. Because Lot chose what he thought was best for himself, Abram had to go to the land that had big hills and rocks. He knew it would be harder to find places for his animals to eat. It would be harder to live there. But Abram was happy because he knew that when he was not selfish he was living God's way. He wanted to please God.

Application

➤ Do you think God was happy with what Abram did? *(yes)* God promised to take care of His friend Abram, and He did. Abram always had a place to live and plenty of animals, servants, and food. God took care of Abram's big family. Abram showed that he loved God by the way he acted. He was loving, kind, and unselfish. God wants us to show our love for Him by being kind and unselfish to others. (BATs: 5a Love; 8a Faith in God's promises)

Catechism

Review Catechism 7.

■ How can you glorify God? *(I can glorify God by loving Him and doing what He commands.)*

➤ Did Abram glorify God in our lesson today? *(Yes, he did.)* How? *(He showed that he loved God by being kind.)* Did God take care of Abram? *(Yes, God did.)*

Song: "Obedience Is," stanza 1

Song: "Trust and Obey"

Lesson 29: Abram's Courage

Bible text: Genesis 14:1–2, 11–24
Doctrinal truth: God
Character trait: Courage
Memory verse: Introduce Proverbs 3:5–6.
Catechism: Introduce Catechism 15.

Opening song: "The Children's Friend"
Introduce stanza 2.

Song: "Trust and Obey"
Review the discussion begun in Lesson 27.

Prayer

Ask God to help us to be brave when we have hard things to do.

Memory verse

Read Proverbs 3:5–6 to the children.

➤ We have been singing about trusting God. What does it mean when you trust someone? *(Answers may vary.)* When we trust someone, we believe him. We believe he will do what he says. We believe he will keep his promises. Do boys and girls always keep their promises? *(no)* Do mommies and daddies *always* keep their promises? They try to, and most of the time they do, don't they? But sometimes they don't; sometimes they can't. Does our Lord God keep His promises? *(Yes, He always does.)* What God says, He will do. (BAT: 8a Faith in God's promises)

The verse says you should "trust in the Lord *with all your heart.*" It doesn't say you should trust in the Lord maybe hoping He will take care of you and do what is best for you. No! It says, "Trust in the Lord with all your heart." We can know for sure with all our hearts and minds that God will keep His promises to us.

Recite the verses several times, having the children join in each time with the first clause of the verse.

Song: "Trust in the Lord"

Bible lesson

Introduction

➤ Remember, God had brought Abram to the land of Canaan. God had promised to take care of Abram. Abram showed his love for God by loving and obeying Him. Remember how kind Abram was to his nephew Lot. Who remembers what he did? *(Abram let Lot have first choice of the land.)*

Lot thought he had chosen the best for himself. When he camped near the city of Sodom, he kept looking at that city and thinking how he would like to live there. He kept moving closer until finally he moved inside the walls of the city. Back in those days all the cities had big tall stone walls around them for protection. Let's listen and see what happened to Lot and his family there.

Lesson

A terrible war was being fought near the city called Sodom where Lot had moved. Four kings brought their soldiers to fight against five other kings near the place where Lot lived in Sodom. The four kings won the battle. They took people and food and other things from the cities they captured. They captured the whole city of Sodom. That means that they captured Lot and his family and everything that was his. Lot's selfish choice really wasn't the best for him after all, was it?

Someone from Sodom was able to escape, and he ran and told Abram what had happened. As soon as Abram heard of the capture of his nephew Lot, he took his own men and planned an attack to rescue him. He and his servants went by night to surprise the enemy soldiers when they were sleeping.

Even though Abram's group of men was much smaller than the great number of enemy soldiers, they were able to get back not only Lot and his family but also all the women and the soldiers and the things that were theirs that had been captured from the city of Sodom. How brave God had helped Abram to be!

The king of Sodom had escaped during the battle. He had hidden in a low, dirty place (slime pit) where no one ever went during the battle. When the king heard what Abram had done, he went to thank him. The king even offered to pay Abram by giving him gold and silver and clothes and cattle. But Abram said, "No." Abram did not want anything from this wicked king. He told the king that he was only doing what God wanted him to do. Abram said that God would take care of him and bless him with all that he needed and even more than he needed.

Application

➤ Abram showed his faith again, didn't he? He believed God would take care of him even in a battle against his enemies. He trusted God with all his heart. God made him brave. And God will give us courage to do hard things for Him too. (BATs: 8a Faith in God's promises; 8d Courage)

Song: "When I Am Afraid"

Catechism

Introduce Catechism 15.

◾ Does God know all things? *(Yes, nothing can be hidden from God.)*

Song: "God Is with Me"

➤ Did God see Lot when he was selfish? *(yes)* Does He see us when we are selfish? *(yes)*

Lesson 30: Abraham's Trust

Bible text: Genesis 15–17

Doctrinal truth: God

Character trait: Trust

Memory verse: Review Proverbs 3:5–6.

Catechism: Review Catechism 7–15.

Materials
- "Thy Word have I hid in mine heart" visual (See the Appendix; also see Lesson 24.)

Opening song: "The Children's Friend," stanza 2

Song: "Whisper a Prayer"

Prayer

Thank God that He lets us talk with Him in prayer.

Memory verse

Read Proverbs 3:5–6 to the children.

Review the discussion from Lesson 29 with questions such as the following:

➤ What does "trust" mean? When we trust God "with all our heart," do we doubt Him? Do we think, "Well, maybe He will do what He says?" Let's say the part of the verse we learned together yesterday. (Recite Proverbs 3:5a.)

Quote Proverbs 3:5b.

➤ This means we need to ask the Lord to help us to know what to say and do. We ought not to depend on what we know. Do we know everything? No, but God does. God is omniscient. Say *omniscient* with me. That's a big word, isn't it? But it just means that God knows *all* things. He knows what happened yesterday and all the yesterdays before. He knows what will happen today here in our class. He knows whether we will obey and listen carefully. He knows what will happen when we go home. He knows what will happen tomorrow, and the next day, and the next day—forever and ever.

Do we know what will happen when we go home today? Tomorrow? Well, we may *think* we do. But we are not always right, are we? (Quote Proverbs 3:5b.)

We cannot depend on our knowing everything, but we can trust in God. He always knows what is best for us. He knows all things. He is omniscient. We can talk to God in prayer and listen to His Word, and He will "direct our paths."

Lead the children in reciting the verse with you several times. You may want to recite verse 5 by pointing to one table or row to stand and say the first phrase, followed by another row saying the second phrase. They may take turns by groups as you direct several times. Then read verses 5 and 6 again.

Song: "Obedience Is," stanza 3

Song: "Trust and Obey"

Catechism

Review Catechism 7–15. Use "Thy Word have I hid in mine heart" visual.

- How can you glorify God? (*I can glorify God by loving Him and doing what He commands.*)

- Why ought you to glorify God? (*I ought to glorify God because He made me and takes care of me.*)

- Are there more gods than one? (*No, there is only one God.*)

- In how many persons does this one God exist? (*God exists in three persons.*)

- Who are the three persons of God? (*The three persons of God are the Father, the Son, and the Holy Spirit.*)

- Who is God? (*God is a spirit and does not have a body like man.*)

- Where is God? (*God is everywhere.*)

- Can you see God? (*No, I cannot see God, but He always sees me.*)

- Does God know all things? (*Yes, nothing can be hidden from God.*)

Bible lesson

Introduction
➤ After God helped Abram rescue Lot and the people of Sodom in the great battle, God spoke to Abram. He said, "Don't be afraid, Abram; I am your shield . . . your protector. I will be your great reward."

Lesson

Then Abram talked to God. He told God what he was thinking about. He told God that he remembered that God had promised to make him the father of many, many people—God's own chosen people of Israel. And yet, he said, "Lord, how can this be? I have no children . . . not even one." He reminded God that all he had was his servant Eliezer. "Is he to be like a son to me? Is he to have all that You have given me?" Abram asked God.

The Lord listened to Abram as they talked together. The Lord knew what Abram was thinking even before he spoke. Then God answered Abram. He told Abram that Eliezer was not to be the same as a son. Many years ago when a father died, he left the oldest son twice as many things as the other sons. So God was saying that Eliezer would not be like a son to inherit all that Abram had.

God told Abram to look up into the sky outside and count the stars, if he could. Then God said, "That is to remind you of all the children and grandchildren and great-great-grandchildren that you will have. They will be so many that they cannot be counted."

Now, that could have seemed impossible to believe, since Abram didn't have even one child. But God's Word tells us that Abram believed and trusted God. And God saw his faith and forgave all his sins. Our God knows all things.

Application

➤ Abram and God talked together many times. One day when they were talking, God reminded Abram again of His promise to him. God said that He was changing Abram's name to Abraham, meaning "Abram, father of many." And Sarai's name was to be Sarah, which means "Princess." He promised that a son, Isaac, would soon be born to Abraham and Sarah.

Abraham was learning to trust in the Lord with all his heart. He didn't understand all that God was telling him. He didn't know everything, but he knew he should lean on God's wisdom and ask God what to do, and that God would take care of him and help him do the right thing. (BAT: 8a Faith in God's promises)

Recite Proverbs 3:5–6, inserting "Abraham"; i.e., "Abraham trusted in the Lord with all his heart."

Song: "Abraham"
After you sing the song, you may want to add additional stanzas, substituting children's names for "Abraham."

➤ _____ believes God's Word,
Believes God's Word,
Believes God's Word.
_____ believes God's Word.
God is faithful.

Song: "God's Way"

Lesson 31: Abraham's Friend

Bible text: Genesis 18
Doctrinal truth: God (faithfulness)
Character traits: Honesty; Courtesy
Memory verse: Review Proverbs 3:5–6.
Catechism: Introduce Catechism 16.
Materials
• Abram and Sarai visuals (See the Appendix; used in Lesson 27.)

Opening song: "The Children's Friend"

Prayer
Ask God to help us remember to please Him in everything we do.

Song: "Learning God's Way," stanza 2

Memory verse
Review Proverbs 3:5–6. Recite the verse together and discuss it.

➤ God tells us that in everything we do we should remember the powerful God who made us to love and serve Him. We should ask Him to help us obey His Word. Let's think of some ways we can do this.

1. When Mother gives you two cookies—one for your friend and one for you—how can you acknowledge God? What would be the right thing to do? *(Allow discussion.)* We should remember what God tells us to do in His Word—"We are to be kind to each other."

2. If mother has told you to play outside in your own yard, and your playmate tries to get you to come to his house or go to the park without getting permission, how can you acknowledge God? *(Allow discussion.)* We should remember that God tells us in His Word to obey our parents.

Continue with other illustrations.

Song: "Trust and Obey"

Bible lesson

Introduction
➤ The doorbell rang. When Kate ran to answer it, there stood Mrs. Luna and Rosa.

"Hello, Kate," said Mrs. Luna with a smile. "Your mother invited us for tea. May we come in?"

Kate stepped back and replied, "Yes, ma'am, come right in and have a seat. I'll run and get Mom." Then she went to the kitchen to get her mother.

Mom was preparing the tea and getting out the cookies. "Thank you, Kate. Tell Mrs. Luna and Rosa that I'll be right in. I just need to put the cookies and napkins on the tray and pour the hot water in the teapot. Then you can help me serve our guests." Mom smiled at Kate as she happily returned to the living room.

➤ Have you ever helped serve guests at your house? *(Allow discussion.)*

Lesson
Display the Abram and Sarai visuals.

One day as Abraham was sitting at the door of his tent-home, he saw three men coming along the road. Abraham quickly got up and hurried to greet them.

He offered to bring water to wash their feet, which were dirty from walking on the dusty road. He asked them to sit down in the shade and rest while he got something for them to eat.

Abraham went into the tent. He called to Sarah, "We have guests. Quickly, have your servants bake cakes and roast meat for them."

While the visitors were eating, they asked Abraham, "Where is your wife Sarah?"

Abraham answered, "In the tent."

Then one of the visitors said, "I will come and visit you again after a year, and Sarah your wife *shall* have a son."

Now Sarah had been listening at the door of the tent. And when she heard this, she laughed and thought to herself, "This cannot be. I am too old to have a child."

Now not just any visitor could see Sarah inside the tent or know her thoughts, but *this* visitor knew she was there and even what she was thinking. So he said to Abraham, "Why did Sarah laugh and say, 'Shall I really have a child when I am an old woman?' Is anything too hard for your God? I will come again in a year, and Sarah *shall* have a son."

Then Sarah and Abraham both knew that these were not just ordinary men. One was really the Son of God who had visited them in a body dressed to look like a man. The others with him were two of God's angels.

Sarah was afraid then. She said, "I did not laugh."

God answered, "But you did laugh."

We can never lie and get away with it. We may tell a lie and be able to fool some people for a while, but God knows all things. How sorry Sarah was that she had lied to God. She was sorry that she had not had faith to believe that God would do what He had said.

Then the visitors left Abraham's home and went toward the city of Sodom. Abraham walked along part of the way with them. He treated his guests courteously, and as they walked along, God reminded Abraham again of how He would bless him. Then God did something very special. He called Abraham His good friend. . . . Abraham was the friend of God.

Application

➤ Abraham gave lovingly and happily to his guests, didn't he? Yes, he did even before he knew one of them was the Son of God and two of them were God's angels. God wants us also to be kind and courteous to others, "to acknowledge Him in all our ways." (BAT: 5e Friendliness)

Wouldn't you like to be called the friend of God? Abraham trusted in God with all his heart. He believed God would do what He said; He loved God and talked to Him.

Poem: "Kind Abraham"

➤ Abraham was kind.
Abraham was good.
Abraham obeyed God.
He did the things he should.

Catechism
Introduce Catechism 16.

■ Can God do all things? *(Yes, God can do all His holy will.)*

Lesson 32: Abraham and Sarah

Bible text: Review.
Doctrinal truth: God (faithfulness)
Character trait: Trust
Memory verses: Review.
Materials
• Student page 8 and cutout
• Scissors
• Glue

Opening song: "The Children's Friend"

Song: "Obedience Is," stanzas 1 and 3

Prayer
Ask God to help us to trust and obey Him.

Song: "Abraham"

Student page 8
Instruct the children to cut out the picture.

➤ Who are the characters in the picture? *(Abraham and Sarah)*

Instruct the children to glue the picture in its space and to color the page. Read the page and lead the children in reciting Proverbs 3:5–6.

Poem: "Kind Abraham"
(See Index of Poetry.)

Memory verses
Review as many memory verses as time allows.

Song: "Trust and Obey"

Lesson 33: Abraham's Prayer

Bible text: Genesis 18–19

Doctrinal truth: Sin

Character trait: Obedience

Memory verses: Review Romans 3:23 and Psalm 37:27.

Catechism: Review Catechism 13–16.

Opening song: "The Children's Friend"

Song: "There Is None That Doeth Good"

Memory verses

Review Romans 3:23.

Review Psalm 37:27 and the verse discussion in Lesson 26. Divide the class into two groups to repeat the verse in choral response (one group reciting the first part of the verse, and the other the last part). This verse may also be sung as a scale song.

➤ De-part from e-vil, and do good;
(do re mi fa sol la ti do)

And dwe-ell for e-ev-er-more.
(do ti la sol fa mi re do)

Prayer

Ask God to help us stay away from sin and obey God's Word.

Song: "God's Way"

Bible lesson

Introduction

➤ After God had called Abraham His friend, He and Abraham talked together. God told Abraham about the terrible sin of the cities of Sodom and Gomorrah. Abraham understood that sin must be punished. The Bible tells us that "Abraham drew near to God." Abraham was thinking of his nephew Lot and his family. He asked God, "If there are any good people who love God in those two cities, would the cities have to be destroyed?"

Lesson

When the two angels of the Lord left Abraham's tent, they walked toward Sodom. Do you remember the name of the city that was near where Lot went to live? *(Sodom)* Lot thought the city life of Sodom looked good, and he kept moving his tent-home closer and closer, until finally he was living inside the city of Sodom.

Now Sodom was a wicked city. The people did many sinful things, and Lot knew all about the sin of Sodom. He should have separated himself from their sin, but he didn't. Lot had even become one of the leaders of the city. He did not obey God's Word, "Depart from evil, and do good; and dwell for evermore."

When the two angels reached Sodom, they found Lot sitting at the gate of the city with the other city leaders.

When Lot saw them, he got up to meet them. He did not recognize that they were angels of God, but he treated them with kindness. Lot asked them to come to his house and be his guests for the night. But the two angel visitors answered, "No, we'll just spend the night in the city." They were probably planning to wrap themselves in their robes and spend the night lying on the street.

Now Lot saw that these visitors were good men, and because he knew about the wickedness of the people of Sodom, he was afraid for these men to sleep in the street. Lot asked them again; he begged them strongly, so they followed him to his house, where he fed them supper.

Before Lot and his guests had gone to bed for the night, the men who lived in Sodom came all around Lot's house and shouted, "Where are the men who have come to you this night? Bring them outside so that we can hurt them and get them to do sinful things with us."

When Lot talked to the evil men and told them, "No," they tried to break the door down. But the two visitors pulled Lot back into the house and closed the door. Then they did something very powerful: they worked a miracle. A miracle is a special work that only God can do. It shows us His power. God gave them the power to make the evil men outside blind so they could not even find the door of the house.

The two visitors told Lot to get his family together and take them out of Sodom because God had sent them to destroy the wicked city. Then Lot knew these men were angels—servants of the God of heaven sent to do His work.

In the early morning, the angels told Lot to take his family and leave the city. But his daughters' husbands only laughed at Lot. They did not believe God would really destroy their city. Lot was so slow in obeying that the angels had to take Lot and his wife and two daughters by their hands and lead them out of the city. The angels warned them, "Run for your lives to the mountains. Do not look back or you will also be destroyed with the wicked people and the city of Sodom."

Lot begged that they might be able to run to a small town nearby because he was afraid to go live in the mountains. So the angels said they could do this.

And immediately God sent an awful punishment to the wicked cities of Sodom and Gomorrah. He sent down brimstone and ashes of fire from heaven to kill the wicked people. (Brimstone is sulphur—a yellow chalklike powder that burns easily.)

Lot and his daughters ran to safety, but the Bible tells us that Lot's wife looked back and she was turned into a pillar of salt. She became a statue of salt. The Bible doesn't tell us why Lot's wife looked back, but she did disobey, and she had to be punished. Sin must always be punished.

Application

➤ Later Abraham came to see the smoke of the destroyed city. How thankful he was that God had answered his prayer—that Lot had been saved from the terrible destruction. God always answers the prayers of those who love and obey Him. (BAT: 6b Prayer)

Song: "Obedience Is," stanzas 1 and 3

Catechism

Review Catechism 13–16 and relate the questions to the characters in this lesson.

▪ Where is God? *(God is everywhere.)*

▪ Can you see God? *(No, I cannot see God, but He always sees me.)*

▪ Does God know all things? *(Yes, nothing can be hidden from God.)*

▪ Can God do all things? *(Yes, God can do all His holy will.)*

➤ What is a miracle? *(A miracle is a special work that only God can do.)*

Lesson 34: Abraham's Obedience

Bible text: Genesis 22:1–19

Doctrinal truth: God

Character trait: Obedience

Memory verse: Review Proverbs 3:5–6.

Catechism: Review Catechism 1–16.

Materials
• "Thy Word have I hid in mine heart" visual (See the Appendix.)
• Student page 9 and cutout
• Scissors
• Glue

Opening song: "The Children's Friend"

Song: "Trust and Obey"

Prayer

Ask God to make us willing to obey no matter how hard it may be.

Memory verse

Review Proverbs 3:5–6.

Bible lesson

Introduction

➤ God kept His promise to Abraham. Abraham's wife, Sarah, had a baby son whom they named Isaac. Abraham was one hundred years old when Isaac was born. His wife was old too, but Abraham had believed that God would do what He said He would do. And God did. (BAT: 8a Faith in God's promises)

Read the poem "Abram."

➤ Abram was rich
In cattle and gold.
And God blessed him
When he was old.

➤ In what special way did God bless Abram when he was old? *(God gave him a son.)*

Lesson

One night God spoke to Abraham, "Abraham."

Abraham answered, "Here I am!"

God said, "Take your only son Isaac, whom you love, up to a mountain in the land of Moriah and offer him on the altar as a sacrifice to Me to show Me how much you love Me."

The Bible tells us that Abraham did not argue with God. He did not say, "But God, I love my son; You wouldn't really ask me to do that, would You?" No, Abraham just started out to do what God said. He obeyed. Abraham got up early the next morning and cut the wood for the altar fire. He took his donkey and two servants and his son Isaac to the place God told him to go. After traveling for two days, Abraham told his servants, "Stay here with the donkey while I take my son up the mountain to worship God, and then we shall return." Now Abraham did not say, "*I* shall return." The Bible tells us that he said, "*We* shall return." How could that be? If Abraham were going to sacrifice Isaac, that means he would have to put him on an altar and kill him for a sin offering to show his love for God.

Again Abraham trusted God. He didn't depend on his own understanding; he just obeyed God. God had asked Abraham to sacrifice his son Isaac instead of a lamb on the altar. But Abraham knew that God had the power to raise Isaac from the dead and make him live again.

So Abraham took the wood for the sacrifice and gave it to Isaac to carry. Then Abraham took the fire and the knife, and the two started together on the rest of the way alone.

Isaac asked his father, "Father?"

Abraham answered, "What is it, my son?"

"Here is the fire and wood, but where is the lamb for sacrifice?"

Abraham answered, "God will provide a lamb for our offering, my son."

And they went on. And when they came to the place to which God had directed Abraham, Abraham built an altar. He laid the wood in order on it. Then he tied up his son and laid him on the wood on the altar. Abraham slowly held up the knife to kill his son when suddenly the Lord called from heaven, saying, "Abraham, Abraham!"

Abraham answered, "Here am I."

And the Lord said, "Lay not your hand upon the lad, neither do anything to him, for now I know that you trust me, and will obey me. And because you have obeyed me, I will bless you and make your children as many as the stars of the heaven and the sands of the seashore. Your family shall be a blessing to all people."

Application

➤ Abraham believed God. He trusted God to do what was right for Him. He obeyed God even when it seemed like a very hard thing to do.

Do *you* always obey God? Are you always kind and helpful to your parents and brothers and sisters? Do you always follow directions in our kindergarten class?

Remember, we glorify God when we love Him and do what He commands. Abraham was a friend of God. He glorified God because he knew God made him and took care of him. (BATs: 2a Authority; 2b Servanthood)

Student page 9

Instruct the children to cut out the picture of the ram and glue it in place. Guide them in a discussion about the picture and read the sentences at the top of the page. Instruct them to listen carefully as you read the sentence at the bottom of the page. Lead the children in "reading" the sentence together.

Song: "Obedience Is," stanzas 1 and 3

Catechism

Review as many catechism questions (1–16) as time allows, using "Thy Word have I hid in mine heart" visual.

Lesson 35: A Servant's Prayer

Bible text: Genesis 24:1–28
Doctrinal truth: Salvation (prayer)
Character trait: Trust
Memory verse: Review Psalm 95:6.
Materials
• "A Servant's Prayer" (Picture Packet)

Opening song: "The Children's Friend"

Song: "Whisper a Prayer"

Memory verse
Review Psalm 95:6.

Prayer
Thank God for always listening to our prayers.

Bible lesson

Introduction
Lead the class in singing "Obedience Is," stanza 3.

Lesson

Many years had passed now. God had blessed Abraham in every way. Abraham was now very old—one hundred and forty years old! His own son Isaac had grown up. Abraham knew that Isaac needed a good wife to help him serve God.

Abraham called the leader of his servants and asked him to go back to the land Abraham had come from to find a wife for Isaac. Abraham was too old to take the long journey, as was the custom—the way they usually did things—in that day, for the parents decided whom their children would marry.

So the servant took ten of Abraham's camels and all sorts of valuable gifts and set out for Haran, where Abraham had come from.

When the servant got to Haran, he made his camels kneel down outside the city by the well of water at evening time. That was the time when the women came to the well to let down their buckets to draw up water to take to their homes. Remember, they did not have water that comes through pipes into faucets in sinks like we have in our homes.

Then Abraham's servant prayed. He wanted to do what was right. He asked the Lord to help him choose the right wife for Abraham's son Isaac. He told the Lord that he would sit there by the well, and as the young women came to the well to get water for their fathers' homes, he would ask them to give him a drink. He would say, "Let down your pitcher, and get water that I may drink." He asked God to have the young woman whom He wanted to be Isaac's wife answer, "Drink, and I will water your camels also." That would be the way he would know whom God wanted Isaac to marry.

And the Bible tells us that before he finished praying, a beautiful young woman named Rebekah came with a pitcher on her shoulder to get water for her father's house. Abraham's servant hurried to meet her at the well and said, "Please, let me drink a bit of water from your pitcher."

And she answered, "Drink, kind sir." And she quickly lowered her pitcher and gave him a drink. After he had drunk, she said, "I will also get water for your camels." Then she quickly ran to bring many pitchers of water for his camels. (Display "A Servant's Prayer" picture.)

When the camels had finished drinking, Abraham's servant gave Rebekah a gold ring and two gold bracelets and asked who her father was. He also asked if there would be a room for him to spend the night at her father's house. She answered that there was room and that they would even have room and food for his animals. She told the servant that she would run ahead and tell her family that he was coming.

Then the servant bowed and thanked God for answering his prayer for bringing him to the right place and to the right young woman to be a wife for Isaac.

Application
➤ God answered the prayer of Abraham's servant. God always answers our prayers. He has promised to hear us when we talk to Him.

When we pray, we talk to God. God tells us that He is happy to hear the prayers of those who love Him (Proverbs 15:8). When we love someone, we want to be with him and talk to him. God loves us. He talks to us in His Word—the Bible. He wants us to love Him and talk to Him in prayer. (BAT: 8a Faith in God's promises)

Song: "How Do We Know?" stanza 7

Lesson 36: Isaac's Wife

Bible text: Genesis 24:29–67
Doctrinal truth: God (attributes of)
Character trait: Trust
Memory verses: Review Psalm 95:6 and Proverbs 3:5–6.

Opening song: "The Children's Friend"

Song: "Whisper a Prayer"

Song: "Pray with Me," stanzas 1 and 2

Memory verses
Review Psalm 95:6 and Proverbs 3:5–6.

Prayer
Thank God for always listening to and answering our prayers.

Song: "Trust in the Lord"

Remind the children that only God knows what is best for those who love Him.

➤ Remember how Abraham's servant did not know which young woman should be Isaac's wife? He asked God to show him. And God did.

Bible lesson

Introduction
➤ At the end of our last lesson, Rebekah ran to tell her family about the servant she had met at the well. After Rebekah told them what the man had said and after she had showed her brother Laban what the man had given her, Laban ran out to the well to meet the man.

Lesson

Laban invited Abraham's servant to come and bring his camels to his father's home. Rebekah's family welcomed the man and offered him water to bathe his feet after his long journey. When they brought him food to eat, he first wanted to tell them why he had come to their land. Then the servant would eat with Rebekah's family.

He told how God had blessed his master Abraham with many things—money, servants, and cattle—and that, even though Abraham and his wife Sarah were very old, God had blessed them with a son named Isaac. He said that now that Isaac had grown to be a man, Abraham had sent him to find a wife for Isaac—a young woman who would love and serve God together with Isaac.

He told them how he had asked God to show him which young woman should be Isaac's wife. How had he asked God to show him who the girl should be? *(She would give water to him and to his camels.)* How did God answer his prayer? *(God sent the beautiful young woman Rebekah.)*

When he had told them everything that had happened, he also told them he had praised the Lord for answering his prayer.

When Rebekah's father and brother heard all that Abraham's servant told them, they agreed that the Lord had led him to the best wife and that they should all obey God's will.

Then the servant gave much gold and silver jewelry and clothes to Rebekah and many expensive gifts to her family also.

The next morning the servant asked her father if he could take Rebekah to Isaac. Her family wanted him to stay a few more days, but the servant said he must obey his master and return immediately.

Do you think Rebekah was happy to go with him—to leave her family and go to a strange land? When her parents told her, she was happy to obey. She knew that God would bless her for loving and obeying Him.

Rebekah and her maidservants rode on camels along with Abraham's servant. When they finally got near Abraham's home, it was evening. Isaac was out in the field when he looked up and saw them coming. When Rebekah saw Isaac, she got down off her camel and asked Abraham's old servant, "Who is this young man?"

When she lifted her veil, Isaac saw the beautiful young girl that God had sent to be his wife. He was very happy. After they were married, God sent Isaac and Rebekah twin sons whom they named Jacob and Esau.

Application
➤ God answered Abraham's prayer and the prayer of his servant many, many years ago in a wonderful way. And God still answers prayer for us today. (BATs: 6b Prayer; 8a Faith in God's promises)

God is faithful. When we talk to Him, He promises to hear and answer our prayers.

Give an illustration of a recent answer to prayer in your own life or an answer to a class prayer.

Song: "Trust and Obey"

Lesson 37: Jacob's Dream

Bible text: Genesis 28:1–5, 10–22
Doctrinal truths: God; Angels; Satan
Character traits: Trust; Thankfulness
Memory verses: Review Psalm 25:4 and Proverbs 3:5–6.
Materials
• Jacob's Dream visual (See the Appendix for the visual and instructions.)

Opening song: "The Children's Friend"

Song: "God's Way"

Song: "Thank God"

Memory verses
Review Psalm 25:4 and Proverbs 3:5–6 with choral response activities and "Show Me Thy Ways" and "Trust in the Lord" choruses.

Prayer
Thank God for all His good gifts to us.

Song: "Thank You, God"

Bible lesson

Introduction
➤ Remember God's promise to Abraham to give him a big family and to bless them and make them His chosen people?

God made this same promise to Abraham's son, Isaac, and many years later to Isaac's son, Jacob. They were all in the big family of God's special chosen people. God told them that they would bring good to the whole world.

Lesson

Our story today is about Abraham's grandson, Jacob. One day Jacob's father, Isaac, called Jacob to come to him. Isaac reminded Jacob of God's promises to their family. He reminded Jacob that he should think and live God's way—that he should love and obey God.

Isaac told Jacob that he was old enough to marry a wife and have a family. Where would Jacob find a wife? The young girls who lived around them did not worship the God of heaven. Isaac told Jacob that he should go back to the place his family came from, to a place where the families loved God, to find a wife. Wasn't that what Abraham's servant did for Isaac?

Jacob had learned to obey his parents as God's Word told him. He knew that God had told him to marry someone who loved and obeyed God. God says it is a sin to marry someone who does not love and serve Him. So Jacob obeyed God and his parents. He got his things ready and went on a trip toward another land.

Jacob walked and walked. He had come a long way. He was away from his family. He was all alone. He was tired. It was nighttime.

He saw a flat place on the ground where he could sleep. He used a stone for his pillow. Then the Bible says that Jacob "lay down in that place to sleep." (Display Jacob's Dream visual, scene 1.)

When he was asleep, he dreamed. (Display Jacob's Dream visual, scene 2.) In his dream he saw a ladder that reached from the earth way, way up to heaven. (Display Jacob's Dream visual, scene 3.)

When he looked closer, he saw the angels of God going up and down the ladder. And the Lord Himself stood at the very top of the ladder.

He heard God's voice say, "I am the Lord God of Abraham, your grandfather, and Isaac, your father. I will give you this land where you are. I will bless—be good to—you and give you a wife and many children who will also love and serve me. Your family will bless all the families of the earth."

Then God went on to say, "Listen carefully. I am with you and will keep you. I will take care of you everywhere you go. I will never leave you. I will always keep my promises to you."

And then Jacob woke up. "Oh," he said, "this place is special. God is here. God has spoken to me in a special way here." Jacob got up early in the morning. He took the stone that he had used for his pillow. He set it up like a marker to help him remember the special place where God had spoken to him. He poured oil on the stone. He called the place Beth-el. *Bethel* means "house of God."

Then Jacob prayed to God. He thanked Him for His promise to be with him always and to take care of him. He thanked God for His promise to give him food and clothes to wear. He promised God that he would love and obey Him and always give back to God part of all he had. Later the Bible tells us that God changed Jacob's name to Israel because Jacob believed God's promises and His power.

Application
➤ That is a wonderful lesson from God's Word. It reminds us of so many things to be thankful for. God is always with those who love Him. He was with Jacob. He will be with us. The angels of the Lord that Jacob saw in his dream remind us that God sends angels to help take care of us. (BAT: 8a Faith in God's promises) Jacob saw God in His heavenly home at the top of the ladder. God has promised us a home in heaven if we trust and obey Him—if we believe that God's Son, Jesus Christ, took the punishment for our sin. (BAT: 1a Understanding Jesus Christ) We should thank and praise God for all His good gifts to us. (BAT: 7c Praise)

Song: "O Give Thanks"

Lesson 38: God Is My Friend

Bible text: Review.
Doctrinal truth: God
Character traits: Trust; Love
Memory verses: Review.
Catechism: Review Catechism 1–16.
Materials
• Simple sketch of a tent for display (for review activity)
• Chalk or crayons

Opening song: "The Children's Friend"

Song: "God's Way"

Prayer
Ask God to help us remember that He will always do what is right for us.

Song: "What Does the Bible Say?" stanza 2

Character story: "New Neighbors"

The Vick family had been wondering for several weeks who would move into the empty house down the street. Kate especially was praying for a five-year-old girl to be in the new family. The Vicks had prayed that God would send just the right neighbors—either a family who loved the Lord or a family to whom they could witness about their Lord.

Kate was skating up and down her driveway. As she turned around, she saw a big moving van coming down the street. It slowed down. As Kate watched, the van pulled into the driveway of a house on the other side of the street. A car drove in behind it.

Kate skated up to the kitchen door and excitedly called to her mother. "Mom, come quickly. I think they are finally here. Hurry!"

Mrs. Vick looked out the back door at Kate, who was pulling and tugging to get her skates off.

"Who's here, Kate? Do we have company? . . . I don't see anyone," Kate's mother said, as she looked down the drive toward the street.

"No, not here, Mom; down there!" Kate pointed toward the moving van. "Let's go meet them, may we?"

"Well, it seems a little soon," Mrs. Vick paused thoughtfully, "but maybe we can help them in some way. Just a minute. I'll get a sweater."

Kate had her shoes on by the time her mother stepped out the door. Mrs. Vick was carrying a box. Kate didn't have to ask what was in the box. She already knew it contained some of the yummy cookies her mother had just baked. Mrs. Vick always tried to take a loaf of homemade bread, a cake, or some cookies to a new neighbor or a sick friend. She had told Kate many times that this was one way to show Christian love and kindness.

As they walked down the street, Kate wished she too had something to give the new family. She wished she could help show their new neighbors that she loved the Lord.

Mrs. Vick and Kate walked up the driveway, and a man and woman carrying a baby came out the front door of the house. They introduced themselves and found that the name of the new family was Rochester. Kate was disappointed to see only a baby who could hardly walk. She had so hoped for a new playmate. Kate smiled at the baby, and the baby smiled back. In fact, the baby held out her arms toward Kate.

Mrs. Rochester said, "I believe Ellen likes you, Kate. Would you like to push her in her stroller?" Kate smiled as she nodded her head. Mrs. Rochester carried Ellen over and put her in the stroller. Kate pushed Ellen up and down the sidewalk. Suddenly she got an idea and pushed the stroller toward her mother. She waited until her mother stopped talking and looked down at her.

"Mom, I want to ask you something." Her mother bent down and listened while Kate whispered something in her ear.

"All right, Kate, I'll ask." Mrs. Vick turned to Mrs. Rochester. "Mrs. Rochester, Kate says if it would help you, she could take care of Ellen while you are busy moving in."

"What a kind offer. You are a thoughtful girl, Kate. We'd be happy to have you watch Ellen. And we'll be happy to have you as a friend for our five-year-old twins, Dot and David. They will be here this weekend. They have been visiting their grandparents this week while we moved."

Kate's mouth fell wide open with surprise. "Two five-year olds to play with," she thought, and then quickly prayed, "Oh, thank you, thank you, Lord. You gave me even more than I asked for." She smiled happily as she pushed Ellen's stroller up and down the sidewalk, talking and singing all the way.

Application
➤ The Vick family loved and obeyed God. They prayed for God to send ~~just~~ the right new neighbors to live on their street.

How did Mrs. Vick and Kate show kindness to their new neighbors? *(by being friendly, taking cookies, and baby-sitting)* They were showing that they wanted to trust and obey God. They wanted to be God's friend— just like Abraham. (BATs: 5a Love; 5e Friendliness)

What did Kate pray for? *(a new neighbor to play with)* Did God answer her prayer? *(Yes; he gave her two new friends.)* (BAT: 6b Prayer)

Review activity
Using the simple tent sketch, direct each child to draw a tent peg at the base of the tent when he quotes a memory verse or answers a catechism question. You may also use two tents for team competition.

Lesson 39: Review—Abraham

Bible text: Review.
Doctrinal truth: God (faithfulness)
Character trait: Trust
Memory verses: Review.
Catechism: Review Catechism 1–16.
Materials
• Tent sketch for display (for review activity; see Lesson 38)
• Student page 10 and cutouts
• Scissors
• Glue

Opening song: "The Children's Friend"

Song: "God's Way"

Prayer
Thank God for always doing what is right for us.

Song
Review any songs used in the unit.

Student page 10
Instruct the children to cut out the pictures of Abraham, Isaac, and Jacob. Remind the children that God called Abraham His friend. Review the ways that God blessed Abraham, Isaac, and Jacob. Read each sentence and guide the children in gluing the pictures in the appropriate spaces.

Review activity
Repeat the tent activity from Lesson 38 with the following questions.

1. Why was Abraham different from everyone around him? *(He loved the one true and living God.)*

2. What did God tell Abraham to do? *(leave his home and go to a country God would show him)*

3. What did God promise Abraham? *(a big family that God would bless)*

4. Why did God change Abram's name to Abraham? *(Abraham means "father of many.")*

5. What does "Sarah" mean? *(princess)*

6. What was the name of Abraham's nephew who went with Abraham? *(Lot)*

7. What kind of homes did Lot and Abraham live in? *(tent-homes)*

8. Who came to visit Abraham in his tent-home? *(three men)*

9. What were these men? *(angels)*

10. Who was one of these men? *(the Son of God)*

11. What did God tell Abraham? *(that he and Sarah would have a baby son)*

12. Why did God tell Abraham that He was going to destroy the city of Sodom? *(The people who lived there were wicked and sinful.)*

13. Who came to Sodom while Lot was sitting by the city gate? *(two angels)*

14. When the bad men of Sodom came to Lot's house, what did the angels do to them? *(caused them to be blind)*

15. What did Lot do when the angels told him they were going to destroy the city of Sodom? *(He went to tell his children.)*

16. What did God send from heaven to destroy Sodom? *(fire)*

17. What did Lot's wife do when they were running away from the burning city? *(She disobeyed God and stopped and looked back.)*

18. What happened to her because she disobeyed God? *(She became a pillar of salt.)*

19. Where did Lot and his two daughters hide? *(in a cave)*

20. What was the name God told Abraham and Sarah to give their little baby boy? *(Isaac)*

21. Why did God ask Abraham to offer his son Isaac on the altar? *(to see if Abraham really loved Him and would obey Him)*

22. What did Isaac ask Abraham as they walked up the mountain? *(Where is the lamb [ram] for the offering to God?)*

23. Whom did Abraham send to get a wife for Isaac? *(his servant)*

24. How did the servant know Rebekah was the young woman God wanted to be Isaac's wife? *(God caused her to offer water to the servant's camels.)*

25. What did Jacob see in his dream? *(a ladder)*

26. Where did the ladder reach to? *(from earth to heaven)*

27. Who spoke to Jacob from the top of the ladder? *(God Himself)*

Review catechism and memory verses as time permits.

God's Care

Joseph: I Trust God

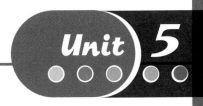
Lesson 40: Joseph Obeyed

Bible texts: Genesis 37:1–11; Ephesians 6:1

Doctrinal truth: God (sovereignty)

Character traits: Obedience; Contentment

Memory verse: Introduce I Thessalonians 5:18.

Materials
- I Thessalonians 5:18 visual 1 (See the Appendix for patterns and instructions.)
- One or more Vick or Hunter children puppets
- "Joseph's Dreams" (Picture Packet)

Opening chorus: "I Trust in God"

Song: "Thank God"

Prayer
Ask God to help us to be happy with what He has given us.

Memory verse
Read I Thessalonians 5:18 to the children. Discuss the meaning of "every thing." Display I Thessalonians 5:18 visual 1. Ask the children to name and discuss these and other things for which they can thank God. Read the verse again.

Song: "In Everything Give Thanks"

Bible lesson

Introduction
Display one or two of the Vick children puppets and have them sing "The Patriarchs." Explain that the name *patriarch* is another name for Abraham, Isaac, and Jacob, the great fathers and grandfathers of God's special people. You could have each puppet pretend to sing two lines and then hold both of them up for the last line.

Lesson

Jacob lived in the land of Canaan where his father Isaac and grandfather Abraham lived before him. Jacob had twelve sons. His ten older sons made him very sad. They sinned and disobeyed God. Jacob's two other sons were Joseph and Benjamin. Their mother had died when Benjamin was a baby.

Now Joseph was a young man who loved and obeyed his father and his God. This made his father Jacob happy. One day Joseph came and told his father a terrible thing that some of his older brothers had done. Jacob was happy that his son Joseph obeyed him and tried to do what was right. He made Joseph a special coat. When Joseph's older brothers saw this coat, though, they were jealous. They were very mean to Joseph.

One night Joseph had a dream. (Display "Joseph's Dreams" picture.) He told his brothers that he had dreamed that they were all out in the field binding sheaves of grain. In his dream, his sheaf had stood up tall and all of their sheaves had bowed down before his.

Oh, this made Joseph's brothers angrier than ever with him. They said, "Are you trying to tell us that you are going to rule over us and tell us what to do?"

Joseph had another dream. This time he dreamed that the sun and the moon and the eleven stars bowed down to him. He told his father about his dream. The sun was his father; the moon, his mother; and the eleven stars, his brothers. His father scolded him. "Is a father to obey his son?" he asked.

How angry Joseph's brothers were then! And even Joseph's father, Jacob, wondered about the meaning of the dream.

Application
➤ Did Joseph obey his father? *(Yes, he did.)* His father loved him very much. Are your mommies and daddies happy when you obey them? *(yes)* Is God happy when we obey them? *(yes)* Listen to what God tells us in Ephesians 6:1. (Read from your Bible.) This is God's plan. This is God's way. (BATs: 2a Authority; 2b Servanthood)

Jealousy is a sin. Have you ever wanted something someone else had? Have you ever been mean to someone because they were able to do something you couldn't do? Jealousy will make us hate instead of love and hurt instead of help. Yes, jealousy is a terrible sin.

God has a special plan for each of us. We should want what He wants us to have, not what someone else has. God gives us just what He knows is best for us to have. We should be happy for our brothers and sisters and friends, even if they have good things we don't have. (BATs: 5a Love; 7d Contentment)

Song: "Obedience Is," stanzas 6 and 9

Action rhyme: "Joseph"

➤ Joseph had a coat,
  (Pretend to put on coat.)
A gift from dad.
  (Hold out one hand palm up.)
His brothers hated him.
  (Look angry; frown.)
You think this made him sad?
(Look sad.)

Joseph had a dream;
  (Lay head on hand, pretend to sleep.)
His brothers frowned.
  (Frown.)
In the field while working
  (Pretend to gather grain.)
Their sheaves to his bowed down.
  (Bow from waist.)

Song: "Oh, Be Careful"

Review activity: Pantomime
Use the following poem to review the lesson.

➤ Joseph put his coat on.
  (Pretend to put arms in sleeves of coat.)
Joseph had a dream.
  (Lay head on hands as if sleeping.)
Joseph's sheaves stood upright.
  (Stand tall.)
His brothers' bowed to him.
  (Bow from waist.)

Lesson 41: Joseph's Brothers Disobeyed

Bible text: Genesis 37:12–35
Doctrinal truth: God (sovereignty)
Character traits: Obedience; Contentment
Memory verse: Review I Thessalonians 5:18.
Catechism: Introduce Catechism 17.
Materials
• I Thessalonians 5:18 visuals 1 and 2

Opening chorus: "I Trust in God"

Song: "Be Ye Doers of the Word," stanzas 4–5

Catechism
Introduce Catechism 17.

■ Where do you learn how to love and obey God? *(I learn how to love and obey God in the Bible alone.)*

Prayer
Ask God to help us to be happy even when things do not go our way.

Memory verse
Review I Thessalonians 5:18, using the I Thessalonians 5:18 visuals 1 and 2. Remind the children that we should thank God even for the hard things and sad things that happen to us. God always knows what is best for us. Choose a few children to take turns (two at a time) holding the visuals and reciting the verse.

Bible lesson

Introduction
Sing "The Patriarchs."

Lead the class in the action rhyme "Joseph" and the pantomiming of "Joseph put his coat on." (See Index of Poetry.).

Lesson

Do you know why shepherds have to move their flocks of sheep around from one place to another? *(to find grass and water for their sheep to eat and drink)*

One day Joseph's older brothers were keeping their father's sheep in Shechem. Jacob called Joseph and asked him to run an errand. His father said, "Joseph, I want you to go up to Shechem to see how your brothers are getting along."

When Joseph came to Shechem, he wandered around in the fields trying to find his brothers. A man saw him and asked what he was doing. When Joseph told the man whom he was looking for, the man said, "I heard your brothers say they were going to Dothan."

So Joseph hurried on toward Dothan. When Joseph's jealous brothers saw him coming toward them, they said, "Here comes the Dreamer. He thinks he is so special. Let's get even with him. We'll kill him and then throw him into a well. Then we'll see what will become of all his dreams."

Joseph's oldest brother, Reuben, did not want to kill Joseph. So the brothers pulled off Joseph's coat and threw him into a dry well. Reuben planned to rescue Joseph from the well when his other brothers were not around to see.

While Reuben was away, the other brothers sat down to eat. As they were eating, they saw a group of merchants riding by on their camels. The merchants were taking spices and perfumes to Egypt to sell. Judah, one of the mean brothers, said, "Let's just sell Joseph to these men, and then we won't have to kill him." That is just what they did. When Reuben returned from taking care of the sheep, he didn't see Joseph in the well. When he found out what his brothers had done, he was scared. "What can we tell our father?" he asked.

The other brothers answered, "We can just tell him that a wild beast attacked and ate our little brother."

So Joseph's brothers took his special coat and dipped it into goat's blood. Then they took the coat back to their father Jacob and told him that they had found it and wondered if it was Joseph's.

When Jacob recognized the coat, he said, "It is my son's coat. An evil beast has eaten him; Joseph surely is torn into pieces." How sad Jacob was. He loved Joseph so much, and now he thought Joseph was gone. The Bible tells us that Jacob was so unhappy that no one could comfort him.

Application

➤ Joseph's brothers were not only jealous but also full of hatred for Joseph. They sold him as a slave, and they lied to their father. Do you think what they did pleased God? Do you think they pleased Satan? Satan wants us to sin also, boys and girls.

God tells us to be content with what we have, to love one another, and to be honest. (BATs: 4c Honesty; 5a Love; 7d Contentment)

Song: "Oh, Be Careful"

Lesson 42: God's Enemy

Bible text: Isaiah 14:12–17

Doctrinal truth: Satan

Character trait: Contentment

Catechism: Review Catechism 17 and introduce Catechism 18.

Materials
• Kate and Sam Vick puppets

Opening chorus: "I Trust in God"

Song: "Be Ye Doers of the Word," stanzas 1, 4, and 5

Catechism

Introduce Catechism 18.

■ Who wrote the Bible? *(Holy men who were taught by the Holy Spirit wrote the Bible.)*

Prayer

Ask God to help us remember that He is stronger than His enemy Satan.

Doctrinal emphasis: Satan

➤ Who is Satan? Satan is God's enemy. Where did Satan come from? Satan once lived in heaven. He was one of God's good angels. His name was Lucifer when he lived in heaven. One day Lucifer became jealous of God. He wanted to be as great as God. He wanted to do the things that only God could do. So God made Lucifer leave heaven. God changed Lucifer's name to Satan. Sometimes Satan is also called the Devil.

Satan hates God. Satan wants everyone else to hate God. He wants each one of us to hate God. Does Satan want us to do what God tells us to do? No, never. Satan *always* wants us to do what God tells us not to do.

Can you think of some things Satan wants us to do? *(disobey our parents, disobey our teachers, be selfish, be jealous, not share our toys, cry when we don't get what we want)* Can you name some things God wants us to do? *(obey our parents, obey our teachers, listen quietly during Bible time, share our toys, be kind to our brothers and sisters, be good helpers at home and at school)*

Sin is doing what God tells us not to do and not doing what God tells us to do. God's Word tells us what to do and what not to do. Not obeying God's Word is sin. Satan will tempt us to sin. He will not come to us looking like a snake—as when he tempted Eve. We cannot see Satan. But he will still try to make us think, say, and do sinful things. Who is stronger, God or Satan? *(Catechism 28: God is stronger.)* (BAT: 8c Fight) We must ask God to help us to do the right thing; we must obey what God tells us in the Bible. What teaches us to love and obey God? *(the Bible)*

God is love. God hates sin, but God loves sinners. Our Bible verses tell us that all of us are sinners. God loves us even when we sin. We all disobey God sometimes. (Recite Romans 3:23.)

• God is holy. He cannot sin.

• Heaven is where God lives and where He wants us to live someday.

• God cannot let sin into heaven.

• That is why God sent His Son, Jesus Christ, to die on the cross to take away our sin—to take the punishment for our sin. (BAT: 1a Understanding Jesus Christ)

Song: "There Is None That Doeth Good"

Character story: Kate's Jealousy

Kate thought angrily, "Sam always gets to do special things." She looked inside his room where he was busily packing for a Sunday school class hike and overnight camp-out. He was whistling happily as he got his camping gear together.

Kate saw the flashlight on his dresser just inside the door. She thought, "I'll play a mean trick on him and hide it." But as she reached for the flashlight, it slipped right out of her hand and dropped to the floor. The glass was shattered—broken into pieces all over the floor.

Sam turned around quickly. "Now, just look what you've done, Kate!" He had started to speak angrily, but when he saw the frightened look on Kate's face, he said quietly, "I'm sure you didn't mean to."

Kate's face clouded up and she started to cry. Sam walked over and put his arm around her. "It's O.K., Kate. Maybe Dad will let me borrow his; don't cry."

Kate was so ashamed. Sam was being so kind. He didn't know how jealous and mean she had felt toward him and that she had really planned to play a mean trick on him. She just had to confess what she had really been doing when she broke his flashlight.

"I'm so sorry, Sam. I was jealous and wanted to hurt you because you were going on a special camping trip. But I know that was wrong. You're a good brother, and I do want good things to happen to you. You must think I'm just awful."

Sam spoke kindly to Kate, "I understand, Kate. Sometimes I have felt the same way, but being jealous is a sin. What you need to do is ask the Lord to forgive you . . . and He will, Kate, because He promised, and God always keeps His promises."

Song: "Oh, Be Careful"

Catechism
Review Catechism 17 and 18.

- Where do you learn how to love and obey God? (*I learn how to love and obey God in the Bible alone.*)

- Who wrote the Bible? (*Holy men who were taught by the Holy Spirit wrote the Bible.*)

Lesson 43: Joseph Trusted God

Bible text: Genesis 39
Doctrinal truth: Satan
Character traits: Obedience; Contentment
Memory verse: Review I Thessalonians 5:18.
Catechism: Review Catechism 17 and 18.
Materials
• I Thessalonians 5:18 visuals 1 and 2

Opening chorus: "I Trust in God"

Song: "Obedience Is," stanzas 1 and 3

Prayer
Ask God to help us to obey and be happy even when things do not go our way.

Memory verse
Review I Thessalonians 5:18 with visuals.

Song: "In Everything Give Thanks"

Catechism
Review Catechism 17 and 18 along with the doctrinal emphasis from Lesson 42.

- Where do you learn how to love and obey God? (*I learn how to love and obey God in the Bible alone.*)

- Who wrote the Bible? (*Holy men who were taught by the Holy Spirit wrote the Bible.*)

➤ We need to learn how to love and obey in order to fight God's enemy, Satan. Satan is God's enemy, but God is stronger than Satan.

Song: "Story Review Song," stanza 1

Bible lesson

Introduction
Sing "The Patriarchs."

Lead the class in the action rhyme "Joseph" and the pantomiming of "Joseph put his coat on." (See Index of Poetry.)

Lesson

The merchant men brought Joseph down to Egypt and sold him as a slave to Potiphar, who was a very rich captain in the Egyptian king's army. The king of Egypt was called *Pharaoh*. A slave is someone who serves his master, the one who bought him and owns him. A good slave works very hard to please his master. Now you might think Joseph would have felt so sorry for himself that he would not do his work well in Potiphar's house. After all, his mean brothers had done a terrible thing to him when they sold him as a slave. But Joseph was a good slave. Most slaves had to work in the fields, but Joseph worked so well that his master, Potiphar, had him work in his house.

The Bible tells us that Potiphar could see that Joseph loved and obeyed his God, and that his God gave him wisdom to do what was right. So Potiphar made him chief of all the servants in his house and also of all of his money. Joseph was honest and did his work so well that he helped his master grow even richer.

Then one day another sad thing happened to Joseph. Potiphar's wife wanted Joseph to disobey God. Joseph knew that it would be a sin, so he didn't listen to this wicked woman. That made her so angry that she told a lie about Joseph. She told her husband that Joseph had done something that he had not done. Potiphar had to punish Joseph. He put Joseph in jail.

Poor Joseph! That just didn't seem fair, did it? He had not done anything wrong. He had obeyed his father and his God. First, his brothers had hated him and sold him. Then when he had obeyed his master, his master's wife had lied about him. He was not only a slave but also a prisoner in jail. You'd think Joseph would have just sat down and pouted or cried. But he didn't. He knew God had a special plan for his life. He became such a good, obedient prisoner that the prison keeper noticed him and gave him the job of being in charge of all the other prisoners. No matter where Joseph was, he let God use him; he glorified God by loving Him and doing what He commanded.

Application

➤ How do you act when things don't go the way you want them to? Do you cry and pout? Or do you ask God to help you to obey Him and to be happy? How do you think Satan wants you to act? What do you think God wants you to do? Let's try to act like Joseph and glorify God by loving Him and doing what He commands. Remember God is always with you and will help you do the right thing.

Song: "Trust and Obey"

Lesson 44: Joseph in Jail

Bible text: Genesis 40–41
Doctrinal truth: God (sovereignty)
Character traits: Self-concept; Contentment
Memory verse: Review Psalm 95:6.
Catechism: Review Catechism 1–3, 7, and 8.
Materials
• "Joseph's Chariot" (Picture Packet)
• Student page 11 and cutouts
• Scissors
• Glue

Opening chorus: "I Trust in God"

Song: "God Is with Me"

➤ Was God with Joseph—even in jail? Is God with you wherever you are?

Ask the children to recall some times and places they have been afraid. Remind them of God's promise to care for them wherever they are.

Song: "Story Review Song," stanza 1

Memory verse
Review Psalm 95:6. Remind the children that God has not only made them but is also always with them.

Prayer
Ask God to help us to remember that He has a special plan for each of our lives. (BAT: 3a Self-concept)

Song: "How Do We Know?" stanza 1

Bible lesson

Introduction
Lead the children in singing "The Patriarchs."

➤ What does the last line of the song say? (*"And God blessed them all."*)

What does "bless" mean? (*give good things to*)

What happened to Joseph in our last lesson? (*He was put in jail.*)

Does that sound like a blessing—a good thing? (*no*)

➤ God had a plan for Joseph's life, just as He has a special plan for each of our lives. Joseph trusted God; he believed that God was doing the best thing for him. And God did.

Lesson

Remember in our last lesson we learned that Joseph was such an obedient prisoner that he was put in charge of all the other prisoners.

One day the king's butler and baker were put into prison where Joseph was in charge. While they were in jail, they each had a dream.

The next morning when Joseph saw them, he asked, "Why do you look so sad?" They told him that they had each had a dream, but they didn't understand what their dreams meant. Joseph said, "My God will tell me what your dreams mean."

After the butler had told Joseph what he had dreamed, Joseph told him his dream meant that in three days the king would take the butler out of jail and put him back in his palace to work for him again as he had before. Joseph asked the butler to remember to tell the king that even though he had not done anything wrong, he was still in jail. Joseph asked the butler to ask Pharaoh if he would release him from jail.

Then the baker told Joseph about his dream. His dream did not have such a happy meaning: Joseph told the baker that in three days the king was going to have him killed.

And sure enough, in three days the king had the butler brought back to the palace to serve him, and he had the baker killed.

But when the butler went back to the palace, he forgot all about poor Joseph. For two years he forgot, until one day when he heard that the king had had two dreams. The king was looking all over his land for someone to interpret his dreams—to tell him what his dreams meant—but he could find no one. *Then* the butler remembered and told the king about Joseph.

Pharaoh sent for Joseph to be brought to him. To go before the king was important, so Joseph shaved, bathed, and put on clean clothes before he went.

Joseph came to the palace before the king. The butler had told Pharaoh that Joseph knew what dreams meant. Joseph said, "I can't, but my God will show me the meaning." So the king told Joseph his dreams.

Pharaoh said he dreamed that he stood by the river and saw several fat cattle come up out of the river and eat grass in the meadow near the river bank. He also saw seven thin, skinny cattle come up out of the river and walk toward the other cattle. Then the seven skinny cattle ate up the seven fat cattle. And Pharaoh said, "I awoke."

Then Pharaoh said that he had a second dream. In this dream he saw seven good ears of corn grow out of one tall stalk. After that, seven thin ears of corn grew out of the same stalk and ate up the seven good ears of corn on the stalk. Pharaoh woke up and knew he had been dreaming again.

Joseph told the king that both dreams meant the same thing: that there were going to be seven years with plenty of corn growing in Egypt and the lands around it, to feed his people. Then there would be seven years without any corn growing to feed the people. Joseph told the king that God had given him two dreams to show that this was a warning from God and that it would happen soon. He also told the king that he should look for a wise man to plan for these years so that no one would be without food during the seven years of famine. A famine is a time when there is not enough food for everyone to eat.

The king knew Joseph must be very wise to know a God that could tell him the meaning of his dreams, so he made Joseph ruler of the land and gave him his own ring and dressed him in fine clothes and put a gold chain around his neck. Everyone was to obey Joseph. He was the highest ruler in the land of Egypt except for the king. He also gave Joseph a beautiful wife and a chariot. (Display "Joseph's Chariot" picture.) Joseph rode out over all the land of Egypt to rule the land.

Application

➤ Well, Joseph wasn't a poor slave in jail anymore, was he? No, instead he was made a ruler of a great land. God had a plan for Joseph's life, and Joseph trusted God to do what was best for him.

Does God have a plan for your life? Yes, He does. You don't know what God may someday want you to do. But you do know He wants you to love and obey Him each day, so that you'll be ready for whatever job God has for you to do as you grow up. (BAT: 3a Self-concept)

Student page 11

Instruct the children to cut out the pictures of the cornstalks. Read the sentences on the page. Allow a volunteer to tell about Pharaoh's first dream. Allow another child to tell what Pharaoh saw in his second dream. Instruct the children to glue the pictures in place (large ears of corn below the fat cows; thin ears below the thin cows).

➤ What was the meaning of Pharaoh's dreams?

Who told Joseph the meaning of Pharaoh's dreams?

Song: "God Made Me"

➤ Joseph knew God would help him to be brave in his big new job as ruler of Egypt. When we have something hard to do, maybe something we have never done before, God will help us to be brave. (BAT: 8d Courage)

Catechism

Review Catechism 1–3 and 7–8.

■ Who made you? (*God made me.*)

- What else did God make? (*God made all things.*)

- Why did God make you and all things? (*God made me and all things for His own glory.*)

- How can you glorify God? (*I can glorify God by loving Him and doing what He commands.*)

- Why ought you to glorify God? (*I ought to glorify God because He made me and takes care of me.*)

Repeat Catechism 1, 3, 7, and 8, substituting "Joseph" for "you."

Lesson 45: Joseph in the King's Palace

Bible text: Genesis 41–42
Doctrinal truth: God (sovereignty)
Character traits: Self-concept; Contentment
Catechism: Review Catechism 12–18.
Materials
• "Joseph's Dreams" and "Joseph's Chariot" (Picture Packet)

Opening chorus: "I Trust in God"

Song: "Story Review Song," stanza 1

Prayer
Ask God to help us to remember how Joseph let God use his life, and ask God to use our lives for His glory.

Song: "Be Ye Doers of the Word," stanzas 1, 4, 5, 7, 9

Bible lesson

Introduction
Review the action rhyme "Joseph." (See Index of Poetry.)

Tell the children that today they are going to find out the meaning of the dreams that Joseph had when he was a young boy. (Display "Joseph's Dreams" picture.)

Lesson

When Joseph was made ruler of Egypt, he traveled all around the country. (Display "Joseph's Chariot" picture.) Just as God had showed Pharaoh in his dreams, during the next seven years there was much food that grew in the land. It was much more than was needed to feed all of the people. So Joseph had his workers gather up all the extra corn and put it in storehouses (like barns) in the land of Egypt.

Then the next seven years began, and, again, just as God had said, there was not enough food grown in the fields to feed the people in Egypt. When the people came crying to Pharaoh for food, he sent them to Joseph. So Joseph opened all the storehouses and sold the food to the people of Egypt.

The famine was also in all the lands around Egypt, so many people came to Egypt to buy corn from Joseph's storehouses. Then something very wonderful happened to Joseph!

About twenty years had passed since his brothers had sold him to be a slave. Oh, how he had missed his father and family! Now when his father Jacob heard that there was corn in Egypt, he sent his ten oldest sons from Canaan to Egypt to buy food for his family. When his brothers came before the ruler of Egypt, they bowed before him, but they did not know that it was Joseph. The king had given Joseph a new name, and besides, he had grown to be a man since they had last seen him, so they did not recognize him as their little brother.

But when Joseph saw his brothers, he knew who they were. He remembered the dream that God had sent him many years ago about his brothers' sheaves bowing down to his in the field. Now he knew why God had let him be sold as a slave, why he had been put in jail, and why he was now living in the palace as a ruler of Egypt.

Even though Joseph knew who his brothers were, he did not act as if he did. He pretended to be an Egyptian; he spoke to them as though they were strangers. "Where did you come from? Who are you?" he asked.

"Our father sent us to buy food for our families. We are from Canaan," they answered.

Joseph accused them of being spies. But they said, "Oh, no, we are all the sons of one man. We have a younger brother at home with our father."

Joseph told them that they must prove to him that they were not spies. He said that he would put nine of the brothers in jail and send the other one back to Canaan to bring their youngest brother to him to prove that they were telling him the truth. The nine brothers were afraid.

Then Joseph told them that he had changed his mind—that he would keep just one brother, Simeon, in jail and let the others go home to bring back Benjamin, their youngest brother. Joseph had his servants fill all of their sacks with corn and also had the money that they had brought to pay for the corn put back into their sacks. Later, on their way home, when they found the money in their sacks of food, they were afraid again. They thought this ruler of Egypt would think they had not paid for their food. They didn't know that it was Joseph who had ordered his servant to put the money into their sacks.

When they came to their home in Canaan and told their father, Jacob, all that had happened, he was very sad. He said, "I can't let you take Benjamin away from me. I've already lost Joseph and now Simeon."

Application

➤ Joseph's brothers were afraid, weren't they? Why? *(Allow discussion.)* Yes, they remembered how they had sinned when they sold Joseph to be a slave. Now they were afraid something bad would happen to them and their family because of their sin. When we sin, we must tell God we are sorry for our sin. If we hurt someone else, we must tell him we are sorry. This helps us to be happy servants of God. (BAT: 6d Clear conscience)

Do you think Joseph forgave his brothers? Why? *(Allow discussion.)* Yes, he was so happy to see that his brothers were sorry for their sin. And he was happy that God could use him to help others. (BAT: 6e Forgiveness)

Song: "Be Ye Doers of the Word," stanza 2

Catechism
Review Catechism 12–18.

- Who is God? *(God is a spirit and does not have a body like man.)*

- Where is God? *(God is everywhere.)*

- Can you see God? *(No, I cannot see God, but He always sees me.)*

- Does God know all things? *(Yes, nothing can be hidden from God.)*

- Can God do all things? *(Yes, God can do all His holy will.)*

- Where do you learn how to love and obey God? *(I learn how to love and obey God in the Bible alone.)*

- Who wrote the Bible? *(Holy men who were taught by the Holy Spirit wrote the Bible.)*

Lesson 46: Joseph's Family United

Bible text: Genesis 42–46

Doctrinal truth: God (sovereignty)

Character traits: Self-concept; Contentment

Memory verses: Review I Thessalonians 5:18 and Psalm 95:6.

Catechism: Review Catechism 7, 8, 15, and 16.

Materials
- I Thessalonians 5:18 visuals 1 and 2
- "Joseph with Brothers" (Picture Packet)

Opening chorus: "I Trust in God"

Song: "Thank You, God"

Memory verse
Read I Thessalonians 5:18 from the Bible. Review the verse with visuals 1 and 2.

Prayer
Ask God to help us give thanks in everything.

➤ We know that God is with us wherever we are. There is a big word that tells us that about God—omnipresent. God is present everywhere. We can pray to Him when we are walking along the sidewalk or outdoors playing. Sometime you might start to say or do something unkind to a friend. You can just stop and whisper a prayer right then: "Dear God, help me to be kind and obey Your Word." We can sit at the dinner table and thank God for our food. We can pray when we are lying in our beds at night and ask the Lord to forgive us for the bad things we did during the day. Anytime, anywhere—we can talk to our God.

There is one special way we can talk to God. We can *kneel* and show Him we praise Him for how great He is. Remember our verse, Psalm 95:6? Let's say it together. (Recite Psalm 95:6.)

This is what we are going to do right now for our prayer time today. I want each one of you to kneel very quietly right by your own chair with your hands on your chair. We will not be looking at anyone else or touching anyone else. That way we can think only of God. Now let us recite our verse again. (Recite Psalm 95:6.)

Ask one or two children to thank God for their homes and mothers and daddies and brothers and sisters. After praying, ask the children to stand up quietly and sit down in their chairs.

➤ I know God is happy to have us praise Him in this special way.

Song: "How Do We Know?" stanza 1

Bible lesson

Introduction
Lead the children in singing "The Patriarchs."

Lesson

When the food that Jacob's sons had brought back from Egypt was all gone, Jacob said to his sons, "Go again and buy us a little food."

Judah reminded his father that the ruler of Egypt had said that he would not help them and he would keep Simeon in jail if they did not bring their younger brother with them.

Jacob asked Judah, "Why did you do this to me? Why did you tell the Egyptian ruler that you had another brother?"

Judah answered his father, "When the man asked us if we had a father who was living and a brother, we answered him honestly. We didn't know that he would ask us to bring Benjamin down to Egypt."

Jacob knew that he must send his sons back to Egypt and let them take Benjamin also, even though he was afraid to do it. Jacob told his sons to take extra money, fresh fruits, spices, and perfumes with them to give to the ruler of Egypt so that he would be kind to them.

So the nine brothers traveled again to the land of Egypt, this time with their younger brother. They took the money they had found in their sacks after their last visit to Joseph. Obeying their father, they also took extra money to buy more food and special gifts to please the leader of Egypt.

When they came before Joseph, Joseph had his servants prepare a special dinner, and he had all of his brothers brought into his home to eat with him.

When Joseph came in, his brothers bowed before him and gave him the gifts they had brought him. He asked them how they were and if their father was alive and well. He greeted Benjamin. Oh, Joseph was so happy that he started to cry. He had to run quickly out of the room. He wanted to be alone so his brothers would not see him cry. Have you ever seen a grown-up cry tears of happiness? Joseph cried because he was happy to see all of his brothers again. Then he washed his face and went back to eat with them.

When the meal was over, Joseph's brothers wanted to go home. They knew their father was anxious to have Benjamin back at home with him again.

So the next morning they took their sacks and started home. But they did not know that Joseph had told his servant to put his own silver cup in Benjamin's sack. They had not traveled far when Joseph's servant caught up with them. He asked them why they had done such an evil thing to his master when he had been so good to them. They declared they had done nothing wrong; they didn't know what the servant was talking about. When they opened their sacks to show the servant, they were surprised to see the silver cup in Benjamin's sack. "How did the cup get into his sack?" they wondered. Now they were more afraid than ever.

They returned to the city to Joseph's house. When they saw Joseph, they bowed before him and tried to explain that they had not stolen the cup. Joseph listened to them and then said that he would have to keep Benjamin as his servant since the cup was found in his sack.

Judah came close to Joseph and begged Joseph to keep him instead and let Benjamin go. He told Joseph how hard it had been for their father to let his youngest son come so far away from home. He said that if they did not take Benjamin back to their father, their father would surely die.

This was just too much for Joseph. He couldn't wait any longer to tell his secret. He told all of his servants to leave the room. (Display "Joseph with Brothers" picture.) Then as he stood before his brothers and told them who he was, again he cried tears of joy.

He said, "I am your brother Joseph whom you sold into Egypt. Do not be afraid or angry with yourselves. God had a special plan for my life. He allowed me to be sold as a slave so that I would be here in Egypt in this palace. Because I am here, I can save your lives during this famine."

Then Joseph told his brothers to go home and bring his father and all his family and cattle to live in Egypt. And they did. Do you think Jacob was happy when he heard that his beloved son Joseph was not dead but alive and a ruler in the land of Egypt?

God spoke to Jacob and told him not to be afraid to go to Egypt. He promised him again to make his family a great people who would bless the whole world. How happy Jacob and Joseph were to see each other again!

Application
> ➤ God used Joseph's life in a special way (Psalm 105:17–24). Joseph trusted God and was happy to obey and serve the Lord, his Maker. He didn't grumble or complain, even when he was made a slave and put in jail.

Did Joseph glorify God with his life? How? *(Allow discussion.)* (BATs: 3a Self-concept; 7d Contentment)

Catechism
Review Catechism 7 and 8 and apply the questions to the life of Joseph.

■ How can you glorify God? *(I can glorify God by loving Him and doing what He commands.)*

■ Why ought you to glorify God? *(I ought to glorify God because He made me and takes care of me.)*

Review Catechism 15 and 16.

■ Does God know all things? *(Yes, nothing can be hidden from God.)*

■ Can God do all things? *(Yes, God can do all His holy will.)*

Song: "Story Review Song," stanza 1

Song: "Trust and Obey"

Lesson 47: God Cared for Joseph

Bible text: Review.

Doctrinal truth: God (sovereignty)

Character trait: Trust

Memory verses: Review.

Catechism: Review Catechism 1–18.

Materials
- Large sketch of Joseph's coat for display (for review activity)
- A completed copy of Student page 1 (for use as a song visual)
- Student page 12 and cutouts
- Scissors
- Glue
- Colored chalk

Opening chorus: "I Trust in God"

Song: "Holy Bible, Book Divine"
Use the completed copy of Student page 1 as a visual.

Prayer
Thank God for the promises in His Word.

Student page 12
Direct the children to look at the pictures and tell you who they see. *(Joseph)* Instruct the children to cut out the pictures and place them in a row in front of them. Ask them to pick up the picture that happened "first" in Joseph's life. Select a volunteer to describe the picture and tell what happened to Joseph. Instruct the children to glue the picture in the space with the letter "A" and pick up the picture that shows "what happened next." Select a volunteer to tell about the second picture. Guide the children in gluing the second picture in space "B." Continue until all the pictures have been discussed and glued. Tell the children that they have just "read" a picture story. Read the sentences on the page and review the story sequence: (A) Joseph wearing his special coat, (B) in the well, (C) being sold by brothers, (D) in prison, (E) in the palace before Pharaoh, (F) in the palace with brothers.

Song: "Story Review Song," stanza 1

Review activity
Direct the children to color a stripe on the sketch of Joseph's coat each time they answer a review question. You may choose to have two teams and two coats for competition. Use the following review questions.

1. How many sons did Jacob have? *(twelve)*

2. How many brothers did Joseph have? *(eleven)*

3. Which son did Jacob love very much? *(Joseph)*

4. What special gift did Joseph's father give him? *(a special coat)*

5. Which one of Jacob's sons was the youngest? *(Benjamin)*

6. What were Joseph's brothers doing when Jacob sent Joseph to find them? *(keeping their sheep)*

7. What did Joseph's brothers do to Joseph? *(sold him to be a slave)*

8. What did they tell Jacob, their father, had happened to Joseph? *(killed by an animal)*

9. To what country was Joseph taken as a slave? *(Egypt)*

10. When Joseph was in jail, what did he do for two of the prisoners? *(He told them the meaning of their dreams.)*

11. Who told Pharaoh about Joseph being in prison? *(the butler, one of the king's workers)*

12. Why did Pharaoh get Joseph out of jail? *(He wanted Joseph to tell him what his strange dreams meant.)*

13. What did Pharaoh's dreams mean? *(There would be seven years of plenty and then seven years of famine when the crops would not grow.)*

14. What honor did Pharaoh give to Joseph for interpreting his dream? *(He made him ruler over all the land of Egypt.)*

15. What did Joseph do to prepare for the seven years of famine that were to come to Egypt? *(built barns and filled them with grain during the seven good years of plenty)*

16. When the years of famine came, what did Joseph do with the grain he had stored in the barns? *(sold it to the people who needed it)*

17. Why did Jacob send his ten sons to Egypt? *(to buy food)*

18. Which brother did Joseph keep in prison while the others went back? *(Simeon)*

19. Why was Jacob afraid to let Benjamin go back to Egypt with all his brothers? *(He was afraid harm might come to him as it had to Joseph.)*

20. What did Joseph do first when his brothers came back the next time? *(had a big dinner for them at his house)*

21. Why do you suppose Joseph had his servant put the cup in Benjamin's sack? *(to find out how the older brothers would treat Benjamin)*

22. How did Joseph let his brothers know who he really was? *(He had his servants go away. When he was alone with his brothers, he told them who he was.)*

23. Who spoke to Jacob in the night and told him to go on to Egypt? *(God)*

24. God is omniscient. What does "omniscient" mean? *(God knows all things.)*

You could also use additional questions about memory verses, choruses, and catechism.

Song: "Obedience Is," stanzas 3 and 9

Lesson 48: God Cares for Me

Bible text: Review

Doctrinal truth: God (omnipresence)

Character trait: Trust

Memory verse: Review I Thessalonians 5:18.

Catechism: Review Catechism 13.

Materials
- Pictures suggested for prayer discussion (or cutouts for Student page 13)
- Student page 13 and cutouts
- Scissors
- Glue

Opening chorus: "I Trust in God"

Song: "Holy Bible, Book Divine"

Doctrinal emphasis: Omnipresence of God

➤ Where is God? *(Catechism 13: God is everywhere.)* Did you know that God can be everywhere—in all places—at the same time? Is God with us here in this room? Is He with your mother and your father whether they are at home or at work right now? *(Allow discussion.)*

God is omnipresent. *Omni* means "all," and when we say *omnipresent,* we mean "present everywhere" or "in all places." God is always present everywhere. Say "omnipresent" with me. What does it mean? *(Allow discussion.)*

There is no place where we can go that God is not with us. He is with us in the daytime. He is with us in the nighttime. God says, "I am with you always."

Prayer

Thank God for always being with us.

Display pictures of children in various circumstances: playing, riding in a car, getting on a school bus, at the beach, in church, and in bed. Distribute these to several children. Let them stand up and hold their pictures.

Discuss each picture. Ask "Is God with us when we are _____?" (Refer to one of the pictures. Repeat, referring to another each time.)

Ask the children holding the pictures to pray a short sentence prayer thanking God for being with us. Give them an example: "Johnny may thank God for being with us as we ride on the school bus."

Song: "God Is with Me"

Student page 13

Remind the children that God took care of Joseph and that Joseph trusted God. Read the sentences at the top of the page. Instruct the children to cut out the pictures and glue them inside the house (any order is acceptable). Ask volunteers to tell what is happening in each of the pictures and answer the question, "Is God with us when we are _____?" Remind the children that God is with each one of them wherever they are, all day and all night.

Song: "I Will Trust in Thee"

Lesson 49: God Cared for Sam

Bible text: Review.

Doctrinal truth: God (sovereignty)

Character trait: Trust

Memory verses: Review.

Catechism: Review Catechism 1–18.

Materials
- Sam and Mom Vick puppets (optional)
- Large sketch of Joseph's coat for display (for review activity; used with Lesson 47)

Opening chorus: "I Trust in God"

Song: "How Do We Know?" stanza 1

Character story: "God Cared for Sam"

Sam was walking home from school one day when he felt something brush against his leg. He quickly looked down and saw a cat staring up at him with big, sad, green eyes. When Sam reached down to pet the cat, he noticed its black fur was all ragged.

"You look like you've been in a fight, poor fellow," Sam said.

"Meow, Me-o-w." The cat seemed to say, "Hello, will you be my friend?"

Sam walked on toward home, but every time he turned around, there was the cat following right behind him.

"I think I'll call you 'Tag-a-long.'" Sam smiled. When they reached home, Sam ran excitedly into the house to tell his mother what had happened.

"Come outside, Mom. Come and see what followed me home."

Mrs. Vick walked out to the back porch, and there it was—that old "tag-a-long" cat.

"Oh, Mom, may I keep him? You know I've always wanted a cat—all for my very own," Sam pleaded.

"Well, Sam, we don't know where the cat came from or whom it belongs to. It really doesn't look too healthy either. Someone else might be missing this cat this very minute. I don't think we should say you can keep it."

Sam was disappointed. He secretly prayed that the cat would stay around and no one else would want him.

The next morning when Sam left for school, he walked outside, and there it was, waiting for him—old "Tag-a-long." Sam was happy; he had so hoped the cat would still be there that he had even stuck a piece of his breakfast muffin in his pocket to feed it.

The cat followed him all the way to school. Sam could hardly get his schoolwork done because he kept wondering if the cat would still be waiting for him. When the dismissal bell finally rang that day, Sam rushed out of school and down the walkway.

Sure enough, there it was, lying all curled up under the shrubbery at the end of the walkway near the sidewalk.

"Hi, 'Tag-a-long,' let's go." The cat got up and curled itself around Sam's legs as if to say hello.

Sam and his cat had a good time playing that afternoon. Sam was even planning to build a cat house and thinking about where he might find some scrap lumber. And that night he remembered to thank the Lord again for his new cat.

The next morning, the two new friends started out together—Sam in front and 'Tag-a-long' not far behind. When Sam turned the corner at the stop light, he saw a friend across the street from his class and yelled, "Hi!" A minute later when he looked back, the cat was gone. He looked up and down the streets and alleys, but he couldn't find "Tag-a-long" anywhere.

Sam hurried on because he didn't want to be late. By the time he arrived at school, he was so disappointed and sad that he was almost crying. When he walked through his classroom door, his teacher noticed his red eyes.

"Sam, is something wrong?" Mrs. Repp asked.

Sam told her all about his new friend, "Tag-a-long", and how he ran away on the way to school.

Mrs. Repp was very kind. She said, "Remember, Sam, God never takes anything away without giving us something better in its place. He always knows what's best for us."

When Sam sat down at his desk, he asked God to help him to trust and obey Him.

That afternoon after school, Sam told his mother what had happened and what Mrs. Repp had said.

"Your teacher is right, Sam. God's Word tells us how the Lord took care of Joseph and made sad things turn out to be for Joseph's good."

One afternoon about a week later, when Sam came home from school, he found his mother in the yard waiting for him with a smile on her face. She told Sam to come over by the bush where she was standing.

"Look what I just found, Sam." Sam bent down and peered through the brushy leaves of the bush. Then he saw something—there was a tiny fluffy gray kitten sleeping all curled up.

"May I pick him up?" Sam whispered.

"I believe it would be O.K. Hold him gently though. He looks like he's not very old, probably the runt of his mother's litter. You'll have to take good care of him for a while to help him grow stronger." Sam threw his arms around his mother, "Oh, Mom, you really mean it—this kitten can be mine—my very own?"

His mother smiled and nodded her head. "Yes, I believe God sent His best for you in this special way, Sam."

In his heart Sam said a special "thank you" to the Lord. He knew God's way is always best.

Prayer: Thank God for His care for us.

Song: "Trust and Obey"

Review activity
Repeat the activity with Joseph's coat from Lesson 47.

God's Leader

Moses: I Obey God's Word

> It may be necessary to skip ahead to Unit 7 (God's Gifts) or Unit 8 (God's Best Gift) to cover lessons that correspond to Thanksgiving or Christmas. Unit 7 should be taught before Thanksgiving and Unit 8 before Christmas. You may want to begin teaching the Thanksgiving memory passage, Psalm 100, before teaching the Thanksgiving lessons; for this reason, all the memory verse instructions for Psalm 100 are located at the beginning of Unit 7.

Lesson 50: A New King

Bible text: Exodus 1:8–22

Doctrinal truths: Man; Salvation (repentance)

Character trait: Trust

Memory verses: Review Romans 3:23 and Psalm 37:27.

Catechism: Introduce Catechism 19–20.

Opening chorus: "I Will Obey"

Prayer

Ask God to help us to always be sorry for our sin.

Bible lesson

Introduction

➤ In our lessons about Joseph, we learned that God told Joseph's father, Jacob, to bring his family to Egypt. Joseph lived for many years with Jacob and his family after they came to Egypt. Remember, Abraham, Isaac, Jacob, and Joseph were Israelites—God's chosen people, whom we are learning about in our Bible lessons. (Lead the children in singing "The Patriarchs." God promised to make their families great and bring them to a special place to live—the promised land.

Lesson

After Joseph died, the Bible tells us that there was a new king of Egypt who did not know Joseph and his family—the Israelites. Remember that, in our lessons about how God took care of Joseph, we learned that the king of Egypt was called "Pharaoh." All the kings of Egypt were called Pharaoh, just like the leader of our nation is called the president. (Name the current president of the United States.)

This Pharaoh was afraid of God's people, the Israelites, because they were growing into a big

family. Do you remember what God had promised to their fathers, to Abraham, Isaac, and Jacob? *(He would bless their families and make them great.)* And God was keeping His promise. He had blessed them with many children, and houses, and lands. They had grown to be a strong people and the new Pharaoh was afraid that they might join with Egypt's enemies and fight against his country.

Pharaoh ordered his soldiers to make the people of Israel work hard to build special cities where he could store his special things. These taskmasters whipped the Israelites to make them work harder and faster. They forced the Israelites to make bricks and build walls and do very hard work. But the more the Egyptian taskmasters beat them and the harder they worked them, the more God's people grew to become an even larger family.

So the king of Egypt spoke to the nurses who took care of the Israelite women when they had their babies. He ordered them to kill all the baby boys who were born to the Israelite mothers. What a cruel, mean thing for a Pharaoh to do! Do you think these nurses obeyed the Pharaoh? No, they did not. The Bible tells us that because the nurses loved and trusted God, they obeyed Him. Because of this, God took care of them and gave them children of their own to make them happy.

Application

➤ Yes, Pharaoh was a cruel, sinful man, but we know the Bible tells us that all people are sinners. To kill is a terrible sin. But there are many other sins. What have we learned that sin is? *(Allow discussion.)* Yes, sin is disobeying God. All sin must be punished. We are all sinners. The punishment for sin is death. How can we escape this punishment? We must trust in God's Son, Jesus Christ, who was sent to Earth to die on the cross for our sin. If we believe that Jesus died for our sin, we can accept Him as our Savior. We must be sorry for our sin and believe that He will forgive us. We must confess our sin to God, turn from it, and live God's way. (BAT: 1b Repentance and faith)

Song: "There Is None That Doeth Good"

Memory verses

Review Romans 3:23 and Psalm 37:27.

Catechism

Discuss sins such as disobeying parents or teachers; being unkind to a brother, sister, or friend; not sharing; or being jealous.

➤ Did Pharaoh transgress God's law? Transgression is another word for sin. Transgression is *not doing* what God's Word *tells* us to do or *doing* what God's Word tells us *not* to do.

God's Word tells us, "Children, obey your parents." Have you *always* done everything your parents told you to do? Not doing what God tells us to do is a transgression. It is failing to do what God commands.

God's Word tells us not to tell lies or steal and not to be jealous or unkind. When we do these things, we are doing what God forbids or tells us not to do and transgressing God's laws.

Introduce Catechism 19 and 20.

■ Who were our first parents? (*Adam and Eve were our first parents.*)

■ Of what were our first parents made? (*God made the body of Adam out of the dust of the ground and formed Eve from the body of Adam.*)

Song: "Oh, Be Careful"

Lesson 51: A Baby in the Bulrushes

Bible text: Exodus 1:22–2:10

Doctrinal truth: God (sovereignty)

Character trait: Trust

Memory verse: Introduce Ecclesiastes 12:13*b*.

Catechism: Review Catechism 1, 7, 8, 17, and 18.

Materials
• "Baby Moses" (Picture Packet)
• Student page 14

Opening chorus: "I Will Obey"

Song: "Be Ye Doers of the Word"

Prayer

Thank God for making us and ask Him to help us glorify Him by the way we live.

Memory verse

Read Ecclesiastes 12:13*b* to the children.

➤ When the Bible says "to *fear* God," it means to believe that God is the great, powerful God of heaven who made us and wants us to love and obey Him. "To keep his commandments" means to obey God's Word. Just like our parents should punish us when we disobey, so God must punish sin.

We should fear God and keep His commandments because this is the reason God made us. When we fear God and keep His commandments, we will be pleasing God. And we will be happy too.

Song: "God Is with Me"

Catechism

Review Catechism 17 and 18.

■ Where do you learn how to love and obey God? (*I learn how to love and obey God in the Bible alone.*)

■ Who wrote the Bible? (*Holy men who were taught by the Holy Spirit wrote the Bible.*)

➤ Where do we find God's commandments? (*in the Bible*)

Bible lesson

Introduction

➤ In our last lesson, what did Pharaoh tell the nurses to do when helping the Israelite mothers have their babies? (*Whenever a baby boy was born, they were to kill him.*) Did the nurses obey the king? (*no*) Whom did they obey? (*God*) So Pharaoh had to think of another way to get rid of God's people, the Israelites. This time Pharaoh told his people and soldiers to throw into the river all of the baby boys who were born into the families of the Israelites.

Lesson

In one of the Israelite families who loved and served God were a mother and father, a daughter named Miriam, and a son named Aaron. And then a little baby boy was born. Oh, how happy the family was, until they remembered the king's rule about baby boys.

They loved their baby. They didn't want the king's men to find out about him. They decided to try to hide their baby in their house so that the king's soldiers could not find him. But the baby grew bigger, and he cried louder. They were so afraid someone would see him or hear him. What could they do?

They asked God to help them.

The mother gathered tall plants called bulrushes that grew by the river. She made a basket. She covered the basket with pitch to keep the water out. She put the baby into the basket and hid him among the tall grass and bulrushes. (Display "Baby Moses" picture.)

The daughter of the king came down to the river to take a bath. The princess saw the basket in the river and sent her servants to get it. How surprised they were to find a baby! She knew why someone had hidden the baby in the basket. She knew about her father's law.

Miriam was hiding nearby. She saw and heard everything that happened. She ran to the princess. She asked if she should get a mother from the families of God's people to feed and take care of the baby for the princess. The princess said yes.

Miriam ran and got her mother—baby Moses' own mother—and together they carried the baby back home. Now no one would dare hurt their son. Everyone knew that the king's daughter, the princess, had found him.

How happy the family was to have their baby Moses at home with them again! God had used a sister to help protect her little brother. This little brother was to grow up some day to be a great servant of God and a great leader of God's people.

Application

➤ God had a special plan for baby Moses. We will hear more stories about how Moses grew up to become God's leader for his people. And just as God had a special plan for Joseph and for Moses, God has a special plan for each of you, boys and girls. He wants you to love and obey Him every day, and He will help you do special work for Him. (BAT: 3a Self-concept)

Student page 14

Guide the children as they connect the dots to complete the picture. Allow them to color the basket. Ask a volunteer to tell how baby Moses stayed safe in the water. Read and discuss the page, reminding the children that God always takes care of us.

Song: "Story Review Song," stanza 2

Catechism

Review Catechism 1, 7, and 8.

- Who made you? (*God made me.*)

- How can you glorify God? (*I can glorify God by loving Him and doing what He commands.*)

- Why ought you to glorify God? (*I ought to glorify God because He made me and takes care of me.*)

Recite Ecclesiastes 12:13*b* again.

Song: "Trust and Obey"

Lesson 52: A Burning Bush

Bible text: Exodus 3–4

Doctrinal truth: God (omnipotence and faithfulness)

Character trait: Obedience

Memory verse: Review Ecclesiastes 12:13*b*.

Catechism: Introduce Catechism 21.

Materials

- Toy or paper snake (Fold a strip of paper in accordion fashion, and add eyes and a tongue. See the illustration below.)
- A white glove marked with a felt-tip marker to resemble the hand of a leper
- Vick family puppets
- Red cellophane or crepe paper
- A piece of a shrub
- A stick
- "Moses" (Picture Packet)
- Apron with large pockets (optional)

Opening chorus: "I Will Obey"

Song: "Obedience Is"

Song: "Story Review Song," stanza 2

Memory verse

Review Ecclesiastes 12:13*b*. Divide the children into three groups or have three children recite the verse in a choral response activity, assigning one phrase of the verse to each group or child. Repeat this activity several times.

Song: "Be Ye Doers of the Word," stanza 1

➤ The Bible tells us, "Children, obey your parents." We *hear* God's Word, "Children, obey." Then we *do* God's Word when we obey our parents. When we obey, we show God and others that we love and fear God and want to grow up God's way.

Prayer

Ask God to help us to be doers of the Word and not hearers only.

Bible lesson

You may wish to wear an apron with large pockets to conceal your visual objects until you are ready to display them. Or you could sit behind a table and use a large piece of cardboard or standing flannelgraph board as a screen.

Introduction

➤ The Vick family sat in front of their fireplace for family devotions. Dad had just walked into the room carrying his Bible.

"I just love to *see* the red and orange flames of the fire," Kate exclaimed.

"I just love to *hear* the fire crackle and pop," added Sam.

Josh jumped up and ran over to his mother and pulled at the sleeve of her dress.

"Could we roast marshmallows tonight after family devotions?" Josh asked. "I just love to *taste* roasted marshmallows."

"Well, I do happen to have a package of marshmallows in the cupboard," Mom answered with a smile.

Then Dad asked, "Children, do you know what happens to the fireplace logs when they burn?"

Sam answered, "They burn up and turn into ashes."

"That's right, Sam. When the fire goes out, there is nothing left but ashes. I'm going to read you a Bible story tonight about a very special fire."

Our story today is the same story that Pastor Vick read to his family for their devotions that night.

Lesson

Who can tell us the story of baby Moses? (Let someone review the story briefly.) What happened to Moses when he was a baby? Why was he hidden in the bulrushes? Who found him? What did the princess do with him? Yes, God took care of baby Moses. He lived a short while with his own family. And then Moses grew up in the king's palace. After Moses grew up to be a man, he moved to another land and became a shepherd taking care of sheep.

One day while Moses was taking care of his sheep, he looked up and saw a bush that was on fire. He came closer to look at the bush. There was something different about it. There was fire coming from the bush, but the bush didn't burn. It stayed the same—there were no ashes. (Display "Moses" picture.)

Then Moses heard a voice calling from the burning bush, "Moses! Moses!" Have you ever heard a bush speak? No, of course not, but Moses did. He answered, "Here I am." The voice from the bush told Moses to stay where he was and not to come any closer. Then the voice told Moses that it was the one true God of heaven who now spoke to him. God was speaking to Moses from the burning bush. Moses was afraid, so he hid his face.

God spoke again. He told Moses that His people needed a leader to take them to their promised land. God's people were living in the land of Egypt because there had been a famine in their land. Remember how Jacob brought his family to live in Egypt? Later, when a mean king was the leader of Egypt, he made God's people work very hard. He even beat them to make them work harder.

God's people prayed and asked God to take them away from Egypt and the cruel king.

So God told Moses to be the leader that would take God's people back to the land He had promised to them.

"Oh," Moses said, "I can't be their leader. They don't even know me. They will not know that You have sent me, Lord."

But God promised to be with Moses and show him what to do. He told Moses that He would do special things called "miracles." A miracle is a special act that only God can do. It shows us God's power.

God told Moses to throw the stick or rod he was holding on the ground. Moses obeyed God. He threw the stick on the ground. (Throw the stick on the ground.) God made the stick become a snake. (Remove the stick quickly and replace it with a toy snake.) Then God told Moses to pick the snake up by its tail. (Pick up the snake.) Moses obeyed. God made the snake turn back into a stick. (Replace the paper snake with the stick.) That was a miracle. Moses could not do that; only God could. Our God can do anything.

Then God told Moses to put his hand inside his coat and pull it out again. (Put the white glove on quickly and demonstrate.) Moses obeyed. Moses looked at this hand. (Look at your hand.) It was all rough and scaly and white with a sickness called leprosy. Moses was afraid. But God told him to put his hand back inside his coat and then pull it out again. (Remove the glove.) Moses obeyed God. His hand had changed back to the way it was before. The rough, scaly sickness was gone. God had worked another miracle.

Moses was still not ready to obey God. Moses told God, "Oh, I cannot lead your people, Lord. I do not talk very well—I will not know what to say." But God promised to help Moses know what words he should say. God also gave Moses a helper. He sent Moses' brother Aaron to help him. So Moses listened to God. He believed God, and he obeyed God. Moses was a *doer* as well as a *hearer* of God's Word.

Application

➤ Sometimes it is hard for us to obey God. For example, when we are outside playing games with our friends, Mother may call us to come in. Sometimes we are having such a good time that we don't want to obey. But we can remember God's Word, "Children, obey your parents." God's Word will help us to be quick to obey Mother. God has promised to be with us always to help us to obey. God helps us to be doers of His Word, and not hearers only. (BATs: 2a Authority; 8a Faith in God's promises)

Song: "Obedience Is"

Catechism

Introduce Catechism 21.

- What did God give Adam and Eve besides bodies? *(God gave them souls that could never die.)*

➤ Our souls are the part of us that lives forever, and the part of us that thinks, acts, and feels.

Lesson 53: A Stubborn Pharaoh

Bible text: Exodus 5–7
Doctrinal truth: God (omnipotence and omniscience)
Character trait: Trust
Memory verse: Review Proverbs 3:5–6.
Catechism: Review Catechism 15–16.
Materials
• "Moses and Aaron" (Picture Packet)

Opening chorus: "I Will Obey"

Song: "My Bible Book," stanzas 1–3

Memory verse

Review Proverbs 3:5–6 and sing the chorus "Trust in the Lord."

Prayer

Thank God for the promises in His Word.

Catechism

Review Catechism 15–16.

- Does God know all things? *(Yes, nothing can be hidden from God.)*

- Can God do all things? *(Yes, God can do all His holy will.)*

➤ We will hear in other Bible lessons about many powerful acts that God did for Moses and His people. A miracle is a special act that only God can do. It shows us His power.

Song: "Story Review Song," stanza 2

Bible lesson

Introduction

➤ When God called Moses to be the leader of His people, God told him to go to the king of Egypt and tell the king that God wanted His people to go away from Egypt and into the wilderness to worship Him. God knows all things. God said to Moses, "I will have to stretch out my hand and punish Egypt with terrible plagues before the king will let you go." God can do all things.

Lesson
Display "Moses and Aaron" picture. (Aaron is the one holding the rod.)

Moses and Aaron went to the palace to see the king of Egypt. They told him, "The Lord God of Israel has said, 'Let My people go out of your land into the wilderness to worship Me.'"

And Pharaoh said, "Who is the Lord, that I should obey Him? I don't know your God, and I will not let your people go."

Isn't that just what God told Moses would happen? *(yes)*

Moses and Aaron told Pharaoh that their God—the God of the Israelite people—had told them to leave Egypt and go into the wilderness to worship Him. They said, "If we do not go now, God will send terrible plagues to punish your land."

Pharaoh wouldn't listen; instead, he answered angrily, "Moses and Aaron, why are you trying to take the people away from their work? Now leave me and return to your own work."

Remember, we learned how hard Pharaoh made God's people work in Egypt (Lesson 50). He had them make bricks to build walls and cities. Well, now the king told his soldiers and taskmasters to make the people work even harder. Instead of giving them the straw to make the bricks, he told his taskmasters to make the Israelites find and gather their own straw to make bricks. He also ordered the Israelites to make just as many bricks each day as they had made before, or they would be punished. Pharaoh thought that if he kept the people busy they wouldn't have time to think about going away to worship their God.

The Israelites came to Moses and Aaron and said, "Instead of getting us out of this land and away from our hard work, you have caused Pharaoh to make us work even harder."

So Moses spoke to the Lord and asked Him why He had let this happen. Does God know all things? *(Catechism 15: Yes, nothing can be hidden from God.)* God knows what is going to happen before it happens. God always knows what is best for us.

Then God spoke to Moses and said, "I am the Lord, Jehovah, God of Abraham, Isaac, and Jacob. I promised to take care of them and bless them, and I did. I also see my people suffering now in Egypt, and I will still keep my promise to take care of them and bring them back to their special land."

Moses told the people what God had said, but they would not listen to Moses.

The Lord spoke to Moses again and said, "Go speak to Pharaoh and tell him to let the children of Israel go out of his land."

Moses answered the Lord, "If my own people won't listen to me, how can I expect the Pharaoh of Egypt to believe what I say?"

God told Moses that Pharaoh would listen to him and Aaron because God was going to work special miracles to show His power. So Moses and Aaron went to Pharaoh again. God told Aaron to throw his rod on the ground before the king, and when Aaron obeyed, the rod became a snake.

Then Pharaoh called for his wise men and magicians. They each threw their rods on the ground, and their rods also became snakes. Then God made Aaron's rod swallow the magicians' rods. Only God can work miracles. This miracle was a sign from God to Pharaoh and his people. It showed God's power. But Pharaoh still would not listen to Moses. He refused to let God's people go.

Next, God told Moses and Aaron to take the rod the following morning to the river when Pharaoh visited it. God told Aaron to put the rod into the river. God told them to tell Pharaoh that the Lord God had sent them again. Moses and Aaron did as God told them. When Aaron's rod touched the river, the river turned into blood.

God had turned all the water of Egypt into blood. There was no water at all in Egypt for the people to drink or take a bath in. And the blood made the fish in the rivers and ponds die. But Pharaoh just went back to his palace. He still would not listen to God.

> The magicians in Pharaoh's court, aided by Satan, duplicated some of Moses' miracles to deceive the people. But they could do only what God permitted. True miracles (as opposed to "lying wonders") can be performed only by God.

Application
➤ God keeps His Word, doesn't He? His Word is powerful. What God says He will do, He does. Our God can do all things; nothing is too hard for Him. God is "omnipotent." *Omnipotent* means "all-powerful." (BATs: 8a Faith in God's promises; 8b Faith in the power of the Word of God)

Song: "God Is with Me"

Lesson 54: God's Miracles in Egypt

Bible text: Exodus 8–10
Doctrinal truth: God (omnipotence)
Character traits: Trust; Courage
Catechism: Review Catechism 15–16.
Materials
• "Moses and Aaron" (Picture Packet)

Opening chorus: "I Will Obey"

Song: "How Do We Know?", stanza 1

Prayer
Thank God that He knows all things.

Song: "Story Review Song," stanza 2

Bible lesson

Introduction
Review Catechism 15 and 16.

■ Does God know all things? *(Yes, nothing can be hidden from God.)*

■ Can God do all things? *(Yes, God can do all His holy will.)*

➤ Did God know what Pharaoh would say and do even before He sent Moses and Aaron to him? Yes, God knows all things even before they happen. Do you think Moses and Aaron might have been afraid to go to the king of Egypt? *(Allow discussion.)* They knew that God would take care of them and do what was best for them because God can do anything. God can do all His holy will. Everything God does is perfect and good because He is perfect and good.

Lesson
Display "Moses and Aaron" picture.

Seven days after God turned all the water of Egypt into blood, Pharaoh still had not changed his mind about letting God's people go. So God told Moses and Aaron to go to Pharaoh again and say, "The Lord says, 'Let my people go that they may serve me.'"

When Pharaoh refused again, Moses told Aaron to wave his rod over the waters of Egypt. This time frogs came out of the ponds and rivers and spread across the land. Frogs were hopping everywhere: into people's houses, into their beds, and even into their food. These frogs were the *second* plague that God sent.

Oh, how Pharaoh had hated the bloody water! And now all of these horrible, pesky, hopping frogs were everywhere. This punishment was terrible. So

Pharaoh begged Moses and Aaron to ask their God to take the frogs away. Pharaoh promised that he would let God's people go to worship if the frogs left. The next day when Moses prayed to God to remove the frogs, the Lord answered his prayer, and all of the frogs in the Egyptians' houses and in the king's palace and on the land died. Only the frogs in the rivers lived. The people of Egypt gathered all the dead frogs and piled them up, and the dead frogs smelled very bad.

But when the frogs were gone, the king changed his mind and decided not to let the Israelites go.

This time the Lord told Aaron to hit the dust of the earth with his rod. When he did, the dust became little bugs like lice that jumped and crawled over all the people and animals in Egypt. These bugs were the *third* plague that God sent.

Again Moses asked the king to let God's people go. This time he said if the king did not obey, God would send swarms and swarms of flies everywhere upon the king, his people, and all over his land, but *not* in Goshen, where God's people lived. Still Pharaoh was very, very stubborn. He would not let the Israelites go. Again the Lord did what He said He would do, and flies swarmed all over Egypt. That was the *fourth* plague. Now, the Egyptians worshiped many gods. They worshiped the sun and even some animals and insects. These flies were also gods to them, so they did not want to kill them. "What are we to do?" they wondered.

Then Pharaoh called for Moses and Aaron and said, "I will let the Israelites worship their God; only they must do it in Goshen." That was the part of Egypt where God's people had lived since Joseph's family had moved there during the famine.

But Moses said, "They cannot worship there. Your people would see them and throw stones at them for worshiping a God whom they do not worship."

So the king said, "I will let you go to worship your God in the wilderness; only you must not go too far away."

Moses answered, "We must travel three days away from here." Then Moses prayed again and asked the Lord to take the flies away.

Do you think Pharaoh did what he said he would do this time? (Shake your head.) No, that stubborn, wicked king changed his mind again as soon as he saw that the flies were gone.

Then God sent a terrible disease on all the cattle that were in the fields: horses, cows, camels, oxen, sheep, and donkeys. The cattle that belonged to the Egyptians died, but God protected the cattle that belonged to His people; theirs did not die.

That was the *fifth* plague God sent on Pharaoh and his land.

Still Pharaoh did not obey. He would not let God's people go. The *sixth* plague God sent was boils. He told Aaron to take ashes from the fire of the furnaces and sprinkle them in the air. This caused boils and sores to break out on the skin of all the Egyptian people and on their animals. Even the king's magicians could not perform a trick that would make this happen. Still the king would not obey God.

Next God said He would send a terrible hailstorm that would kill all the people and animals of Egypt who did not stay inside their houses and barns for protection. And God did what He said He would do. There was terrible lightning, thunder, and a hailstorm that killed fruit trees, animals, and even people who did not obey God's warning to stay inside. That was the *seventh* plague. The storm really scared Pharaoh. He called for Moses and Aaron and said, "I have sinned. Your God is good and holy, and my people and I are wicked and sinful. Please ask your God to stop the storm, and I promise I will let you go at once." It sounded like the king was finally sorry for his sin, didn't it?

But he wasn't. When the storm stopped and the sky was sunny and clear again, what do you think he did? He changed his mind. He still did not listen to God's warning or obey Him. He was a very stubborn man; the Bible says that "he hardened his heart."

Then God said He would send locusts to eat any plants and fruit trees that were still alive after the hailstorm. Even the people of Egypt begged their king to let the Israelites go then. They were very afraid of God's wonders. They were afraid that they would all be destroyed.

So Pharaoh asked Moses and Aaron whom they would take with them into the wilderness. Moses answered, "All of our people and our cattle."

Pharaoh shouted, "No, you cannot all go. I will let you go if you will take only your men with you and leave your women and children here." The king was so angry that he had his soldiers throw Moses and Aaron out of his palace.

So the Lord sent a wind to bring the locusts upon the land. And all the plants and trees in Egypt were eaten. That was the *eighth* plague.

Quickly Pharaoh called for Moses and Aaron. Again the king said he had sinned in not obeying their God. "Please don't let me and my people die," Pharaoh begged.

This time after Moses prayed, the Lord sent a strong wind from across the sea, and it blew the locusts into the Red Sea. But still Pharaoh would not obey God.

So God sent yet another plague. This was to be the *ninth* plague. God told Moses to hold up his hand toward heaven, and a great darkness came upon the land. There was not even the sun to shine in the day or the moon and stars to give light at night. For three days there was darkness where the Egyptians lived, but not for God's people. God gave His people light.

Pharaoh certainly did not like the darkness, so he called for Moses again. This time he told Moses that he would let God's people go, but they could not take their cattle with them. Now Moses told the king they had to have cattle to sacrifice to the Lord when they worshiped. That made the king so angry that he yelled at Moses and Aaron to go away because he did not want to see them again. He said if he saw them again, he would have them killed. What a wicked man!

And the Bible tells us that Moses answered the king, "You have spoken the truth—we will *never* see you again."

Application
➤ What an exciting story! Our God can do all things. He gave Moses and Aaron courage to go before Pharaoh. Moses and Aaron knew that nothing could hurt them unless God allowed it to happen.

Sometimes we have to do things that are hard or make us afraid. The same God who was with Moses has also promised to be with us and help us to be brave. (BATs: 8a Faith in God's promises; 8d Courage)

Song: "When I Am Afraid"

Lesson 55: God's Final Plague

Bible text: Exodus 11–13:19

Doctrinal truth: God (omnipotence)

Character trait: Trust

Catechism: Review Catechism 9 and 14–16.

Materials
• Kate Vick puppet

Opening chorus: "I Will Obey"

Song: "How Do We Know?", stanza 1

Prayer
Thank God that He can do anything.

Catechism
Review Catechism 9 and 14–16.

■ Are there more gods than one? *(No, there is only one God.)*

■ Can you see God? *(No, I cannot see God, but He always sees me.)*

■ Does God know all things? *(Yes, nothing can be hidden from God.)*

■ Can God do all things? *(Yes, God can do all His holy will.)*

➤ There is only one true God. But the people of Egypt worshiped many gods. They worshiped the sun, moon, and many kinds of animals. Could their gods help them or answer their prayers? No, their gods had no power; *our* God made those things.

We cannot see God, but we know He made the sun and moon and all living things. Only the God of heaven knows and sees all things and can do all His holy will.

Song: "God Is with Me"

Bible lesson

Introduction
Use the Kate puppet to recite the following rhyme.

➤ Kate wants to recite a poem she learned in Sunday school.

> God showed His power
> Upon that king's land.
> Ten awful plagues
> Were sent by God's hand.

What land do you think Kate's poem is about? *(Egypt)*

Lesson

God told Moses that, after He sent one more plague upon Egypt, Pharaoh would be sure to let God's people go. He told Moses to tell the people to be ready to leave quickly. He also told Moses what was going to happen and what the people should do.

Moses told God's people to ask for silver and gold jewelry from their neighbors. He told the people that God wanted the father of each family to kill a lamb and sprinkle the blood of the lamb on the door frames of his house. This reminds us of Jesus Christ, God's Son, who shed His blood on the cross so that we might have a Savior from sin. One of Jesus' titles—one of His many names—is the "Lamb of God who takes away the sin of the world."

Then Moses told the people that at midnight—in the middle of the night—God would send an angel throughout the land. When the angel came to a home that did not have the blood of a lamb sprinkled on the doorposts, the oldest son in that home would die.

Moses told the mothers in each home to cook the lamb meat with some vegetables for their family to eat just before midnight. All of the families were to be dressed and ready to travel as they stood around the table eating. This midnight supper was called "the Passover" because God's angel would pass over each home that had obeyed the Lord God and had put the blood on the doorposts of their houses. God told His people to have a special passover supper every year after that to help them remember how God had brought them out of Egypt.

Just as God had said, at midnight He sent the angel into every house that did not have blood on the doorpost. The oldest son of each Egyptian family died because they had not put blood on their door frames. There was a great noise of crying in Egypt, for there was not a single Egyptian family in which there was not one son dead.

When Pharaoh found his oldest son dead, he cried out, and he sent a messenger to run to Moses and Aaron in Goshen to tell them to leave the country at once and take everything with them. He told them all to go quickly and leave nothing behind. God's people were finally free to leave Egypt.

Application
➤ Why did the Israelites want to leave Egypt? They wanted to leave because they were slaves and had to work hard for the king. At last they were really on their way. God had given them Moses and his brother Aaron to lead them. God had kept His promise.

Have you ever been afraid in the dark or in a storm? Does God promise to take care of you, boys and girls? *(yes)* He tells you that He is with you wherever you are, and He will take care of you. He says He will never leave you. (BAT: 8a Faith in God's promises)

Song: "When I Am Afraid"

Lesson 56: The Red Sea

Bible text: Exodus 13:17–14:31

Doctrinal truth: God (omnipotence)

Character traits: Trust; Thankfulness

Memory verse: Review Ecclesiastes 12:13*b*.

Catechism: Review Catechism 16.

Materials
• "Crossing the Red Sea" (Picture Packet)
• Student page 15 and cutouts
• Scissors
• Glue

Opening chorus: "I Will Obey"

Song: "How Do We Know?" stanza 1

Prayer
Thank God for always being with us to take care of us.

Memory verse
Review Ecclesiastes 12:13*b*. Review that we are to know who God is, and we are to love Him, trust Him, and obey His Word.

Song: "Trust and Obey"

Song: "Story Review Song," stanza 2

Bible lesson

Introduction
Lead the children in the following action rhyme, "The Ten Plagues." Use it as a story rhyme and have them mimic your actions. Do not expect the children to memorize it.

➤ God chose Moses
   (Point toward heaven.)
His leader to be.
God sent Moses
   (Step in place.)
A great king to see.
   (Point to eyes.)

"King," said Moses,
   (Cup one hand to side of mouth.)
"Let God's people go."
   (Shake pointer finger.)
The king refused.
   (Shake head, "No.")
The great king said, "No."
   (Cup one hand to side of mouth.)

God showed His power
   (Point toward heaven.)
Upon that king's land.
   (Raise arms and then lower to ground.)
Ten awful plagues
   (Hold up ten fingers.)
Were sent by God's hand.

Water to blood,
Then frogs, lice, and flies;
   (Hop and crawl fingers of one hand back and forth on the opposite arm.)
Cattle were sick;
Boils came from on high.
   (Point toward heaven.)

A storm brought fire
And hail from the sky.
  (Raise arms and then lower to the ground.)
And locusts came
As God's wind blew by.
  (Swish arms as blowing wind.)

God showed His power
  (Point toward heaven.)
Upon that king's land.
  (Raise arms and then lower to ground.)
Ten awful plagues
  (Hold up ten fingers.)
Were sent by God's hand.

When darkness came
To cover the land,
  (Put hands over eyes.)
The king still said,
"No!" to God's command.
  (Shake head, "No.")

The last plague—death
Of the oldest son—
From God above.
Ten plagues were done.
  (Hold up ten fingers, and then bring both hands together.)

God showed His power
  (Point toward heaven.)
Upon that king's land.
  (Raise arms and then lower to ground.)
Ten awful plagues
  (Hold up ten fingers.)
Were sent by God's hand.

Lesson

Finally Pharaoh had to let God's people go. God led Moses, Aaron, and His people in the way He wanted them to go. He sent them two special signs to show them which way to go. When it was daytime, the Lord went before them in a cloud, and when it was nighttime, the cloud was like a bright fire. At any time during the day or night, God's people could look up and see the signs and know their God was with them to lead them in the right way.

So God led them to the Red Sea and then the cloud stopped. The people thought that meant that they would be resting there for the night. But suddenly they heard noises, and when they looked around, they saw Pharaoh's soldiers riding in chariots, as fast as they could, coming toward them.

The people cried unto the Lord and they complained to Moses. They said, "What have you done? Have you brought us this far just to let us die? Why, we were better off being slaves in Egypt. We should have just stayed there."

Moses answered the people, "Don't be afraid. Just stand still and see what God is going to do for us. You see the Egyptian soldiers coming? Well, you will never see them again. The Lord shall fight for you."

Then God showed His power in a wonderful way. He told Moses to tell the people to move forward. He told Moses to hold out his rod over the Red Sea, and Moses obeyed. (Display "Crossing the Red Sea" picture.) When Moses held the rod over the water, God sent a strong wind and divided the sea so that there was a wall of water on one side, and a wall of water on the other side, and a path in between— not a wet, muddy path, but *dry* ground for His people to walk across to the other side of the Red Sea. Our God can do anything. (Demonstrate this with your arms.) Our God can do all His holy will.

God not only worked that miracle but also moved the cloud between His people and the soldiers. The cloud made it dark where the Egyptian soldiers were. They could not see God's people walking across the water.

Then God lifted the dark cloud. When the Egyptian soldiers saw the Israelites walking on dry land through the sea, they rushed after them. But God brought all kinds of troubles to the Egyptians. Their chariot wheels came off, and they became very frightened. They feared the God of Israel who was able to work such miracles. They decided to turn around. But when they did, it was too late. The Lord told Moses to hold out his hand over the sea again, and the walls of water ran back together, and the soldiers of Pharaoh were drowned in the sea. (Pause.) But *God's* people were safe on the other side of the sea.

When God's people saw what great things God had done for them, they trusted Him and thanked Him for taking care of them. Moses wrote a song praising God for what He had done for them, and they all sang together.

Application
➤ Can God do all things? *(Catechism 16: Yes, God can do all His holy will.)* The God that long ago separated the waters of the Red Sea for His people is the same God who made us and loves us. He is always with us to lead us and to take care of us. Let's praise Him now with a song like the Israelites did long, long ago. (BAT: 7c Praise)

Song: "Praise Him, Praise Him"

Student page 15
Instruct the children to cut out the pictures. Guide them in gluing Moses in place. Remind the children to put the glue only in the "glue space" on the left side when gluing the Israelites to the page. Read the page, allowing the children to manipulate the picture to see how God cared for His people.

Lesson 57: Review—Moses (Birth to Red Sea)

Bible text: Exodus 1–15 (review)

Doctrinal truth: God

Character traits: Trust; Thankfulness

Memory verses: Review.

Catechism: Review Catechism 1–21.

Materials
• Student page 16 and cutouts
• Pencils or crayons
• Scissors
• Glue

Opening chorus: "I Will Obey"

Prayer
Stand and pray the Lord's Prayer together.

Song: "Story Review Song," stanza 2

Student page 16

> In this lesson the children will begin making a booklet about Moses. You may wish to have the children wait to cut apart the booklet pages on Student page 16 until they complete Student page 18 in Lesson 67. This step will help to prevent pages from being misplaced.

Instruct the children to cut out the pictures. Discuss each booklet page while guiding the children in gluing the pictures. Remind the children to write their names at the top of the student page. Collect the page, keeping it for the completion of the activity in Lesson 67.

Action rhyme: "The Ten Plagues"
(See Index of Poetry.)

Memory verses and catechism
Review memory verses and catechism as time allows.

Lesson 58: Review—Moses (Birth to Red Sea)

Bible text: Exodus 1–15 (review)

Doctrinal truth: God

Character trait: Trust

Memory verses: Review.

Catechism: Review Catechism 1–21.

Materials
• Sketches of a cloud and a pillar of fire for display (for review activity)
• Red and white chalk or crayons

Opening chorus: "I Will Obey"

Prayer
Ask God to help us to obey His Word.

Review activity
Divide the class into two teams. Display the sketches of a large cloud for one team and a pillar of fire for the other team. Remind the class of how God used the cloud and the fire to lead His people. Children may color sections of the cloud white and the fire red when they answer questions correctly. Ask the following questions and tally the correct answers for each side.

1. What did the new Pharaoh (king of Egypt) do to God's people after Joseph died? *(made them slaves)*

2. When Pharaoh grew afraid because God's people, the Israelites, had grown to be so many, what did he do? *(He told the nurses who took care of Israelite babies to kill all baby boys; then he told his soldiers to throw all boy babies into the river.)*

3. What baby boy was hidden in a basket and then put by the side of the river? *(Moses)*

4. Who watched nearby to take care of baby Moses? *(his sister, Miriam)*

5. Who came to the river? *(the king's daughter, the princess)*

6. What did the king's daughter decide to do with the baby? *(take him to the palace to live with her)*

7. What did Miriam ask the princess? *("Would you like me to find a lady to take care of the baby for you?")*

8. Whom did Miriam take the baby to? *(to his own mother)*

9. Did Moses forget his God and his people when he went to live in the palace? *(no)*

10. Moses finally went away from the palace. What did he become? *(a shepherd)*

11. What strange thing happened to Moses one day while he was taking care of his sheep? *(God spoke to him from a burning bush.)*

12. What did God want Moses to do? *(lead His people out of Egypt)*

13. What two acts did God have Moses perform to show the people that God had sent him? *(He turned Moses' rod into a snake. Moses' hand became white with disease—leprosy—and then it became well again.)*

14. Who went to Pharaoh with Moses? *(Aaron, Moses' brother)*

15. What were some of the terrible plagues that God sent to Egypt because Pharaoh would not let the Israelites leave? *(water turned into blood, frogs, lice, flies, cattle sickness, boils, a great storm, big locusts, and great darkness)*

16. What was the very last wonder that God did? (*The angel of death came and the oldest son of every Egyptian family and animal died.*)

17. What saved the oldest sons? (*sprinkling of lamb's blood on the sides and top of the doorway*)

18. What does that remind us of? (*Jesus the Lamb of God, who shed His blood on the cross that we might live*)

19. Which signs did God use to lead the Israelites out of Egypt? (*cloud, fire*)

20. What happened when they came to the Red Sea? (*Moses held out his shepherd's stick over the water. The waters rolled back and left a dry path to cross.*)

21. Why couldn't the soldiers of Egypt see? (*God put a cloud between them and God's people so that the Egyptians were in darkness.*)

Use verses, songs, and catechism questions for other review ideas.

Lesson 59: Trust and Obey

Bible text: Exodus 15:22–27

Doctrinal truth: God (faithfulness and omnipotence)

Character traits: Trust; Obedience

Memory verse: Review Proverbs 3:5–6.

Materials
• Moses and Children of Israel visuals (See the Appendix for visuals and instructions.)
• Sam and Dad Vick family puppets
• Blue cloth or towel (for water) and limb of tree for visual demonstration (optional)

Opening chorus: "I Will Obey"

Song: "Be Ye Doers of the Word," stanzas 1 and 4

Prayer

Ask God to help us to remember always to trust and obey Him.

Song: "Even a Child Is Known"

Replace "so do your work" with "so obey God's Word."

Bible lesson

Introduction

➤ Mrs. Vick had just come home from the hospital. She had been sick for a long time. Grandma Brown had taken care of Josh, Kate, and Sam and cooked for the whole family while their mother was in the hospital.

After a few weeks, when Mom felt better, Grandma went home. Then all of the Vick children and their father helped their mother by doing extra chores so she

could get the rest she needed. (Display Sam and Dad puppets.)

One day when Dad came home from work, Sam asked him for money to get his bicycle painted. But his father answered, "I'm sorry, Sam, but we just don't have any money for extra things right now. Mother's medicine and hospital bills cost quite a lot of money when she was sick. We'll just have to wait awhile until I am able to pay all of those bills."

Sam looked worried. "What if Mom gets sick again, or what would happen if you got sick? Where would we get the money we need to buy food?"

His dad answered, "That is why it is so wonderful to love the Lord and trust Him to take care of us. Remember Proverbs 3:5–6, 'Trust in the Lord with all thine heart; and lean not unto thine own understanding. In all thy ways acknowledge him, and he shall direct thy paths.' The Lord will take care of us because He has promised to supply all our needs. He will give us everything we need."

Sam smiled at his father. "And God always keeps His promises?"

"Yes. He knows what is best for us," his father added.

Lesson

Display Moses and Children of Israel visuals.

God began to lead the people from the Red Sea through the wilderness toward the land He had promised them. They had not found any water for three days. They had marched a long way and were all very tired and thirsty.

Finally they came to a spring of water called Marah. Everyone could hardly wait to get a drink of water from the spring. But when they tasted the water, they were disappointed. (Pretend to scoop handfuls of water up from a spring [blue cloth] and drink; then grimace.) The water didn't taste good. It was too bitter to drink. Again the people began to blame Moses for their troubles. "What shall we drink?" they complained.

Moses prayed to the Lord and asked the Lord God to help them. God always hears His people when they pray, doesn't He?

The Lord showed Moses a tree nearby, and He told Moses to cut it down and throw it into the spring of bitter water. (Put the tree limb on the "water.") When Moses obeyed, the water was sweet. All of the people drank until they were filled. And they gave water to all their thirsty animals also. (Pantomime the actions of this paragraph.)

God told His people that He wanted this to be a lesson to them. They could remember how God had given them water to drink. And that would remind them that their God would always take care of them on their journey if they would obey Him and do what was right.

Then He led them to a beautiful place with many palm trees and twelve wells of water, where they could pitch their tents and camp under the trees and drink from the many wells of water. How happy God's people were to trust and obey their great and powerful God!

Application
➤ God's people were always forgetting to trust in God's promise to take care of them. This time they listened when He said they should obey His Word and do that which was right. And that's the same thing God says to His people today—to you and to me—"trust Me and obey Me." (BATs: 8a Faith in God's promises; 2a Authority)

Memory verse
Review Proverbs 3:5–6 and sing the chorus, "Trust in the Lord."

Song: "Trust and Obey"

Lesson 60: Manna from Heaven

Bible text: Exodus 16

Doctrinal truths: God (faithfulness); Salvation (repentance)

Character traits: Trust; Obedience

Memory verses: Introduce Psalm 38:18 and review Romans 3:23.

Catechism: Introduce Catechism 22.

Materials
• Tents and manna visual (Put sand into a flat box or a pan. Fold sheets of construction paper into tents, and arrange as in sketch. Use puffed-grain cereal or scraps of Styrofoam for manna.)
• Cloud and Pillar of Fire visuals (See the Appendix; copy, cut out, and color.)
• Moses, Aaron, and Children of Israel visuals (See the Appendix.)

Opening chorus: "I Will Obey"

Song: "What Does the Bible Say?"
Sing the second stanza, "Trust in God."

Prayer
Ask God to help us to be sorry when we sin and to believe He will forgive us.

Memory verses
Read Psalm 38:18 to the children.

➤ What does "iniquity" mean? (*sin, disobeying God's Word*)

Guide a discussion about some sins your students may have committed (e.g., disobeying, being unkind). Recite

Romans 3:23 together. Then have the children take turns reciting Psalm 38:18.

Song: "There Is None That Doeth Good"

➤ When we are really sorry for our sins, we will ask God to forgive us.

Catechism
Introduce Catechism 22.

▪ Do you have a soul as well as a body? (*Yes, I have a soul that can never die.*)

➤ Our soul is the part of us that will live somewhere forever.

Song: "Nothing but the Blood"

Bible lesson

Introduction
➤ The Israelites had a good rest under the palm trees near the twelve wells of water, but God told them it was time to take down their tents and travel on. Do you remember how they knew it was time to go and which way to go? What signs did we say God used to lead His people? (*cloud and fire*) (Display Cloud and Pillar of Fire visuals.) Yes, God's cloud lifted up higher in the sky and began to move in the direction He wanted the Israelites to go.

Lesson
Display Moses, Aaron, and Children of Israel visuals.

God's special cloud led them into the wilderness, into a dry, sandy land with lots of rocks, only a few trees, and very little water. Since it was sandy and dry, it was hard to find plants and fruit trees or even animals for food. So the people started complaining to Moses about being hungry. They were afraid they would starve and die of hunger. Again they complained and said, "We wish we had never left Egypt. It would have been better for us to have stayed there and been slaves. We would at least have had enough to eat."

What were God's people forgetting? They forgot how many times God had taken care of them in special ways. They were afraid. They forgot God's promise to take care of them. They were sinning. It is a sin to not trust God—to not believe His promises.

So God had to remind them again of His promise and His power. He told Moses that He would not let His people die of hunger. He said, "I will send them many birds called quail in the evening for supper and a special bread from heaven in the morning."

That's just what He did. The people had quail meat for supper, and in the morning, when they looked out of their tent doors, they saw something white all over the ground. (Display the tents and manna visual.) They asked, "What is this?" They had never seen anything like it before.

And Moses said to them, "This is the bread that the Lord has given you to eat." So they called it *manna,* which means "What is this?" It tasted like a sweet wafer or cookie.

Moses told the people that God had commanded them to take just what they needed to eat for each day. They were not to store or save it for the next day, except on the sixth day of each week.

Only then were they to take twice as much so that they would have enough for the seventh day, the Sabbath, the day they worshiped God. God wanted His people to trust Him, to believe that He would give them each day just what they needed.

But do you know that some of the Israelites still did not believe God? They were afraid they would not have enough to eat. They did not trust God. Instead, they gathered up more manna than they needed and tried to keep it until the next day. But the bread spoiled, and worms got into it, and it wasn't good to eat.

Application

➤ God is always faithful. Every morning during their trip to the promised land He sent manna to His people. But God's people would forget God's promise. They often complained and grumbled about many things. It is a sin to complain. God will always give us what is best for us. (BAT: 7d Contentment)

God has promised to give us everything we need to live happy lives for Him. He wants us to trust Him. God is always faithful to keep His promises to us. He always knows what we need. Sometimes, just like the Israelites, we forget God's promises to us. (BAT: 8a Faith in God's promises)

Song: "When I Am Afraid"

Lesson 61: Mount Sinai

Bible text: Exodus 19–20

Doctrinal truths: God; Bible

Character trait: Obedience

Catechism: Review Catechism 17–18.

Materials
- Mountain, Lightning, Cloud, and Tablets of Stone visuals (See the Appendix; copy, cut out, and color.)
- "Moses and the Law" (Picture Packet)
- Kazoo (See note in next column.)
- Student page 17 and cutout
- Scissors
- Glue

You may prepare a kazoo by cutting several small holes in the middle of a paper-towel tube. Cover one end of the tube with a large piece of waxed paper taped in place or held in place with a rubber band. (The child will place his fingers on the holes and hum in the open end of the kazoo to make the sound of a trumpet.)

Opening chorus: "I Will Obey"

Song: "Be Ye Doers of the Word"

Action rhyme: "God's Word"
(See Index of Poetry.)

Song: "Holy Bible, Book Divine"

Prayer
Thank God for His Word.

Song: "My Bible Book"
Replace "He loves me, He loves me" with "Obey God, Obey God."

Bible lesson

Introduction
➤ God's people had followed His cloud for about forty-five days when they decided to stop. They pitched their tents and rested in the wilderness near a high hill called Mount Sinai.

Lesson

While the people were putting up their tents, Moses climbed up the high hill to talk to God. (Display "Moses and the Law" picture.) God reminded Moses how He had brought them out of Egypt and taken care of them on their journey. He told Moses that, if His people would continue to obey Him, He would bless them in a special way.

When Moses came down from the hill, he told the people that God was going to speak to them in three days from the top of the high hill. He told them everything God had said to him on the mount. And the people said, "All that the Lord has spoken we will do." They said, "We want to be His special people; we will obey."

In the morning on the third day, God sent thunder and lightning and brought a thick, dark cloud down on top of the mountain. The people heard the sound of a trumpet. (Display Mountain, Lightning, and Cloud visuals and play the kazoo.) God's people were afraid. God had told them not to climb up the mountain and not even to touch it because He, their holy God, was there. As the sound of the trumpet got louder, God came down upon the top of the mountain with smoke and fire and called Moses to come up to the top. Moses obeyed and went up.

(Display Tablets of Stone visual.) On the high hill, God gave Moses some rules called *commandments* for His people to obey. God knew that if His people would love Him and obey His rules, the commandments, they would be happy. These are some of the rules that God gave Moses:

Do not love anyone or anything more than Me.

Do not make any wooden or stone idols to worship.

Remember to worship God on His special day.

Honor your father and mother. (We honor our parents when we love and obey them.)

Do not kill.

Do not steal.

Do not tell lies.

And there were many more commandments. Moses read these commandments to the people. Moses told God's people that God had given them these rules to help them keep from sinning. God knew what was best for His people. God knows what is best for us.

Application
➤ The Bible is God's rule book. The commandments that God gave to His people, as well as many other rules and promises, are all written in the Bible for us to obey and trust. (BATs: 8a Faith in God's promises; 8b Faith in the power of the Word of God)

Student page 17
Discuss the picture on the page. Ask the children, "How did the Israelites know that God was on the mountain?" Instruct them to cut out the picture. Remind them to put the glue only in the "glue space" on the left side when gluing the picture to the page.

Catechism
Review Catechism 17–18.

■ Where do you learn how to love and obey God? (*I learn how to love and obey God in the Bible alone.*)

■ Who wrote the Bible? (*Holy men who were taught by the Holy Spirit wrote the Bible.*)

➤ Moses was one of those men whom God told to help write our Bible. Moses wrote the first five books of the Bible, called the Law or Pentateuch—Genesis, Exodus, Leviticus, Numbers, and Deuteronomy.

Song: "Books of Moses"

Lesson 62: The Golden Calf

Bible text: Exodus 24–34
Doctrinal truths: Bible; Salvation (repentance)
Character trait: Obedience
Memory verse: Review Ecclesiastes 12:13*b*.
Catechism: Review Catechism 17, 18, and 22.
Materials
- "Moses and the Law" (Picture Packet)
- Moses, Mountain, Tablets of Stone, Aaron, Children of Israel, and Golden Calf visuals (See the Appendix; copy, cut out, and color.)
- Small piece of facial tissue

Opening chorus: "I Will Obey"

Action rhyme: "God's Word"
(See Index of Poetry.)

Song: "Holy Bible, Book Divine"

Catechism and memory verse
Review Catechism 17.

■ Where do you learn how to love and obey God? (*I learn how to love and obey God in the Bible alone.*)

Review Ecclesiastes 12:13*b* with the children.

➤ The commandments are our duties toward God and toward other people. They tell us what to do and what not to do. When we "fear" God, we believe that He is the one true, holy, and all-powerful God. We believe that He is the God of heaven who made us and loves us and sees our sin. When we "fear" Him, it means that we want to show Him how much we love and honor Him by obeying Him.

What are some of God's commandments or laws? (*Don't love any other person or thing more than God; don't make idols; don't pray to other gods or idols; honor and obey your parents.*)

Song: "My Bible Book"

Bible lesson

Introduction
Review Catechism 18.

■ Who wrote the Bible? (*Holy men who were taught by the Holy Spirit wrote the Bible.*)

➤ Our Bible lessons have been about one of these men. Do you know his name? (*Moses*)

Song: "Books of Moses"

Lesson
Display "Moses and the Law" picture.

God called Moses to climb Mount Sinai so that He could give Moses His law. Moses stayed with God for forty days and forty nights. During this time

God wrote His law on two tablets of stone with His own hand—the Bible says the commandments were written "with the finger of God."

While Moses was listening to God on the mountaintop, the people were waiting below. They were impatient. They soon grew tired of waiting. They wondered why Moses was taking so long. They were afraid he might be dead or that he might never come back. They were afraid that they had lost their leader. Moses was gone and the cloud that God had sent to lead them was up high resting on the mountain. "Who is going to lead us?" they asked. So they went to Aaron and asked him to make them an idol for a god to lead them on their journey. (Display Aaron, Children of Israel, and Golden Calf visuals.)

Aaron listened to them, and he asked them to bring their gold earrings to him. Aaron built a fire and melted all the gold earrings together. Then he took a carving tool and shaped the gold into the shape of a calf. God's people bowed down and worshiped and prayed to the golden calf.

Only forty days before, God had told Moses to tell His people not to make any graven images or idols like this calf. He told them to worship only Him—the one true God of heaven Who had created the world and all things. Were they obeying God's commandments? *(no)*

Then the Lord told Moses that it was time for him to go down from the mountain. God said, "My people have sinned. They have made a golden calf and are worshiping it."

So Moses went down from the mountain, carrying the two tablets of stone with God's Laws written on them. When Moses saw what the people were doing, he became so angry that he threw down God's two tablets of stone and they broke into pieces. (Display Moses, Mountain, and Tablets of Stone visuals.) Then he took the golden calf and burned it in the fire. He ground the melted gold into powder, threw the powder into the water, and made the people drink it. God caused many people to get sick and die. God must always punish sin because He is a holy God. God's holiness means that God never sins.

Moses prayed for God's people. He asked God to forgive them. He asked God to be with them and lead them. God forgave all who were truly sorry for their sin. God promised again to lead them to the special land He had promised to Abraham, Isaac, and Jacob.

The Lord God told Moses to cut two more tablets of stone and go back up on the mountain. And Moses obeyed. God wrote His commandments again on the two tablets. The Bible also tells us that God showed Moses His glory. Moses was in the presence of God. After forty more days and nights, Moses finally came down the mountain again with the two tablets of stone. When the people looked at Moses, they were afraid because his face shone with a strange light so bright that it hurt their eyes to look at him. Moses knew that his face glowed because he had been with God, so he put a veil over his face when he talked to God's people. (Use Moses visual; cover the face of Moses with a small piece of tissue.) Moses had been so close to God that he knew how wise and powerful God is. He knew how great our God is. And the people knew that he had been with God.

Application

➤ Do you think God's people were sorry for their sin? *(Answers may vary.)* Did God forgive those who were sorry? Does God punish sin? When we sin, we must be sorry for our sin and ask God to forgive us and believe that He will forgive us. (BAT: 1b Repentance and faith)

Catechism
Review Catechism 22.

■ Do you have a soul as well as a body? *(Yes, I have a soul that can never die.)*

➤ What happens to our souls when we die? *(Allow discussion.)* Why do we need to be sorry for our sin? *(Allow discussion.)* When we ask God to be our Savior, He has promised that, when we die, He will take our souls to heaven to live with Him forever.

Lesson 63: The Tabernacle

Bible texts: Exodus 25–31; Leviticus 1–9

Doctrinal truth: Church

Character trait: Thankfulness

Memory verse: Review Psalm 95:6.

Catechism: Review Catechism 21–22.

Materials
• Tabernacle and Church visuals (See the Appendix; copy and color.)
• A completed copy of Student page 4
• Cloud and Pillar of Fire (See the Appendix.)

Opening chorus: "I Will Obey"

Song: "The Wonder Song"

Song: "Praise Him, Praise Him"

Prayer
Thank God for our churches where we can worship Him.

Memory verse
Review Psalm 95:6. Use Student page 4 for a review visual.

➤ We can worship God by praying, singing, and listening to His Word in Bible time, in family worship, or at church. We can worship God by giving. God loves a cheerful giver. We should be happy to give our money and ourselves to God. (BATs: 6a Bible study; 6b Prayer; 5b Giving)

Catechism

Review Catechism 21–22.

■ What did God give Adam and Eve besides bodies? *(God gave them souls that could never die.)*

■ Do you have a soul as well as a body? *(Yes, I have a soul that can never die.)*

➤ Our soul is the part of us that will live with God forever.

Bible lesson

Introduction

➤ Pastor Vick announced in church that they were going to take up a special offering in a few weeks. They needed more Sunday school rooms for their church, so the pastor was asking everyone to give an extra, special offering for this project.

Kate listened thoughtfully every time her dad talked about giving for God's house. She wanted to be able to give a special gift for this offering. She had asked the Lord Jesus to be her Savior from sin, and ever since then, she had tried to live God's way. She had learned that giving for God's work was one way of worshiping Him. She thought and thought about where she could get extra money for her part of the church offering.

One day as she was playing in the front yard, she noticed one of her neighbors, Mrs. Babb, had forgotten to take her trash container to the back door.

The trash container was still in front of Mrs. Babb's house, where she had placed it that morning for trash pickup. Kate liked Mrs. Babb and knew she lived alone and was often tired when she got home from work. Kate walked over and took hold of the handle of the trash can and pushed it back to where Mrs. Babb usually kept it, by the back door.

Just then Mrs. Babb drove up and saw what Kate was doing. She got out of her car and smiled at Kate. She said, "That was a very thoughtful thing to do. I'm always in such a hurry when I get home from work that I sometimes forget that job." Mrs. Babb paused and then added, "You know, if you would be willing, Kate, I would like to hire you to do this job for me. I could give you a quarter every week to do it and also to pick up the newspapers and put them on the back porch for me."

Kate's eyes got as big as saucers, and she said, "Do you really want me to, Mrs. Babb? I asked the Lord to help me to get some money for a special church offering, and now I know He has answered my prayers. Oh, thank you, and I'll try to do a good job too." Kate turned quickly and hurried home to tell her mother how God had answered her prayer.

Our Bible lesson today is about how God's people gave and worked to build God's house.

Lesson

God wanted His people to have a special place to worship Him. He told Moses to tell the people to bring gifts to help build a tabernacle. They brought gold, silver, pieces of cloth, animal skins, wood, oil, and many other gifts for God's house. (Display Tabernacle visual.)

God even told Moses how His tabernacle was to be built. It was to be built like a tent so that it could be taken apart and moved when the people traveled toward the promised land. God told them how to make the furniture for His tabernacle. One of these pieces of furniture was like a box or chest. It was to be covered on the inside and the outside with gold. It was a box called the Ark of the Covenant in which God told Moses to put the two stone tablets. These were the tablets on which He had written His commandments.

God's people obeyed and brought gifts. They worked hard for two years to finish the tabernacle. God chose the family of Levi to take care of the tabernacle after it was built. Aaron and his sons were to be the priests of the tabernacle. They were to offer the sacrifices to God to have their sins forgiven.

When the tabernacle was finished, God moved His cloud over the tabernacle, and the glory of the Lord filled it. From that time on, when God wanted His people to travel, He would move His cloud by day or His fire by night from the tabernacle. His people would fold up their tents while the Levites folded up the tabernacle, and they would all follow God's sign.

Application

➤ God's people had a special place to worship God in the tabernacle. We have a special place to worship God in our church. We should thank God for our churches. (BAT: 7c Praise)

Display Church visual.

Lesson 64: Spies in the Land

Bible text: Numbers 13–14

Doctrinal truth: God

Character traits: Obedience; Trust

Memory verse: Review Proverbs 3:5–6.

Opening chorus: "I Will Obey"

Song: "Trust and Obey"

Prayer
Thank God for His promises.

Song: "When I Am Afraid"

Memory verse
Review Proverbs 3:5–6, and sing the chorus "Trust in the Lord."

Bible lesson

Introduction

➤ Ron woke up in the middle of the night. It was very dark. He had had a bad dream and was scared. He called, "Daaa-dy, Daaa-dy."

His father got out of bed and walked into Ron's bedroom. "What is it, son?" he asked softly.

"I think I had a bad dream. I'm scared . . . and I don't want to be alone," Ron whispered.

"Well, now, Ron, don't you remember the verse we read from God's Word about how God is always with us? We read it for family devotions last week. Can you help me say it, Ron?" his father asked.

Mr. Lee began to recite the verse, and Ron joined him on the parts he remembered, "Be not afraid, . . . for the Lord thy God is with thee whithersoever thou goest."

"Who said that, Ron?"

"God," Ron answered.

"Does God mean what He says, or does He sometimes forget His promises?" Father asked.

"Oh, no, God never forgets. I guess I'm the one who forgot," Ron admitted.

"Yes, just remember, wherever you are and whatever you have to do, God is always with you to take care of you because He made you and He loves you." Then his father bent over and kissed Ron and hugged him and said, "Isn't that a good promise to remember, Ron? Keep thinking about it until you fall back asleep."

Lesson

God led His people through the wilderness to a place near Canaan, the land He had promised them. Here the Lord told Moses to send twelve men to spy in the land of Canaan. He told them to go secretly to see what the land and people were like. He also told them to bring back some of the fruit that grew in Canaan.

For forty days the spies looked over the land. They saw a beautiful land with plenty of food to eat. They saw strong people and cities. When they were ready to return to tell Moses and the people what they had seen, they cut down one cluster of grapes so big that it took two men to carry it. They also took other fruit back with them.

When the spies returned, they told the people, "We went to Canaan and saw a land that flows with milk and honey. It is a rich land. Just look at this fruit we brought back from it. The people who live in Canaan are strong, and they have very large walls around their cities."

One of the spies, Caleb, said, "Let us go at once and capture the land, for with God's help, we are strong enough." Another spy, Joshua, agreed with Caleb.

But the other ten spies argued, "We are not strong enough. The people we saw were like giants. They were so big that they make us look like little grasshoppers."

When God's people heard this, they were afraid. They said, "We would have been better off to have stayed in Egypt, or even in the wilderness, and to have died there." They even began to plan to choose a new leader to lead them back to Egypt.

Only two of the spies, Caleb and Joshua, had faith that God would take care of them when they went into Canaan. So, along with Moses and Aaron, Caleb and Joshua begged God's people to obey God and trust His promises.

Moses had to pray that God would forgive the people's unbelief. And God answered Moses' prayer. God said because His people did not trust Him, they could not go into Canaan. God said He would punish them by making them live in the wilderness until all of the people who had complained were dead. Only their children, when they had grown up, could go into Canaan. God also said that He would let the two spies who had trusted God, Caleb and Joshua, live so that they could go into the promised land.

But the next morning, the people got up early and went to the top of the mountain and said, "We have changed our minds; we will go into the land as God first told us to." But Moses cried out,

"Don't go now; it's too late! The Lord is not with you; you will be defeated!"

The people did not listen. They went on to fight the people of Canaan, even though God had told them they must wait. The people of Canaan fought them and drove them out of the land.

Application

➤ Which of the twelve spies trusted God and were not afraid? *(Joshua and Caleb)* God wants us to be faithful servants and trust Him. (BATs: 2c Faithfulness; 8a Faith in God's promises)

Why wouldn't God let His people go into the promised land of Canaan? *(because they had sinned by not trusting God)* God rewarded Joshua and Caleb because they believed Him. They would be allowed to go into the promised land later. (BAT: 4a Sowing and reaping)

Recite Proverbs 3:5–6 and sing "Trust in the Lord" again, relating it to Joshua and Caleb.

Song: "My Bible Book"

Lesson 65: Moses' and Aaron's Sin

Bible text: Numbers 20:1–13

Doctrinal truth: Salvation (repentance)

Character traits: Obedience; Trust

Memory verse: Review Romans 3:23.

Catechism: Review Catechism 3, 7, 8, and 17.

Materials
• Moses, Aaron, and Children of Israel visuals (See the Appendix.)

Opening chorus: "I Will Obey"

Song: "Holy Bible, Book Divine"

Prayer

Ask God to help us use our eyes, ears, tongues, hands, and feet to obey Him.

Memory verse

Review Romans 3:23.

Song: "There Is None That Doeth Good"

Catechism

Review Catechism 3, 7, 8, and 17.

■ Why did God make you and all things? *(God made me and all things for His own glory.)*

■ How can you glorify God? *(I can glorify God by loving Him and doing what He commands.)*

■ Why ought you to glorify God? *(I ought to glorify God because He made me and takes care of me.)*

■ Where do you learn how to love and obey God? *(I learn how to love and obey God in the Bible alone.)*

Song: "Trust and Obey"

Bible lesson

Introduction

➤ Where were the Israelites in our last lesson? *(still wandering in the wilderness)* Why didn't the Lord let them enter the promised land when they were so near it? *(They sinned in not believing that God would be with them to conquer the people who lived in Canaan.)* How many times did the Israelites not trust God? *(The Bible tells us of many times when they forgot that God was with them.)* They would become afraid and not believe in God's Word and His promises.

Lesson

Display Moses, Aaron, and Children of Israel visuals.

In our lesson today, we find the same thing happening again. The Israelites were camping at Kadesh, and the wells of water had dried up. There was no water at all for the people and their cattle to drink.

The people gathered themselves together to complain to Moses and Aaron. Again they asked Moses, "Why didn't you just let us die with the rest of our people? Why did you bring us this far to die of thirst? This is no place to find fruit. Seeds can't even grow into plants here because there is no water. Why have you done this to us?"

Now what do you suppose Moses and Aaron did? Why, they did what they always did when the people would not trust and obey God. They went to God's house, the tabernacle, and prayed. God showed His presence there to them in the cloud.

The Lord spoke to them and said, "Take Aaron's rod from the tabernacle where I told you to keep it. Then get all of my people together around the rock. And while they are looking at you, speak to the rock and you will see a miracle. Water will come out from the rock and there will be enough water for the people and their cattle to drink."

So Moses took the rod from the tabernacle and called the people to come to the rock. But instead of speaking to the rock as God commanded, Moses angrily said to the people, "Hear now, you unbelievers, must we bring you water out of this rock?" Then Moses lifted up his hand, and with the rod he hit the rock twice. Water came out of the rock—so much water that there was enough for all the people and their cattle.

But God was not happy with Moses and Aaron. Why? Because they had not obeyed Him when He said all they needed to do was speak to the rock.

God said, "Because you did not obey Me, you made the people think the water came by your power and not mine; I must punish you. I will not let you lead my people into the promised land of Canaan. I will choose someone else."

Application
➤ Moses struck the rock. He disobeyed God. Moses was angry at the people and hit the rock instead of controlling himself and obeying God. Moses and Aaron had to be punished for their disobedience. (BAT: 4a Sowing and reaping)

Song: "Obedience Is"

Lesson 66: God Took Moses

Bible texts: Numbers 27:12–14; Deuteronomy 31–34

Doctrinal truth: God

Character trait: Trust

Catechism: Review Catechism 18, 21, and 22, and introduce Catechism 23–25.

Materials
• Moses and Children of Israel visuals (See the Appendix.)

Opening chorus: "I Will Obey"

Song: "Jesus Loves Me"

Prayer
Thank God for His love.

Song: "Oh, Be Careful"

Bible lesson

Introduction
Display Moses visual.

➤ Moses had been a good leader for God's people, the Israelites, for many, many years. He had brought them out of Egypt and led them into the wilderness. He knew that he was about to die. He had asked the Lord to choose another leader for His people. God had answered that it would be Joshua. Remember, Joshua was one of the twelve spies whom Moses had sent into the Promised Land when God's people were camped close by. He and Caleb were the only ones who had faith to believe God would help them conquer the land. God knew Joshua wanted to love and serve Him and would be a good leader for His people.

Lesson
Display Moses and Children of Israel visuals.

So Moses called God's people together. He told them many important things. He reminded them that God loves them, had brought them out of Egypt, and had taken care of them on their journey. He reminded them of their sin in not believing and trusting God even though He had made them, loved them, and had taken care of them. He told them again that our God is a holy God, without sin. God is perfectly holy, set apart from sin. Moses' words are written in the book of Deuteronomy in the Bible. Who wrote the Bible? *(Catechism 18: Holy men who were taught by the Holy Spirit wrote the Bible.)* Whom did God have write His words in Genesis, Exodus, Leviticus, Numbers, and Deuteronomy? *(Moses)* (You may wish to sing "Books of Moses.")

Finally, Moses told the people that he was one hundred twenty years old, and it was time for him to die. He reminded the people that because of his sin of hitting the rock instead of speaking to it, as God had commanded, he could not lead them into the promised land of Canaan.

But Moses said, "The Lord your God will go with you to help you capture the land, and Joshua will be your leader. Be strong and of good courage; don't be afraid of the people who live in Canaan. God will never leave you."

The people listened carefully to Moses. They loved Moses. He had been their faithful leader for many, many years. They would miss him. It made them sad to know he was leaving them.

Then Moses climbed to the top of Mount Nebo. There the Lord God showed him all the beautiful land of Canaan that He had promised to Abraham, Isaac, and Jacob. So Moses, God's special servant and leader, died there on the mountain, and the Lord Himself buried Moses. The Bible tells us that no one has ever known where God buried Moses. The Bible also tells us that there was never so great a leader of God's people as Moses. We remember Moses as the great leader for God. Moses talked to God and saw the glory of God on Mount Sinai.

Application
➤ God loved Moses very much, and Moses loved God. God took Moses' soul to heaven to live with Him. (BAT: 8a Faith in God's promises)

What did God give Adam and Eve besides bodies? *(Catechism 21: God gave them souls that could never die.)* Do you have a soul as well as a body? *(Catechism 22: Yes, I have a soul that can never die.)*

Our soul is the part of us that will never die. Did Moses have a soul? *(Yes, Moses had a soul that could never die, and God took Moses' soul to heaven to live with Him.)*

God loves you and me. He sent His Son to die on the cross for our sins. If we accept Jesus as our Savior from sin, then someday, when we die, God will take our souls to heaven to live with Him forever.

> This might be a good time to review the plan of salvation to see if any children are ready to accept Jesus as Savior. (See "Leading a Child to the Lord" in the Introduction to this teacher's edition.)

Catechism
Introduce Catechism 23–25.

- In what condition did God make Adam and Eve? (*God made them holy and happy.*)

- Did Adam obey God? (*No, Adam chose to disobey God.*)

- How did God punish Adam's disobedience? (*Adam's punishment was death and separation from God.*)

➤ We are sinners like Adam, and that is why we need a Savior from sin. When we ask Jesus to forgive our sins, then we do not have to be separated from God. Because Jesus took our punishment, someday we can live forever with God.

Song: "Nothing but the Blood"

Lesson 67: Review—Moses' Life

Bible texts: Exodus 1–40; Numbers 13, 14, 20, 27 (review)
Doctrinal truth: God
Character traits: Trust; Obedience
Catechism: Review Catechism 19–25.
Materials
- Each student's completed Student page 16 (from Lesson 57)
- Student page 18 and cutouts
- Scissors
- Glue

Opening chorus: "I Will Obey"

Song: "Oh, Be Careful"

Prayer
Thank God for the lessons about God's leader Moses. Ask God to help us be obedient followers.

Song: "Trust and Obey"

Student page 18
Instruct the children to cut out the pictures. Review Moses' life while guiding the children in gluing the pictures. Give each child his completed Student page 16 from Lesson 57. Instruct the children to cut out the booklet pages on both sheets. Lead them in a sequencing activity to put the pages of their Moses booklets in order. Staple the pages together on

the left side. Direct the children to write their names on the back of their booklets. Allow the children to take their Moses booklets home.

Catechism
Review Catechism 19–25.

- Who were our first parents? (*Adam and Eve were our first parents.*)

- Of what were our first parents made? (*God made the body of Adam out of the dust of the ground and formed Eve from the body of Adam.*)

- What did God give Adam and Eve besides bodies? (*God gave them souls that could never die.*)

- Do you have a soul as well as a body? (*Yes, I have a soul that can never die.*)

- In what condition did God make Adam and Eve? (*God made them holy and happy.*)

- Did Adam obey God? (*No, Adam chose to disobey God.*)

- How did God punish Adam's disobedience? (*Adam's punishment was death and separation from God.*)

Song: "Nothing but the Blood"

Lesson 68: Josh Is Sorry for His Sin

Bible text: Review.
Doctrinal truth: Salvation (repentance)
Character trait: Obedience
Memory verses: Review Psalm 38:18 and Ecclesiastes 12:13*b*.
Catechism: Review Catechism 15, 17, and 18, and introduce Catechism 26.
Materials
- Kate, Josh, and Mom Vick family puppets

Opening chorus: "I Will Obey"

Song: "Be Ye Doers of the Word"

Prayer
Ask God to help us listen to and obey His Word.

Catechism
Review Catechism 15, 17, and 18.

- Does God know all things? (*Yes, nothing can be hidden from God.*)

- Where do you learn how to love and obey God? (*I learn how to love and obey God in the Bible alone.*)

- Who wrote the Bible? (*Holy men who were taught by the Holy Spirit wrote the Bible.*)

Introduce Catechism 26.

- What is sin? *(Sin is the transgression of the law of God.)*

➤ Sin is *not doing* what God commands, and it also is *doing* what God forbids. When God forbids something, He is telling us *not* to do it.

Memory verse
Review Psalm 38:18.

Song: "Nothing but the Blood"

Character story: "Josh Is Sorry for His Sin"

Kate and Josh were building with blocks in the den. Mom was baking cookies in the kitchen. She called to the children, "Come and get a treat."

Kate and Josh both hurried into the kitchen, trying to see who could get there first.

"Well," Mom said as she looked up from her work, "I believe you think I must have something special for you."

"Mmm," Kate said, "those peanut butter cookies smell so good."

"How many can we have, Mom?" asked Josh eagerly.

"Let's see, now, what time is it?" Mom asked as she looked at the kitchen clock. "Hmmmmm, well, we won't be eating supper for two hours yet; I guess I can let you each have three." Mom got two napkins out of the cupboard, laid them on the kitchen table, and placed three cookies on each napkin. "I hope you like them, children," she said as she smiled.

"Yummy! We will. We will!" Josh exclaimed.

"Thank you, Mom," Kate said as she picked up her cookies. "May we take them into the den to eat while we play with our blocks?"

"I guess so, if you'll try to be careful not to get crumbs on the carpet," Mom answered.

As Kate and Josh returned to the den, Josh began eating one of his cookies. "Oh, boy, are these good." He gulped one down.

And when he sat down on the floor, he gobbled up his other two cookies as fast as he could.

Kate placed the napkin with her three cookies on the floor by her blocks. She picked up one and began nibbling around the edge of it while she added two more blocks to the bridge she was building.

"Rrrrrring," went the doorbell.

"Kate," Mom called from the kitchen. "I have cookie dough on my hands. Will you please see who is at the door?"

"Yes, ma'am," Kate answered as she jumped up and ran to the front door.

Kate opened the door and smiled as she saw their neighbor. "Come in, Mrs. Berg. Mom is in the kitchen. She will be here in just a minute." Then Kate ran into the kitchen to tell her mother who had come.

When Kate had left the den to answer the door, Josh looked at the two cookies that were left on her napkin. He had eaten his so quickly, and hers smelled so good that it made his mouth water. Josh thought, "Maybe Kate won't notice if just one of hers is missing." Quickly, he reached out, grabbed one of Kate's two cookies, and popped it into his mouth.

Just then Kate came running back from the kitchen and kneeled down beside the blocks. When she reached for one of her cookies, her eyes blinked. "Josh!" she said angrily, "Did you eat one of mine?"

"No," Josh said. He lied.

"Well, then who did?" Kate asked.

"How should I know?" Josh answered. Josh began to feel very guilty.

"You did too take one of my cookies," Kate yelled.

"No, I didn't," Josh shouted back.

Mother was just passing the door on her way to get something from a hall closet, and she heard the children arguing. "Kate, Josh, what is going on?"

"Josh took one of my cookies," cried Kate.

Josh's face was beginning to turn red; he didn't say anything.

"Josh," Mother asked sadly, "did you take one of Kate's cookies? You know that it is a sin to take something that belongs to someone else, and it is also a sin to tell a lie."

"How do you know?" asked Josh, with tears in his eyes.

"That's why God gave us commandments in His Word, the Holy Bible. His commandments are rules that tell us what to do and what not to do. We should obey His rules to show God that we love Him; that will make us happy Christians. Sin is the transgression of the law of God. Sin is failing to do what God commands and doing what God forbids or tells us not to do. Remember your memory verse, 'Fear God and keep his commandments: for this is the whole duty of man' (Ecclesiastes 12:13b)."

"I'm sorry I disobeyed God's commandments," Josh said softly. "I'm sorry I took one of your cookies, Kate."

"I'm glad you told us you're sorry, but it's more important that you tell God that you are sorry," his mother said.

Song: "Obedience Is"

Lesson 69: Review—God's Law

Bible text: Review.

Doctrinal truth: God; Bible; Salvation

Character traits: Trust; Obedience

Memory verses: Review.

Catechism: Review Catechism 1–26.

Materials
• Large sketch of tablets of stone for display (for review activity)
• Student page 19
• Crayons or chalk

Opening chorus: "I Will Obey"

Song: "God's Way"

Prayer
Stand and pray together the Lord's prayer.

Song: "My Bible Book"

Student page 19
Read the sentences at the top of the page. Instruct the children to put their pointer finger on the numeral one and read the commandment. Direct them to the pictures at the end of the row. Allow a volunteer to identify the picture of the Lord. Instruct the children to circle the Lord's picture. Complete the page following the same procedure (2. idol; 3. bowing to idol; 4. church; 5. parents). Read the entire page with the children.

Review activity
Display the sketch of the tablets of stone. You may make two or more for team competition. Instruct children to add a mark on the tablet for each question they answer correctly.

1. What did God's people call the special food He sent from heaven? *(manna)*

2. How much were the Israelites to take? *(just enough for one day except on the sixth day, when they should take enough for two days)*

3. Did all the people obey God? *(no)*

4. What happened to the manna when the Israelites disobeyed God by taking more than enough for one day? *(The manna became spoiled and full of worms.)*

5. What was God trying to teach His people? *(to obey and trust Him)*

6. Why did Moses go to the top of Mt. Sinai? *(to receive the laws, or commandments, for His people)*

7. Whom did Moses choose to be the leader of the people while he was on the mount? *(his brother, Aaron)*

8. What did the people ask Aaron to do? *(make an idol to worship)*

9. What did Aaron have the people bring to him? *(their golden earrings)*

10. What did Aaron make? *(a golden calf)*

11. What did the people do with the golden calf? *(They worshiped it.)*

12. Could that idol hear their prayers and take care of them? *(no)* Why? *(Idols are just pieces of wood and stone; they cannot hear or answer prayers.)*

13. What happened when Moses came back down the mountain? *(He was angry, and God was angry. God caused the people to be sick, and some even died.)*

14. What was God trying to teach His people? *(that they were to worship only Him)*

15. What were some of the things the people brought to Moses to help build their tabernacle? *(silver, gold, wood, soft animal fur, jewels)*

16. Who was the high minister or priest? *(Aaron)*

17. When the people of Israel came near the promised land, what did God tell Moses to do? *(send twelve men ahead to see what it was like)*

18. What do we call these twelve men? *(spies)*

19. What did they bring back with them? *(big bunches of grapes and other fruits)*

20. What did the spies say the people in Canaan were like? *(giants)*

21. Which two spies were not afraid of the giants and knew God would help them? *(Caleb and Joshua)*

22. Why wouldn't God let His people go into the promised land of Canaan? *(because they had sinned and had not trusted and obeyed God)*

23. Whom would God allow into the promised land? Why? *(Joshua and Caleb—They believed and trusted God.)*

24. How did Moses sin? *(God told him to speak to the rock for water, but instead Moses struck [hit] the rock.)*

25. Where did God take Moses to show him the land of Canaan? *(Mount Nebo)*

26. Who buried Moses? *(God)*

27. Where did Moses' soul go? *(to heaven)*

28. Which books of the Bible did God have Moses write? *(Genesis, Exodus, Leviticus, Numbers, and Deuteronomy, which together are the Law, or Pentateuch)*

Review catechism and memory verses.

Song: "Books of Moses"

God's Gifts

Thanksgiving: I Praise God

Psalm 100

You may want to introduce Psalm 100 before teaching the four lessons in Unit 7 to allow more time for teaching and reviewing the psalm. The booklet, "Our Thanksgiving Psalm," included in the Student Packet, is used in the following lesson procedures as well as in Lesson 73.

The following are four lesson procedures for introducing the five verses of the psalm.

> These four memory verse lessons and "Our Thanksgiving Psalm" booklet include Scripture in the King James Version. If you use a different version of the Bible, you may need to adapt the lessons.

Memory verse lesson 1—Psalm 100:1–2

➤ We are going to begin learning our special Thanksgiving psalm today. Listen as I read it from the Bible. Remember the book of Psalms is almost in the middle of the Bible. (Demonstrate this as you turn to the psalm.)

Read Psalm 100 aloud. Display your copy of "Our Thanksgiving Psalm" booklet. Turn the pages of the booklet as you recite the psalm again. Tell the children that they will each have a booklet like yours to take home at Thanksgiving after they have learned the verses of the psalm. (See Lesson 73.) Discuss verses 1–2.

➤ "Make a joyful noise unto the Lord." How can we make a joyful noise unto the Lord? How can we praise Him? *(Answers may vary.)* Yes, when we sing songs about God and His Word and when we talk to God in prayer and thank Him for all His goodness, we are praising Him.

The Lord made us. The Lord takes care of us. Everything we have comes from God. We have so much to thank Him for.

➤ The verse also says, "All ye lands," which means that everyone everywhere in the world should make a joyful noise or sing and praise the Lord.

But some boys and girls and mothers and fathers have never heard about our God. People who do not know that God sent His Son to be their Savior do not have happy hearts. They cannot thank God with a joyful noise.

➤ "Serve the Lord with gladness: come before his presence with singing." How can we serve the Lord with gladness? *(Answers may vary.)* We can serve the

Savior. We must always remember to pray for our missionaries and pray that God will send even more missionaries around the world to tell the good news of His Son.

We can also be good missionaries ourselves right here in (name your city) and tell those who have never heard that God made us all, that He loves us, and that He sent His Son Jesus to die for us. (BAT: 5c Evangelism and missions)

Because God has been so good to us, we should serve Him with a happy heart. Let's come before His presence with singing right now.

Sing "Rejoice, Ye Pure in Heart," stanza 1.

Display the Christian flag. Explain the symbol of the cross—it reminds us of God's Son, Jesus Christ, who died on the cross for the sins of everyone in the world.

➤ *Rejoice* means "be happy"; *pure in heart* means "our sins have been forgiven."

Memory verse lesson 2—Psalm 100:3

Read Psalm 100 from your Bible. Direct the children to join in as you recite verses 1–2 several times.

➤ God wants the people of all lands and nations to believe that He is God and to sing praises to Him.

Discuss verse 3, using the booklet page.

➤ "Know ye that the Lord he is God: it is he that hath made us, and not we ourselves." In the beginning God made the heavens and the earth; all things were made by Him.

Do you think that Abraham, Joseph, and Moses knew that the Lord is God and that He made them? Yes, and they glorified God by loving Him and doing what He commanded them to do.

➤ "We are his people, and the sheep of his pasture." Little lambs and sheep look to their shepherd to lead them to good places and take care of them. The God of heaven takes care of us just as a shepherd takes care of his sheep.

Recite verse 3 several times, asking the children to say it with you. Read verses 1–3 from your Bible, and have the children recite Psalm 95:6 with you. Lead the class in a prayer of thanks. Lead them in singing "Rejoice, Ye Pure in Heart."

Memory verse lesson 3—Psalm 100:4

Read the entire psalm from your Bible. Ask one of the children to come and hold the Bible as you read it. Discuss verse 4, using the booklet page.

➤ "Enter into his gates with thanksgiving, and into his courts with praise: be thankful unto him, and bless his name."

Thanksgiving Day is coming soon, and we have so many things to thank God for. Can you name some things you are thankful for? *(Answers may vary.)*

This verse reminds us that we should go to church and praise and thank God for all His gifts to us. And we also should remember to thank God anytime and anywhere for all His goodness.

Recite the verse together. Have a few of the children recite the psalm with your prompting. Lead the children in singing "Rejoice, Ye Pure in Heart."

Memory verse lesson 4—Psalm 100:5

Read the entire psalm from your Bible. Ask one of the children to come and hold the Bible as you read it. Discuss verse 5, using the booklet page.

➤ "For the Lord is good; his mercy is everlasting; and his truth endureth to all generations." The Lord is good. God is so good; there is none as truly good as God is. He sent His Son, Jesus Christ, to be born in a manger to grow up and die on the cross to be our Savior from sin. Is Jesus still dead? No, He arose from the tomb where they buried Him. Where is Jesus now? He is in heaven with God the Father. He is praying for us who trust Him as our Savior.

Our God is perfectly holy and good. He is loving, kind, and forgiving. He always keeps His promises. He never forgets. His mercy and kindness to us will never stop; they are forever. That is what *everlasting* means. God's truth—what He says—will never change because He never changes.

Divide the children into two or more groups, and lead them in reciting Psalm 100 in choral response.

Lead the children in singing "Rejoice, Ye Pure in Heart."

Lesson 70: O Give Thanks unto the Lord

Bible text: Psalm 105

Doctrinal truth: God (sovereignty)

Character trait: Trust

Memory verse: Introduce (or review) Psalm 100.

Materials
- "Our Thanksgiving Psalm" booklet (One copy for the teacher from the Student Packet—cut on dashed line, fold on solid line, and staple to make booklet.)
- A completed cornucopia from Student pages 20–21 (for use as a sample)
- Student pages 20–21
- Large sheet of construction paper (12" × 18") for each student
- Scissors
- Glue

Opening hymn: "Father, We Thank Thee for the Night," stanza 1

Memory verse

Refer to the Psalm 100 lessons at the beginning of this unit, and to the "Our Thanksgiving Psalm" booklet, to introduce or review Psalm 100.

Prayer

Ask God to help us always remember to thank Him for all He has done for us.

Song: "O Give Thanks"

Doctrinal emphasis: Sovereignty of God

Read the following verses of Psalm 105 from your Bible and discuss them.

➤ *Verse 1:* Tell everyone what great things our God has done for you. This psalm was written to remind God's people that they should remember to thank God and tell others about the many wonderful things He has done for them.

Verse 2: Sing songs of thanks and praise to God.

Verse 5: Don't forget about what great and good things God has done for you.

Verses 8–14: God didn't let anyone, not even kings, hurt His people.

Verses 16–17: Joseph was put into jail.

Verses 20–23: Pharaoh made Joseph ruler of all that Pharaoh had, and Jacob, Joseph's father, came to the land.

Verse 24: God made his people stronger than their enemies.

Verses 26–27: Moses and Aaron showed God's signs in Egypt.

Verses 28–36: God sent hail and locusts, and He killed the oldest son in the families of the Egyptians.

Verses 37–38: God brought His people forth out of Egypt, and the people of Egypt were glad when they left because they were afraid of God's people and their powerful God.

Verse 39: God provided a cloud to cover His people and fire to give them light in the night.

Verses 40–41: The people asked for food, and God sent quail and manna, bread from heaven. He brought water from a rock.

Verses 42–45: God remembered His promise. He gave His people the lands that they might listen to His Word and obey His laws.

Song: "Praise Him, Praise Him"

Action rhyme: "All Things Bright and Beautiful"

➤ Each little flower that opens,
   (Hold fingers of both hands up in a fist and then open fingers slowly.)
   Each little bird that sings,
   (Flap both arms like wings.)
   God made their pretty colors.
   (Hold fingers of both hands up in a fist and then open fingers slowly.)
   He made their tiny wings.
   (Flap both arms like wings.)

   –Adapted from the poem by Cecil Francis Alexander

Praise time

Encourage a few children to stand and tell what God has done for them.

Song: "Rejoice, Ye Pure in Heart"

Student pages 20–21

Student pages 20–21 for Lesson 70 may be completed in two days. The cornucopia may be cut and glued during Lesson 70, and the fruit and vegetables may be added as part of Lesson 71.

Using the sample, show the children the cornucopia they will be making. Instruct the children to cut out their cornucopia and the fruits and vegetables. Guide the children in gluing the cornucopia to the left side of the construction paper. Allow the children to add the fruits and vegetables to the cornucopia so that the pictures are visible. Encourage the children who did not have an opportunity to tell what God has done for them during the praise time to share something from their picture for which they are thankful.

Lesson 71: Our Great Provider

Bible texts: James 1:17; Psalm 107:8
Doctrinal truth: God
Character trait: Thankfulness
Memory verses: Review Psalm 100 and I Thessalonians 5:18.

Opening hymn: "Father, We Thank Thee for the Night," stanza 1

Action rhyme: "All Things Bright and Beautiful" (See Index of Poetry.)

Song: "O Give Thanks"

Prayer
Thank God for all the good gifts He gives to us.

Song: "Praise Him, Praise Him," stanzas 1–3

Character story: "Give Thanks"

Mrs. Robinson enjoyed teaching her kindergarten class. They were such sweet boys and girls. They loved to learn new things and usually were happy and kind to each other. But this week was different. The children seemed restless, and Mrs. Robinson noticed that several of the children had started to complain.

"I wish I didn't have to wear this raincoat," moaned Rosa. "Why can't it be sunny? Now we can't even go outside for recess."

"Oh no, not another banana!" whined Ron at snack time. "I wish Mama wouldn't give me a banana for my snack every day. Look at all the brown spots on it. Why can't I have something good like chocolate chip cookies?"

"Mrs. Robinson," Kate cried during recess, "Amy wants me to play house with her at the home center. She says she won't be my friend any more if I don't do what she wants to do. But I don't want to play house I want to color this picture."

Mrs. Robinson was very concerned. This was the week before Thanksgiving. She knew the children wanted to do what was right. But she also knew that whining and complaining did not please God. Mrs. Robinson wanted to teach the children in her class the importance of being thankful for all God has given to us. She silently prayed and asked God to show her a way to help the boys and girls.

"Children," Mrs. Robinson said, "I have heard several of my boys and girls grumbling and complaining this week. We have been learning that complaining does not please God. He wants us to be thankful. God tells us this in His Word when He says, 'In everything give thanks' (I Thess. 5:18). I know you boys and girls want to please God," said Mrs. Robinson. "God has given me an idea for a way we can learn to be more thankful. Whenever anyone starts to complain, we will all stop what we are doing and everyone will say, 'In everything give thanks, I Thessalonians 5:18.' Then we will all sing 'Thank Him, Thank Him.' Let's make a class book of things for which we are thankful now. I want each of you to think of something you would like to thank God for. Then, as you draw a picture of it, I will come around and write a sentence about your picture on the bottom of your paper. I will use your pictures to make a book. Later this morning we will read our story. Let's see how many different things we can think of to be thankful for, including our friends, bananas, and even the rain."

Application

Guide a discussion, using the following questions:
    Who sent the rain?
    Why does God send the rain?
    Where did the banana come from?
    Who do our friends come from?

Recite I Thessalonians 5:18 together (BAT:7c Praise).

Memory verse
Continue introducing or reviewing Psalm 100 with "Our Thanksgiving Psalm" booklet and lessons at the beginning of this unit.

Song: "Rejoice, Ye Pure in Heart"

Lesson 72: Turkey for Thanksgiving

Bible texts: Jeremiah 33:3; Philippians 4:19
Doctrinal truth: God
Character trait: Thankfulness
Memory verse: Review Psalm 100.
Materials
• "The Wonder Song" visuals (See the Appendix.)
• A cornucopia or basket
• Student page 22

Opening hymn: "Father, We Thank Thee for the Night"

Action rhyme: "All Things Bright and Beautiful" (See Index of Poetry.)

Song: "O Give Thanks"

Memory verse
Continue the Psalm 100 lessons (at the beginning of Unit 7).

Song: "The Wonder Song"
Choose children to hold the visuals and to place them in a cornucopia or basket after each corresponding stanza has been sung.

Character story: "Turkey for Thanksgiving"

Emily was feeling sad. She knew that tomorrow was the last day the children in her kindergarten class would be able to bring their canned goods to school for the Thanksgiving basket. The day before yesterday, Mrs. Sommers had said, "Boys and girls, you may begin bringing your food for the Thanksgiving basket tomorrow. There are some families in our town that will not have a happy Thanksgiving because they will be hungry."

Emily sighed a little when Mrs. Sommers said that. Her family could be that family. They often did not have much to eat, but as her father had said many times, "God will always provide for His children." Emily was not so sure this time, though. She knew that there was no turkey waiting in the freezer for Thanksgiving Day at her house. And besides that, she did not have a thing to put into the Thanksgiving basket at school.

The day had begun as usual in kindergarten. First, the class said the pledge to the American flag, then the pledge to the Christian flag, and then they prayed. Prayer was not new to Emily. Her father and mother prayed with her often, and she had accepted Jesus Christ as her Savior on the Friday of the first week of school. Just the same, she had never really seen one of her own prayers answered. She wondered if Jesus answered when she prayed by herself with no one listening but God.

The morning went by quickly, and soon it was time for recess. On the way out, she stopped to look at all the cans of food piled up like building blocks in the Thanksgiving basket. "Tomorrow is the last day to bring some food for the Thanksgiving basket, and I still don't have anything to put in," she thought. "Maybe if I ask Jesus, He will help." Right then and there she prayed. She prayed in her heart so no one could hear but God. "Dear Jesus, please give me something to put in the Thanksgiving basket before tomorrow because tomorrow is the last day. In Jesus' name. Amen."

The class began playing "Duck, Duck, Goose." That was one of Emily's favorite games. Her friend Susan was "It," and Emily was tapped. Around the circle she flew as fast as her feet would take her. Since she did not tap Susan in time, she had to be "It" next. "Duck . . . duck . . . GOOSE!" The little blond-haired boy who sat next to her in class was chasing her now. Around they went. As she dropped into the empty space in the circle, she spotted something shiny in the grass. "Teacher, Teacher! Look what I found!" she shouted.

"Why, where did you find those quarters?" Mrs. Sommers asked in her usual soft way.

"Right in front of me in the grass. May I keep them?" Emily asked excitedly.

The teacher asked if anyone had lost the quarters. Jeff said that he had lost one once at his grandmother's house. Linda was sure she had lost two pennies on the way to her friend's house yesterday. But no one claimed the quarters.

"Well, Emily, since you found the quarters and we are unable to find their owner, you may keep them," Mrs. Sommers announced.

"Wow!"

"You're lucky!"

"What are you going to buy with them, Emily?"

"You could get some candy!"

"I would get gum if they were mine."

Almost every child in the class had a comment to make about Emily's quarters. When Mrs. Sommers asked her what she planned to do with them, Emily slowly and thoughtfully fingered the quarters. Then she said, "It's a secret."

Emily knew exactly what she was going to do with the quarters. Walking to and from school each day, she passed a neighborhood store. Her mother had sent her there for a loaf of bread last week. That is where she would spend her quarters.

As soon as school was out, she hurried down the street to the store. As she walked down the aisles, she came to a shelf neatly lined with soup cans. Soup was something she liked a lot. She often had it at home. Sometimes that was all her family had. At least they had soup, though, and she was thankful for that. The people who would receive the Thanksgiving basket probably didn't have that much. That is why she carefully took one can of soup off the shelf and carried it to the lady at the check-out. Her quarters disappeared into the cash register drawer, and the lady gave Emily the soup can in a brown paper bag. Now she, too, could put something in the Thanksgiving basket at school.

The next morning Emily happily laid the can of soup in the Thanksgiving basket. Mrs. Sommers, who had been watching, came over and put her hand on Emily's shoulder. "Thank you for putting something in the basket, Emily," said Mrs. Sommers with a kind voice. She spoke as if she knew about Emily's prayer. But she couldn't know be-

cause Emily had prayed so that no one could hear but God. Emily knew that for sure.

"God answered my prayer, Mrs. Sommers—the prayer I prayed all by myself without anyone listening but God,"she announced matter-of-factly. "My mother couldn't spare any food for the Thanksgiving basket, so I prayed that God would give me something to put in the basket and He did! He gave me the quarters that I found on the playground yesterday, and I bought a can of soup with them."

"I'm very proud of you, Emily. You could have bought gum or candy, but instead you chose to give to someone else," Mrs. Sommers said as she gave Emily a gentle pat. Her teacher was quiet for a minute and then went on to say, "You know, every year the school gives each of us teachers a turkey for Thanksgiving. This year I am going to be eating Thanksgiving dinner with some friends. Do you think your family could use my turkey?" Emily almost screamed with delight. She was sure her mother would be thrilled to serve her family turkey. She also knew that her father would say, "Praise the Lord!"

Before everyone went home from school that day, Mrs. Sommers asked the children to tell the class something they were thankful for.

Emily raised her hand immediately. "I have two things that I am especially thankful for this Thanksgiving. One is that God answered the prayer I prayed yesterday about the Thanksgiving basket. The other is that we are going to have turkey for Thanksgiving."

Song: "Praise Him, Praise Him," stanzas 1–3
Read Philippians 4:19 from your Bible.

Student page 22
Allow the children to draw some things for which they are thankful. Give them an opportunity to tell about their pictures.

Song: "Rejoice, Ye Pure in Heart"

Lesson 73: Our Thanksgiving Psalm

Bible text: Psalm 100

Doctrinal truth: God

Character trait: Thankfulness

Memory verse: Review Psalm 100.

Materials
- "Our Thanksgiving Psalm" booklet for each student and the teacher (Student Packet—cut on dashed line, fold on solid line, and staple to make booklet.)
- Several pieces of real or artificial fruit
- A cornucopia or basket

> The teacher's copy of "Our Thanksgiving Psalm" booklet will be used again in Lessons 135 and 155.

Opening hymn: "Father, We Thank Thee for the Night"

Action rhyme: "All Things Bright and Beautiful" (See Index of Poetry.)

Song: "Thank You God," stanzas 1–3

Prayer

Thank God for His blessings.

Direct the children to bow their heads and sing "Thank You, God" for prayer time today.

Praise time

Allow the children to take turns coming to the front of the class and telling one thing for which they are thankful. After each child tells a blessing or gift God has given to him, he may pick a piece of fruit from a box or bag and place it in the cornucopia or Thanksgiving basket. After the cornucopia is filled, you may empty it and begin again with other children.

Song: "Praise Him, Praise Him"

Student Packet: "Our Thanksgiving Psalm" booklet
Distribute "Our Thanksgiving Psalm" booklet to each child. Lead a discussion about the cover of the booklet. Read the title. Guide the children in "reading" it with you. Encourage them to "read" the pictures as you proceed through the book.

Guide the picture reading on page 2 by asking the following questions. Recite Psalm 100:1 together.

➤ What do you see on this page? *(children)*

   What else do you see? *(a picture of the world, a globe)*

   Where do you think the children live? *(in different countries or lands all over the world; notice their dress and facial features)*

   Did God make all the children of the world? *(yes)* Does God love them? *(yes)*

   Do you think everyone in the world knows about God and His Son? *(no)* Who is supposed to tell them? *(We are.)* God wants everyone everywhere to love and serve Him. That is why God made us.

Lead the children in singing "Jesus Loves the Little Children."

Guide the picture reading on page 3 by asking the following questions. Recite Psalm 100:2 together.

➤ What do you see on this page? *(children)*

   What are they doing? *(reading the Bible, praying, and singing)*

   How can you serve the Lord? *(Allow discussion.)*

Guide the children in reading page 4 by asking the following questions. Recite Psalm 100:3a together.

➤ What do you see on this page? *(the Lord Jesus and children)*

   Who made us? *(God the Father, Son, and Holy Spirit)*

   To whom do we belong? *(God; we are His people.)*

Guide the children in reading page 5 by asking the following questions. Recite Psalm 100:3b together.

➤ What do you see on this page? *(the Lord Jesus with a lamb and sheep)*

   Who made the lambs? *(the Lord God)*

   Who takes care of sheep? *(a shepherd)*

   What does the psalm say we are like? *(The sheep of His pasture; our Lord takes care of us as a shepherd takes care of his sheep. God's Son is the Good Shepherd.)*

Guide the children in reading page 6 by asking the following questions. Recite Psalm 100:4 together.

➤ What do you see in this picture? *(a family)*

   What are they doing? *(going to church)*

   Is a church the only place where we can thank God for His good gifts to us? *(no; at home, at school, in the car, everywhere)* We can talk with God any time and anywhere.

   Why do we go to church? *(God tells us to meet to-gether with others who love Him to serve and praise Him together.)*

Guide the picture reading on page 7 by asking the following questions. Recite Psalm 100:5 and John 3:16.

➤ What do you see on this page? *(manger, cross, open tomb, heaven)* These are picture symbols that remind us of how good the Lord is.

   What does the manger remind us of? *(God loved us and sent His Son.)*

   What does the cross remind us of? *(God's Son died on the cross to be our Savior from sin.)*

   What does the open tomb remind us of? *(God's Son arose from the grave.)* When we accept Him as our Savior from sin, we know that when we die, we can live again with Him forever.

Song: "Rejoice, Ye Pure in Heart"

God's Best Gift

Christmas: I Thank God

Lesson 74: God Planned for Our Savior

Bible text: Luke 1:26–38

Doctrinal truths: God the Son; Salvation

Character traits: Wisdom; Thankfulness

Memory verse: Introduce John 3:16.

Catechism: Review Catechism 19–26.

Materials
- Wristband bells (Use wide elastic to make a wristband. Sew three or four jingle bells on the wristband.)
- John 3:16 visual (See the Appendix for the visual and instructions.)

Opening chorus: "Ring the Bells"

Direct the children to stand, hang their arms down in front of them, and clasp their hands together, swaying them like a bell clapper.

After the song is taught, you may choose one child to "play" an introduction with the wristband bells and accompany the children as they sing.

Song: "Jesus Christ Is Born"

Prayer

Thank God for loving us so much that He sent His own Son to be our Savior from sin.

Song: "Jesus, Born in Bethlehem," stanza 1

Memory verse

Read John 3:16 to the children.

➤ Who knows what this verse is saying? It says that God sent to this world His Son, who had always lived in heaven. Jesus Christ, God's Son, was born in this world to grow up and take the punishment for our sin. Because God's Son took the punishment for our sin when He died on the cross, someday we can live in heaven with God forever. God's Son shows us the way to heaven. He is the way to heaven for everyone who believes in Him. (BAT: 1a Understanding Jesus Christ)

Display the John 3:16 visual as you recite the phrases of the verse.

➤ Manger—"For God so loved the world, that he gave his only begotten son,"

Cross—"that whosoever believeth in him"

Open tomb—"should not perish,"

Heaven—"but have everlasting life."

Song: "How Do We Know?" stanzas 2–3

Bible lesson

Introduction

➤ Why is Christmas such a happy time? Because at Christmas we remember when Jesus came down from heaven. Jesus had always lived in heaven with God the Father and God the Holy Spirit. But He left His home in heaven to come to earth. We celebrate Jesus' birthday at Christmas. Christmas is a happy time because we think about how much God loves us. God loves us so much that He "sent his only begotten Son into the world, that we might live through him" (I John 4:9). Jesus Christ, God's Son, is the gift God gave to us. Jesus Christ, God's Son, came to show us God's great love and kindness—a kindness we do not deserve.

Lesson

Do you remember what happened to Adam and Eve after they had sinned in the Garden of Eden? God promised them that someday He would send a Savior to take the punishment for their sin. (Review Catechism 19–26.)

- Who were our first parents? *(Adam and Eve were our first parents.)*

- Of what were our first parents made? *(God made the body of Adam out of the dust of the ground and formed Eve from the body of Adam.)*

- What did God give Adam and Eve besides bodies? *(God gave them souls that could never die.)*

- Do you have a soul as well as a body? *(Yes, I have a soul that can never die.)*

- In what condition did God make Adam and Eve? *(God made them holy and happy.)*

- Did Adam obey God? *(No, Adam chose to disobey God.)*

- How did God punish Adam's disobedience? *(Adam's punishment was death and separation from God.)*

■ What is sin? (*Sin is the transgression of the law of God.*)

God kept reminding His people of His promise. He reminded Noah, Abraham, Isaac, Jacob, Moses, and David. Oh, how God's people happily looked forward to that special time when the Savior would come! No one knew when He would come, but they knew that God would fulfill His promise when it was the right time. God always does the right thing at the right time because God is holy—without sin—and God knows all things.

One day God said, "This is the time. I will send my only Son from heaven down to Earth—just as I have promised." So God sent His special angel, Gabriel, as a messenger down from heaven to a little city called Nazareth. God told the angel Gabriel to go to a young woman named Mary who lived in Nazareth. God told Gabriel to tell Mary that she was going to be the mother of the promised Son of God.

Mary was a young woman who loved and obeyed the Lord God of heaven. She knew that *she* needed a Savior from sin. She knew that the whole world needed a Savior to take the punishment for their sins. Maybe Mary was thinking about these things when suddenly—she looked up and saw someone. It was God's angel, Gabriel. Gabriel was bright and shining; Mary was afraid.

Gabriel said, "Don't be afraid, Mary. God loves you. He has a special job He wants you to do. He wants you to be the mother of the Son of God, whom He promised so long ago. You will have this baby in a very special way."

Gabriel told Mary that she should name the baby "Jesus" because *Jesus* means "Savior," and God sent His Son to "save his people from their sins."

Mary did not know what to say. She was so happy and so surprised. She knew she must obey God because she loved Him. She told the angel Gabriel, "Whatever the Lord God wants me to do, I'll do it." Then the angel went away from her.

Mary praised God. She thanked Him for promising to send a Savior. She thanked Him for keeping His promise. God always does what He says He will do.

Application
➤ We should thank God for His best gift to us—His only begotten Son. That's why Christmas is such a happy time. Christmas is our Savior's birthday. It reminds us of God's mercy and great kindness toward us, which we do not deserve. (BATs: 1a Understanding Jesus Christ; 7c Praise)

Song: "Away in a Manger"

Lesson 75: God Sent His Messenger

Bible text: Luke 1:26–38 (review); Psalm 106:1; I John 4:9b
Doctrinal truths: Salvation; Angels
Character traits: Wisdom; Thankfulness
Memory verses: Review John 3:16 and introduce Luke 2:11.
Catechism: Introduce Catechism 27–29.
Materials
• John 3:16 visual (See the Appendix.)
• Role-playing costumes: band of tinsel to fit child's head for Gabriel's halo, towel or robe for Gabriel's robe, large scarf for Mary's head (optional)

Opening chorus: "Ring the Bells"

Song: "Jesus Christ Is Born"

Prayer
Thank God for sending His Son to show us God's love and kindness.

Song: "Away in a Manger"

Memory verses
Read John 3:16 to the children. Direct the children to recite the verse with you. Sing "John 3:16." Read Luke 2:11 aloud.

➤ Where does this verse tell us the Lord Jesus was born? (*city of David*) The name of that city is Bethlehem. When he was a young boy David lived and took care of his sheep very near this little town.

Review activity: Role play
Select and costume two children—one to be Gabriel and one to be Mary.

Direct Mary to sit and the angel Gabriel to stand. Instruct them to repeat their lines after you each time, either phrase by phrase or sentence by sentence.

➤ Teacher: God sent the angel Gabriel to the city of Nazareth to tell Mary the good news.

Gabriel: (*Hold up one arm in greeting.*) Don't be afraid, Mary. God says you will have His special Son and "call his name Jesus: for He shall save His people from their sins" (Luke 1:31 and Matt. 1:21).

Mary: Whatever God says, I will do. (*Gabriel exits while Mary folds hands to pray.*)

Class: (*Recite John 3:16.*)

Teacher: (*Read I John 4:9b and Psalm 106:1 to the children.*)

Class: (*Sing* "O Give Thanks.")

Repeat this activity, giving as many children as possible an opportunity to participate.

Doctrinal emphasis: Angels

➤ Where do angels come from? *(God created angels.)* We don't know when. The Bible doesn't tell us. But we know that God created the angels before He created the world. Angels are not like us. They do not have bodies as we have.

Angels are very wise; they know many things. Angels do different works for God. Some angels take care of God's throne; some fight sin and Satan for God. All good angels serve God in a special way. All angels worship and praise God. The Bible tells us that angels even help us. They take care of us even though we cannot see them.

Do you remember what we learned about Satan? Who is Satan? *(Catechism 27: Satan is an evil spirit who is the enemy of God and all Christians.)* Yes, he was one of God's angels. His name was Lucifer when he lived in heaven. What happened? One day the angel Lucifer became jealous of God. He wanted to be as great as God. So God made Lucifer leave heaven. God changed Lucifer's name to Satan. Satan is God's enemy. Satan hates God. Satan wants everyone else to hate God. Who is stronger, God or Satan? *(Catechism 28: God is stronger.)*

Who is Gabriel? *(The angel that God sent to tell Mary that she was going to have a very special baby in a very special way.)* Who was that baby? *(God's Son)* Why did He come from heaven to this world? *(to be our Savior from sin)* Do you think Satan was happy to see God's Son come to this world as our Savior? Does Satan want God's will to be done? *(Catechism 29: No, Satan always wants people to do the opposite of what God wants them to do.)*

Gabriel's name means "mighty one of God." Gabriel was God's special messenger to bring good news. He is an angel of joy that stands in the presence of God in heaven.

Why do you think we decorate our homes with angels at Christmas time? *(to remind us of the angel that brought the good news of God's Son)*

Song: "Gabriel Told"

Lesson 76: God Sent His Son

Bible texts: Matthew 1:20–21; Luke 2:1–7

Doctrinal truths: God the Son; Salvation

Character traits: Wisdom; Trust

Memory verses: Review John 3:16 and Luke 2:11.

Catechism: Review Catechism 26–29.

Materials
- Cardboard, wood, or ceramic nativity pieces
- Doll wrapped in strips of cloth—swaddling bands (You may prefer to use picture visuals from a flannel-graph Christmas series.)
- Student page 23 and cutouts
- Scissors
- Glue

Opening chorus: "Ring the Bells"

Song: "How Do We Know?" stanza 2

Prayer
Thank God for His Son, who is the way to heaven.

Catechism
Review Catechism 26–29.

■ What is sin? *(Sin is the transgression of the law of God.)*

➤ Does God want us to sin? *(no)* When we disobey Mother or Daddy, is that sin? *(yes)* God's Word tells us, "Children, obey your parents." When we are unkind to someone, is that sin? *(yes)* God's Word tells us, "Be ye kind one to another."

■ Who is Satan? *(Satan is an evil spirit who is the enemy of God and all Christians)*

■ Who is stronger, God or Satan? *(God is stronger.)*

➤ When we do not do what God tells us to do, we sin or transgress God's law. When we do something that God tells us not to do, we sin or transgress God's law. *Transgression* is another word for sin.

God's Son came to show the power of God, that God is stronger than Satan.

■ Does Satan want God's will to be done? *(No, Satan always wants people to do the opposite of what God wants them to do.)*

➤ Did Satan want the Lord Jesus to come to be the Savior of the world? *(no)* Does Satan wants us to obey God and trust God's Son? *(no)*

Song: "Christmas Is a Happy Time"

Memory verses
Review John 3:16 with the song "John 3:16" and Luke 2:11 with a choral-response activity. Divide the class into three or four groups and have each group recite portions of the verse in sequence.

Bible lesson
As you tell this story, add pieces (Mary, Joseph, angel, stable, manger, animals, Christ child) to the nativity scene. Show the doll wrapped in pieces of cloth to illustrate "swaddling clothes."

Introduction
➤ Mary and Joseph both knew that God was sending them His Son to take care of. The angel Gabriel told Mary, and an angel also told Joseph the good news. Mary and Joseph looked forward to the time when the baby would be born. All babies are gifts from God. Everyone loves little babies. But God's Son was to be the most special baby of all. And God's Son was to be born in a very

special way. Even though Joseph was Mary's husband, he was not the father of Jesus. Our Lord had no earthly father; His father is God, the heavenly Father.

Lesson

Long ago when Mary and Joseph lived, the ruler of their land gave an order. This ruler was the leader of a great land. He had decided that he wanted to know how many people lived in his land. He said everyone should go to his hometown, the place where he was born, to be counted. When the people got to their hometowns, they were to tell their names, what kind of work they did, and how many family members lived in their homes. They were also to tell what they owned, such as a donkey, a house, or a camel. Then the tax collector would tell them how much money they should pay the ruler of the land. This was called tax money. Our mothers and fathers still pay taxes today.

So Joseph took Mary and went toward Bethlehem where he had been born. Bethlehem is sometimes called the "city of David" because it was the place where King David was born many, many years before. Since David grew up to be the king and was such an important man, everyone called his hometown—the town where he was born—"the city of David." Mary and Joseph were in the family of David. That means David would have been their great, great (and we could add many more "greats") grandfather.

Mary and Joseph had traveled for a long time. They were tired. "Clippety-clop, clippety-clop" is the sound the donkey made as he walked along the road carrying Mary.

> Although there is no Scriptural evidence that Mary rode on a donkey, the custom of the day was that people relied heavily on the donkey for transportation.

It was almost time for the baby to be born. Finally they reached Bethlehem. Quickly, Joseph began to look for a place to stay for the night. He knocked on the door of an inn where people who were traveling could sleep for the night. An inn is like a hotel. The innkeeper came to the door. He said, "I'm sorry; my rooms are all full. I don't have any rooms left at all."

The innkeeper saw that Mary was going to have a baby soon. He knew she was tired and needed to rest; so he said, "You may make a bed in the hay out in the stable where I keep my animals."

Mary and Joseph did not have much money, and they were very tired. They were very happy for any place to rest—even with the animals. They piled up some hay for a bed and lay down to sleep.

Outside the inn the stars shone brightly; the nighttime was quiet, but soon, inside the stable, there was a tiny sound. (Pause and then whisper.) A baby's cry! God's Son was born. God had kept His promise.

Mary and Joseph thanked God for His Gift. They wrapped the baby in pieces of cloth, called swaddling clothes. (Display doll wrapped in strips of cloth.) Then they laid the tiny baby in a manger, a feeding place for the animals.

Sing "Away in a Manger," verse 1, pretending to rock a baby in your arms.

Student page 23

Instruct the children to cut out the pictures of baby Jesus and the shepherds. Direct them to glue the pictures in place. Recite or sing "John 3:16" and read the sentence.

Lesson 77: Angel Messengers Told of the Way

Bible text: Luke 2:8–20

Doctrinal truths: God the Son; Angels; Church

Character trait: Love

Memory verses: Review John 3:16 and Luke 2:11.

Materials
• Shepherd figures to add to nativity scene begun in Lesson 76

Opening chorus: "Ring the Bells"

Song: "Jesus Christ Is Born"

Song: "Christmas Is a Happy Time"

Prayer
Thank God that Jesus loved us so much that He left His heavenly home to come to die on the cross for us.

Song: "Jesus, Born in Bethlehem," stanzas 1–2

Bible lesson

Introduction
➤ Angels are God's messengers. God sent an angel to tell Joseph about the coming Savior. God sent Gabriel to tell Mary about the coming Savior. Gabriel was a bringer of joy and good news. His name means "the mighty one of God." Today we'll hear how other angels told of the birth of God's Son.

Lesson
Read Luke 2:8–16 slowly and with much expression. You might add "of sheep" after "flock" in verse 8 and "of many, many angels" after "host" in verse 13.

This is a beautiful story from our Bible. It tells us that some shepherds were out on a hillside at night taking care of their flocks of sheep.

The night was beautiful and quiet with stars shining all around in the sky. These shepherds were on a hillside near the little town of Bethlehem. They were near the very same place where David the shepherd boy had taken care of his sheep many years before.

Suddenly there was a bright, shiny light all around the shepherds. Then the shepherds saw an angel sent from God. The angel said, "Don't be afraid; I bring you good news. God has kept His promise. He has sent the Savior. You will find the holy Baby wrapped in swaddling clothes lying in a manger in Bethlehem, which is called 'the city of David.'"

Suddenly there was a big choir of angels praising God. They sang, "Glory to God in the highest."

When the angels had gone away, the shepherds said, "Let's go to Bethlehem right now and see what the angels have told us."

So they hurried toward Bethlehem, and when they found Mary, Joseph, and the Baby, they praised and thanked God for His love. (Add shepherds to the nativity scene.)

When they returned to their work and their homes, they told everyone about the good news of God's Son.

Application
➤ God loves us very much. We should remember to tell our friends that God sent His Son at Christmas time many years ago to be our Savior from sin. (BAT: 5c Evangelism and missions)

Song: "Away in a Manger"

Memory verses
Review John 3:16 and Luke 2:11.

Song: "Shepherds Came"
Lead the children in pretending to be shepherds as they march around the nativity scene and sing the four stanzas of the song.

➤ As soon as the shepherds saw the newborn Savior, they went out to tell the good news. We have heard about God's Son in our homes, in Sunday school and church, and at school. God wants us to tell this good news to others. He wants us to tell others that Jesus is the way to heaven. (BAT: 5c Evangelism and missions)

Lesson 78: Wise Men Brought Gifts

Bible text: Matthew 2:1–23
Doctrinal truth: Salvation (sanctification)
Character trait: Giving
Memory verses: Review John 3:16 and Luke 2:11.
Materials
• Foil star to hang above nativity scene
• Wise men to place near (but not in) the nativity scene

Opening chorus: "Ring the Bells"

Song: "Away in a Manger"

Memory verses
Review John 3:16 and Luke 2:11.

Song: "John 3:16"

Prayer
Ask God to help us show Him and others that we love Him by giving some of what we have to others.

Song: "Jesus, Born in Bethlehem," stanzas 1 and 3

Bible lesson

Introduction
Lead the action rhyme "God's Star."

➤ God's star so bright,
See up high.
(Cup hands around eyes for binoculars.)
God's star twinkling,
Up in the sky.
(Reach high on tiptoes.)

Lesson

When Jesus was born in Bethlehem, there were wise men who lived in a faraway land. These men studied many books and had learned many things.

These wise men had probably heard God's people tell about God's promised Son. They had learned much about the stars in God's sky. They may have heard about the "Star out of Jacob" who was to be the Savior of the world (Numbers 24:17). The Star of Jacob is another name for God's Son.

One day when these men were looking at the stars in the sky, they saw a bright, bright star—a star so bright that they thought it might be the star that God had promised to send to tell of His Son's birth. The wise men followed God's star. The star did not stand still. It moved before them.

They went to the big city of Jerusalem. Now, there was a wicked king who lived in Jerusalem. His name was Herod. The wise men did not know how wicked King Herod was, so they went to him. They asked the king, "Where is He that is born to be King of the Jews? We have seen His star from far, far away. We want to see this new king and worship Him."

Herod answered that he did not know anything about the new king. So he called for the leaders and teachers from the temple in Jerusalem. The teachers told Herod what God's Word said about His Son's birth. They told the king that the Son of God was to be born in a small town called Bethlehem.

So Herod told the wise men to go to Bethlehem. The king said, "When you have found the king, come back and tell me where He is so that I may go worship Him also."

When the wise men learned that God's Son was not in the big city of Jerusalem, they followed the star on to the little town of Bethlehem, which was very near Jerusalem. The star showed them the way to a house, not the manger. Joseph had moved his family from the stable near the inn to a house in Bethlehem. When the wise men came to the house, they saw the Holy Child, the Son of God, and His mother, Mary. When the wise men saw God's Son, they bowed down and worshiped Him.

These wise men brought God's Son special gifts. One of the gifts was gold. (Point to gold in a ring.) The gold reminds us that Christ is King of heaven and earth. Everything belongs to our God. The other gifts were frankincense and myrrh—these are perfumes. The frankincense reminds us that the Lord Jesus is holy and without sin. The myrrh reminds us that God's Son died for our sin. The wise men gave these gifts to God's Son to show Him that they loved Him.

That night, after the wise men had worshiped the Christ Child, they went to bed. God spoke to them in a dream. He said, "Do not go back to Jerusalem to tell Herod where the Christ Child is." God knew that Herod was wicked and jealous of the newborn King. He knew Herod wanted to kill the Baby Jesus.

So the wise men obeyed God. They avoided Jerusalem and went back to their home another way.

Application
➤ The wise men showed how great God's Son was when they worshiped Him and gave gifts to Him. God wants us to tell Him we love Him by praying. He wants us to show Him that we love Him by giving to Him and sharing Him with others. (BATs: 5b Giving; 6b Prayer)

Song: "Wise Men Came"

Song: "My Gift"

Lesson 79: Christmas Brings Joy

Bible texts: Matthew 1:20–21; 2:1–11; Luke 1:26–28; 2:1–20
Doctrinal truths: God the Son; Salvation
Character traits: Giving; Thankfulness
Memory verses: Review John 3:16 and Luke 2:11.
Catechism: Review Catechism 27–29.
Materials
• Nativity figures (flannelboard, card stock, or ceramic)
• Vick family puppets

Opening chorus: "Ring the Bells"

Song: "Away in a Manger"

Action rhyme: "My Gift"
Recite the song, "My Gift," as an action rhyme.

➤ What can I give Him
   (*Stretch out your hands and turn your palms up.*)
   Poor as I am;
   (*Pretend to turn your pockets inside out.*)
   If I were a shepherd,
   (*Pretend to hold a staff.*)
   I would give Him a lamb.
   (*Fold your arms across your waist and pretend to carry something.*)
   If I were a wise man,
   (*Form a crown by holding your hands in a "halo" above your head.*)
   I would do my part.
   (*Kneel and pretend to offer a gift.*)
   But what can I give Him?
   (*Point to yourself.*)
   I will give my heart.
   (*Draw a heart shape in the air.*)
                                    –*Christina Rossetti*

Song: "My Gift"
Discuss how we can give our lives by, for example, obeying God's Word, sharing, and telling others about God's Son.

Song: "O Come and Let Us Worship"

➤ The wise men worshiped the newborn Savior. We can worship God's Son, our Savior, who is the way to heaven.

Review the meaning of "worship": to pray, to sing, to listen to God's Word, to give money so that other people can hear about God. (BAT: 7c Praise)

Prayer

Thank God for Christmas and for giving His Son.

Review activity

Quickly and secretly remove a piece from the nativity scene (e.g., shepherd, angel, star, wise man, manger). Choose a child to tell what is missing. Allow him to review the part of the Christmas story that the piece reminds him of. Continue the review with other children participating, using other objects.

Include review of John 3:16 (with manger) and Luke 2:11 (with shepherd) in this activity. Also, when the angel is picked, remind the children that Satan was once an angel created by God, but because of his sin, God made him leave heaven. Then review Catechism 27–29.

- Who is Satan? (*Satan is an evil spirit who is the enemy of God and all Christians.*)

- Who is stronger, God or Satan? (*God is stronger.*)

- Does Satan want God's will to be done? (*No, Satan always wants people to do the opposite of what God wants them to do.*)

Character story: "He Did Come"

Everyone in the Vick family was busy with Christmas preparations. Dad took Sam and Josh to look for a Christmas tree. While Mom was baking Christmas cakes and cookies in the kitchen, Kate sat at the table coloring, cutting, and pasting. She scooted back in her chair to rest and look over the three Christmas cards she had already completed.

On Grandma and Grandpa Vick's card she had drawn a church and then glued tiny bits of cotton on the blue sky above it to make it look like falling snow. On Grandma Brown's card was a manger to remind her of Baby Jesus' birth. Kate had very neatly placed some sheep and cow stickers around the manger on the card.

Best of all, Kate liked her angel card. She had made it for their neighbor, Mrs. Babb. She had drawn several angels on the blue construction paper and had sprinkled some shiny glitter all around the card. It reminded her of her kindergarten verse: "For unto you is born this day in the city of David a Savior, which is Christ the Lord" (Luke 2:11).

She thought, "How happy the shepherds must have been to hear the angel choir's good news." Christmas was such a happy time in her home because her family loved the Son of God who had come to be their Savior. Suddenly she thought, "What if the Lord Jesus had not come!" She thought it so hard that she whispered out loud, "What if Jesus had not come?"

"What did you say, Kate?" her mother asked.

"Uh, well, I was just wondering about something. What if Jesus had not come down from His home in heaven to be our Savior? What would it be like?"

"Well, for one thing, Dad and your brothers would not be out looking for a tree to decorate. We always have an evergreen tree at Christmas to remind us of the eternal life we can have because God sent His Son at Christmas time. And you would not be drawing a picture of a church for Grandma Vick on a Christmas card, either. There would be no churches where we could sing, pray, and hear lessons from the Bible about God's Son. I wouldn't be baking these Christmas goodies for the people at the nursing home because we wouldn't have this special Christmas time to remember by giving to others.

"The saddest thing is that we would not have the home in heaven waiting for us—the one that Jesus promised to build for those of us who ask Him to be our Savior from sin."

Suddenly, Mom stopped talking and listened. There was music coming from somewhere.

It was the choir from the church down the street. They were practicing to go caroling.

Kate ran over and hugged her mother as she whispered, "And there would be no beautiful Christmas songs to sing either. Oh, Mom, let's just bow our heads right this minute and thank God that Jesus did come . . . that 'God so loved the world, that he gave his only begotten Son, that whosoever believeth in Him should not perish, but have everlasting life.'"

Lesson 80: The Best Birthday

Bible text: Review.

Doctrinal truth: God the Son

Character traits: Wisdom; Thankfulness

Catechism: Review Catechism 1–29.

Materials
- Student page 24 and cutouts
- Scissors
- Glue
- Question Mark visual (Draw a large question mark on poster board. Make or punch holes in the question mark and insert into the holes 2- to 3-inch segments of drinking straws, each labeled with a number from 1 to 29.)

Opening chorus: "Ring the Bells"

Song: "Away in a Manger"

Prayer

Allow the children to share prayer requests.

Character story: "My Best Friend"

It was the week before Christmas and all of the Hunters were busy. Mr. and Mrs. Hunter and the children had arrived at Grandpa and Grandma Hunter's house two days before. This was a special time for the Hunters. It was special because they would spend the next few days getting ready to celebrate Jesus' birth. Just as they had done for as long as Dave could remember, he and his family had come to the farm to help Grandpa and Grandma decorate and get ready for Christmas Day. Early Christmas morning all his aunts, uncles, and cousins would begin arriving for a fun-filled day of caroling, games, and delicious food. But these few days before Christmas were the days Dave liked best. It was fun spending so much time with Grandma and Grandpa. There was shopping to do, a Christmas tree to find, decorations to put up, and lots of cooking and baking to be done. Each day everyone would become more excited as the house began to look and smell more like Christmas.

Yesterday Dave had gone with Grandpa, Dad, and Grant to look for a Christmas tree while Mom and Grandma had strung popcorn and cranberries. The tree was so big that Grandpa and Dad could barely get it in the door.

This morning Christmas music floated through the house as everyone looked forward to decorating the tree.

After breakfast, Grandpa and Dad put the lights on the tree while Mom and the children helped Grandma clean the kitchen. Then everyone helped trim the tree. Mom and Grandma carefully draped the long strands of popcorn and cranberries around the tree. Grant and Dave put on the ornaments, helped by Dad and Grandpa who hung ornaments on the higher branches. Even Abby was able to hang some ornaments on the lower branches with Mom's help.

When all the ornaments had been hung, everyone found a comfortable seat and quietly looked on while Grandma carefully unpacked the pieces of the manger scene. Gently she placed each piece in exactly the right place under the tree. The manger was placed in the center of the stable, Mary kneeling on one side while Joseph stood lovingly taking in the precious sight. The shepherds appeared to be walking towards the stable eager to see the special babe of whom they had heard the angels sing. An angel, hovering from a branch, was right over the place where Jesus would lay. But the manger would remain empty until Christmas Eve when the family would gather around the tree and listen to Grandpa read the Christmas story. Then Grandma would tenderly lay the Baby Jesus in the manger while everyone sang "Silent Night."

Now lunch was finished. The house was quiet and Abby was taking a nap. Grandma and Mom were busy making Christmas cookies. Soon the house would be filled with the aroma of cinnamon and gingerbread.

This was one of Dave's favorite times. This was when he and Grandpa would curl up on the sofa and admire the tree. Grandma would bring them some freshly baked cookies and some nice cold milk. Then Grandpa would read a story. After the story, he and Grandpa would have a quiet talk. Today Grandpa asked Dave a question. "Now that the tree is decorated, what else do you plan to do while you are here, Dave?" Dave thought carefully. "I am going to celebrate the birthday of my very best friend," replied Dave. "You are? And whose birthday would that be?" Grandpa asked with a twinkle in his eye. "Why Jesus, Grandpa! You remember when I asked Jesus to be my Savior last summer don't you, Grandpa?" Grandpa nodded. "Well, that makes Jesus my best friend. Next week, when we celebrate Christmas, we will be celebrating the birthday of my best friend. That's the best birthday of all!"

Song: "Happy Birthday to You"

Sing "Happy Birthday to You," inserting the words "dear Jesus" at the end of the third line.

Student page 24

Instruct the children to cut out the Christmas story sequence pictures. Referring to the bells in the spaces for placement, guide the children in gluing the pictures in order on the Christmas wreath. Reinforce the important fact that Christ came from heaven to die for our sin. Read and discuss the page. (BAT: 1a Understanding Jesus Christ)

Song: "John 3:16"

Catechism

Use the Question Mark visual to review Catechism 1–29 as time allows. After a child pulls out a straw from the visual and reads the number on it, ask the corresponding catechism question and allow the child to answer it.

Lesson 81: Review—Christmas

Bible text: Review.

Doctrinal truth: God the Son

Character traits: Wisdom; Thankfulness

Memory verses: Review.

Catechism: Review Catechism 1–29.

Materials
- Two Christmas trees cut from poster board (or small artificial trees)
- Christmas stickers (or tree ornaments)
- Student page 25
- Yellow and blue crayons
- Glue
- A completed copy of Student page 4 (for use as a visual; used in Lesson 17)

Opening chorus: "Ring the Bells"

Prayer
Thank the Lord for His best Gift.

Student page 25
Read the two sentences aloud.

➤ How did the wise men find the baby Jesus?

➤ Use a yellow crayon to color all the shapes that have a 1, 2, or 3 inside. Use a blue crayon to color all the shapes that have a 4 or 5 inside.

Review the story of the wise men as the children color the star puzzle. Remind the children that the wise men came to worship Jesus. Review the aspects of worship, using the completed copy of Student page 4.

Song: "Away in a Manger"

Review activity
Display Christmas trees and provide stickers/ornaments. As a child answers a review question, have him place a sticker on his team's tree.

1. What was the name of Jesus' mother? *(Mary)*

2. What was the name of the angel who came to tell Mary of Jesus' birth? *(Gabriel)*

3. Who is Jesus' Father? *(God)*

4. What is the name of the man that God chose to be Mary's husband and to help Mary take care of Jesus? *(Joseph)*

5. What town was Jesus born in? *(Bethlehem)*

6. Why did Mary and Joseph go to Bethlehem? *(The king said everyone was to go to the city where they were born to be counted.)*

7. Who told the shepherds of Jesus' birth? *(angels)*

8. Give the Bible reference for "For God so loved the world." *(John 3:16)*

9. Quote Luke 2:11.

10. Sing your choice of one of the Christmas choruses we have learned. *(The whole team may join in.)*

11. What does the name "Jesus" mean? *(Savior)*

12. Who gave Him that name? *(God)*

13. Whose Savior is He? *(everyone who will believe)*

14. Where was Jesus before He came to Earth? *(heaven)*

15. Why did Jesus come to Earth? *(to die; to take the punishment for our sin; to save us from our sin)*

16. What did He leave behind in heaven? *(beautiful home, His Father, angels, glory, and riches)*

17. Who followed the star to where Jesus was? *(the wise men)*

18. What gifts did the wise men bring the Christ Child? *(gold, frankincense, and myrrh)*

19. What big city did the wise men go to first to look for Jesus? *(Jerusalem)*

20. Who in Jerusalem did the wise men ask about the new-born King? *(King Herod)*

21. Where did the Jewish teachers say Jesus was to be born, according to the Old Testament Scriptures? *(Bethlehem—Micah 5:2)*

22. Where were Mary, Joseph, and Jesus when the wise men found them? *(in a house)*

23. Did the wise men go back to tell King Herod where the Christ Child was? *(no)*

24. Why not? *(God came to them in a dream and warned them that Herod wanted to hurt Jesus.)*

Review memory verses and catechism as time allows.

God's Helpers

Joshua to Jonah: I Will Help

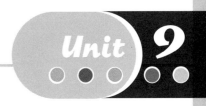
Lesson 82: Captain Joshua

Bible texts: Joshua 1–4; Psalm 91:15; Isaiah 58:9a; Jeremiah 33:3

Doctrinal truth: God (omnipotence)

Character trait: Courage

Memory verse: Introduce Joshua 1:9.

Catechism: Review Catechism 16.

Materials
• "Crossing the Jordan" (Picture Packet)

Opening chorus: "I Will Trust in Thee"

Song: "What Does the Bible Say?" stanza 2

Song: "My Bible Book," stanza 5

Prayer

Thank God that He is always with us.

➤ Do you know that God always hears us when we pray? Yes, He promises many times in the Bible that He hears us. Listen while I read some of these promises.

Read Isaiah 58:9a; Psalm 91:15; Jeremiah 33:3.

Does God always do what He says He will do? *(yes)* Let's thank God that He always hears us when we pray.

Song: "My Bible Book"
Replace "He loves me, He loves me" with "He hears me, He hears me."

Bible lesson

Introduction

➤ Remember how God chose Moses to lead His people out of the land of Egypt? When God's leader Moses died, God chose another leader to lead His people. He spoke to Joshua, who had already served God as a helper to Moses. God told Joshua that He wanted him to lead His people—the children of Israel—back into the land that He had promised to Abraham, Isaac, and Jacob.

God told Joshua to go across the Jordan River and conquer the land—to take it because it belonged to the Israelites. God had already given it to them.

God promised Joshua that He would be with him and take care of him, just as He had been with Moses and had taken care of him. God said, "Be strong and of a good courage; be not afraid . . . for the Lord your God is with you whithersoever you go."

Lesson

So Joshua commanded his soldiers, "Tell our people to prepare food for a trip, because in three days we are going to pass through the Jordan River to go in and conquer the land God has given to us."

Joshua told his men that they were going to leave the women, children, and their cattle behind while they crossed over the river to fight for their land.

And the men answered Joshua, "All that you command us we will do, and wherever you send us, we will go. We will obey you just as we obeyed God's leader, Moses."

So Joshua sent two men to secretly spy out the land of Jericho—which is where the Israelites were going—and see how many soldiers there were and how strong they were. When the spies returned, they told Joshua that the king of Jericho and his people were afraid of them because they heard how God had taken care of the Israelites and had brought them out of Egypt.

So Joshua led his people to the Jordan River. God told Joshua to order the priests who took care of the house of God to take the ark of the covenant and walk into the river. Remember, the ark was a special sign to remind God's people that He was with them. (Display "Crossing the Jordan" picture.)

As the men who carried the ark stepped into the water of the Jordan River, God worked another great miracle. He caused the water from both sides to back up so that while these men stood there, Joshua's army, and later, all of God's people, could walk through the river on dry ground.

Later, when all the people had crossed the river, the Lord told Joshua to choose twelve men to take twelve stones from the river. These stones would be placed on the other side of the river. Another set of stones would be placed in the river where the priests had stood. He said that this was to remind the people of God's great power. When the Israelites saw these stones in years to come, they would remember how God had held back the water so that they could walk across the Jordan River.

Application

➤ What an exciting story! That reminds me of how God helped His people cross the Red Sea. Our God is a great and powerful God. Can God do all things? *(Catechism 16: Yes, God can do all His holy will.)* God had a plan for the children of Israel, and He told them not to be afraid. He promised to be with them and take care of them.

Is our God the same God who took care of Joshua and the children of Israel? Does God have a plan for our lives? Will He always be with us and help us not to be afraid when we have hard things to do? *(Allow discussion.)* (BAT: 8d Courage)

Memory verse

Read Joshua 1:9 from your Bible.

➤ God is telling us, "Haven't I told you? Be strong and have courage. Don't be afraid, don't be fearful; because I am with you wherever you go."

Recite the verse again.

➤ This is one of God's promises. This is what God told Joshua, the new leader of His people. Remember that when Moses died and God took his soul to heaven, God told Joshua to be the new leader for His people.

Instruct the children to recite the first part of the verse several times with you. Ask the children to think of things they are sometimes afraid of or something that may be hard for them to do.

After the children share their responses, have the class recite Joshua 1:9 together.

Song: "When I Am Afraid"

Lesson 83: Battle of Jericho

Bible text: Joshua 5:13–6:20

Doctrinal truth: God

Character traits: Trust; Obedience

Memory verse: Review Joshua 1:9.

Materials
• Dave, Abby, and Mom Hunter puppets
• Several toy blocks (optional)
• Kazoo (See Lesson 61.)
• "Battle of Jericho" (Picture Packet)

Opening chorus: "I Will Trust in Thee"

Song: "My Bible Book," stanza 5

Memory verse

Review Joshua 1:9. Repeat the activity from Lesson 82.

Song: "My Bible Book"
Replace "He loves me, He loves me" with "Be brave, be brave."

Prayer

Thank God for being with Moses and Joshua many years ago and for helping them to be brave servants.

Bible lesson

Introduction

Use the Dave, Abby, and Mom Hunter puppets. You may want to place a few blocks to form a square wall around which you march the Dave and Abby puppets.

➤ Dave and Abby built a wall in the den with their blocks. They then stood up and began to march around the wall of blocks.

"Once," Abby said, and Dave blew his horn. (Blow kazoo.)

"Twice," Abby said, and Dave blew his horn again. (Blow kazoo.)

"They marched around three four . . . five . . . six . . . and finally seven times," Abby continued.

And each time they walked around the block wall, Dave blew his horn. (Blow kazoo.) But after the seventh march around the block wall, they both shouted as loudly as they could.

Mom came rushing from the kitchen into the room. "What's the matter?" she said. "What happened?"

Abby and Dave looked surprised. Abby answered, "Oh, we're sorry, Mom. We forgot we were inside. We were playing the story about Jericho, and we were marching like God's soldiers. And, well, Joshua told God's people to shout as loud as they could on the seventh day after they had gone around the wall seven times. You know that Bible story, Mom."

Mom smiled at Dave and Abby and said, "I surely do. What happened after the people shouted?"

"The walls came tumbling down!" Dave and Abby shouted together. "I just love that Bible story," said Dave.

Lesson

After Joshua had led the Israelites across the Jordan River, they pitched their tents near the city of Jericho. While they were there, they had the Passover supper as God had told them. They remembered the night God brought them out of Egypt. Since then, they had wandered in the wilderness for forty years. Oh, how happy they were to be in this special land that God had given them! Now they wouldn't need the manna God sent them from heaven. Instead, they could eat the fresh fruits and vegetables that grew in their new land of Canaan.

As the people looked at the strong wall that went all the way around the city of Jericho, some of them must have wondered, "How will we ever conquer that city?"

But the Lord God had a plan. He told Joshua that He, the Lord God of heaven, would be the Captain of His people's army, and His people would conquer the city of Jericho if they obeyed His commands. And then God told them what He wanted them to do. (Display "Battle of Jericho" picture.)

The soldiers were to march all the way around the walls outside the city, one time each day for six days. Each day the priests were to blow their trumpets. (You may add sound effects with a kazoo at the appropriate times throughout the lesson.) And Joshua told the rest of the people to be very quiet and not to make a sound. On the seventh day, the Lord said that the soldiers were to march around the city seven times; then the priests were to carry the ark of the covenant and blow their trumpets. When God's people heard long, loud trumpet sounds, they were all to shout as loud as they could.

So that's what they did. The first day the soldiers lined up to follow Joshua as they marched around the walls of Jericho. Then the priests blew their horns and the people were very quiet. At the end of the day, they all went back to their tents.

The second day they marched—tramp, tramp, tramp, tramp—around the walls of the city. Again the trumpets blew and everyone was quiet. On the third, fourth, fifth, and sixth days, they again marched around the walls, blew their trumpets, and then became quiet.

Then on the seventh day, as God commanded, they lined up again—the soldiers, the priests with their trumpets, and last of all the priests carrying the ark of the covenant from the tabernacle.

Tramp, tramp, tramp, tramp—they marched around once, blew the trumpets, and (whisper) not a word was spoken.

Tramp, tramp, tramp, tramp—they marched around twice, blew the trumpets, and (whisper) not a word was spoken.

They marched four more times around the city, each time following God's instructions. They were now ready for the seventh march around the walls of the city.

Tramp, tramp, tramp, tramp they marched, and the trumpets blew. Joshua then said to the people, (increase volume) "Shout! for the Lord has given you the city!"

And God's people shouted loudly, and the walls around the city fell down to the ground so that the people could walk across them. At last they had captured the city.

Application

➤ That was an exciting lesson, wasn't it? Would you have been afraid to march around a strong city where brave soldiers lived? God promised His people that if they would obey Him and do just what He told them, He would win the battle for them. They trusted and obeyed God, and He kept His promise. (BAT: 8a Faith in God's promises)

Song: "Trust and Obey"

Lesson 84: Joshua and the Battle of Jericho

Bible text: Joshua 1–6 (review)

Doctrinal truth: God

Character traits: Trust; Obedience

Memory verse: Review Joshua 1:9.

Catechism: Review Catechism 16.

Materials
- Blocks or empty milk or juice cartons to build walls for the city of Jericho. Masking tape may be used to simulate the lines of Jericho's walls on the floor.
- Kazoos (See Lesson 61.)
- Student page 26

Opening chorus: "I Will Trust in Thee"

Song: "Be Ye Doers of the Word," stanzas 1 and 4

Prayer
Ask God to help us to be brave when we have hard things to do.

Memory verse
Let the children take turns blowing a kazoo before and after they recite Joshua 1:9.

Song: "Obedience Is"

Review activity: Role play
Lead the children in reenacting the battle of Jericho. Use blocks to "build" the walls of Jericho. Choose children to speak and to pantomime the actions of the following characters and blow their kazoos as you read the narration.

Characters: Joshua, Priests (no more than seven), Soldiers, and People

➤ Narrator: And the Lord said unto Joshua, "Be strong and of good courage; be not afraid, neither be dismayed; for the Lord your God is with you wherever you go."

All of the soldiers shall go around the city of Jericho once each day for six days. The priests will follow and then blow their trumpets.

On the first day, Joshua led the parade of priests and soldiers to march around the walls of Jericho one time. The priests blew their trumpets and all the people were very quiet—(whisper) they didn't say a word. They then went back to their camp.

On the second day, they marched around the city *once* and the priests blew the trumpets. They then returned to camp. The people marched this way on the third day, the fourth day, the fifth day, and the sixth day.

On the seventh day, they rose early in the morning and marched around the city *seven* times and when the priests blew their trumpets the seventh time, Joshua said unto the people,

Joshua: "Shout, for the Lord has given you the city."

Narrator: So the people shouted with a great shout.

People: (shout)

Narrator: And the walls of Jericho fell down flat, and the people went into the city over the walls and captured the city. Can God do all things?

People: Yes, God can do all His holy will. (Catechism 16)

Student page 26

Read and discuss the page. Guide the children as they use their pencils to track around the walls of Jericho seven times.

Lesson 85: David, the Shepherd

Bible texts: I Samuel 16:11; 17:34–36; Psalm 23; John 10:3–5

Doctrinal truth: God (faithfulness)

Character traits: Diligence; Trust

Memory verse: Introduce Psalm 23:1.

Catechism: Review Catechism 13 and 14.

Materials
• A completed copy of "The Lord is My Shepherd" booklet—Student pages 28–30 (for use as a visual)
• "David the Shepherd Boy" (Picture Packet)

Opening chorus: "I Will Trust in Thee"

Prayer

Thank God that He takes care of us like a shepherd takes care of his sheep.

Song: "Savior, Like a Shepherd Lead Us," stanza 1

Use "The Lord is My Shepherd" booklet as a visual. Introduce additional stanzas during the unit if time permits.

Memory verse

Introduce Psalm 23:1 by reading it from your Bible. Tell the children that God told David to write these verses in the Bible. Remind them that if they love the Lord, He is their

Good Shepherd, and He takes care of them like a shepherd takes care of his lambs and sheep. Instruct them to recite the verse with you several times.

Tell the following story, "My Shepherd."

A Scottish minister was teaching a small boy to read the Twenty-third Psalm in the home of one of his parishioners. The little boy began, "The Lord is my Shepherd."

The old minister interrupted him. He said, "No, no, you don't read it right!"

Again, the little boy began. Slowly and earnestly, he said, "The Lord is my Shepherd."

"No, you don't read it right," said the old minister. "Now watch me." The minister held up his left hand. He placed the forefinger of his right hand on the thumb of his left hand and said, "The!" Then he placed the forefinger of his right hand on the next finger and said, "Lord!" Then, he placed it on his third finger and said, "Is!" And then, grasping hold of the fourth finger of his left hand, he said, "My! You take hold of the fourth finger and say, 'My.' "

"Oh," cried the little boy, "I see. It's 'The Lord is MY Shepherd.' " *(1,001 Stories for Children and Children's Workers)*

Song: "The Lord Is My Shepherd"

Song: "I'm His Little Child"

Replace the last word of each stanza, "child," with the word "lamb."

Catechism

Review Catechism 13–14.

■ Where is God? *(God is everywhere.)*

■ Can you see God? *(No, I cannot see God, but He always sees me.)*

Song: "God Is with Me"

➤ God is always with us. Our heavenly Father sees all that we do. God is everywhere. He knows when we do our work well, and that pleases Him.

Bible lesson

Introduction

➤ Do you know what a shepherd is? Yes, he is someone who takes care of his sheep. Do you know that a good shepherd names each of his sheep and little lambs? A lamb is a baby sheep. A shepherd knows each one, and he even calls each by its own name.

A good shepherd also leads his sheep. He goes in front of them, and his sheep follow him. The shepherd takes them to safe places. He takes them where there are little streams of water from which to drink.

A good shepherd is brave. He protects his sheep from their enemies, from wild animals, such as lions and bears that might try to catch them and eat them. A good shepherd is kind to his sheep. He puts medicine on the sores and scratches that his sheep get from sharp rocks and thorns. A good shepherd builds a special home for his sheep called a sheepfold. At night he takes his sheep into their sheepfold to sleep.

Sheep love the shepherd who takes care of them. They even know his voice. If another shepherd calls them, they will not follow him. They know it is not the voice of their own shepherd. But when their shepherd calls, they know his voice, and they follow him where he leads them.

Lesson

Display "David the Shepherd Boy" picture.

> Our Bible lesson today is about a young boy named David. David took care of his father's sheep. Now young David was a good shepherd.

> He listened and learned from his father. He learned what a good shepherd should do for his sheep, and he did it. David worked hard and did his job well. He knew his sheep; he was kind to his sheep. He was a brave shepherd.

> One day when David was out in the country on a grassy hillside, a lion sneaked up quietly and tried to steal one of the lambs. David heard the little bleating "baa-baa" of the lamb's voice.

> David loved his lambs. He knew it was his job to protect them. So brave David ran to where he heard the sound. He saw a lion with one of his lambs, and he killed the lion. What a brave, young shepherd David was!

> The Bible also tells us that later, another enemy tried to steal a lamb from David's flock. This time it was a bear. In the country where David lived, shepherds were even more afraid of bears than of lions. When David hurried to protect his lamb, the strong, angry bear stood up on his back legs and fought David. David was very brave, wasn't he? The Bible tells us that David killed that bear.

Application

> ➤ David was brave, and he was also a hard worker. He did his job well. David knew that the Lord God of heaven had promised to take care of him. David trusted God. He believed God's promise. He knew that God always does what He says He will do. (BATs: 2e Work; 8a Faith in God's promises)

Song: "My Bible Book"

Lesson 86: David Anointed

Bible text: I Samuel 16:1–13
Doctrinal truth: God (sovereignty)
Character traits: Diligence; Self-concept
Memory verse: Introduce Psalm 23:2.
Materials
- A completed copy of "The Lord is My Shepherd" booklet (for use as a visual; used in Lesson 85)
- A staff, bathrobe, and headpiece for shepherd costume (for review activity)
- Large blocks for sheepfold (Masking tape could also be used to simulate the outline of a sheepfold on the floor.)

Opening chorus: "I Will Trust in Thee"

Song: "My Bible Book"

Prayer
Ask God to help us finish the jobs we have to do.

Song: "Obedience Is," stanza 5

Memory verse
Read Psalm 23 from your Bible.

Read verse 2 again. Display page 1 of "The Lord is My Shepherd" booklet. Point to the picture of the sheep eating grass and drinking water.

Read Psalm 23:2*a* to the children.

> ➤ The psalm tells us that just as sheep eat grass to help them grow and be happy, so we need to know God's Word, the Bible, to help us grow in God's way. Who leads the sheep to green grass to eat and cool water to drink? *(the shepherd)* The Lord Jesus is just like a shepherd to us. We can listen to His Word in the Bible and pray to Him each day. That helps us to grow to love and serve Him better.

Read Psalm 23:2*b* aloud.

> ➤ Sheep also need shade from the hot sun and water to drink, so their shepherd leads them to brooks of water. That reminds us that we need God, the Holy Spirit, to show us through God's Word where to go and what to do.

Point to the picture of Jesus and the children on page 1 of the booklet to illustrate this verse. Lead the children in reciting the first two verses of the psalm together.

Song: "The Lord Is My Shepherd"

Bible lesson

Introduction

> ➤ David certainly had many exciting things happen to him when he kept his father's sheep out on the hillside near Bethlehem, didn't he? Who can remember some of these? (Briefly review the last lesson.)

God's Helpers

David watched his father's sheep in the fields. But do you know he also played the harp? He had plenty of time to practice and play his harp while his sheep were eating grass on the hillside.

Lesson

Now after God's people had conquered the land of Canaan and moved into their new land, they called it the land of Israel. Do you remember that God had changed Jacob's name to Israel? And today that is still the name of the land God led His people to many, many years ago. And we call the people who live there Israelites.

Well, when the Israelites were settled in their new land, they looked around and saw other countries who had kings for their leaders. So they told God that they wanted a king. They forgot that their God was a better leader than any king on Earth—that He was all powerful and knew all things.

But the Lord did give his people a king. The king's name was Saul. The Lord chose Saul to be the first king of Israel.

At first King Saul was a good king who loved and obeyed God. But then Saul began to turn away from obeying God. He didn't listen to God or to God's preacher, Samuel. God knew Saul would not rule his people well if He didn't trust in God to help him. So God told the preacher Samuel to go to Bethlehem, where he would find the young man God had chosen to be the next king for His people. God told Samuel that the king would be one of Jesse's sons, and He said He would show Samuel which one.

One by one, Samuel had each of Jesse's older sons come to stand before him. As he looked at each son, God told him, "This is not the one."

So Samuel said to Jesse, "Are these all of your children?"

And Jesse answered, "There is one more—my youngest who is out on the hillside keeping my sheep."

Samuel said, "Send for him at once."

So on that day, as David watched his father's sheep, he heard a noise. When he looked up, he saw someone running across the field toward him. It was someone bringing a message from his father. The messenger said that David was to go to Bethlehem at once. When David came to Bethlehem and Samuel saw him, Samuel heard the voice of God say, "Get up and anoint him: for this is he whom I have chosen to be the new king."

So Samuel poured a little oil on David's head as a sign to everyone that God was to be with David to make him a great leader of Israel, for soon he would be the new king.

Application

➤ David faithfully kept sheep for his father. And God gave David bigger and harder jobs to do. Soon David was to be the king of Israel. God promised He would be with David to help him do what was right.

God also tells you to obey your parents and teachers and do your work well. And God has a plan for each of you. God may want some of you to be preachers of God's Word, or to be missionaries to go far away to tell others about God and His Son. God may want you to be teachers, firemen, policemen, mothers, or fathers. Whatever God calls you to do, He wants you to be faithful in serving Him now. (BATs: 2e Work; 3a Self-concept)

Review activity

Choose one child to be David, the shepherd boy. Put a piece of cloth on his head, using a belt or sash to hold it in place. You may also provide a bathrobe and staff for additional costuming.

Make a simple sheepfold by lining up blocks in a large square and leaving an opening.

Direct "David" to stand at the door to the sheepfold. As the children answer review questions, let them crawl quietly into the sheepfold to rest.

1. What animals did David kill to protect his sheep? *(lion, bear)*

2. Who takes care of us like a shepherd takes care of his sheep? *(The Lord; the Lord Jesus is our Good Shepherd.)*

3. Does the shepherd know all his sheep? *(Yes, he has a name for each one.)*

4. Does Jesus know each one of us? *(yes)*

5. Do the sheep know their shepherd's voice? *(Yes, they will not follow another shepherd.)*

6. Where do we hear our Good Shepherd's voice? *(in God's Word, the Bible)*

Continue with memory verse and catechism review as time permits.

Song: "Savior, Like a Shepherd Lead Us"

Lesson 87: Brave David

Bible text: I Samuel 17

Doctrinal truth: God

Character trait: Courage

Memory verse: Introduce Psalm 23:3.

Catechism: Review Catechism 13.

Materials
- A completed copy of "The Lord is My Shepherd" booklet (for use as a visual)
- A completed copy of Student page 27 (for use as a visual). The teacher's name should be written on the handwriting line at the bottom of the page.
- Student page 27

Opening chorus: "I Will Trust in Thee"

Song: "Savior, Like a Shepherd Lead Us"

Song: "When I Am Afraid"

Catechism

Review Catechism 13.

■ Where is God? (*God is everywhere.*)

Song: "I'm His Little Child," stanzas 4 and 6

Prayer

Ask God to help us trust Him and not be afraid.

Memory verse

Read Psalm 23, using "The Lord is My Shepherd" booklet to illustrate each verse.

Read verse 3 again.

Bible lesson

Introduction

➤ God chose David to do a big job for Him. God told David that He wanted him to be the king over His people, the Israelites. Even after God told David that he was to be a king, David went back to his job of keeping sheep. God was not ready for David to be the new king yet. So David kept busy doing what God told him to do. He learned many lessons that would help him serve God as a great leader someday.

Lesson

Remember, Saul was the king of God's people. One day the army of an enemy—the Philistines—came to fight Saul's army. Saul's army of soldiers was on one side of a mountain, and the army of the enemy was on the other side. There was a valley—a lowland—between them.

Now the enemy army, the Philistines, had one soldier who was very tall and very strong. He was a tall, tall man—a giant—named Goliath. Goliath liked to fight. He was proud of his great strength. Goliath came down from the side of the mountain to call up to Saul's army. (Cup hand to mouth.) He called out, "I dare any one of you to come down and fight me. If any one of your men can kill me, then all of our people will be your servants. You will win the battle."

Well, the soldiers in Saul's army were afraid. They knew that none of them were big enough or strong enough to win a fight with such a soldier as the giant Goliath.

One day David's father asked him to run an errand. He gave David some corn and cheese and bread to take to his brothers who were soldiers in Saul's army.

David got up early in the morning. He left his sheep with another shepherd. Then he went to the place on the mountain where his brothers were camping with the other soldiers in Saul's army. While he was talking to one of his brothers, he heard someone shouting and making fun of God's people. David asked, "Aren't you going to do anything about this? Aren't you going to send someone to fight Goliath? Are you going to let him make fun of your God like that?"

But everyone was afraid.

David told King Saul, "I will fight the giant."

Saul said, "You can't; you are just a boy. Goliath is a strong soldier."

Then David told Saul how God had helped him kill a lion and a bear when he was taking care of his sheep. David said, "The Lord took care of me then; He will take care of me *now.*"

"Well, then," Saul said, "Go, and the Lord be with you."

So David went to meet the giant. And when he went, he took only his shepherd's staff and his sling. He picked up five smooth stones from a brook nearby and put them into his bag, and away he went. He was ready. He was not afraid. He knew God would help him.

When Goliath saw David, he laughed at him and made fun of him because he was so small. Goliath didn't know that God was going to win the battle for David.

The giant began to walk toward David. But David ran toward the giant. He put his hand into his bag and took out one stone and quickly put it into his sling. He whirled the sling around and around and threw the stone at Goliath. The stone hit Goliath on his forehead, and he fell forward to the ground. The giant was dead.

God had given David the courage to fight. He had helped David kill the giant, and Saul's army won the battle.

Application

➤ Well, I am glad we don't have to fight giants. But we need courage to be brave to do other hard things for the Lord, don't we? God has promised to give us courage to do and say the right things, even when it is hard. (BATs: 8a Faith in God's promises; 8d Courage)

Song: "The Lord Is My Shepherd"

Student page 27

Allow the children to connect the dots to complete the picture. Read and discuss the sentences at the top of the page. Remind the children that God is with each one of them, just as He was with David, and we need to trust God too. Read the sentences at the bottom of the page (and insert your name to complete the first sentence). Instruct the children to write their names on the handwriting line to complete the sentence. Ask several volunteers to read the sentences.

Lesson 88: David's Friend

Bible texts: I Samuel 18:1–9, 28–30; 19:10, 20; II Samuel 1:4, 12:9

Doctrinal truth: God

Character trait: Love

Memory verse: Introduce Psalm 23:4.

Catechism: Review Catechism 27–29.

Materials
• A completed copy of "The Lord is My Shepherd" booklet (for use as a visual)

Opening chorus: "I Will Trust in Thee"

Song: "Savior, Like a Shepherd Lead Us"

Prayer
Thank God for our friends.

Song: "Be Ye Doers of the Word," stanzas 6–7

Memory verse

Read Psalm 23.

Read verse 4 again.

Display page 3 of "The Lord is My Shepherd" booklet and point to the illustration of the sheep with their shepherd on the cliff. Remind the children that the shepherd is showing his sheep the safe way to go. Help the children identify the rod and the staff. Tell them the shepherd used his rod and staff to protect his sheep from danger.

Direct the children's attention to the picture of the child during a storm. Lead the children in reciting the first four verses of the psalm. Remind the children that God is always with us and will take care of us—that He is our best Friend.

Song: "Oh, Be Careful"

Bible lesson

Introduction

Review the lessons, "David, the Shepherd" (Lesson 85) and "Brave David" (Lesson 87).

➤ David still watched the sheep for his father in the fields near the little town of Bethlehem, even though he knew God had chosen him to be the next king of Israel. Whom did we say God chose to be the first king of Israel? (Saul) We learned that, at first, Saul served God, but later he turned away from the Lord.

Lesson

Saul was no longer a happy king serving the Lord. He was worried and could not think clearly. Because his head hurt so much, his servants thought that music might help him. So they found a young man to play a harp to make Saul feel better. And do you know whom they brought to the palace to play the harp for Saul? Yes, it was David, the shepherd boy. And when David came to the palace and played his harp and sang for Saul, he helped Saul get better, so Saul loved David.

Now Saul had a son named Jonathan. Since Jonathan was the son of a king, he was a prince—Prince Jonathan. Jonathan and David became good friends. Of course Jonathan lived in the palace and had many beautiful clothes and other nice things. But David was only a very poor shepherd boy.

Jonathan had a loving heart. Since Jonathan loved his friend David, he wanted to share some of the things he had with his friend. He gave David a beautiful robe, a sword, and his own bow for shooting arrows. And David was a good friend to Jonathan. They helped each other in many ways and promised to be good friends always.

After David fought and killed the giant Goliath, everyone was talking about how strong and brave David was. Some of the people were even saying David was greater than the king. When Saul heard what they were saying, he became jealous of David.

Saul became so angry with David that he told all his servants and his son Jonathan that he wanted them to kill David. Jonathan was afraid for his friend. Why, he couldn't kill David! Jonathan loved him. He hurried to warn David to hide from his father. Jonathan also pleaded with his father not to kill David. He reminded him of how David had played the harp for him and had served him. King Saul listened to his son. He was sorry for his anger and jealousy, and the king promised that he would not hurt David.

But later, when David became even more popular and all the people loved him, Saul knew that God was going to make David the next king instead of his own son, Prince Jonathan. Saul became angry again. Jonathan knew God's plan also, but he wasn't jealous of David. He even helped David escape from his father's soldiers. When David and Jonathan said goodbye, they promised to be friends always.

Many years later, after Saul and Jonathan had been killed in a battle and David had become the king, David found out that Jonathan's son was crippled. He remembered his promise to Jonathan to care for Jonathan's family. He invited Jonathan's crippled son, Mephibosheth, to come with his family to live in the palace.

Application
➤ David and Jonathan were good, loving friends. They kept their promise to be kind to each other always.

One of God's gifts to us is our friends. God wants us to remember that "a friend loves at all times." If we love someone, we are kind and thoughtful to him or her. We pray for our friends and want to share what we have with them. (BATs: 5a Love; 5b Giving; 5e Friendliness)

Poem: "My Friend"
Read the following poem.

➤ Holding hands and counting sidewalk squares
(Being careful not to step on cracks);
And taking turns with playing hide-and-seek
(Or maybe Simon Says, or maybe jacks).
I give you half my peanut-butter sandwich
And pour a cup of milk (we call it tea);
And then I bow my head and thank dear Jesus
For giving food to us, and you to me.

–*Becky Henry Davis*

Catechism
Review Catechism 27–29.

■ Who is Satan? (*Satan is an evil spirit who is the enemy of God and all Christians.*)

■ Who is stronger, God or Satan? (*God is stronger.*)

■ Does Satan want God's will to be done? (*No, Satan always wants people to do the opposite of what God wants them to do.*)

➤ Does God want us to be kind to our friends? (*Yes, God tells us, "Be ye kind one to another."*)

Does Satan want us to be kind to our friends? (*No, Satan always wants us to do the opposite of what God wants us to do.*)

Lesson 89: The Twenty-Third Psalm

Bible text: Psalm 23

Doctrinal truth: Salvation

Character trait: Trust

Memory verse: Review Psalm 23 (emphasizing verses 5–6).

Materials
- A completed copy of "The Lord is My Shepherd" booklet (for use as a visual)
- Student pages 28–30
- Scissors

> This lesson may be taught over two days. The booklets may be made one day and then the pictures of the shepherd and his sheep may be "read" and discussed the next day. An alternative is to have the children make the booklets during Lesson 89, and then "read" and discuss both the biblical concepts (from Lesson 89) and the application of each verse during Lesson 90.

Opening chorus: "I Will Trust in Thee"

Song: "The Lord Is My Shepherd"

Song: "I'm His Little Child"
After you remind the children that the Lord is our Good Shepherd and that He takes care of us as a shepherd takes care of his lambs and sheep, change the word "child" to "lamb," and sing the chorus again.

Prayer
Thank God for sending His Son to be our Good Shepherd.

Student pages 28–30
Instruct the children to cut the pages of their booklets along the cutting lines. Guide them as they put their booklet pages in order. Staple the booklets together. Direct the children to write their names on the cover of their booklets.

Guide the picture reading for Psalm 23:1–2 by asking the following questions and teaching the following biblical concepts. Then recite the verses. (Use the same method for verses 3–6.)

➤ What do you see in the first picture? (*Answers may vary.*)

What do we call a man who takes care of sheep? (*a shepherd*)

What are the sheep doing? (*eating grass, drinking water*)

Who leads them to the grass and water? (*the shepherd*)

A shepherd takes care of his sheep.
He leads his sheep to green grass to eat.
He leads his sheep to water to drink.

Guide the picture reading for Psalm 23:3. Then recite the verse.

➤ What do you think the shepherd is doing for this lamb? *(petting him, comforting him, loving him)*

The shepherd leads his sheep.
He comforts them when they are frightened or hurt.

Guide the picture reading for Psalm 23:4. Recite the verse.

➤ What do you think the shepherd is showing his sheep? *(Answers may vary.)*

The shepherd is showing his sheep the safe way to go. The shepherd used his rod and staff to protect his sheep from danger.

Identify the rod and the staff in the picture.

Guide the picture reading for Psalm 23:5. Recite the verse.

➤ What is the shepherd doing to his sheep? *(putting oil, like medicine, on a cut)*

What do you see at the back of the picture? *(a well)*

What do you think the dog does? *(helps the shepherd)*

The shepherd puts medicine on the cuts of the sheep.

Guide the picture reading for Psalm 23:6. Recite the verse.

➤ Where are the sheep? *(in their sheepfold home)*

Who brought them home safely? *(their shepherd)*

Do you think the sheep love their shepherd? *(Allow discussion.)*

The shepherd takes his sheep to their sheepfold home.

Collect the booklets for use in Lesson 90.

Role-play activity

Encourage the children to imitate your actions as they pretend to be shepherds doing the following:

1. Walking down a path *(Walk in place.)*
2. Climbing over rocks *(Step high, reach, pull up, repeat.)*
3. Looking behind bushes *(Shade eyes.)*
4. Peeking into holes *(Look through circle made by thumb and index finger.)*

Song: "Savior, Like a Shepherd Lead Us"

Lesson 90: Review—Our Loving Shepherd

Bible texts: Psalm 23; John 10:3–5; Luke 15:4–6
Doctrinal truth: Salvation
Character trait: Trust
Memory verses: Review Psalm 23; Psalm 25:4; I Thessalonians 5:18; Psalm 38:18; Joshua 1:9.
Catechism: Review Catechism 7 and 27–29.
Materials
• Teacher's copy of "The Lord is My Shepherd" booklet (for use as a visual)
• Each student's copy of "The Lord is My Shepherd" booklet (completed in Lesson 89)
• Role-playing costumes (optional): bathrobe, red scarf and sash, shepherd's crook, bag, bottle, green rug or towel, blue rug or towel, cardboard stand-up for sheepfold or chairs arranged in outline of sheepfold

Opening chorus: "I Will Trust in Thee"

Song: "Thank God"

Prayer
Thank God for loving and caring for us.

Song: "Jesus Loves Me"

Song: "I'm His Little Child"

Bible lesson review
Recite Psalm 23, using your copy of "The Lord is My Shepherd" booklet.

Review activity: Role play
Choose one child to wear the shepherd's costume. Choose two or three to pretend to be sheep following the shepherd as you narrate the following or the teacher could be the shepherd, with all of the class participating as sheep.

Sing "Tiptoe Quietly," stanza 4, replacing "round the room" with "quietly."

➤ A good shepherd takes his sheep to green grass to eat. *(Walk to the green rug.)*

Sing "Tiptoe Quietly," stanza 4, replacing "round the room" with "quietly."

➤ A good shepherd takes his sheep to cool water to drink. *(Walk to the blue rug.)*

A good shepherd pours medicine on the sores and cuts that his sheep get. *(Shepherd pretends to pour medicine on the cuts of his sheep.)*

Sing "Tiptoe Quietly," stanza 4, replacing "round the room" with "quietly."

➤ A good shepherd takes his sheep to their sheepfold to sleep at night. *(All except one sheep walk inside sheepfold as the shepherd counts them.)*

A good shepherd goes and finds his lost sheep. *(Lost sheep follows shepherd to sheepfold.)*

Song: "The Lord Is My Shepherd"

Student pages 28–30

Guide the picture reading for the application of Psalm 23:1–2. Recite the verses. (Use the same method for verses 3–6.)

➤ The Lord takes care of me.
I can read His Word. He talks to me.
I can pray to Him. I talk to Him.

➤ Just as sheep need grass to eat to help them grow and be happy, so we need to read and listen to God's Word to help us grow God's way. We need to obey God's rules and believe His promises, and then we can be happy Christians.

Guide the picture reading of Psalm 23:3. Recite the verse.

➤ When I am sad, He makes me glad.
The Lord will make me feel happy and content.
The Lord shows me His way.

➤ When sheep get cut or hurt on rough rocks, their shepherd takes care of them. When we are sick, the Lord can heal us. When we feel sad or when we have sinned, we can pray to the Lord and He will forgive us and make us happy. His Word shows us how to live God's way. Remember that Psalm 25:4 tells us that we should want God to teach us His ways. (Lead the children in reciting the verse.) We are to honor and glorify our God by the way we live. Why did God make you? *(God made me for His own glory.)* How can you glorify God? *(Catechism 7: I can glorify Him by loving Him and doing what He commands.)*

Recite I Thessalonians 5:18 and Psalm 38:18 with the children.

Guide the picture reading of Psalm 23:4. Recite the verse.

➤ God is always with me.
I don't need to be afraid.
He will take care of me.
My God can do anything.

➤ The shepherd takes care of his sheep with his rod and staff. When his sheep are disobedient, he punishes them. When they are attacked by a wild animal, he defends them with his rod and staff. When the sheep run away, he brings them back.

God will give us courage when we are in danger. No matter what troubles we have, we will not fear when we remember the Lord is with us.

Guide the picture reading of Psalm 23:5. Recite the verse.

➤ The Lord gives me everything I need.
The Lord gave Himself to be my Savior.
I am very happy because Jesus is my Shepherd.

➤ What enemies do sheep have? *(wild animals like bears and lions)* Remember that David once killed a lion and also a bear that were about to attack his sheep.

Who are our enemies? *(Satan, sin, unbelief)*

Review Catechism 27–29.

▪ Who is Satan? *(Satan is an evil spirit who is the enemy of God and all Christians.)*

▪ Who is stronger, God or Satan? *(God is stronger.)*

▪ Does Satan want God's will to be done? *(No, Satan always wants people to do the opposite of what God wants them to do.)*

➤ The Lord is with us and will take care of us even when troubles come. Just as a shepherd puts oil on his sheep's cuts and bruises to make him better, so the Lord is with us to make us happy and content. He gives us more than we need.

Guide the picture reading of Psalm 23:6. Recite Joshua 1:9 and Psalm 23:6.

➤ God's mercy (love and kindness) to me will never stop. He loves me so much He sent His Son to be my Savior. The Lord had a home in heaven waiting for me. There is no sin or trouble, no darkness or sickness in heaven.

➤ A good shepherd is always with his sheep; even at night he takes them to the sheepfold where they will be safe.

The Lord Jesus is always with us and will someday take us to His heavenly home to live with Him there forever. God's mercy and goodness are always with us, His goodness will give us all that we need, and His mercy and kindness will forgive us when we confess our sin to Him. The Lord even sends guardian angels to keep us safe. When we feel sad, we can recite this psalm. It will help us feel glad.

Song: "Savior, Like a Shepherd Lead Us"

> Allow the children to take their booklets home today. Encourage them to "read" the booklets to their parents.

Lesson 91: God's Word Was Found

Bible texts: II Kings 22:1–20; 23:1–3; II Chronicles 34:1–33

Doctrinal truth: Bible

Character traits: Wisdom; Obedience

Memory verse: Review Psalm 25:4

Catechism: Review Catechism 13–15 and 17–18.

Materials
- A model of a scroll (rolled up piece of paper; optional)
- "King Josiah" (Picture Packet)

Opening chorus: "I Will Trust in Thee"

Song: "Holy Bible, Book Divine"

Prayer

Ask God to help us to remember the words of the Bible.

Poem: "God's Book"

Read the following poem.

➤ The Bible is God's Book.
  Its every word is true.
  It teaches me God's way,
  And tells me what to do.

  The Bible is God's Book.
  It's better far than gold.
  It tells me of God's love
  That never will grow old.

  The Bible is God's Book.
  Its words I will obey.
  It shows me how to grow.
  I want to grow God's way!

Song: "Learning God's Way," stanzas 1 and 2

Bible lesson

Introduction

➤ Did you ever lose something? Have you ever found something that was lost? *(Allow discussion.)* It usually makes us sad when we lose something, doesn't it? But we are happy when we find something that was lost. Our Bible lesson today is about something special that was lost and then found.

Lesson

Josiah became the king of Israel when he was only eight years old. He was the leader of the land where God's people lived. He grew up to be a good king because he loved the Lord God of heaven. Most of the people had forgotten about God. They were worshiping other gods. But Josiah did not worship idols or love and serve any other gods. He told his people not to worship idols. He told them to love and serve the one true God of

heaven. Josiah wanted to do the things that would please God. Because Josiah did not have a Bible, he did not know everything God wanted him to do.

But King Josiah did know one special job he could do for God. He sent one of his helpers to the leader of the temple. He told the leader to bring the money that God's people had given at the temple. He told him to tell the workers to come to the temple. Then King Josiah told his people that they were going to repair God's house.

All the workers became busy doing their jobs. The carpenters were hammering wood, and other builders were laying stones in place. As they worked hard, one day the leader of the temple found something. It was under a lot of dust and dirt in a closet or corner of the temple they were cleaning. It was a piece of paper rolled up like a scroll. (Display model of scroll.) The leader wondered what it was. He very carefully shook the dust off the scroll and began to unroll it. (Pantomime this action with your scroll.) The leader began to read. "Oh," he thought, "I know what this is. This is God's Book!"

Everyone got excited. Someone ran to tell the king what had been found. This was not just any book. It was the Word of God. It had been lost in the temple so long that the people had forgotten about it. The king was very happy to see God's Book.

But when the king saw the book and heard the words that were written in it, he was so sad. He was sorry that he and his people had forgotten God's Word. He was sorry that they had not been obeying God's Word.

King Josiah told the Lord that He was sorry. He called all the people of his land to come to the temple, God's house. (Display "King Josiah "picture.) When the people came, the king read God's Word from the scroll. The people quietly listened. The king talked to God right there in front of all his people. He told God that he would read and obey His Word. The people listened. They all stood up to show God that they, too, were sorry for their sin. They would listen and obey God's Word. The king and his people were all happy that God's Scroll Book had been found. They knew God's Word would show them God's way.

Application

➤ We have many, many Bibles in the world today. We can read God's words in our Bible at home, at school, at church, or anywhere. You boys and girls are just learning to read now. But you can listen when your parents, your Sunday school teacher, or the preacher teaches Bible lessons. You can be good listeners during our Bible time here in kindergarten too. God wants us to listen and obey His Word. (BATs: 2b Servanthood; 6a Bible study)

Song: "Trust and Obey"
Repeat the chorus, followed by one child or the class reciting Psalm 25:4 each time.

Catechism

Review Catechism 13–15 and 17–18.

- Where is God? (*God is everywhere.*)

- Can you see God? (*No, I cannot see God, but He always sees me.*)

- Does God know all things? (*Yes, nothing can be hidden from God.*)

- Where do you learn how to love and obey God? (*I learn how to love and obey God in the Bible alone.*)

- Who wrote the Bible? (*Holy men who were taught by the Holy Spirit wrote the Bible.*)

➤ Whom did God have write Psalm 23? (*David*)

Song: "How Do We Know?"

Lesson 92: The Lost Book Was Found

Bible texts: II Kings 22:1–20; 23:1–3; II Chronicles 34:1–33
Doctrinal truth: Bible
Character traits: Wisdom; Obedience
Memory verses: Review.
Catechism: Review Catechism 1–29.
Materials
• A paper scroll
• A toy or paper crown

Opening chorus: "I Will Trust in Thee"

Songs: "My Bible Book"; "God's Way"

Action rhyme: "God's Word"
(See Index of Poetry.)

Memory verse
Review Psalm 25:4.

Prayer
Ask God to help us remember the words of the Bible.

Review activity
Secretly hide a paper scroll somewhere in the room. Choose one child to be King Josiah. Put the crown on his head and let him sit on a chair. Direct all the other children to pretend to be sawing, hammering wood, sweeping, and cleaning to repair the temple as they sing "Fixing God's House."

Choose one child to look around the room to find the hidden scroll as the children sing. When he or she finds it, have him or her take it to the king. Prompt King Josiah to recite Psalm 25:4. Prompt all the children to answer with, "I will not forget thy word" (Psalm 119:16).

Continue this activity to review all your memory verses and catechism questions.

Song: "Learning God's Way"

Lesson 93: God Delivered Three Men

Bible texts: Daniel 1; 3:1–28
Doctrinal truth: God (omnipotence)
Character traits: Trust; Courage
Memory verse: Review Joshua 1:9.
Materials
• "Daniel's Friends" (Picture Packet)

Opening chorus: "I Will Trust in Thee"

Song: "When I Am Afraid"

Prayer
Thank God for His promise to be with us always.

Bible lesson

Introduction

➤ Long, long ago, Nebuchadnezzar was the king of a great country called Babylon. King Nebuchadnezzar had taken his army into the land where God's special people lived. God's people had disobeyed God again; they had sinned. God must always punish sin. Do you know how God punished His people?

God let the army of King Nebuchadnezzar of Babylon win the battle. After the battle, the king took some of God's people back to Babylon to work for him in his palace. Some of these people were young men. The king wanted these young men to learn to speak his language and serve him in his palace home.

Lesson

One of these young men was Daniel. Daniel had three friends named Shadrach, Meshach, and Abednego. Those are strange names, aren't they? Say them with me. God helped all of these young men to know and to learn to do many things.

God's Word tells us that Daniel decided he was going to love and serve the Lord even in a strange land. The great, powerful king of the land always knew what Daniel did because Daniel lived in the palace home of the king. Because Daniel was faithful to God, God gave him very important jobs and helped him do special things for the king. That made the king happy. He did not love the God of heaven, but he knew Daniel served a great God. The king made Daniel one of his palace leaders. Daniel also helped his friends get important jobs in the king's land.

Nebuchadnezzar was a very powerful king. He had much money and much land. He began to think so much about how great he was that he even had a golden idol—a statue of himself—built. Then he sent for all the leaders of his great land to come to the palace and worship his idol. He gave the order that, when everyone heard the musical instruments play, they were to fall down and worship this statue. The king said that anyone who did not obey must be thrown into a furnace of fire.

Daniel's three friends—Shadrach, Meshach, and Abednego—did not obey King Nebuchadnezzar's rule. They loved the Lord God of heaven. They knew that God had commanded them not to bow down and love and worship any other gods but the one true God of heaven. They knew they must obey God rather than just a man, even though that man was a very powerful king.

When the proud king found out, he was very angry with Shadrach, Meshach, and Abednego. He commanded that the fiery furnace be made even hotter. He had his strongest soldiers tie the three young men and throw them into the burning fiery furnace. Do you think these young men were afraid? Would you have been afraid? These young men trusted their God to take care of them.

When the soldiers took Shadrach, Meshach, and Abednego to the furnace, the fire was so hot that the heat from the flames killed the soldiers. But the three men remained alive in the hot burning fire.

The great King Nebuchadnezzar looked into the furnace. Why, he could not believe what he saw! He stood up quickly. He asked his servants, "Didn't we throw three men into the furnace?"

They answered, "Yes, O King, that's true."

He answered, "But, look, I see *four* men walking in there . . . and they are not even hurt . . . and one of them looks like the Son of God."

Then the king walked over to the furnace and called out, "Shadrach, Meshach, and Abednego, servants of the most high God, come out of the furnace: come here."

Then the king and princes and all the leaders of the land came up close to see these three young men. They saw that the fire had not touched them. Not one hair on their heads was burned.

Their clothes were not burned, and they did not even smell like the smoke of the fire.

King Nebuchadnezzar praised the God of Shadrach, Meshach, and Abednego, who had sent His all-powerful Son to keep these three young men safe in the furnace of fire.

Application

➤ What an exciting story! What courage these three young men had! What power the Son of God has!

The Lord God of heaven gave these young men the courage to do the right thing. God has promised to give us courage to do and say the right things. (BATs: 8a Faith in God's promises; 8d Courage)

Memory verse

Review Joshua 1:9.

➤ Did Daniel's three friends trust God? Was their God with them? Were they afraid? *(Allow discussion.)*

Song: "Be Ye Doers of the Word," stanzas 4 and 9

Lesson 94: God Delivered Daniel

Bible text: Daniel 6:1–23
Doctrinal truth: Angels (assist man)
Character trait: Courage
Memory verses: Review Joshua 1:9 and Psalm 23.

Opening chorus: "I Will Trust in Thee"

Song: "My Bible Book"

Prayer

Ask God to help us show that we believe in Him by trusting Him when we are afraid.

Song: "When I Am Afraid"

Bible lesson

Introduction

➤ The king of this land learned that Daniel was a wise and honest young man. He gave Daniel important jobs to do because Daniel was a good worker. Daniel knew that when he did his work well, other people would know that he loved God. He did his work so well that the king made Daniel the most important leader in his land—next to the king himself, of course. This made the other leaders jealous. They wanted Daniel's job. They wanted to be the most important leader, like Daniel. They decided to try to make Daniel do something wrong so the king wouldn't trust him anymore.

Lesson

Daniel grew up in a home where he learned about the one true God. He knew that God had created him. He knew God had planned his life. He had learned to pray when he was very young. He talked to God each day.

The king's leaders knew that Daniel worshiped and prayed to the Lord God of heaven. They had seen him praying at the window of the house he lived in. Daniel prayed every morning, noon, and night. He asked God to help him to depart from sin and evil and do good things all day long.

So these jealous men went to their king and pretended to be doing him a great honor. They bowed down before him and said, "We think there should be a law [rule] in our land that everyone should pray only to you, King. And if someone prays to any other god, he should be thrown into a den [cage] of lions."

Well, the king thought that sounded very good. After all, he was an important man. The king didn't know that God tells us in His Word that we should worship only the one true God of heaven. So the king made the law.

Daniel heard about the law. Everyone in that land heard about it. But Daniel loved God and obeyed His Word. He knew that God's law says, "Thou shalt have no other gods before me. . . . Thou shalt not bow down thyself to them, nor serve them." So every day, three times a day, he continued to go to his room to pray.

The jealous leaders were watching. They saw what Daniel did.

"Aha," they said. "Now Daniel is in trouble. Let's go tell the king." They told the king what Daniel had done—Daniel had prayed to his God and not to the king. Daniel had not obeyed the new law. The king was sorry he had made the law because he loved Daniel. He didn't want to punish Daniel. He didn't want to have him thrown into the den of lions, but the king did not know what else to do. The rule was made, and he had to obey it.

The king told Daniel that only his God could help him now. So the king's soldiers threw Daniel into the den of lions, and a stone was rolled in front of the den, making it impossible for Daniel to escape.

Do you think Daniel was afraid? Would you have been afraid? Daniel remembered that God had promised to be with him and take care of him wherever he was. So Daniel prayed and asked God to help him.

The poor king was so sad that he could not sleep that night. He got up early in the morning and hurried to the lion's den. He called out to Daniel, "O Daniel, servant of the living God, is thy God, whom thou servest continually, able to deliver thee from the lions?" (Daniel 6:20)

Daniel told the king that his God had sent an angel to shut the lions' mouths so that they would not hurt him.

Application

➤ "So Daniel was taken up out of the den, and no manner of hurt was found upon him, because he believed in his God" (Daniel 6:23). Daniel trusted in God, and God took care of him. God had sent an angel to take care of Daniel. Whenever we are afraid, boys and girls, we need to remember that God will be with us and help us wherever we are. (BATs: 8a Faith in God's promises; 8d Courage)

Memory verses
Review Joshua 1:9 and Psalm 23.

Song: "Savior, Like a Shepherd Lead Us"

Lesson 95: Review—Delivered from Lions

Bible text: Daniel 6:1–23
Doctrinal truth: Angels
Character trait: Courage
Materials
• Student page 31
• Red, yellow, orange, brown, and green crayons

Opening chorus: "I Will Trust in Thee"

Song: "Be Ye Doers of the Word," stanzas 4 and 9

Prayer
Thank God for taking care of Daniel and taking care of us.

Song: "When I Am Afraid"

Character story: "A Real Campout"

Grant found himself singing as Dad pulled the car into the parking space at the bottom of the mountain.

A-camping we will go.
A-camping we will go.
We'll fish all day, talk the night away.
A-camping we will go.
(Tune: "The Farmer in the Dell")

He had been looking forward to this weekend for a long time.

He had been camping many times before with his family, but this was different. This time it was just he and his dad, a real father-son campout. Grant thought about how they would sleep under the stars . . . cook over a campfire . . . catch fish for supper every night . . . have devotions by firelight. What fun they were going to have!

Dad had even borrowed a special tent for the trip. It was small, so small that only Grant and his dad would be able to fit inside. The tent was light too. It had to be because they were backpacking and Dad needed to carry the tent in his backpack.

As Grant lifted his backpack out of the trunk of the car, he was glad that he had listened when Dad said, "Pack carefully, Grant. Make sure you take only what you will need. Remember that we will be parking the car at the ranger station and hiking all the way to our campsite. You'll want to be sure you can carry your backpack all the way there. We want to be able to keep moving so that we arrive at our campsite around one o'clock. Then we will have plenty of time to put up our tent, gather firewood, and catch some fish for supper."

Grant's backpack was light enough as he and his father started up the trail. But before long he realized that it was beginning to feel heavier and heavier. He was sure that by the time they reached the campsite, he would be very ready to put his backpack down.

After hiking for several hours, Grant and his father neared their campsite. Both were very tired. It had been a long hike, and they were ready to take a short break before setting up their campsite.

As they rounded the bend leading to the campsite, Mr. Hunter tripped over a thick root that was curling up out of the ground. He tried to catch himself as he fell, but his foot caught on the root and his ankle twisted.

Grant tried to help his father get up, but Mr. Hunter realized that his ankle was too badly injured to allow him to stand. He knew he needed help. But Mr. Hunter knew he would never be able to walk all the way back to the ranger station. It was just too far!

Mr. Hunter had learned to trust God several years ago. He knew that God would take care of them, but he could see from the look on Grant's face that Grant was worried.

"Grant," he said, "I know you are concerned, but God will take care of us."

Grant nodded. "I know, Dad. In Sunday school we are learning that we don't ever need to be afraid, because God is with us all the time. I know God is here with us now. It's just that I don't see how we

are ever going to get help for you, Dad. We haven't seen anyone since we left the ranger station this morning. How is anyone going to know that you are hurt?"

"Grant, I am going to need you to be a brave helper," said Dad. "I am going to need you to walk down to the ranger station to get help. It's a long hike and I know you are tired, but you can do it, Grant."

Grant felt like crying. "But I don't want to leave you alone, Dad! And how will I get to the ranger station? I don't even know the way!"

"I'll be fine, Grant," replied Mr. Hunter, trying to comfort Grant. "And you'll do fine too. The path is downhill and doesn't have too many turns. You and the ranger will be back in no time. Let's pray and ask the Lord to help us both."

As Dad prayed aloud, Grant prayed silently to himself. "Dear Lord, thank You for being with us all the time. Please help me to trust You to take care of Dad while I'm gone. And please help me to know the right trail so I can get help quickly. In Jesus' name I pray. Amen."

Grant gave Dad a hug and started down the path. He didn't like walking through the woods without Dad. The trail seemed strange. And it was so quiet. Grant was starting to feel very lonely. He didn't want to admit it, but he was scared.

Suddenly Grant froze. What was that noise? Oh, how Grant wanted to turn and run back to Dad! But Dad needed his help. He had to keep going.

Again, Grant prayed, "Dear Lord, You know Dad needs my help. I know You are with me all the time. Please help me not to be afraid. Help me to trust You to keep me safe. Amen."

Grant started down the path again. His feet moved faster now. He knew that the Lord was with him, guiding each step that he took.

A short time later, as Grant rounded a bend in the trail, he yelled for joy. There, walking up the trail towards him, was a ranger from the station.

Whispering, "Thank you, Lord," Grant ran towards the ranger. Now he would not need to hike all the way down to the ranger station. Now the ranger would be able to help Dad.

Daniel trusted in his God, and God took care of him. Grant trusted God, and God took care of him.

Student page 31

Read the sentences at the top of the page. Guide the children in finding the hidden picture. Instruct them to color the numbered sections using the color key: 1—red, 2—yellow, 3—orange, 4—brown, 5—green.

Guide the children as they track the words "trust" and "not." Read the text together.

Lesson 96: God Sent a Big Fish

Bible text: Jonah 1–3

Doctrinal truths: God; Salvation (repentance)

Character trait: Obedience

Memory verses: Review Romans 3:23 and Psalm 38:18.

Catechism: Introduce Catechism 30–31 and review Catechism 27–29.

Materials
- A fish bowl with live fish or a picture of a fish bowl
- Jonah diorama (See the Appendix for patterns and instructions.)

Opening chorus: "I Will Trust in Thee"

Song: "Jesus Loves Me," stanzas 1 and 4

Prayer
Ask God to help us to be sorry when we disobey.

Song: "There Is None That Doeth Good"

Memory verses
Review Romans 3:23 and Psalm 38:18.

Bible lesson

Introduction
Sing the following poem, "Big Fish," to the tune of "I'm a Little Teapot." Display a fish bowl with fish.

➤ Here's a little bowl,
Oh, see the fish.
See how their fins go
Swish, swish, swish.
Here's a special fish.
Who made him so?
It was the God of heav'n;
This I know.

➤ Our Bible story today tells how God made a special, big fish to help one of His servants learn to obey.

Lesson
Use the Jonah diorama to visualize the story.

One day God said to His servant Jonah, "I want you to go to a city called Nineveh. The people who live in that big city are wicked and sinful. I want you to tell them that I am going to punish them for their sins."

Well, Jonah did not obey God. He tried to run away and hide from God. Jonah got on a big ship to sail far away from where God told him to go. But Jonah could not hide from God. God is everywhere.

God saw what Jonah did. He saw him get on the ship. God knew Jonah was disobeying Him. God loved Jonah, but He knew He must punish him.

So God sent a big wind and a terrible storm to stop Jonah. The winds blew, and the waves got higher. The ship rocked back and forth. The sailors on the ship were afraid. They prayed to their gods; they did not know the true God of heaven. Their gods could not answer their prayers. The sailors began to throw barrels and boxes over the sides of the ship into the sea. They hoped that would help to keep their ship from sinking into the deep water.

Do you know what Jonah was doing while the sailors were doing all these things? He was sleeping. He was the only one who was not afraid. He did not know the winds were blowing so hard. He did not know the storm was making the waves very high. When the shipmaster—the captain of the ship—found Jonah asleep, he woke him up. He said, "Wake up and pray to your God. Ask Him to save us before we are all killed."

Jonah knew then that he was in trouble. He knew that he had disobeyed the Lord God. Jonah had to tell the men on the ship what he had done. He told them that he worshiped the one true God of heaven who made the sea and land, but that he had disobeyed God. He told them he was not a doer of God's Word. He told them that he was trying to run away and hide from God.

Then the captain and the men on the ship knew that God had sent the storm to punish Jonah. They said, "Jonah, what shall we do?"

Jonah said, "Throw me into the sea." The sailors did not want to do this to Jonah, so they tried to row to shore. They rowed and they rowed, but they couldn't get to land. (Dramatize.) Finally, they decided they must do what Jonah said. They picked Jonah up and threw him over the side of the ship—down, down, into the high waves and deep waters. And when they did this, the wind suddenly quit blowing, and the sea became calm and quiet. The men knew then that Jonah's God was the true and powerful God of heaven, for even the winds and the sea obeyed Him.

Now what would happen to Jonah in the deep waters of the sea? God had prepared a great fish—a special fish, a fish big enough to swallow a man, a fish big enough to swallow Jonah. This big fish just opened his mouth. (Place palms of hands together and move fingertips apart like a fish opening its mouth.) Gulp! (Make swallowing gesture

and clamp hands back together again quickly.)
And quickly Jonah was in the big, dark stomach of
the fish. For three days (hold up three fingers) and
three nights he was in that big, dark, awful place.

What do you suppose Jonah did? Jonah knew God
was punishing him because he had disobeyed. He
was sorry for his sin. He asked God to forgive him.
He told God that he would obey His Word. He
asked God to help him.

God loved Jonah. He wanted Jonah to obey and
serve Him. So God told the fish to go near land
and spit Jonah out. (Place palms of hands together; move hands in swishing manner. Separate
palms to pretend to open mouth of fish.) Jonah
landed safely on the dry land. Jonah knew that
God had answered his prayer.

God came again and said to Jonah, "I want you to
go to the city of Nineveh. Tell the people there
that they will be punished for their sin if they do
not tell Me they are sorry for their sin and ask Me
to forgive them." Do you think Jonah obeyed God
this time? Yes, he did. Jonah was a doer of God's
Word and not a hearer only. He went to Nineveh
and preached the Word of God. The people of
Nineveh believed God. They told God they were
sorry for their sin. Even the king of that city believed God and confessed his sin. When God saw
what they did—that they turned from doing sinful
things to obeying His Word—God said He would
not punish them. Our God is a kind and merciful
God. (BAT: 7a Grace)

Application
➤ Could Jonah hide from God, boys and girls? No. God is
  everywhere. God knows all things. God can do anything. He knew where Jonah was. He knew why Jonah
  was running away. He made the storm come. He made a
  big fish to swallow Jonah.

  That same God is with you. He knows all about you. He
  sees you when you obey. He sees you when you disobey. God tells you to be sorry for your sin and ask Him
  to forgive you. God wants you to love and obey His
  Word. (BATs: 2a Authority; 6e Forgiveness)

This may be a good time to review the plan of salvation with
the children. Offer them an opportunity to come to you if
they desire to accept Jesus as their Savior from sin.

➤ Jonah could not hide from God. We cannot hide our sin
  from God. (BATs: 1a Understanding Jesus Christ; 1b
  Repentance and faith)

Song: "Obedience Is"

Action rhyme: "Jonah Ran Away"
Repeat the following rhyme several times.

➤ Jonah ran away,
    (Run in place.)
  And that was bad.
    (Shake finger, pretending to scold.)
  Jonah disobeyed
    (Shake head "no.")
  And made God sad.
    (Point to heaven; make sad face.)
  Along came a big fish
    (Place palms of hands together, and move hands in
    swishing manner.)
  And swallowed Jonah. Ohhhh!
    (Move fingers of hands apart like a fish opening its
    mouth and clamp back together again quickly.)
  God sent the fish to punish Jonah.
    (Point to heaven.)
  The Bible tells me so.
    (Place hands side by side with palms up for open
    Bible.)

Song; "Be Ye Doers of the Word"

Catechism
Introduce Catechism 30–31.

▦ What was the sin of our first parents? (*Adam and Eve
  disobeyed God and ate the fruit that God told
  them not to eat.*)

▦ Who tempted Adam and Eve to sin? (*Satan tempted
  Eve, and she gave the fruit to Adam.*)

➤ What happened to our first parents when they had
  sinned? (*They had to leave their beautiful garden
  home; they had to work; they needed a Savior
  from sin.*)

Review Catechism 27–29.

▦ Who is Satan? (*Satan is an evil spirit who is the
  enemy of God and all Christians.*)

▦ Who is stronger, God or Satan? (*God is stronger.*)

▦ Does Satan want God's will to be done? (*No, Satan
  always wants people to do the opposite of what
  God wants them to do.*)

Relate these catechism questions to the lesson about Jonah.

Lesson 97: Kate Is Sorry

Bible text: Review.

Doctrinal truths: God; Salvation (repentance)

Character trait: Obedience

Memory verses: Review.

Catechism: Review Catechism 1–31.

Materials
- Large sketch of a fish (about 18" long and sectioned as shown below) for display (for review activity)
- Student page 32 and cutout
- Scissors
- Glue

Opening chorus: "I Will Trust in Thee"

Song: "God's Way"

Prayer
Ask God to help us to listen to God's Word and obey it.

Review activity
Display the sketch of the fish. As each child answers a review question, direct him to color in one section of the fish with a piece of chalk or crayon.

1. Where did God tell Jonah to go? *(Nineveh)*

2. What did God tell Jonah to do in Nineveh? *(tell the people that they must be sorry for their sins or God would punish them)*

3. Did Jonah obey God? *(no)*

4. What did Jonah do instead of obeying God? *(He got on a ship and went away.)*

5. What did God send to stop Jonah? *(a storm)*

6. What was Jonah doing during the terrible storm? *(He was sleeping.)*

7. What did the ship's captain tell Jonah to do after he woke up Jonah? *(to pray to his God; to ask God to save them from the storm)*

8. What did Jonah tell the men to do to him? *(throw him into the sea)*

9. What happened to the storm after the sailors threw Jonah into the sea? *(The wind stopped; the sea became calm and quiet.)*

10. What happened to Jonah after he was thrown into the sea? *(A great fish swallowed him.)*

11. How long was Jonah in the fish? *(three days and three nights)*

12. What did Jonah tell God while he was in the fish? *(He asked God to forgive him; he told God that he would obey His Word; he asked God to help him.)*

13. How did God answer Jonah's prayer? *(The fish went near the land and spit Jonah out.)*

14. What did Jonah do when God again asked him to go to Nineveh? *(Jonah obeyed; he preached God's Word to the people of Nineveh.)*

15. What happened in Nineveh because Jonah obeyed God? *(The people believed God and turned from their sin; God did not punish the people.)*

Add memory verses and catechism to this review.

Action rhyme: "Jonah Ran Away"
(See Index of Poetry.)

Character story: "The Red Scissors"

Kate was so excited. She was riding down the street in the Lunas' car with Rosa and her mother. "This is going to be a great afternoon," she thought.

Mrs. Luna had called last night to ask Mrs. Vick if Kate could come to their house after kindergarten today—not just for one or two hours, but for the whole afternoon. Mrs. Luna had told Kate's mother that Rosa and her father would watch Kate walk home after supper that evening.

Kate could hardly wait to get there. There were always so many toys to play with at the Lunas' house. Kate knew she would have a good time. Kate liked Mrs. Luna. She always made Kate feel special.

When they got out of the car, Mrs. Luna suggested that the girls might first like to play outside for a while, since the sky looked as though rain might come soon.

Kate and Rosa took turns pulling each other in the wagon. Then they rocked on the teeter-totter and swung side by side on the swing set in the Lunas' big back yard. Before long it began to sprinkle. When the raindrops began to fall, the girls chanted, "Rain, rain, go away; Rosa and Kate want to play." Then they giggled together as they ran toward the back porch.

Mrs. Luna had a snack of cookies and milk waiting for them in the kitchen. Then they hurried into Rosa's room, where they stayed busy all afternoon. They played dolls, built a palace with blocks, listened to some story records, and worked a few puzzles. Then Rosa got some paper and crayons, a couple of old magazines, and two pairs of scissors—one with blue handles and the other with red handles. The girls laid everything out on the little table in Rosa's room and sat down across from each other to color and cut.

There was nothing that Kate liked any better than to cut paper with scissors, especially since she didn't have her own scissors at home. She colored dogs and houses and trees and cut out each one.

Soon Mrs. Luna came to the door and said, "Time to put everything away, girls. Get cleaned up for supper now."

The girls sang one of their kindergarten songs as they began putting everything back in its place.

> We put our toys away.
> We put our toys away.
> We'll make all our things look nice.
> We put our toys away.
> *(Tune: "The Farmer in the Dell")*

Kate was taking care of the things on the table while Rosa put her dolls back on the shelves. Kate picked up the blue pair of scissors in one hand, and as she looked at the bright red-handled pair, she thought about how nice it would be to have her own pair of scissors. She slowly rubbed her fingers over the shiny scissors and finally picked them up. After she put the blue scissors in the drawer, she looked at the red ones still in her other hand and then quickly put them into the pocket of her dress. She walked slowly over to where Rosa was finishing her job.

Just then Mr. Luna stuck his head in the door and said, "Hi there, young ladies. It looks like you have done a good job. And just in time too. Mother says supper is on the table."

Rosa took hold of her daddy's hand and told Kate to hold his other hand. As they walked down the hallway toward the kitchen, Rosa was chattering away, telling her daddy everything that she and Kate had been doing that afternoon.

Kate bowed her head to pray as Mr. Luna returned thanks at the table. But instead of praying in her heart while Mr. Luna prayed aloud, she just kept thinking of God's commandment: "Thou shalt not steal; thou shalt not steal."

Kate didn't eat much for supper, and she was very quiet. Mrs. Luna looked at her and asked, " Kate, do you feel all right?" Kate nodded her head yes, but she felt awful. She really did feel sick—sick with guilt. She felt as if those red scissors were burning a hole in her dress pocket.

Later, when Mrs. Luna went into the kitchen to get the special chocolate pie for their dessert, Kate felt sick all over. This had been such a good afternoon; she should be happy. Instead, she had spoiled it. She thought, "I am a thief, a thief, a thief, . . ." and she began to cry.

"What's the matter, Kate?" asked Rosa. But Kate got up and ran into the kitchen.

"Mrs. Luna," Kate sobbed. "I have done an awful thing. I have broken one of God's laws. I have sinned. I'm so sorry." She reached into her pocket and pulled out the bright red scissors and quickly laid them on the table.

Mrs. Luna looked at the scissors, and then at Kate, and then she knew what had happened.

"Oh, Kate, I'm sorry too. Now I know why you looked so sad at the supper table. But I'm very happy you are sorry for what you did. And the Lord is too. He wants us to confess our sin to Him and tell others we are sorry when we do something to hurt them." Mrs. Luna gave Kate a hug and took a Kleenex and wiped her tears away. "Now, would you help me take the dessert to the table?" she asked.

"Yes, ma'am," Kate whispered. Kate returned to the table carrying two servings of chocolate pie—one for Rosa and one for herself. This time she had a smile on her face and a smile in her heart.

Song: "Be Ye Doers of the Word"

Student page 32
Instruct the children to cut out the picture of Jonah and glue it inside the large fish. Read the page and lead the children in reciting the verses, Romans 3:23 and Psalm 38:18.

God's Son

Life of Christ: I Believe Jesus Is God

Lesson 98: Who God Is

Bible texts: Genesis 1:1; John 1:14; Psalm 19:1

Doctrinal truths: Bible; God the Son; Salvation

Character trait: Trust

Catechism: Review Catechism 18.

Materials
- "Tell Me About God" booklet for each student and the teacher (Student Packet—cut on dashed line, fold on solid line, and staple to make booklet)
- *Days of Creation* visual, Day 3

Opening song: "Tell Me the Stories of Jesus," stanza 1

Song: "God's Way"

Song: "How Do We Know?" stanzas 1–6

Song: "Learning God's Way," stanza 1

Prayer
Thank God for His Word, the Bible, that tells us about His Son.

Song: "Who God Is," stanzas 1–3

Doctrinal emphasis: How do we know what God is like?
Use the song "Who God Is" to emphasize that God tells us about Himself through the Bible, His written Word; through His Son, the Living Word who lived on Earth to show us what God is like; and through God's creation, or nature, which shows us His power. Continue to review these truths throughout this unit.

Display your Bible.

➤ What do I have in my hand? Yes, the Bible, God's Holy Word. Who wrote the Bible? *(Catechism 18: Holy men who were taught by the Holy Spirit wrote the Bible.)* Long, long ago, God told special men to write down what He told them. They wrote God's words, not their own. God's Word is always true and holy (without sin). In the Bible, God tells us what we need to know about Him.

There are two main parts to the Bible—the Old Testament and the New Testament. (Point to each section.)

The lessons about God's Son coming from heaven to be born as a baby, and His life in this world, are written in the beginning of the New Testament. (Show the four Gospels.) The books of Matthew, Mark, Luke, and John tell us about God's Son when He lived here in this world. God sent His Son, Jesus, to show us what God is like (John 1:14).

Our next Bible lessons are found in the New Testament part of the Bible in the first four books. (Show the place in the Bible.) These are the books that tell us about Jesus when He lived on this Earth. They tell us what He did while He lived here.

The names of these books are *Matthew, Mark, Luke,* and *John.* We call them the Gospels because they tell us the good news of Jesus' coming to be our Savior from sin. *Gospel* means "good news."

Song: "The Gospels"

Student Packet: "Tell Me About God" booklet
Distribute a "Tell Me About God" booklet to each child.

Lead a discussion about the cover of the booklet.

➤ What do you think the child is thinking about? Where is she looking? *(up to heaven)* She wants to know who God is. The title of our booklet is "Tell Me About God."

Let's turn to the first page and read what questions this child is asking about God.

Guide the picture reading on page 2 and read the text on the page together.

➤ What do you think is happening in this picture? *(The children are asking their parents about God.)*

Guide the picture reading on page 3 and read the text on the page together.

➤ What do you see on this page? *(a child reading a Bible)*

Continue in a similar manner with pages 4–7.

> The booklets will be reviewed in Lesson 101. Therefore, wait until after Lesson 101 to send the booklets home with the children.

Lesson 99: The Boy Jesus Listened

Bible text: Luke 2:40–52

Doctrinal truths: God; Salvation

Character trait: Obedience

Memory verse: Introduce John 10:30.

Catechism: Review Catechism 9–11 and 19–25.

Materials
- "Boy Jesus in Temple" (Picture Packet)

Opening song: "Tell Me the Stories of Jesus," stanza 1

Song: "God's Way"

Prayer

Thank Jesus that He is God and can help us to do right.

Song: "I'm His Little Child"

Song: "Jesus Loves the Little Children"

Catechism

Review Catechism 19–25.

- Who were our first parents? *(Adam and Eve were our first parents.)*

- Of what were our first parents made? *(God made the body of Adam out of the dust of the ground and formed Eve from the body of Adam.)*

- What did God give Adam and Eve besides bodies? *(God gave them souls that could never die.)*

- Do you have a soul as well as a body? *(Yes, I have a soul that can never die.)*

- In what condition did God make Adam and Eve? *(God made them holy and happy.)*

- Did Adam obey God? *(No, Adam chose to disobey God.)*

- How did God punish Adam's disobedience? *(Adam's punishment was death and separation from God.)*

Bible lesson

Introduction

➤ What was the promise that God gave Adam and Eve after they disobeyed? *(Allow discussion.)* Yes, that He would send His only begotten Son who lived in heaven—who was God Himself—down to this world to be the Savior from sin for all people who will trust and believe in Him. At Christmas each year we remember how God's Son came to be our Savior.

Lesson

When Jesus was a little boy, He lived in His home in the little town of Nazareth with His mother, Mary, and His father, Joseph. Joseph was a carpenter. Jesus watched him make things out of wood. He learned many things and was always ready to be a good helper at home. Mary and Joseph took very good care of Jesus. They taught Him God's Word in their home. They took Jesus to the synagogue, which was like a school at church, where He learned to read and write. He learned the Bible words well so that He would not forget them.

One day when Jesus was twelve years old, Mary and Joseph took Him to a special meeting in the big temple in the city of Jerusalem. They had to travel many miles to get there. Jesus had gone to the temple before, but now that He was twelve years old, He was old enough to go every year.

Many other families were going at this same time. They traveled together on the road to Jerusalem. All the young boys who were old enough to go were very excited. They had heard about the beautiful temple, and they could hardly wait to see it with their own eyes.

Everyone listened and learned as the preachers and teachers taught God's Word in the temple.

As Jesus grew up, He knew why God, His Father, had sent Him from heaven. He knew God had a special plan for His life here in this world. He knew God had sent Him to be the Savior for all the world.

When the temple services were over, all the families got their things packed, and they started home. Jesus was not with Mary or Joseph. Since men traveled with men and women traveled with women, it is likely that each parent thought that Jesus was with the other one. But when nighttime came, they began looking for Him. They asked everyone, "Have you seen Jesus?" But no one had seen Jesus. Then Mary and Joseph began to worry. Where was He? They knew that Jesus was a special child whom God had given them to take care of. So they turned around and traveled back to Jerusalem, looking and asking for Jesus along the way.

Finally they found Jesus—and do you know where He was? (Display "Boy Jesus in Temple" picture.) In the temple—God's house—listening to the great teachers preach God's Word. Jesus was not only listening but also was asking very good questions. He wanted to know all about God's Word and God's way. The teachers were surprised that this young boy knew so much about God's Word.

Application

➤ Jesus is the Son of God. Jesus is God. That is very hard for even our mommies and daddies to understand. But we believe God's Word. We know that God sent His only Son down from heaven to be born in a manger as the Baby Jesus. Jesus grew up knowing and living God's way. Jesus Christ, God's Son, never sinned because He is God. And when Jesus grew up to be a man, He died on the cross. He took the punishment for your sin and for my sin. Is Jesus dead now? No, He arose from the dead and now lives in heaven.

Song: "Even a Child Is Known"

➤ Even when Jesus, the Son of God, was a child, He showed how much He loved God, His Father, by the way He listened and learned in the temple. He showed how much he loved God by the way He always obeyed Mary and Joseph when He was a child.

Action rhyme: "God's Word"
(See Index of Poetry.)

Catechism

Review Catechism 9–11.

■ Are there more gods than one? *(No, there is only one God.)*

■ In how many persons does this one God exist? *(God exists in three persons.)*

■ Who are the three persons of God? *(The three persons of God are the Father, the Son, and the Holy Spirit.)*

Read Luke 2:52 from your Bible. Explain that the verse says that as Jesus grew up, He learned more of God's Word, His body grew taller, He loved God the Father more each day, and He was kind, helpful, and thoughtful to everyone.

➤ Remember, Jesus is God. Jesus was with God the Father and God the Holy Spirit when they created the world together. The Bible tells us there is only one God. But the Bible also tells us that God is three persons. That is hard to understand. But we believe what the Bible says. The three persons of God are God the Father, God the Son, and God the Holy Spirit. We call God a Trinity—that means three persons in one. All three persons of God worked together to create the world.

Memory verse

Read John 10:30 aloud. Let the children know that this is Jesus speaking.

➤ In our verse today, Jesus says that He and God the Father are One. God the Father and God the Son are one God. We know this is true because God's Word tells us so, and God's Word is true and never changes.

Direct the children to say the verse with you several times.

Song: "One God"

Song: "The Trinity"

Lesson 100: Jesus Was Baptized

Bible texts: Matthew 3:1–17; Mark 1:9–11; John 1:19–34
Doctrinal truth: God the Son
Character traits: Trust; Love
Memory verse: Review John 10:30.
Catechism: Review Catechism 9–11.
Materials
• "Jesus' Baptism" (Picture Packet)

Opening song: "Tell Me the Stories of Jesus"

Prayer
Thank God for sending His Son to be our Savior and our example of how to live God's way.

Song: "Oh, How I Love Jesus"

Song: "How Do We Know?" stanzas 1–3

Catechism

Review Catechism 9–11.

■ Are there more gods than one? *(No, there is only one God.)*

■ In how many persons does this one God exist? *(God exists in three persons.)*

■ Who are the three persons of God? *(The three persons of God are the Father, the Son, and the Holy Spirit.)*

Memory verse

Recite John 10:30 together.

Song: "One God"

Bible lesson

Introduction

➤ At the same time the Lord Jesus lived on Earth, there was a preacher of God's Word, named John, who preached in the wilderness near the Jordan River. He preached that people should repent, which means be sorry and turn away from their sin, and trust and obey the one God of heaven.

Lesson

Many people came to hear John preach. They were surprised when they saw him. He was not dressed as they thought a preacher should be dressed. He didn't have fine clothes. He wore only a rough robe made of camel's hair. He didn't have fine food to eat either. He ate dried locusts and wild honey, which was food that he could find in the country where he preached.

Some people who heard John thought he might be Elijah or the promised Messiah. So they asked John who he was. They wondered why he was preaching God's Word and why he was in the Jordan River baptizing those who repented and told God they were sorry for their sin. Because John baptized believers in the river, people called him "John the Baptist."

One day when John was preaching, he saw Jesus standing in the crowd. John pointed to the Lord and said, "This is the Lamb of God that takes away the sin of the world." The Lord Jesus came to John and asked John to baptize Him. John answered, "Why, I should not baptize You; You are much greater than I. Instead, You should baptize me."

But the Lord Jesus told John that this was God's way—it was what God had planned. (Display "Jesus' Baptism" picture.) So John took the Lord Jesus into the river and baptized Him. As the Lord Jesus came out of the river, God sent a dove from heaven to come and light or land upon Jesus. And God's voice spoke from heaven and said, "This is my beloved Son, in whom I am well pleased."

Application
➤ Have you ever seen your pastor baptize someone in church? Do you know why people are baptized? It is to show others that they have accepted Jesus Christ as their Savior from sin, that they have turned away from their sin to live for God. Jesus was baptized to show to us what we should do. He was our example.

God sent the dove to show that Jesus is God and that the Holy Spirit of God was with His Son. Remember there are three persons in God. Who are the three persons of God? *(Catechism 11: The three persons of God are the Father, the Son, and the Holy Spirit.)*

Someday after you have accepted the Lord Jesus as your Savior from sin, you will want to be baptized to show to others you believe in God's Son. (BATs: 1a Understanding Jesus Christ; 1b Repentance and faith)

Song: "The Trinity"

Lesson 101: Jesus Is God

Bible texts: Genesis 1:1; John 1:14; Psalm 19:1
Doctrinal truth: God the Son
Character traits: Trust; Love
Memory verse: Review John 10:30.
Catechism: Review Catechism 9–11.
Materials
• "Tell Me About God" booklets (used in Lesson 98)

Opening song: "Tell Me the Stories of Jesus"

Song: "God's Way"

Prayer
Ask God to help us listen carefully to Bible words to learn what God tells us about His Son.

Song: "The Doxology"

Song: "How Do We Know?" stanzas 1–6
➤ We know all these things because God's Word tells us.

Song: "Who God Is," stanzas 1–2

Song: "The Gospels"

Doctrinal emphasis: Jesus is God
➤ God sent His Son, the Lord Jesus Christ, to live on this Earth. When the Lord Jesus grew to be a man, He walked through the countryside and the towns telling people about God's Word and God's way. The Lord Jesus did many wonderful things while He lived on this Earth. We will hear about some other wonderful miracles He worked. The Bible tells us many of the things that God's Son did. Which part of the Bible tells us the most about the life of Jesus Christ—the Old Testament or the New Testament? *(the New Testament)*

The Bible also tells us that God's Son is God. He is God's Son, and He is also God. The Lord Jesus said, "I and my Father are one" (John 10:30). That is hard even for mommies, daddies, and teachers to understand. But because we believe in God's Word, we know it is so. God cannot lie; God always speaks the truth.

The Bible tells us that God is one God. But the Bible also tells us that God is three persons in one. The three persons are God the Father, God the Son, and God the Holy Spirit. In the beginning all three persons of our God created the world and all things.

How many gods do we serve? *(We serve one God who is three persons.)* Who are the three persons that are the one true God of heaven? *(They are God the Father, God the Son, and God the Holy Spirit.)* Why do we believe our God is three persons in one? *(We believe this because the Bible tells us so, and the Bible is true and holy.)*

Catechism
Review Catechism 9–11.

■ Are there more gods than one? *(No, there is only one God.)*

■ In how many persons does this one God exist? *(God exists in three persons.)*

■ Who are the three persons of God? *(The three persons of God are the Father, the Son, and the Holy Spirit.)*

Song: "The Trinity"

Student Packet: "Tell Me About God" booklet
Review the booklet activity in Lesson 98.

Lesson 102: Jesus Obeyed the Father

Bible texts: Matthew 4:11; Mark 1:12–13; Luke 4:1–13;
I John 2:16
Doctrinal truths: Angels; Satan
Character trait: Obedience
Memory verses: Review Ecclesiastes 12:13*b* and Psalm 95:6.
Catechism: Review Catechism 9–11 and 27–29.

Opening song: "Tell Me the Stories of Jesus,"
stanza 1

Song: "Obedience Is"

Memory verse
Review Ecclesiastes 12:13b.

Prayer
Lead the children in reciting Psalm 95:6 and then kneeling
to sing "The Doxology" for their prayer time today.

Catechism
Review Catechism 9–11.

- Are there more gods than one? *(No, there is only one God.)*

- In how many persons does this one God exist? *(God exists in three persons.)*

- Who are the three persons of God? *(The three persons of God are the Father, the Son, and the Holy Spirit.)*

Song: "One God"

Song: "The Trinity"

Bible lesson

Introduction
➤ We've learned that when our Lord Jesus was baptized
by John the Baptist in the Jordan River, the Holy Spirit
came upon Him. And right after that, the Holy Spirit led
the Lord Jesus into the wilderness. Remember, we
learned that the wilderness was a hot, dry place, something like a desert.

Lesson

The Lord Jesus knew why God the Father had sent
Him to live in the world. He knew that He was to
be the Lamb of God that takes away the sin of the
world. He was to die on the cross to take the punishment for my sins and for your sins so that we
would not have to be punished and be separated
from God forever. He knew that He had a great
work to do.

While He was alone in the wilderness, He thought
about God's plan and prayed to God the Father
for strength to do His work. The Bible tells us that
the Lord Jesus did not even eat during the forty
days He was in the wilderness. He fasted. Fasting
means to go without eating food. Our Lord was so
busy talking to God the Father that He didn't even
think about eating for forty days.

When the Lord was very weak and hungry from
not eating for so long, Satan came to Him. He
knew Jesus was weak from not eating. So Satan
said to Him, "If you are really the Son of God, just
command, just say the word, and these stones will
become loaves of bread."

Jesus answered him, "The Word of God says, 'Man
shall not live by bread alone, but by every word of
God.' " Even though Jesus was hungry, He would
not use the power of God just for Himself. He
knew that His Heavenly Father would give Him
what He needed, so He trusted in Him.

When that temptation did not work, the Devil—
Satan—took the Lord Jesus to Jerusalem and sat
Him on the top of the temple. This time Satan
said, "If you really are the Son of God, show how
powerful you are. Jump off the temple. God's
Word says His angels will protect you from harm."

The Lord Jesus again refused to listen to Satan. He
answered, "God's Word also says, 'Thou shall not
put the Lord thy God to the test.' I don't need to
prove God's power."

And finally the Devil took Jesus up on a high
mountain and told Him to look around and see all
the lands, cities, and kingdoms of the world. Satan
said, "All of these things I will give to you if you
will fall down and worship me."

The Lord Jesus answered him, "Be gone, Satan; for
the Bible says, 'Thou shalt worship the Lord thy
God, and Him only shalt thou serve.'"

Satan tried three times to tempt the Lord Jesus to
do something that would not please God the Father. Satan wanted our Lord to obey him instead
of God the Father. At last Satan went away; he left
Jesus alone. And God the Father sent angels from
heaven to take care of Jesus.

Application

➤ Who is Satan? *(Catechism 27: Satan is an evil spirit who is the enemy of God and all Christians.)* Who is stronger, God or Satan? *(Catechism 28: God is stronger.)* Does Satan want God's will to be done? *(Catechism 29: No, Satan always wants people to do the opposite of what God wants them to do.)*

Did the Lord Jesus obey Satan? *(No, He trusted and obeyed God the Father.)* Whom should we obey, Satan or God? *(God)* Yes, we should love and obey God— "Fear God and keep his commandments." We must work and fight against sin and use God's Word as our weapon against the Devil. (BAT: 8c Fight)

Song: "Oh, Be Careful"

Lesson 103: The Tempter

Bible texts: Matthew 13:39; John 8:44; I Peter 5:8; I John 3:8; 4:4; Ephesians 6:11–12, 16
Doctrinal truth: Satan
Character trait: Obedience
Catechism: Review Catechism 27–31 and introduce Catechism 32.

Opening song: "Tell Me the Stories of Jesus," stanzas 1–2

Song: "Be Ye Doers of the Word," stanzas 1, 4, and 5

Prayer
Thank God that He is stronger than Satan.

Song: "Obedience Is"

Doctrinal emphasis: Satan
Review the doctrinal emphasis about Satan in Lesson 42.

Song: "Oh, Be Careful"

Catechism
Review Catechism 27–31.

■ Who is Satan? *(Satan is an evil spirit who is the enemy of God and all Christians.)*

■ Who is stronger, God or Satan? *(God is stronger.)*

■ Does Satan want God's will to be done? *(No, Satan always wants people to do the opposite of what God wants them to do.)*

■ What was the sin of our first parents? *(Adam and Eve disobeyed God and ate the fruit that God told them not to eat.)*

■ Who tempted Adam and Eve to sin? *(Satan tempted Eve, and she gave the fruit to Adam.)*

Introduce Catechism 32.

■ What does every sin deserve? *(Every sin deserves the wrath and curse of God.)*

Explain that "curse" is another word for *punishment*.

Song: "God's Way"

Lesson 104: Jesus Called His Disciples

Bible texts: Matthew 4:18–22; Mark 1:16–20; John 1:35–51
Doctrinal truths: God the Son; Church (service)
Character traits: Obedience; Diligence
Memory verse: Review John 10:30.
Catechism: Review Catechism 26 and 32.

Opening song: "Tell Me the Stories of Jesus," stanzas 1–2

Song: "One God"
Repeat several times, having one row or group of children recite John 10:30 each time after this chorus and the following song are sung.

Song: "The Trinity"

Prayer
Stand and pray the Lord's Prayer together.

Bible lesson

Introduction

➤ What have we learned about John the Baptist? *(Allow discussion.)* Yes, he told people to repent—to be sorry for their sin and to hate and forsake it because God hates sin. Do you remember what John said about Jesus when he saw Him? He said, "Behold the Lamb of God, which taketh away the sin of the world."

Lesson
Dramatize the actions of the story as you walk around telling it.

Two of the men who heard John say this about Jesus began to follow Jesus. They wanted to see and hear more about this man of God. When Jesus saw them following Him, He asked them whom they were looking for. Then they asked the Lord where He lived. He answered them, "Come and see."

The two men talked to the Lord all day. One of the young men was named Andrew. Andrew was so happy and excited to listen to the Lord Jesus that he ran to get his brother, Simon Peter, and brought him to see Jesus also. Jesus preached to them, and then they knew that He was truly the Son of God—the promised Savior of the world.

On another day, as Jesus walked down the road to preach God's Word, he saw another man. His name was Philip. Jesus said to him, "Follow me." Philip immediately stopped what he was doing and obeyed. He went and found his friend Nathanael and told him about the Lord Jesus. Nathanael also came and followed the Lord.

Later when the Lord walked by the Sea of Galilee, He saw Simon Peter and Andrew. They were throwing their fishing nets into the sea. The Lord said to them, "Follow me, and I will make you fishers of men." They obeyed and immediately left their nets and followed the Lord.

As they walked along, they saw two other fishermen, James and John, in a boat near the shore. They were with their father mending their fishing nets. The Lord also called them, telling them to come and be His disciples. So James and John put down their fishing nets, left their father, and followed the Lord.

Jesus also called other men to follow Him. He called twelve disciples to be with Him. He preached God's Word to them and taught them God's Way.

Application
➤ Jesus called these men to work with Him. He wanted them to be "fishers of men"—to "catch" people for Jesus—and tell people about Jesus. They were His workers or helpers. We call them "disciples." They were willing and obedient. (BAT: 2b Servanthood)

The disciples left their homes and families to serve Jesus because they knew He is God. God wants us to be good workers for Him. (BAT: 2c Faithfulness)

Song: "There Were Twelve Disciples"

Song: "A Helper I Will Be"

Catechism
Review Catechism 26 and 32.

■ What is sin? *(Sin is the transgression of the law of God.)*

■ What does every sin deserve? *(Every sin deserves the wrath and curse of God.)*

➤ When John the Baptist preached to the people that they should repent and be sorry for their sin, I'm sure he told them about how God had made man without sin. He told them how the first man, Adam, and the first woman, Eve, had disobeyed God. How unhappy and miserable they were after they had sinned! Because of

their sin they deserved the wrath and curse—the anger and punishment—of God.

So when John the Baptist pointed to the Lord Jesus and said, "Behold . . . look . . . the Lamb of God, who takes away the sin of the world," many people were happy to know that God had sent His promised Son to be their Savior from sin. Because of our sin, we deserve God's punishment. But because of God's love and mercy, we can accept His Son as our Savior and have the gift of eternal life instead of God's punishment. (BAT: 1a Understanding Jesus Christ)

Direct the children to join in as you recite the catechism questions and answers several times.

Lesson 105: Review—Jesus Is God

Bible text: Review.
Doctrinal truth: God the Son
Character traits: Trust; Love
Memory verses: Review.
Catechism: Review Catechism 1–32.
Materials
• Two vegetable or fruit mesh bags (for review activity)
• Sixteen or more construction-paper fish (for review activity)
• Student page 33 and cutout
• Scissors
• Glue

Opening song: "Tell Me the Stories of Jesus," stanzas 1–2

Song: "The Gospels"

Prayer
Ask the Lord to help us be good workers and tell others that Jesus loves them.

Student page 33
Instruct the children to cut out the picture of the disciples and glue only the left side of the picture to the page. Read the page and recite John 10:30. Allow the children to simulate the disciples coming to the Lord.

Song: "There Were Twelve Disciples"

Review activity
Display mesh bags (nets) and provide paper fish. Each child who answers a question correctly may add a paper fish to his team's net. Use the questions below.

1. In which town did Jesus live with His mother and father? *(Nazareth)*

2. How old was Jesus when Joseph and Mary took Him to the temple at Jerusalem? *(twelve)*

3. What did Jesus do in the temple? *(talked to the teachers)*

4. Recite John 10:30.

5. What are the four Gospels? *(Matthew, Mark, Luke, and John)*

6. Why are they called Gospels? *(They tell the good news that Jesus came to die and take our punishment for sin.)* (Sing together "The Four Gospels.")

7. Are there more gods than one? *(No, there is only one God.)*

8. Who is God? *(Catechism 12: God is a spirit and does not have a body like man.)*

9. How many persons is our God? *(three persons in one)*

10. What do we call our God? *(the Trinity)* (Sing together "The Trinity.")

11. Who is Satan? *(Catechism 27: Satan is an evil spirit who is the enemy of God and all Christians.)*

12. Who is stronger, God or Satan? *(Catechism 28: God is stronger.)*

13. Does Satan want God's will to be done? *(Catechism 29: No, Satan always wants people to do the opposite of what God wants them to do.)*

14. Name one of the men Jesus called to be His disciples. *(Peter, Andrew, James, John, etc.)*

15. What does "I will make you fishers of men" mean? *(We can tell others about Jesus' coming from heaven to be our Savior. We can "catch" people for Jesus—we can show others how to become God's children.)*

16. Does Satan want us to tell others about Jesus? *(no)*

Review other memory verses and catechism questions as time allows.

Lesson 106: The Wedding at Cana

Bible text: John 2:1–11
Doctrinal truth: God (omnipotence)
Character trait: Trust
Memory verse: Introduce Hebrews 13:6.
Catechism: Review Catechism 16.

Opening song: "Tell Me the Stories of Jesus," stanzas 1–2

Song: "How Do We Know?" stanzas 1–2

Song: "The Trinity"

Prayer
Thank God that Jesus is God and can do all things.

Song: "Oh, How I Love Jesus"

Bible lesson

Introduction

➤ Rosa was so excited. She was going to be a flower girl in her cousin's wedding. She could hardly wait. Her mother had made her a pretty long pink dress, and she was going to carry a basket of rose petals as she walked down the aisle of the church.

She was to walk in front of the bride and drop the rose petals along the way to make a path for the bride to walk over. After the wedding, there would be cake and punch and little sandwiches at the wedding reception.

Have you ever been to a wedding? (Let the children share some of their experiences.) Our Bible story today is about a wedding that took place long, long ago when Jesus lived on Earth.

Lesson

It was a happy day for a family in the city of Cana. One of the family members was getting married, so the family was giving a wedding dinner. They had invited many people to the wedding feast. Jesus and His disciples were invited as well as the mother of Jesus. Many years ago it was the custom for a wedding feast to go on for several days, sometimes for even more than a week.

A terrible thing happened during this feast. The family giving the dinner ran out of wine for their guests. Maybe it was because they were poor and didn't have money to buy more; or it could be that they had more company come to the wedding than planned.

Now when Jesus' mother heard what had happened, she told her Son, the Lord Jesus. Mary was a kind and helpful woman and wanted her Son to help their friends. She told the servants of the house to do whatever her Son told them. She knew Jesus was really the Son of God—the promised Savior of the world. She knew He would do what was best.

So the Lord Jesus pointed to six empty water jugs that were nearby, and He said to the servants, "Fill those water jugs with water." And they did; they filled them to the brim—to the very top.

Then the Lord said, "Pour some into a cup and take it to the governor of the feast." The governor was in charge of the feast.

When the servants poured from the water jugs, they were amazed. "Why," they said, "it is no longer water!" The Lord Jesus had changed the water into wine, which is made from the juice of grapes. Quickly they took the cup to the governor of the feast. It was the custom for the person to taste everything before it was served to other guests.

When the governor of the feast tasted the water that was made wine, he didn't know where it came from or what the Lord had done. But he called the bridegroom over to him and said, "Usually people serve their best wine first and save what isn't as good until last, but you have kept the best wine and served it last."

Application

➤ This was the first miracle Jesus performed on Earth. It showed His power and caused His disciples and His friends to believe even more that He is the Son of God. A miracle is a special act that only God can cause to happen. It shows His power. (BAT: 7b Exaltation of Christ)

Memory verse and catechism
Read Hebrews 13:6 from your Bible.

➤ Who helped the family at the wedding? (*Jesus*) Yes, the Lord Jesus. Jesus is God and can do all things. Our God is a great and powerful God. Can God do all things? (*Catechism 16: Yes, God can do all His Holy will.*) It was God's will to change the water to wine so that the people at the wedding feast would see the power of God.

The Lord will help us. Wherever we are, and whatever we do, we can ask God to be with us. We should never be afraid because our God will not let anyone or anything hurt us unless it is in His plan for our lives. (BAT: 8d Courage)

Guide the children in reciting the verse after you. Later, you may divide the class into two or three groups and recite sections of the verse in choral response.

Lesson 107: Jesus Healed a Nobleman's Son

Bible text: John 4:46–54
Doctrinal truths: Bible; God the Son; Salvation
Character trait: Trust
Memory verse: Review Hebrews 13:6 and John 10:30.
Catechism: Introduce Catechism 33 and review Catechism 18.
Materials
• "Nobleman's Son" (Picture Packet)

Opening song: "Tell Me the Stories of Jesus," stanzas 1–2

Song: "God's Way"

Song: "How Do We Know?" stanzas 1–6

Song: "Learning God's Way," stanza 1

Prayer
Thank God for His power.

Song: "Learning God's Way," stanza 2

Doctrinal emphasis: How do we know what God is like?
Review this doctrinal emphasis from Lesson 98.

Song: "Who God Is"

Bible lesson

Introduction
Display your Bible.

➤ Our lesson today is found in John, one of the four Gospel books. It is in the New Testament part of the Bible. It tells about the Lord Jesus' growing up to be a man and doing many wonderful works to show people God's power.

> Distinguish magic from miracles in the mind of a child. Magic is using tricks to make it seem like something that is impossible really happens. A miracle is a supernatural act—something that only God can cause to happen.

Lesson

God's Son went to another country (Galilee) to preach, teach, and work more miracles so that people could hear and see the power of God. A miracle is a special work that only God can do. It shows us His power. It shows us that He is God.

A nobleman who was a very important leader in his country came to the Lord Jesus. He asked the Lord to come and heal his son who was very, very sick. The boy was so sick that the father was afraid he might die.

This nobleman had heard of the great miracles worked by the Lord. He had faith in God's Son. He believed that the Lord could work another miracle and save his son's life. The nobleman said again, "Sir, come before my child dies." The nobleman knew that no one else could help him. He knew that this Man, Jesus Christ, sent from God, could heal his son.

Jesus, God's Son, saw that the nobleman had faith in Him. He knew that the nobleman believed that He could do all things. So He said, "Go your way; your son will live."

The nobleman didn't ask the Lord, "Are you sure he will get well?" or "How do you know?" The Bible tells us the man believed the words that the Lord Jesus had said to him, and he went back home. He knew Jesus would do what He said He would. He could "boldly say, the Lord is my helper, and I will not fear." The Lord was twenty-five miles away—a long way from the nobleman's home in a town named Capernaum. That did not matter to the Son of God. It didn't matter how far away the sick boy was. God could still make him well because our God can do all things. And Jesus is God. He said, "I and my Father are one."

As the nobleman traveled along the road toward his home, he looked up and saw some of his servants hurrying to meet him. They told him, "Your son is well. He is alive." (Display "Nobleman's Son" picture.)

How the nobleman praised God! He believed that Jesus was God and could do all things. And the Bible tells us something else very wonderful. Not only did the nobleman believe that Jesus Christ is God's Son, but his family and the servants who worked in his house also believed in God's Son.

Application

➤ Our God has the power to heal people and to work miracles. But the greatest thing He can do for us is to change our lives when we ask Him to be our Savior from sin. Just as the nobleman and his family believed in Jesus Christ as the Way to heaven, we can believe in Jesus Christ too. God wants us to do these things:

1. Believe He made us and all things.

2. Believe we have sinned.

3. Believe God sent Jesus Christ to die for our sin, and believe that the Lord Jesus lives again in heaven today.

4. Ask Jesus, God's Son, to forgive our sin right now.

5. Know that someday we can live in heaven forever and ever, always with God, because we asked Jesus Christ to be our Savior from sin. (BATs: 1a Understanding Jesus Christ; 1b Repentance and faith)

Catechism

Introduce Catechism 33.

■ What does God require of man before he can go to heaven? *(No one can enter heaven unless his heart is changed.)*

➤ The nobleman and his family let Jesus change their hearts and lives. Could they go to heaven? *(yes)* What does God require of us before we can go to heaven? *(a change of heart)*

Song: "Who God Is," stanza 2

Avoid any formal group invitation with five-year-olds. Being great imitators, they will often raise a hand in response to an invitation because another child does so. They are also most eager to please and may show a desire to accept the Lord just to please you, their teacher. Salvation is a personal decision. Let God's Holy Spirit motivate their decision in accordance with God's timing for their lives. If a child sincerely approaches you about his desire to be saved, then joyfully and prayerfully take the child aside and again simply review God's plan with him.

No pressure should be put upon children to force them into a premature experience of accepting Christ as their personal Savior. Although some five-year-olds are ready for this important decision of their lives, most are not. Make the plan of salvation simple and repeat it periodically throughout the year.

Lesson 108: Jesus Helped Some Fishermen

Bible text: Luke 5:1–11

Doctrinal truths: God the Son; Salvation

Character traits: Trust; Love

Memory verses: Review.

Materials
• Mesh bags and construction-paper fish (for memory verse review; used in Lesson 105)
• Chalkboard and chalk or large sheet of paper and crayon to draw simple story sketch
• Toy boat (optional)
• Stick figures for display (See Bible lesson below.)

Opening song: "Tell Me the Stories of Jesus," stanzas 1–2

Song: "God's Way"

Prayer
Thank the Lord that Jesus, God's Son, is our Helper.

Song: "The Gospels"

Memory verses
Review John 10:30, Hebrews 13:6, and other verses as time permits. Every time a child says a verse, have him place a paper fish in the mesh bag "net."

Song: "God's Son," stanza 4

Bible lesson

Introduction

➤ Have you ever gone fishing? Did you catch any fish? Did your daddy catch any? What did you use to catch your fish? Some people fish with fishing poles that have lines and hooks. Some people use long spears to throw at big fish, and some people go fishing with nets. In our Bible lesson today, we'll hear about four fishermen who went fishing with big nets.

Lesson
Draw stick figures for appropriate
scenes while telling the story.

(Scene 1)
One day the Lord Jesus Christ,
God's Son, was standing
beside a beautiful lake—the Sea of Galilee. He had
preached to many, many people that day as they
sat and stood along the hillsides beside the lake.
But now there were so many people who had
come to hear the Son of God preach that there
was almost no place for the Lord to stand. The
people were crowding closer; Jesus was being
pushed closer to the lake.

As the Lord looked around for a place to stand and
preach, He saw two fishermen's boats by the lake.
The fishermen were not in their boats. They were
washing their fishing nets. They had been out fishing all night and now they were cleaning their
nets and putting their fishing gear (tools) away.

(Scene 2)
The Lord saw Simon Peter and got
into his boat. He asked Simon to
row his boat out a little way from the shore so that
He could go on preaching to the many, many
people who were crowded around the lake. Simon
Peter obeyed, and the Lord sat down and taught
the people from Simon's fishing boat.

When the Lord Jesus had finished preaching to the
many people on the shore, He told Simon Peter to
row out into the deeper water and let down his
fishing nets to catch fish.

Now Simon and his fishermen friends had fished
the night before. Simon told the Lord that they
had not caught even one fish. Simon said, "Master, we have been working all night trying to catch
some fish, and we haven't caught anything. But if
you really want us to, we'll try again."

(Scene 3)
So Simon obeyed. He did
what the Lord said. The nets
made a swishing sound as
the fishermen threw them into the air and they
dropped into the water. The nets sank slowly to
the bottom of the lake as the fishermen watched.

And then a wonderful thing happened. So many
fish were caught in the fishing net that Simon had
to call for help. He called to some friends in the
other fishing boat and asked them to come and
help pull all the fish in. They came and began filling both of the boats with fish until they were so
heavy and full that they began to sink.

When Simon Peter saw what was happening, he
fell down on his knees in front of the Lord. He

knew then that Jesus Christ was not just a good
teacher and preacher; he knew Jesus is God's Son.
Simon Peter knew that only God could work such
a miracle. He knew he was standing in the presence of the one true God of heaven. Simon Peter
was afraid. He knew that he was a sinner and that
God's Son is holy and without sin.

The Lord Jesus told Simon Peter and the other fishermen not to be afraid. He told them He had a job
for them to do, and it wasn't just catching fish.
The Lord told these fishermen that He wanted
them to be fishermen for Him—to be His followers
to preach and teach God's way to others.

The Lord used this great miracle that only He
could do to show His power. These fishermen
learned a lesson. They knew Jesus was truly the
Son of God.

Application
➤ God calls each of us to be His followers, to obey Him,
and to go His way. He wants us to tell others about the
Bible and about how to live God's way. (BAT: 5c Evangelism and missions)

Song: "Fishers of Men"

Song: "Even a Child Is Known"

Song: "There Were Twelve Disciples"

Song: "This Is the Way We Row Our Boat"
Sing stanzas 1–3.

Read Luke 5:4 to the children and then sing stanza 1 again.

Recite Hebrews 13:6 together with the class and then sing
stanza 4.

Review activity

➤ Today we're going to review our lesson in a different
way. I am going to say a sentence about the story and
leave out at least one word. Then we'll see who can tell
me the word or words that will make our sentence complete.

You may want to pass around a toy boat for each child to
hold as he or she answers the questions.

1. One day the Lord Jesus was standing on the shore beside the _____ *(water, Sea of Galilee, lake, etc.).*

2. The Lord was _____ *(preaching, teaching, speaking,
   talking, etc.)* to many people that day on the hillside by
   the lake.

3. It was very crowded with so many people. So the Lord
   had to look around for a place to _____ *(stand, sit,
   preach).*

4. As He looked around, He saw two _____ *(boats)* by the lake.

5. The Lord got into a boat and asked one of the fishermen, Simon Peter, to _____ *(row the boat out into the water)*.

6. When the Lord finished preaching, He told Simon Peter to row out into the deeper water and _____ *(let down his nets, go fishing)*.

7. Simon Peter obeyed, and when the disciples had thrown the nets over the side of the boat, _____ *(many fish were caught in the net)*.

8. The fishermen pulled up the nets and filled their boats with fish until their boats were so full that they began _____ *(to sink)*.

9. The fishermen were afraid. They knew that Jesus was truly _____ *(the Son of God)*.

10. Then God's Son told the disciples that He had a very important job for them to do, a job more important than catching fish. He wanted them to _____ *(be fishers of men, catch people)*.

Review what "fishers of men" means.

Lesson 109: Jesus Healed a Sick Man

Bible texts: Matthew 9:2–8; Mark 2:1–12; Luke 5:16–26
Doctrinal truths: God the Son; Salvation
Character traits: Trust; Love
Memory verse: Review John 10:30.
Catechism: Introduce Catechism 34.
Materials
• "Four Friends" (Picture Packet)

Opening song: "Tell Me the Stories of Jesus," stanzas 1–2

Song: "God's Way"

Song: "The Trinity"

Memory verse
Review John 10:30.

Song: "One God"

Prayer
Thank God for His Son, who came to show us God's love and power.

Song: "The Gospels"

Bible lesson

Introduction

➤ Have you ever seen an ambulance or a rescue or emergency squad come to carry a sick or injured person to the hospital? How do the emergency workers usually carry the person who is sick? They carefully pick up the sick person and put him on a stretcher or cot, which is like a bed that isn't very heavy. This makes it easier to carry the sick person. Then they take him to their ambulance and drive him to the hospital.

Lesson

One day long ago, the Lord Jesus was teaching and preaching. Many, many people had come from the cities and towns all around to see and hear Him. The people had heard what great powers the Lord Jesus had. They had heard what great miracles He had worked. They wanted to see the One who could do so many wonderful things.

Our Lord was preaching in a house that day. People kept entering the house until there was no more room for anyone else to squeeze through the door.

There were some men who had a friend who was very sick. He had a sickness called "palsy." He was so sick that he could not walk to where the Lord Jesus was. The sick man's friends wanted to help him, so they brought a stretcher and carefully laid their sick friend on it. Then they carried the sick man to the house where the Lord was preaching.

When they got there, they found the house was so full of people that there was not enough room to get inside to take their friend to the Lord. Do you think these men gave up and went home? No, they didn't give up. They thought of a way to finish their job. They lifted the sick friend onto the flat roof of the house.

The friends of the sick man then began picking up some of the tiles that covered the top of the house. The men moved away enough tiles so that they could lower a cot down through the hole they had made. Then they tied ropes to the cot and began to slowly lower their sick friend down into the room. (Display "Four Friends" picture.)

During this time the Lord Jesus had been preaching and healing the people who were crowded into the house where He was. Everyone looked up. They watched as the cot came slowly down and settled on the floor near the Lord. Everyone was very still. They wondered what the Lord would do.

The Bible tells us that when the Lord Jesus Christ saw how these friends and the sick man believed in Him, He said to the man, "Your sins are forgiven. Pick up your bed and walk." And immediately, the man who was sick got up, picked up his bed, and went home. As he went along the way, he thanked and praised God. He told everyone that he believed in the power of the Son of God.

Only God could do such a great miracle. Jesus Christ is God's Son, but He is also God. Our God is one God in three persons—God the Father, God the Son, and God the Holy Spirit. God's Word tells us so, and we believe God's Word. God's Word is always true.

Application

➤ These four men brought their sick friend to the Lord. They had faith in God's Son. They believed in God's power. They believed Jesus is God. Do you pray for your friends when they are sick? Do you believe the Lord can help them? God tells us to "pray one for another." God tells us to have faith and believe Him. He will always do what is best for us. (BAT: 6b Prayer)

These four men brought their friend who needed to have his sins forgiven to the Lord Jesus Christ. Do you know someone who does not love and obey God? God wants you to pray for him or her and tell him or her about His Word and His Son who is the way to heaven. (BAT: 5c Evangelism and missions)

Song: "Even a Child Is Known"

Song: "Who God Is"
Remind the children that God tells us about Himself in the Bible; He shows us what He is like in His Son; and we can see His great power in the heaven and earth that He created.

Role-play activity
Choose two children to use God's Word to dramatize telling others of Him. Prompt them to repeat the following dialogue.

➤ Child 1: (Hold a Bible) Do you know God's Son as your Savior from sin?

Child 2: Why do I need a Savior?

Child 1: Because "there is none that doeth good, no, not one . . . ; for all have sinned and come short of the glory of God."

Child 2: Who is the Savior?

Child 1: "For God so loved the world, that he gave his only begotten son, that whosoever believeth in him should not perish, but have everlasting life."

Child 2: "I will be sorry for my sin." (Bow head to pray.) "Show me thy ways, O Lord; teach me thy paths."

Class: (Sing "The Doxology.")

Catechism
Introduce Catechism 34.

■ Who can change a sinner's heart? (The Holy Spirit can change a sinner's heart.)

➤ Was the sick man's heart changed in our lesson today? (yes) Who changed his heart? (The Holy Spirit—because of the love and kindness of God in sending Jesus to die on the cross for our sins.)

Recite Catechism 34 several times.

◗ Lesson 110: Jesus Calmed the Storm

Bible texts: Matthew 8:23–27; Mark 4:35–41; Luke 8:22–25

Doctrinal truths: God the Son (omnipotence); Salvation (faith)

Character trait: Trust

Memory verse: Review Hebrews 13:6.

Catechism: Review Catechism 13–16.

Materials
• Storm visual (See the Appendix for visual and instructions.)
• Stick figures for display (See Bible lesson below.)
• Student page 34 and cutouts
• Scissors
• Glue

Opening song: "Tell Me the Stories of Jesus," stanzas 1–2

Song: "I'm His Little Child," stanzas 1 and 4

Prayer
Thank God for His care.

Bible lesson

Introduction
➤ Have you ever been out in a boat when the waves got very, very tall?

Let's hold our arms straight out from our sides and pretend that they are waves as we move them up and down.

Choose one child to close his eyes and answer the last line of the following action rhyme.

➤ Sometimes the waves are very, very small.
(Stoop low to ground, waving arms out from sides.)
Sometimes the waves are very, very tall.
(Stretch tall, waving arms out from sides.)
Sometimes small, sometimes tall,
(Repeat directions for first and second lines.)
Guess which they are now.
(Choose either the first or the second line directions to imitate.)

➤ Who created all the oceans and seas and lakes? *(God did.)* Is Jesus God? *(Yes, He is.)* He was in the beginning with God the Father and God the Holy Spirit and helped to create all things in heaven and in earth. It is hard for us to understand, but God the Father, God the Son (Jesus Christ), and God the Holy Spirit are one God.

Lesson

Draw stick figures for appropriate scenes while telling the story.

(Scene 1)
Our Lord's days on Earth were very busy. He was always preaching and healing and helping everyone who came to Him. One day after He had been preaching and healing in the city of Capernaum, it was evening. The Lord Jesus and His disciples were tired. The Lord said to His disciples, "Let us sail over to the other side." The Lord went to a quiet place in the back of the boat and fell asleep on a pillow.

(Scene 2)
Suddenly a strong wind brought dark clouds and a terrible storm over the lake. The wind was howling; the waves were crashing against the boat. The wind blew so hard and the waves got so high that water splashed into the boat. Many of the disciples were fishermen. They were good boatmen; they usually knew what to do in a storm. But the wind and the waves were so strong that they were afraid. They didn't know what to do. Their boat was filling up with water—they were afraid that their boat would sink and that they would drown.

The Lord was still quietly sleeping. He knew there was nothing to worry about, because He knew that God the Father was watching over them even in the storm. He knew that God would not let anything happen to them that was not for the best.

Finally, the disciples were so afraid that they woke the Lord Jesus. They said, "Lord, save us or we'll all be killed in this storm."

(Scene 3)
The Lord Jesus got up, walked to the side of the boat, and spoke to the winds and the waves. He said, "Peace, be still—be silent, be quiet." And suddenly the wind quit blowing, and the waves were quiet and calm. The Lord scolded His disciples. He said, "Why is your faith so small—are you forgetting to trust in Me?"

Then the disciples believed again in the power of God's Son. The Lord Jesus had worked another miracle. A miracle is something special that only God can do. It shows us His power. These disciples were sorry they had been afraid. They were sorry they had forgotten how great the Lord Jesus was. They knew He was not like any other man. They knew He was God. Only God could make the wind and the sea obey Him.

Application

➤ Sometimes we forget how great our God is. We forget His promises to take care of us wherever we are. Even when we are afraid at night in bed in the dark, who has promised to be with us? Yes, the Lord. Even when we get lost in a store, who has promised to be with us and take care of us? Yes, the Lord says, "I am with you always." God the Father and God the Son always do what They say They will do. (BAT: 8a Faith in God's promises)

Song: "God Is with Me"

Catechism

Review Catechism 13–16.

- Where is God? *(God is everywhere.)*

- Can you see God? *(No, I cannot see God, but He always sees me.)*

- Does God know all things? *(Yes, nothing can be hidden from God.)*

- Can God do all things? *(Yes, God can do all His holy will.)*

Song: "When I Am Afraid"

Memory verse

Review Hebrews 13:6. Have children take turns holding and manipulating the Storm visual as they recite the verse.

➤ This reminds us of how the Lord Jesus took care of His disciples.

Student page 34

Instruct the children to cut out the sequencing pictures. Referring to the cloud symbols in each section of the page, guide the children in sequencing and gluing the pictures. Read the sentences at the top of the page. Allow a volunteer to tell how Jesus calmed the storm.

Lesson 111: Jesus Showed That He Is God

Bible text: Review.

Doctrinal truth: God the Son

Character trait: Trust

Memory verses: Review.

Materials
- Mesh bags and paper fish (for review activity; used in Lessons 105 and 108)
- Student page 35 and cutouts
- Scissors
- Glue (and wet paper towels for cleanup)
- Props for role-play review
  Sick man: a doll
  Cot: piece of cardboard or box approximately 18" × 24" to hold the doll, ropes tied to four corners of cot
  Blanket: piece of cloth or towel to cover the doll
  House: large cardboard packing or appliance box, with hole cut out of top and four or five overlapping cardboard pieces—tiles—to lay over the hole. Draw a front door or cut an opening in the front of the house.

Opening song: "Tell Me the Stories of Jesus," stanzas 1–2

Prayer
Stand and pray the Lord's Prayer together.

Song: "God's Son," stanzas 1, 2, and 4

Review activity
Call on the children individually or by groups to review the following.

➤ Which miracle did Jesus do for the rich man's son? *(made him well)*

Recite Hebrews 13:6.

➤ What happened one day after Peter, James, and John went out fishing at night? *(They could not catch any fish. Jesus told them the next day to go out into deeper water. They caught so many fish that their boats began to sink.)*

What was the first miracle Jesus did while He was on Earth? *(changed water to wine at the wedding feast)*

Review memory verses using the activity with mesh bags and paper fish in Lessons 105 and 108.

Song: "This Is the Way We Row Our Boat"

Student page 35
Instruct the children to cut out the pictures and lay the pictures in a row in front of them. Ask them to listen carefully as you review each story in a clue-giving manner. Allow the children to hold up the picture that goes with the story as soon as they recognize it. Check to make sure that each child is holding up the correct picture. Then guide the children in gluing the picture in the appropriate space. (Jesus and the nobleman in the space labeled A; Jesus helping the fishermen—B; Jesus healing the sick man—C; Jesus calming the storm—D) Read the sentences on the page. Ask a volunteer to tell how Jesus showed He is God in each picture.

Song: "The Gospels"

Song: "Who God Is," stanza 2

Review activity: Role play
Open your Bible as you begin the narration. This is a paraphrase of Mark 2:1–12. Prompt the children by suggesting action to dramatize, using props. Choose four children to be the "four friends." More children may be involved by having some sit in front of the "door."

➤ Teacher: Jesus "entered in Capernaum." He was in a house. Immediately many people "were gathered together, insomuch that there was no room to receive" everyone into the house. And four men came to the Lord, bringing one who was sick of the palsy.

Four friends: *(Four children dramatize walking to the front door of the house.)*

Teacher: "And when they could not" come near to Him because of the crowd of people, they went up on top of the house—on the roof.

Four friends: *(Dramatize turning away from front door to go behind the box house and climb platform [steps, chairs] to be seen from behind box.)*

Teacher: They "uncovered the roof where he was" and let down the bed on which the man sick with palsy lay.

Four friends: *(Dramatize lifting tile away and letting the cot down through the hole in the roof.)*

Teacher: "When Jesus saw their faith, he said unto the sick of the palsy, 'Son, thy sins be forgiven thee. . . . I say unto thee, Arise, and take up thy bed, and go thy way into thine house'."

Song: "Be Ye Doers of the Word," stanzas 6–7
Repeat the role-play review with different children participating as many times as your schedule permits.

Lesson 112: Many Believed

Bible texts: Matthew 14:13–21; Mark 6:30–44; Luke 9:10–17; John 6:1–14

Doctrinal truth: God the Son (omnipotence)

Character trait: Love

Catechism: Review Catechism 16.

Opening song: "Tell Me the Stories of Jesus," stanzas 1–2

Song: "God's Son"

Song: "What Does the Bible Say?" stanza 3

Prayer
Ask God to help us to be kind and share with others.

Song: "Obedience Is," stanza 6

Bible lesson

Introduction
Recite the action rhyme "God's Son" several times.

➤ Jesus preached His Father's Word.
   (Point to heaven, place hands side by side with palms open for Bible.)
   He told of things to come.
   (Cup hands at side of mouth.)
   He fed the crowds.
   (Pretend to distribute food from cupped hand.)
   He calmed the storms.
   (Hold arms up and out.)
   He healed the deaf and dumb.
   (Touch ears and then mouth.)

➤ Have you ever gone on a picnic? Whom did you go with? Has your mother ever packed a lunch in a basket for you to eat out in the yard by yourself or with a friend? **(Allow discussion.)**

We're going to hear a Bible lesson today about a little boy's picnic lunch.

Lesson

Every day Jesus Christ and His disciples were busy preaching and teaching God's Word and God's way. God's Son, Jesus Christ, had healed many people who were sick. More and more people wanted to hear Him preach. They wanted to see the One who could work such wonderful miracles. Remember, a miracle is a special work that only God can do. It shows us His power.

One day many, many people had followed Jesus Christ and His disciples. They had stayed to hear Him preach. It was getting late in the day. It was evening, and it was time to eat.

The disciples told the Lord to send the people away so that they could go to the farms or towns nearby to get some food to eat. The Lord Jesus knew that the people were tired. He knew they were hungry. The Lord felt sorry for them.

He said to one of His disciples, "You feed them."

His disciples answered, "Where can we buy enough bread to feed these people?"

One of the disciples, whose name was Philip, said, "Lord, we could never have the money to buy enough bread to feed so many people."

Now, God's Son knew what He was going to do. He just wanted to see if His disciples trusted Him. He said to them, "Go, see if anyone here has any food to share with everyone."

Andrew answered, "There is a young boy here who has his picnic lunch. He has five small loaves of bread and two small fish, but that would not be enough for all of these thousands of people."

The Lord Jesus told His disciples to bring the boy's lunch to Him and then to have everyone sit down on the grass. There were about five thousand men besides all the women and children. He told the disciples to have all the people sit down in small groups. That would make it easier for the disciples to take food to everyone.

Then the Son of God took the five loaves and prayed. He thanked the heavenly Father for them and gave them to the disciples to take to the people.

Do you know that God's Son kept handing out bread and fish until every one of those many, many people had eaten? How could five loaves and two small fish feed so many? God's Son had worked another miracle. He made the little bit of bread and fish become more and more until the many, many people there had eaten all they wanted.

There was so much to eat that the disciples gathered up twelve baskets full of leftover bread. The Lord Jesus Christ had made one little boy's lunch become more than enough to feed thousands of people. That was another miracle. Only God can work miracles. Jesus is God.

When all the people saw what God's Son had done, they saw His power, and many believed He was God.

Application

➤ Do you think the little boy wanted to give his lunch to the Lord Jesus? Yes, I'm sure he did. He knew that God's Son could do great things. The boy wanted to show that he believed in God by giving.

Because the little boy was willing to give to God, many, many people saw God's power and believed in Him. Can God do all things? **(Catechism 16: Yes, God can do all His holy will.)**

God wants us to give to His work. We can give money in our churches to help missionaries and preachers tell others of God's Word and His way. God used a little boy long ago, and He wants to use you today. When we obey the Lord, He can use our lives for His glory. (BATs: 3a Self-concept; 5b Giving)

Song: "God's Son," stanza 5

Action rhyme: "The Hungry Crowd"
Recite the following action rhyme.

➤ Once Jesus had preached
    (Cup hands to mouth.)
To the crowds all day.
His disciples said,
"Lord, send them away."
    (Pretend to dismiss with back of hand.)

Jesus said, "No, you
    (Shake head.)
Give them some bread."
"Food for so many?
How can all be fed?"
    (Extend hands out with palms up, in questioning manner.)

Five loaves and two fishes,
    (Hold up five fingers on one hand and two on other.)
A lad with a lunch.
    (Extend hand out from waist, palm down.)
Food for so many?
Now that wasn't much.
    (Shake head slowly.)

"Bring them here to me.
    (Beckon with hand.)
Have all to sit down."
    (Sit on floor.)
The Lord gave thanks
    (Clasp hands to pray.)
And the food passed 'round.
    (Pretend to pass food.)

They all were fed,
Five thousand and more.
    (Make sweeping motion with arms.)
With twelve full baskets
Of food left o'er.

Song: "Tiptoe Quietly," stanzas 1 and 4
Allow the children to move around the room, pretending to be the little boy carrying his lunch as he goes to hear the Lord Jesus speak.

Lesson 113: Jesus Made a Girl Live Again

Bible texts: Matthew 9:18–26; Mark 5:22–43; Luke 8:41–56
Doctrinal truth: God the Son
Character trait: Trust
Memory verse: Introduce John 14:6.
Catechism: Introduce Catechism 35.

Opening song: "Jesus Loves Even Me," stanzas 1–2

Song: "God's Way"

Song: "Obedience Is"

Prayer
Thank God for the promise of eternal life in heaven.

Song: "The Wonder Song"
Replace "a flower" with "the dead live."

Song: "God's Son"

Bible lesson

Introduction
Recite the action rhyme "God's Son." (See Index of Poetry.)

Lesson

One day Jesus was standing by the Sea of Galilee, preaching and teaching. Suddenly a man came and knelt down before the Lord. This man was a leader in the synagogue. His name was Jairus. Jairus said to the Lord, "My daughter is very sick. She is going to die. She is only twelve years old. Please come and touch her that she may be well again and live."

The Lord Jesus went with Jairus. Many other people followed along the way also. They wanted to see what great things the Lord could do. While they were on the way to Jairus's house, crowds of people were all around the Lord Jesus; it was hard for Him to find room to walk along the way.

In the crowd, there was one woman who was trying to get near enough to God's Son to touch Him. This woman had been sick for many years. None of the doctors could help her. She had spent all her money, and she was still getting sicker and sicker. She had heard of the Lord Jesus' great power. She thought, "If I could just get close enough to touch His clothes—the robe He is wearing—I know I will be made well." And she did; she touched His robe, and immediately she was made well.

The Lord Jesus is God. He knows all things. He knew what had happened. He asked, "Who touched my clothes?"

"Why," His disciples said, "look at all the people so close around you. It could have been many people." But Jesus didn't mean that. He knew that the woman had touched His robe, believing in His power, and was healed. He wanted the woman to tell Him that she had touched Him.

The woman was afraid. She fell down on her knees in front of the Lord and told Him what she had done. Now Jesus already knew what she had done, but He wanted her to show her faith in His power to everyone who was watching and listening. Then he told her, "Daughter . . . child of mine, be of good comfort—be happy; your faith has made you well."

As soon as the woman went on her way, some people from the synagogue ran up to Jairus and said, "Don't bother Jesus anymore. It's too late. Your daughter has already died."

When Jesus heard the servants, He said to Jairus, "Don't be afraid. Just believe in me." And they walked on toward Jairus's house. When the Lord and some of His disciples came into Jairus's house, the family and friends of Jairus were all crying and feeling very sad.

The Lord said, "Why are you all crying? The little girl is not dead. She is just sleeping."

The people laughed at Jesus. Then the Lord Jesus had all the people leave the house, and He took Jairus and his wife with Him into the room where their daughter was lying.

God's Son took their daughter's hand and said, "Little girl, I say unto you, arise—get up."

Right away the little girl got up and walked. Everyone was very surprised. They knew the Lord could heal, but this girl was not just sick; she had been dead. God's Son had raised her from the dead. He had made her live again. Then the Lord Jesus told them to give her something to eat because He knew she would need food to keep her strong and healthy.

Application
➤ The Lord Jesus could not only heal the sick but also make dead people come to life again. What power God's Son has! Our God can do all things. Do you believe God can do anything? Let's praise Him for His great power right now. (BATs: 7c Praise; 8b Faith in the promises of God)

Song: "Praise Him, Praise Him"
Replace "God is love" with "God is great."

Memory verse
Read John 14:6 to the children.

➤ This is what Jesus said. He tells us that He is the only way to heaven. No one can be saved by his own works. Some people think that if they are kind, they will go to heaven some day. Some people think that if they give money to the church, they will deserve to go to heaven.

But Jesus tells us in this verse that He is the only way to heaven. He is the one true God, and He can give us eternal life.

Catechism
Introduce Catechism 35.

■ What is grace? (*Grace is God's kindness to us when we deserve punishment.*)

➤ Because of our sins, we deserve eternal punishment, but because of God's grace or kindness He sent His own Son, Jesus, to be punished in our place. Jesus took the punishment for my sin. Jesus took the punishment for your sin. When we ask Jesus to be our own Savior from sin, we are saved by the grace or kindness of God. We do not deserve salvation; it is the gift of God. Jesus is the only way to heaven.

Lesson 114: Jesus Walked on the Waves

Bible texts: Matthew 14:22–23; Mark 6:45–52; John 6:16–21
Doctrinal truth: God the Son (omnipotence)
Character trait: Trust
Memory verse: Review Hebrews 13:6.
Materials
• "Jesus Walked on the Water" (Picture Packet)

Opening song: "Jesus Loves Even Me," stanza 1

Prayer
Thank God that He is always with us wherever we are.

Memory verse
Review Hebrews 13:6.

Song: "God's Son," stanza 5

Bible lesson

Introduction
Sing "The Gospels."

Lead the class in the action rhyme "The Hungry Crowd." (See Index of Poetry.)

Lesson

The Bible tells us that after Jesus had fed over five thousand people with the little boy's lunch, He sent His disciples away and went up into the hills to be alone with God. There he prayed to the heavenly Father. God the Son prayed to God the Father. While He was praying, His disciples were having trouble. The Lord Jesus had sent His disciples away out on the lake in a boat to rest. They had been working hard all day. The Lord knew they were tired. But while they were out on the lake, a storm came. The winds blew and the waves tossed their boat. They could not make their boat go where they wanted it to go.

Now, even though the Lord was on the hillside praying, He knew His disciples were having problems. He knew they were rowing as hard as they could, but they were not able to get anywhere. Remember, Jesus is God's Son, but He is also God. And God knows all things. So God's Son got up from His prayer time with God the Father, and He went to help His disciples. (Display "Jesus Walked on the Water" picture.)

Do you know how He came to them? They were out in the middle of the lake in a boat with the wind and the tall waves all around. The Lord Jesus didn't have a boat, but He didn't really need one. He just walked out onto the water. He walked across the waves on top of the water and never even sank into that water. Oh, what power God's Son has! He can do anything. He was walking on the water! He was working another miracle, doing something only God can do, to show His power.

It was nighttime now. As the Lord Jesus walked near the disciples' boat, the disciples saw Him. They thought what they saw looked like the Lord, but they didn't think it really could be. How could He be walking on the water? They knew something or someone was out there in the dark, and they were afraid, but the Lord Jesus said, "It is I; don't be afraid."

The disciples were so happy to see their Lord; they took Him into their boat. The strong wind and big waves became quiet immediately. Then the disciples remembered. They remembered all the other miracles the Lord Jesus had done. They knew they had nothing to fear because the Lord God of heaven was there with them. The same God who had created the rivers, lakes, and oceans in the beginning of the world was right there with them to help them. Oh, how they worshiped this powerful Son of God! And the Bible tells us that immediately the boat came to the shore where they were going.

Application

➤ God's Son, the Lord Jesus Christ, knows all things. Jesus knew His disciples were in trouble. He went to help them. He even showed His great power by walking on the water to them.

Jesus is God. He sees each of you. He knows all about you. He has promised to take care of you when you're in trouble. You don't need to be afraid, because your God can do all things. He wants you always to remember that He can do anything, and He has promised to take care of you. (BAT: 8a Faith in God's promises)

Song: "God's Son," stanza 6

Doctrinal emphasis: God

➤ Jesus knew His disciples were in danger. Even though Jesus was up on the hillside praying, He knew what was happening to His disciples in the boat out on the lake.

Jesus has the power to do anything. There is nothing too hard for Him. He calmed the storm; He walked on the water; He made sick people well; He fed many, many people.

God knows all things. He sees each of you. He knows your names. He knows when you are sick. He knows when you are sad. He knows when you are in danger.

When we are sad or afraid, we can just pray—talk to God—and He will hear us. He has promised to be with us always, just as He was with His disciples.

Isn't our God a great and good God! (BAT: 8a Faith in God's promises)

Song: "Who God Is," stanzas 1–3

Song: "When I Am Afraid"

Song: "The Tossing Boat"

Lesson 115: A Son Was Sorry

Bible text: Luke 15:11–32

Doctrinal truth: Salvation (repentance and faith)

Character traits: Trust; Obedience

Memory verses: Introduce I John 1:9 and review Romans 3:23, Psalm 37:27, and Psalm 38:18.

Catechism: Review Catechism 32–35.

Materials
• Student page 36
• 4" × 18" strip of construction paper for each child
• Scissors
• Glue

Opening song: "Jesus Loves Even Me," stanza 1

Song: "God's Way"

Song: "Even a Child Is Known"

Prayer
Ask God to help us show Him that we love Him by the things we do.

Memory verse
Read I John 1:9 from your Bible.

➤ When we confess our sins, we tell God that we are sorry to have sinned and we want Him to forgive us. We want Him to forgive all of our unrighteousness—that's another big word for sin. Remember God is *righteous*—without sin. But we are *unrighteous;* we sin.

Song: "There Is None That Doeth Good"
Divide the children into two groups. Instruct one group to sing the chorus, followed by the other group reciting Romans 3:23*a.* Repeat several times, reversing their parts.

Bible lesson

Introduction
Sing scale song to review Psalm 37:27. (See Lesson 33.)

Lesson

The Bible tells a story about a father who had two sons. The father lived in a beautiful home with his sons. He was a very rich man. He had a lot of money, land, and houses. The father was kind to his sons and gave them a happy home. But best of all, the father loved and served the Lord God of heaven.

His younger son wanted to leave home. He wanted to go someplace where he could do what he wanted to—with no father to obey and no work to do. He wanted to spend his money and have fun. He was selfish and was thinking only about himself.

One day the younger of the two sons said to his father, "Give me the money you promised me when I was a little boy. I want to go away and live somewhere else."

The young son should have stayed home and obeyed his father. He should have worked to help his father. But he left his beautiful home. He decided to go his own way. He forgot that to be happy he should live God's way.

The young man took his money and went to a country far away. The people there did not worship the Lord God of heaven. The young man bought a lot of nice clothes; he had big parties and a lot of good food to eat. Soon he had spent all of his money. He did not even have any friends. The people he met were sinful and selfish. They thought only of themselves. They liked him only when he had money to spend and good food to eat.

The young man became very sad. After a while, he didn't have enough money to buy food to eat. He didn't have a home to live in or a nice bed to sleep in. He got a job feeding some pigs.

One day when the young son was feeding the pigs, he was so hungry that he almost ate the pigs' food. Then he began to think about the nice home where his father lived. He thought about his good father who had loved him and had been so good to him. He thought, "All the servants in my father's house are living and eating better than I am. How foolish I was to run away from a loving father who wanted to take care of me and teach me God's way. I have sinned. I must go back to my father and tell him that I am sorry for my sin. I will ask him if I can work for him like a servant to show how sorry I am for my sin."

But even before the young son got to his father's house, his father saw him coming. His father had been hoping that his son would come home. He had been waiting for him. The loving father was so happy to see his son that he ran to meet him and hugged and kissed him, The young son told his father how sorry he was for his sin. He told his father that he knew he did not deserve to be his son anymore.

But the father was very happy to have his son come home. He was so happy that his son was sorry for his sin that he called to his servants. He told them to prepare a special dinner party. He had the servants bring nice clothes for his son to wear. He was happy that his lost son was found.

Application
➤ This young son learned that God's way is best. He learned that going his own way and living selfishly and sinfully made him unhappy. He was sorry for his sin. He asked his father to forgive him.

This story reminds us that God, our heavenly Father, is always near to take care of us and give us the things we need. Our heavenly Father wants us to obey our mommies and daddies. He wants us to love and obey Him (Point up.) and learn His way from His Word. (Hold up Bible.)

When we sin, He wants us to tell Him that we are sorry. He wants to clean us from all unrighteousness. What did we say that big word means? *(sin)* Let's say, "I will be sorry for my sin." (Direct the children to recite Psalm 38:18*b* and I John 1:9 with you.) When we are really sorry for our sins, we will try hard to stop doing sinful things. We will listen to God's Word to learn God's way. We will want to live and obey our heavenly Father. (BAT: 1b Repentance and faith)

Song: "Trust and Obey," chorus
Lead the children in singing the chorus several times, reciting Psalm 38:18b each time the chorus is sung.

Student page 36

Instruct the children to cut out the pictures for the parable of the Prodigal Son. Distribute the strips of construction paper. Direct the children to lay the pictures in a row above the construction paper. Ask them to hold up the picture that shows what happened first in the story (father talking to two sons). Allow a volunteer to tell what is happening in the picture while you check to see that each child is holding the correct picture. Guide the children in gluing the picture on the left end of the construction paper. Instruct the children to hold up the picture that shows what happened second (younger son leaving home). Check for the correct picture while a volunteer tells about the picture. Guide the children in gluing the picture in the second position. Continue to direct the sequencing in the same manner (son with friends, feeding pigs, returning home).

Catechism

Review Catechism 32–35.

- What does every sin deserve? (*Every sin deserves the wrath and curse of God.*)

- What does God require of man before he can go to heaven? (*No one can enter heaven unless his heart is changed.*)

- Who can change a sinner's heart? (*The Holy Spirit can change a sinner's heart.*)

- What is grace? (*Grace is God's kindness to us when we deserve punishment.*)

Song: "Nothing but the Blood"

Lesson 116: One Man Thanked God

Bible text: Luke 17:11–19

Doctrinal truth: God the Son (omnipotence)

Character trait: Thankfulness

Memory verses: Review I Thessalonians 5:18 and John 10:30.

Catechism: Review Catechism 9.

Materials
• I Thessalonians 5:18 visuals 1 and 2 (See Lesson 40.)
• "One Man Thanked God" (Picture Packet)

Opening song: "Jesus Loves Even Me," stanzas 1–2

Song: "God's Way"

Song: "Praise Him, Praise Him"

Memory verse

Review I Thessalonians 5:18. Divide the children into two groups. Direct the first group to say the first part of the verse and the second group the second part of the verse.

Prayer

Thank God for all His blessings.

Use I Thessalonians 5:18 visuals 1 and 2.

Song: "God's Son," stanza 7

Bible lesson

Introduction

➤ When God's Son, Jesus Christ, lived in the world, He went everywhere preaching and teaching God's way. He did many, many good and kind things for people. He worked many miracles. A miracle is a special act that only God can do. It shows us God's power.

Recite "God's Son" action rhyme. (See Index of Poetry.)

Lesson

One day Jesus and His disciples—His helpers—were walking along the road going to the big city, Jerusalem. They were going to preach God's Word. As they were walking near a small town on their way to Jerusalem, they saw something very sad. They saw ten men who were sick with leprosy. Leprosy is a sickness that makes the skin scaly and rough. When the sickness gets very bad, it makes the skin fall off the person's body.

No one could help these men. Even doctors did not have medicine to make them well. No one wanted to go near them. Everyone was afraid he might get the sickness also. These sick men loved their families and did not want them to get leprosy. So they had to leave their homes and families and friends. They lived in caves outside the town away from other people. When they saw someone coming, they would call out, "Unclean, unclean," to warn people not to come near them. How sad these ten men with leprosy must have been.

As Jesus and His disciples were walking along the road, they heard the words, "Unclean, unclean." The ten sick men had heard about the power of Jesus Christ, the Son of God. They had heard how He healed crippled people and made blind people see again. They had probably even heard how Jesus had healed others who had leprosy. So when they saw Jesus coming along the road, they called out, "Jesus, Master, have mercy on us." They asked the Son of God to make them well.

Jesus answered their prayers for help. He told them to give thanks to God and then go and show themselves to the priest in the temple. The priest was the one who could tell all the other people that these men had been healed. These men believed that God's Son could make them well. They believed that God could do all things. They had faith in Him. They hurried on their way toward the temple. As they walked along, they looked down and saw that they were healed. They looked at each other. God's Son had made them all well. How happy they were. Their prayers had been answered.

But do you know what happened? The Bible tells us that only one of those ten remembered to turn around and go back to Jesus to thank Him. Only one man bowed down before the Son of God and praised Him—that means he told Jesus how great and good and powerful He is. Jesus was so happy that this man remembered to say thank you. But Jesus asked, "Where are the other nine men? Why didn't they come and thank me? Only this one man thanked me." Then Jesus told the man, "You are well because you believed me. You trusted me. Go on to the temple now."

Application

➤ How happy those ten men were. God's Son had answered their prayers. They were well. Now they could go back to their homes and families and work. But only one of them had remembered to say thank you to Jesus.

We ask God to help us get well when we're sick, don't we? We pray for others when they are sick. God gives us everything we have—our families, our homes, our churches, our school, our food, and toys. Everything we have God gives to us.

Do you always remember to thank Him for answering your prayers? Do you remember to thank Him for the food when you sit down at the table to eat? The Bible says, "O give thanks unto the Lord, for he is good." (BAT: 7c Praise) Instruct the children to recite I Thessalonians 5:18 with you.

Song: "O Give Thanks"

Song: "God's Son," stanza 7
Recite John 10:30 and review Catechism 9.

■ Are there more gods than one? *(No, there is only one God.)*

➤ Jesus worked a miracle when He healed the ten sick men. Jesus is God, and our God can do anything.

Lesson 117: A Kind Neighbor

Bible text: Luke 10:30–37

Doctrinal truth: Salvation

Character trait: Love

Memory verse: Introduce I John 4:19.

Catechism: Review Catechism 7.

Materials
• Props for role-play review (optional): sweater or jacket, purse, coins (enough for two children), Bible, broom and dustpan, Band-Aids

Opening song: "Jesus Loves Even Me," stanzas 1–2

Song: "Be Ye Doers of the Word," stanzas 6–7

Memory verse
Read I John 4:19 to the children.

Prayer
Ask God to help us show love to our family and friends.

Song: "Politeness Is"

➤ Being polite shows love.

Bible lesson

Introduction

➤ The Lord Jesus told many wonderful stories when He taught and preached here on earth. One time He told this story.

Lesson

One day there was a man who was walking along the road from a city called Jerusalem to another city called Jericho. Step, step, step, step, he walked along the road. He didn't have a car to ride in because no one had a car that long ago. He didn't even have a donkey to ride. He had to walk. While the man was walking along the way, bad men came along. They grabbed the man and tore off his coat. They hit him many, many times with sticks. They kicked him and took his money. Then they left him all alone by the side of the road. The poor man was hurt so badly that he could not move. Oh, how he hoped someone would come by and help him.

Not long after that happened, a priest came walking by. When he saw the hurt man, he crossed over to the other side of the road. He did not try to help the hurt man. Instead, he pretended not to see him. "Oh," thought the hurt man, "he didn't even stop to see how badly hurt I am." Boys and girls, do you think that priest really loved God?

Soon the injured man heard another man come along. This man was not a priest, but he did serve God as a helper in the temple. When he walked by, he saw the hurt man and came near to look at him to see who he was. But he didn't stop to help him. He also went on by—without even a kind word to the poor, pitiful man who was hurt. How sad the hurt man was! He was afraid he would just lie there and die. Wasn't there anyone who would be kind enough to help him?

Finally, a third man came walking by. This man was not even one of God's people who loved and served Him. He lived in another country called Samaria. And yet, when he saw the hurt man lying on the road, he felt sorry for him. He went over to him and put medicine and bandages on his cuts and bruises.

Then he did another very kind thing. He put the man on his own mule and took him to an inn, a place like a hotel, where he could rest in bed and have food and water to help him grow strong and well again. The next day before he left, this kind neighbor gave the hotel keeper some money and asked him to take care of the hurt man until he was well and able to get up and take care of himself.

Application

➤ When the Lord Jesus finished telling this story, he asked, "Which of these three men do you think was a good neighbor to the hurt man?" Why, of course, you know, don't you? The man from Samaria was kind, even though he did not know the Lord God of heaven.

The Lord tells us to be a good neighbor like the Samaritan man. We know God made us and loves and takes care of us. Because He has done so much for us, we should be kind to others. The Lord wants us to show our love for Him by showing love to others. We can do this with the kind words we speak and the kind things we do. (BAT: 5a Love)

Catechism

Review Catechism 7.

■ How can you glorify God? (*I can glorify God by loving Him and doing what He commands.*)

➤ Did the man from Samaria glorify God? How?

Song: "What Does the Bible Say?" stanza 5

Review activity: Role play

Narrator: Teacher, reading from open Bible

Characters: Injured man (wearing jacket or sweater), two robbers, a priest, a temple helper, a loving neighbor

Read the following narration while children pantomime actions.

➤Narrator: A certain man went from Jerusalem to Jericho, and some robbers took his clothes and money. They beat him until he was almost dead.

Man: (*One child walks along road.*)

Robbers: (*Two children pretend to hit the man and take his sweater and money.*)

Man: (*Lies still on the ground*)

Narrator: And by chance there came a certain priest that way; and when he saw him, he passed by on the other side.

Priest: (*Walks by, looks away, and crosses over to other side as he passes hurt man*)

Narrator: When a temple helper came to that place, he also looked at the hurt man and passed by on the other side.

Temple helper: (*Carrying broom and dustpan, walks by, looks at hurt man, and then walks on*)

Narrator: But when another man who was not one of God's chosen people came by and saw him, he felt sorry for him. He went to him and put medicine and bandages on his cuts. Then he put the man on his mule and took him to an inn. He gave the owner of the inn some money to take care of him.

Neighbor: (*Walks along, comes near the hurt man, pretends to put medicine and Band-Aids on the man. Helps him stand and walks over to the innkeeper. Gives innkeeper money.*) (BAT: Love)

Narrator: (Read Ephesians 4:32 to the children.) "How can you glorify God?"

Class: I can glorify God by loving Him and doing what He commands. (Catechism 7)

Repeat as your schedule permits. It may be profitable to "rehearse" this type of lesson review several times.

Lesson 118: Mary and Martha Believed

Bible text: John 11:1–45

Doctrinal truth: God the Son (omnipotence)

Character trait: Trust

Memory verse: Review I John 4:19.

Opening song: "Jesus Loves Even Me," stanzas 1–2

Memory verse

Review I John 4:19.

➤ God made each one of us. He created us to live forever because He loves us. We can live in heaven with Him if we believe that Jesus, God's Son, died for our sin, and then trust in Him.

Song: "Jesus Loves Me"

Song: "God's Way"

Prayer
Thank God for His great power to make all living things and to give life to each of us.

Song: "O Give Thanks"

Bible lesson

Introduction
➤ We have heard many lessons on God's Son. We have heard of His miracles of healing the sick. We have heard of His miracles on the sea, of his feeding the many people with one boy's lunch. And then we have heard how He made a widow's son and Jairus's daughter live again. Today we are going to hear how God's Son helped some of His friends in a special way.

Lesson

There were two sisters named Mary and Martha who lived with their brother Lazarus in a little town named Bethany. They were good friends of the Lord Jesus. The Lord often visited them in their home.

One day Lazarus got sick. He didn't get well. He got even sicker. Mary and Martha were afraid that their brother would get so sick that he would die. Mary and Martha loved their brother, and they wanted to help him. They thought of God's Son, Jesus Christ. They knew he had healed many people who were sick. They wished He were there to help. But the Lord was away in another town preaching and teaching God's Word.

The two sisters sent someone to find the Lord Jesus and to tell Him about their sick brother, Lazarus.

The messenger told the Lord that Lazarus—Jesus' friend whom He loved—was very, very sick.

The Lord Jesus did not go right away to help Lazarus. He stayed two more days where He was, preaching God's Word and teaching His disciples. When the Lord Jesus and His disciples finally came to the home of Mary and Martha, Lazarus had already died and was buried. Many of their friends had come to tell the sisters how sorry they were.

When Martha saw the Lord coming, she ran out to meet Him. She cried, "Oh, Lord, if You had only been here, You could have made Lazarus well, and he would not have died." The Lord told Martha

that her brother would live again. The Lord Jesus asked Martha if she believed that He was the Son of God.

"Oh, yes," Martha answered. "I believe You are God's Son that came from heaven to this world. I believe that You can do anything."

Martha ran to get her sister, Mary. Mary said the same thing Martha had said: "Lord, if You had been here, my brother would not have died."

Mary and Martha took the Lord to the place where Lazarus's body had been buried. There was a stone like a door in front of the place. The Lord Jesus told some friends of the family to roll the stone away.

The Lord prayed and thanked His heavenly Father for helping Him. He asked God to help everyone who was there to believe that He was the Son of God.

Then the Lord called out with a loud voice, "Lazarus, come forth." What do you think happened? Did Lazarus come out of the tomb where they had buried him? Yes, he did. Can God's Son raise the dead to life again? Yes, He can. The Lord Jesus said that He and God the Father are One. We know that nothing is too hard for God. God can do anything. Many of Mary and Martha's friends believed that day that Jesus was the Son of God.

Application
➤ There is nothing too hard for God. Our God who can do all things is here in our room right now. He is with us wherever we are. He sees you. He knows all about you. He takes care of you. You don't ever need to feel alone—even at night when it's dark—because God is with you and has promised always to take care of you. (BATs: 8a Faith in God's promises; 8d Courage)

Song: "God's Son," stanza 8

Lesson 119: The Lost Sheep

Bible texts: Psalm 23; John 10:3–5; Luke 15:4–6
Doctrinal truth: Salvation
Character trait: Trust
Memory verses: Review Psalm 23 and I John 4:19.
Materials
• A completed copy of "The Lord is My Shepherd" booklet—Student pages 28–30 (for use as a visual; used in Lessons 85–90)
• Shepherd costume
• Green and blue rugs or towels (optional)

Opening song: "Jesus Loves Even Me," stanzas 1–2
Recite I John 4:19 after each stanza.

Song: "Growing, Knowing, Showing"

Song: "I'm His Little Child"

Song: "Jesus Loves Me"

Prayer

Thank God for loving and caring for us.

Song: "Thank God"

Bible lesson

Introduction

➤ Do you remember the lesson about David, the shepherd boy? What wild animals did brave David protect his sheep from? *(a lion and a bear)*

Let's see if we can remember what else we learned in our Bible lessons about David.

➤ What does a shepherd do? *(He takes care of sheep.)*

Does a shepherd know his sheep? *(Yes, he calls them each by name.)*

How does a shepherd lead his sheep? *(He walks before them and they follow him.)*

Do sheep know their shepherd's voice? *(Yes, they won't follow the voice of other shepherds.)*

What does a shepherd do for his sheep? *(He takes them where there is green grass to eat and water to drink, puts medicine on their cuts, protects them from lions and bears, and takes them to their sheepfold to sleep at night.)*

Lesson

When Jesus lived here in this world, He told many stories. One of these was a story about another good shepherd.

This good shepherd was kind to his sheep. This good shepherd had one hundred sheep. That's a lot of sheep, isn't it? Every day he would take his sheep out to eat the green grass and drink the cool water. He led them to safe places where they wouldn't fall on sharp rocks. He watched for robbers—bad men who might try to steal his sheep. Whenever a little lamb would start to wander away from the flock—the family of sheep—he would call him back.

Every night he led his sheep back to the sheepfold he had built for them. As the sheep walked into their sheepfold home, the shepherd watched and counted them to be sure all of his one hundred sheep came safely home.

One night this good shepherd called to his sheep. His sheep knew his voice, and they came to follow him home to their sheepfold. They were tired after their busy day and were ready to sleep.

When the shepherd and sheep got to their sheepfold, the shepherd opened the door. He watched and counted as the sheep walked through the doorway. "1, 2, 3, 4, 5," he counted the sheep. "Count with me, . . . 6, 7, 8, 9, 10," etc., to 99. (Stop abruptly.) "99, 99, 99, only 99?" That was all! One sheep was missing. Where was his one hundredth sheep?

The shepherd was tired. He wanted to rest. But he loved his sheep—every one of them. So he took his staff and went back out into the dark night. He went over the hills, by the streams, and back to where they had been during the day. He called his lost sheep by name. He listened. (Pause.) But he didn't hear anything. He walked on—up and down and all around—stopping to call and listen. (Pause.) This time he heard a sound. He heard a soft little "baa, baa." The poor little lamb was so tired he could hardly "baa" anymore.

The good shepherd found his lamb. He patted him, picked him up, and laid him on his shoulder. He carried him the long way back to the sheepfold. He opened the gate and laid the tired little lamb in the sheepfold. "One hundred," he said. Now he was happy because his lost sheep was found. The Bible tells us that he hurried to tell all his neighbors and friends the good news. He loved his sheep and was happy even though the sheep had caused him so much trouble.

Application

➤ Jesus tells us that He is our Good Shepherd, and we are His little lambs. Just like the shepherd in the story loved and took care of his sheep, so Jesus, our Good Shepherd, takes care of us. He loves us; He knows us; He wants us to hate sin and love Him; He wants us to ask Him to be our Savior from sin. "We love him, because he first loved us" (I John 4:19).

Every time a little boy or girl or mommy or daddy tells Jesus he is sorry for his sin and asks Him to be his Savior, it makes Jesus happy—just like the good shepherd was happy when he found his lost sheep. (BAT: 1b Repentance and faith)

➤ Why was the shepherd happy? *(because he had found his lost lamb that he loved)*

Who did Jesus say is our Good Shepherd? *(He is.)*

What makes Jesus happy? *(when someone asks Him to be his Savior from sin)*

Memory verse

Review Psalm 23 with "The Lord is My Shepherd" booklet.

Song: "The Lord Is My Shepherd"

Review activity: Role play

Place the rugs or towels on the floor to represent grass and water. Choose one child to wear the shepherd's costume. Direct all of the children (or choose two or three) to pretend to be sheep. Direct the sheep to follow the shepherd as you narrate the following. The teacher could be the shepherd, with all of the class participating as sheep.

Sing "Tiptoe Quietly," stanza 4, replacing "round the room" with "quietly."

➤ A good shepherd takes his sheep to green grass to eat. *(Walk to green rug.)*

Sing "Tiptoe Quietly," stanza 4, replacing "round the room" with "quietly."

➤ A good shepherd takes his sheep to cool water to drink. *(Walk to blue rug.)*

A good shepherd pours medicine on the sores and cuts that his sheep get. *(Shepherd pretends to pour medicine on the cuts of his sheep.)*

Sing "Tiptoe Quietly," stanza 4, replacing "round the room" with "quietly."

➤ A good shepherd takes his sheep to their sheepfold to sleep at night. *(All except one sheep walk inside sheepfold as the shepherd counts them.)*

A good shepherd goes and finds his lost sheep. *(Lost sheep follows shepherd to sheepfold.)*

Song: "Savior, Like a Shepherd Lead Us"

Lesson 120: Jesus Loves Children

Bible texts: Matthew 19:13–15; Mark 10:13–16; Luke 18:15–17

Doctrinal truth: God (His love)

Character traits: Trust; Contentment

Memory verses: Review I John 4:19 and John 14:6.

Catechism: Review Catechism 13–15 and introduce Catechism 41. (Catechism 41 is taken out of order to follow the lesson theme.)

Materials
• "Jesus Blessing Children" (Picture Packet)
• Student page 37

Opening song: "Jesus Loves Even Me"
Recite I John 4:19.

Song: "Jesus Loves the Little Children"

Song: "Jesus Loves Me"

Catechism

Introduce Catechism 41.

■ Does Christ care for little children? *(Yes, for He says in Mark 10:14, "Suffer the little children to come unto me, and forbid them not: for of such is the kingdom of God.)*

Song: "I'm His Little Child"

Prayer

Thank God that He loves us and sent His Son, Jesus Christ, to take the punishment for our sins.

Bible lesson

Introduction

Sing "Where Is Jason?" substituting "Jason" with the names of children in your class. Each time you sing to a child, you could ask that child to recite I John 4:19 or answer Catechism 41.

Lesson

One day God's Son, Jesus Christ, was preaching in the country along the roadside. People came from everywhere to hear the words He spoke. Some came to Him because they were blind. Only Jesus, God's Son, could heal the blind and make them see again. Some came to Jesus because they could not walk. They believed God's Son would be able to heal them. And He did. Jesus Christ did many wonderful miracles while He lived on this earth. A miracle is something special that only God can do. It shows us His power.

But some people came just to hear Jesus preach God's Word. They were sorry for their sins, and they wanted to know about God's way. The Lord Jesus Christ, God's Son, told these people how God had created mothers and fathers and boys and girls to love and obey Him. He told them that "there is none that doeth good, no, not one . . . ; for all have sinned and come short of the glory of God." He told them that sin must be punished. But He also told them that God had a plan to forgive them of their sin. Jesus told them that He was God's Son and that He was the way to heaven. (Recite John 14:6.)

The people listened. They wanted to hear the Word of God. Mothers and fathers even brought their children to see and hear God's Son. They wanted Jesus to touch their boys and girls. They wanted Him to pray to God the Father and ask Him to help their children to grow up to know God's way and to love and obey Him.

As the children came nearer to where Jesus Christ was, they got very excited. They had heard their parents talk about the great Son of God. Now they could see Him. Maybe He would even touch them. There were happy smiles on their faces. They could hardly wait to get up close to God's Son.

Then suddenly Jesus' helpers came and started pushing the children away. They said, "Don't bother God's Son with these little ones. He has more important things to do. He is teaching these older people."

Oh, how unhappy those words made the parents and their children. Their happy smiles disappeared. Was Jesus really too busy to bless the small children? *(No, He loves and cares for everyone.)*

Now Jesus heard what His disciples had said, and He saw what they had done. (Display "Jesus Blessing Children" picture.) He said, "Let the children come to me. Don't send them away. These children love and trust me. They believe what I say. No one can live in heaven with God the Father unless he believes and trusts me, just like these little children."

How happy the parents and children were to have Jesus bless them. Jesus not only touched them and prayed for them, but He also picked them up in His arms, held them, and talked to them.

Application

➤ You boys and girls cannot sit on Jesus' lap today. You cannot feel His hand touch you on the head. But even though you cannot see Him, you can talk to God anytime and anywhere. When you pray, you talk to God. You can also hear God speak to you when you listen to Bible words. (BATs: 6a Bible study; 6b Prayer)

God's Word tells you that Jesus Christ, God's Son, loves you very much. He is always with you wherever you are. Even though you cannot see Him, He sees all that you do. Jesus loves you even more than your mothers, fathers, grandmothers, and grandfathers love you.

Lead the children in reciting I John 4:19.

Student page 37

Instruct the children to draw a picture of themselves in the picture of Jesus blessing the children. Lead them in reciting I John 4:19. Read and discuss the page. Direct the children to write their names on the handwriting line at the bottom of the page. Allow several volunteers to read the sentence.

Song: "Jesus Loves the Little Children"
Recite Catechism 41 again.

Catechism

Review Catechism 13–15.

- Where is God? *(God is everywhere.)*

- Can you see God? *(No, I cannot see God, but He always sees me.)*

- Does God know all things? *(Yes, nothing can be hidden from God.)*

Lesson 121: Jesus Healed a Blind Man

Bible text: Luke 18:35–43
Doctrinal truths: God the Son (omnipotence); Salvation (faith)
Character traits: Trust; Thankfulness
Memory verse: Review I John 4:19.
Catechism: Review Catechism 41.
Materials
- "A Man Born Blind" (Picture Packet)

Opening song: "Jesus Loves Even Me"

Song: "Learning God's Way," stanzas 1–2

Memory verse
Review I John 4:19.

Song: "I'm His Little Child"

Catechism
Review Catechism 41.

- Does Christ care for little children? *(Yes, for He says in Mark 10:14, "Suffer the little children to come unto me, and forbid them not: for of such is the kingdom of God.")*

Prayer
Thank God for making us, loving us, and taking care of us.

Action rhyme: "God Made Me Wonderfully"
Read the following action rhyme.

➤ My feet are made for walking.
  (Point to feet.)
They walk from here to there.
  (Step in place.)
My hands are made for helping
  (Hold out hands.)
And showing that I care.
  (Place hands over heart.)
My head is made for thinking.
  (Point to head.)
My eyes are made to see.
  (Point to eyes.)
My ears are made for hearing.
  (Point to ears.)
God made me wonderfully.
  (Point to heaven.)

Bible lesson

Introduction
Sing "My Eyes Can See a Flower."

Sing about something you can see in the room, replacing "a flower" with the object.

Ask a child to sing about something he can see.

➤ God made us with eyes so that we can see. Some people are blind. They are blind and cannot see because God made them that way. If they love God, they know His way is best.

Lesson

One day the Lord Jesus was walking and talking with His disciples on the way to Jerusalem. As they walked near the city of Jericho, crowds of people came to see Jesus. A blind man was sitting beside the road.

Do you know what it means to be blind? Everyone close your eyes for a moment. Can you think how it might be if you had never seen a tree or a flower, or if you had never seen your mother or daddy or friends? How sad that would be. You would need someone to help you in many, many ways.

In our story the blind man was begging. He was asking people to give him money to buy food. He couldn't work to make money or to buy what he needed. He had to beg for everything he needed.

When the blind man heard the noise of the crowd of people walking near, he asked someone what was happening. Some told him that Jesus of Nazareth was walking by and that many people were with Him. "Oh," thought the blind man, "I've heard about this great man sent from God. He has worked many miracles. He has healed the sick and even raised the dead. I know He can help me also."

The blind man called out, "Jesus, have mercy on me." The blind man asked the Lord for mercy. He wanted Jesus to heal him. Mercy is kindness that we don't deserve.

The people who were walking in front of Jesus told the man to be quiet, but the blind man did not listen to them. He called even louder, "Thou Son of David, have mercy on me."

Did Jesus hear him? Yes, of course He did. Jesus is God. He knows all things. Jesus told some of the people there to bring the blind man to Him. Oh, how excited the blind man must have been to come so near to the Son of God. If only he could see Him!

Jesus asked him, "What do you want Me to do for you?"

The blind man answered, "Lord, that I might be able to see."

Jesus said, "You can see because you believe in Me." And the man's eyes immediately were healed—he could see. He saw the Son of God who

had healed him. He saw the people all around; he saw the trees, the sky, the birds—all of God's creation. He was so happy.

What do you think the man did? Yes, he praised and thanked God. And everyone who had been watching praised God also.

Application

➤ The blind man believed that the Son of God could do anything. God wants us to believe His Word. He says He will take care of us and always be with us and show us what to do. (BAT: 8a Faith in God's promises) Let's thank God for His promises and kindnesses to us. (BAT: 7c Praise)

Song: "A Blind Man"

Song: "O Give Thanks"

Song: "God's Son," stanzas 1–3

Lesson 122: Jesus Helped Zacchaeus

Bible text: Luke 19:1–10

Doctrinal truths: God the Son; Salvation

Character trait: Love

Memory verses: Review John 14:6; I John 1:9; and John 3:16.

Catechism: Introduce Catechism 36–37.

Materials
• Stick figures for display (See Bible lesson below.)
• Student page 38 and cutout
• Scissors
• Glue

Opening song: "Jesus Loves Even Me"

Song: "Growing, Knowing, Showing"

Song: "Jesus Loves the Little Children"

Song: "Jesus Loves Me"

Prayer

Thank God for His love in sending His Son and for loving us even when we disobey.

Memory verses

Review John 14:6 and I John 1:9.

➤ Jesus, God's Son, tells us that He is the only way to heaven. He tells us that if we confess our sins, He will forgive us. Do you believe what God's Son tells you in His Word? We learned that to trust someone is to believe him. When we trust someone, we believe that he will do what he says. We believe that he will keep his promises.

Do boys and girls always keep their promises? *(no)* Do mommies and daddies always keep their promises? They try to, but sometimes they can't. Does God always keep His promises? Yes, He always does. Because God can do anything, He can always do what He promises. We know He will do what He says He will. (BAT: 8a Faith in God's promises)

Bible lesson

Introduction
Sing or recite the chorus "Oh, How I Love Jesus."

➤ The Lord Jesus was always showing His love to others when He lived in this world. Can you tell me some ways He showed His love? *(He healed the sick, calmed the storms, and blessed the children.)*

Lesson
Draw stick figures for appropriate scenes while telling the story.

(Scene 1)
One warm spring day the Lord Jesus was walking along the road through the city of Jericho. The new green leaves were filling the branches of the trees all around the countryside. Many people had heard that Jesus was coming. They had come to see this great man who worked so many miracles. Some of these people believed Jesus was the Son of God, but many did not.

There was a man named Zacchaeus who lived in Jericho. Zacchaeus was a rich man. He had much money. He had a very important job. His job was to collect taxes; that means he took money from the people to give to the leader of the land they lived in. The people did not like this leader. Many times Zacchaeus had cheated the people. He had taken some of their money for himself. The people did not like Zacchaeus either. They did not even want to be near Zacchaeus or speak to him. They called him bad names. Zacchaeus was a lonely man. He did not have many friends who loved him.

Now Zacchaeus had heard that Jesus had come to Jericho. He wanted to see this Jesus whom he had heard so much about. Zacchaeus was a very, very short man. He was not tall enough to see over all the people who were standing by the roadside where the Lord Jesus walked. What was he to do?

Zacchaeus thought of the tall trees by the roadside. He had probably climbed them when he was a little boy. He saw a tall tree by the side of the road where he knew the Lord Jesus was to walk. He ran and quickly climbed the tree. He scooted

his way out onto a strong limb of the tree that stretched out over where the Lord was to walk. There he hid in the leaves of the tree while he watched and waited.

(Scene 2)
Soon the Son of God came to the place where Zacchaeus was hiding. The Lord knew where Zacchaeus was. He didn't have to look up to see Zacchaeus. The Lord always sees us wherever we are because He is God. The Lord even knew that Zacchaeus was thinking, "Can God really love me and forgive my sins?" The Lord always knows what we are thinking and how we feel because He is God.

Because the Lord knew Zacchaeus was there, He "looked up, and saw him, and said to him, 'Zacchaeus, make haste [hurry], and come down; for today I [am going to your house]'."

Zacchaeus could hardly believe his ears. What had he heard? The Lord Jesus was really coming to his house. Now he could talk to the Lord and learn God's way.

Joyfully, Zacchaeus came down from the tree just as quickly as he could. And happily he ran to take the Lord to his house.

"Humpf!" grumbled the people who were watching. "Jesus is going to eat with that terrible sinner." They wondered why Jesus would go to the home of such a wicked man. The synagogue leaders probably were jealous that the Lord had not asked to come to one of their houses.

When Zacchaeus took the Lord to his house, he said, "Lord, I'm not good enough to have you come to my house." Zacchaeus confessed that he had done many sinful things.

Do you think that stopped Jesus? No, Jesus already knew Zacchaeus was a sinner—"for all have sinned." The Lord loved Zacchaeus and wanted to tell him God's Word and the way to heaven. He wants to show us that He loves everyone—no matter who he is or what he has done. (Recite John 3:16.) So the Lord Jesus went with Zacchaeus to his house. Zacchaeus was certainly a sinner—he did not know how to get to heaven. But Jesus told him the way. (Recite John 14:6.)

Application
➤ God's Son came to show us how much God loves each one of us. That's why God sent His Son into this world. (BAT: 1a Understanding Jesus Christ)

He tells us in His Word that because He loved us so much, we should also love each other. (BAT: 5a Love)

Student page 38

Guide the children in connecting the dots to complete the figure of Jesus. Instruct them to cut out the picture of Zacchaeus and glue it in place. Read and discuss the page.

Song: "Zacchaeus"

Action rhyme: "Zacchaeus"

➤ "Zacchaeus, Zacchaeus,
    (Cup hand to one side of mouth, calling.)
   Way up in the tree."
    (Shade eyes and look up.)
   Our Lord called, "Zacchaeus,
    (Point to heaven and cup hand to one side of mouth, calling.)
   Come and walk with me."
    (Beckon with hand; walk in place.)

Catechism

Introduce Catechism 36–37.

➤ Why did God send His Son into the world? *(to live a perfect life without sin and to die on the cross and take the punishment for our sins)*

■ Can anyone be saved by his own works? *(No one can be saved by his own works.)*

■ Did Christ ever sin? *(No, Christ was holy, sinless, and undefiled.)*

Relate the catechism questions to the Zacchaeus lesson.

Lesson 123: Review—Life of Christ

Bible text: Review.

Doctrinal truth: God the Son

Character trait: Love

Memory verses: Review.

Catechism: Review Catechism 1–37 and 41.

Materials
• Student page 39
• Question Mark visual (used in Lesson 80)

Opening song: "Jesus Loves Even Me," stanzas 1–2

Prayer

Stand and pray the Lord's Prayer together.

Song: "Tell Me the Stories of Jesus"

Song: "One God"

Song: "The Trinity"

Song: "The Gospels"

Character story: "Running Errands for Jesus"

A little boy once said, "Mother, I wish that Jesus lived on earth now!"

"Why, my darling?" asked the mother.

"Because I would like so much to do something for Him."

"What could a little fellow like you do for Him?" asked the mother. The little boy replied, "I could run errands for Him."

"So you could, my child," said Mother, "and so you shall. Here are a glass of jelly and some oranges that you can take to poor old Margaret. That will be doing an errand for Jesus. When Jesus was on earth, He said, 'Inasmuch as you have done it unto one of the least of these . . . , ye have done it unto me' (Matthew 25:40). My darling, remember that when you do a kind deed for someone because you love Jesus, it is just the same as doing it for Jesus. You can run errands for Him every day!" *(1,001 Stories for Children and Children's Workers)*

Student page 39

Review the story represented by the first picture. Ask the children, "Does the picture show something that happened in the story about the lost sheep?" *(yes)* Instruct them to draw a smile on the face at the top of the picture. Lead them in reciting the verse at the bottom of the picture. Review in the same manner the stories represented by the remaining pictures. If the picture did not happen in the story, instruct the children to leave the face blank or to draw a frown on the face (the story about Jesus walking on the water—no; the story about Jesus helping Zaccheus—no; Jesus blessing the children—yes). Read the sentence together.

Song: "Jesus Loves the Little Children"

Review activity: Question Mark visual

Review all verses and catechism with the Question Mark visual.

God's Son Lives

Easter: I Believe Jesus Lives

Lesson 124: Jesus Rode into the City

Bible texts: Matthew 21:1–11; Mark 11:1–11; Luke 19:29–40

Doctrinal truth: God the Son

Character trait: Thankfulness

Memory verses: Introduce I Corinthians 15:3*b*–4 and review Hebrews 13:6.

Catechism: Review Catechism 36 and introduce Catechism 38, 45, and 46.

Materials
- Construction-paper palm branch for each student (Roll a 9" × 12" green sheet of construction paper into a tube. Tape, and then fringe at one end.)

Opening chorus: "Easter Time"

Song: "Christ Arose," stanza 1
Be sure the children understand the meaning of the words. "Arose" could easily be misinterpreted as a flower.

Prayer
Tell the Lord that you love Him.

Song: "Praise Him, Praise Him"

Memory verse
Read I Corinthians 15:3*b*–4 from the Bible. Recite the verses several times and have the children join you on the first phrase.

Action rhyme: "God's Son"
(See Index of Poetry.)

Bible lesson

Introduction
➤ The Lord Jesus had been preaching God's Word and working wonderful miracles. He had healed the sick, made blind men see, and made crippled people walk. He had even raised the dead and made them live again.

Lesson

The Lord was walking with His disciples toward the city of Jerusalem. When they came near the city, the Lord Jesus said to two of His disciples, "Go into that little village over there and you will find a little donkey. Untie it and bring it to me. If anyone asks you what you are doing, say the Lord needs it."

The disciples did as Jesus commanded them. They found the donkey tied just as the Lord had said they would. When someone saw them and asked what they were doing, they said what the Lord Jesus had told them to say. And they took the donkey away.

When they brought the donkey to the Lord, they put a coat on the donkey's back. Jesus then sat on the donkey. While the Lord rode on the donkey toward Jerusalem, His disciples walked along the road beside Him. As they went along the road, people came to see who it was. When they saw that it was the Lord, some of them took off their coats and put them on the ground to make a carpet for the Lord to ride over.

When many people heard that the Lord Jesus was coming to Jerusalem, they took branches of palm trees and spread them on the road in front of the Lord.

More and more people joined the group as they went along the way. Everyone was so happy to be with the Lord. He had preached and had done so many wonderful miracles that they began to sing praises to God and thank Him for His wonderful power.

They sang, "Hosanna! Blessed be the King who comes in the name of the Lord." And when the Lord Jesus and his disciples came into Jerusalem and the people saw them, many people asked, "Who is this?"

Then those who knew the Lord Jesus answered, "This is Jesus, the prophet who grew up in the little town of Nazareth in Galilee."

Not all the people praised Jesus and wanted Him to be their king. There were some Pharisees— wicked men who came to say bad things to Jesus and about Jesus. But they could not stop the people. The people just went on praising God's Son.

The Pharisees believed they could go to heaven because they knew God's laws. They were so proud of themselves. They were thankful for how good they thought they were instead of how good

God is. They really didn't love God or His Son. They didn't think they were sinners and needed a Savior. Can anyone be saved by his own works? *(Catechism 36: No one can be saved by his own works.)*

Will knowing about God's Word get us to heaven? No! We must confess our sin and ask Jesus Christ, God's Son, to be our Savior. The Lord Jesus is the only way to heaven.

Do people act like Pharisees today? *(Answers may vary.)* Some people believe that going to church will save them. Some believe that if they give money to help the poor people, they will be saved. Jesus says, "I am the way"—the only way to heaven.

Application
Distribute palm branches.

➤ The people in our lesson today gave praise to Jesus, God's Son. Mothers and fathers and children sang and waved palm branches. God wants us to praise His Son too. Let's sing "Praise Him, Praise Him." Let's stand and pretend to be waving palm branches to greet Jesus into Jerusalem as we sing our song.

Sometimes when you sing a song about God or Jesus Christ, God's Son, or tell someone that God loves him and Jesus died to save him from his sin, some boy or girl may laugh at you or say bad things about God's Son. Should that stop you from doing the right thing? No! We should love and obey God's Son no matter what anyone else says or does. God will help us to be brave when we do the right thing. (Recite Hebrews 13:6.) (BAT: 8d Courage)

Catechism
Introduce Catechism 38, 45, and 46.

▪ For whom did Christ obey and suffer? *(Christ obeyed and suffered for sinners.)*

▪ Did Christ remain in the tomb after His crucifixion? *(No, Christ rose bodily from the tomb on the third day after His death.)*

▪ Will Christ come again? *(Yes, Christ has promised to return to take us to be with Him.)*

Lesson 125: Jesus Died

Bible texts: Matthew 27:11–36; Mark 15:1–15; Luke 23:13–24; John 19:6–16

Doctrinal truths: God the Son; Man; Satan

Character traits: Trust; Thankfulness

Memory verse: Review I Corinthians 15:3b–4.

Catechism: Review Catechism 27, 29, 38, 45, and 46.

Materials
• "Christ on the Cross" (Picture Packet)

Opening chorus: "Easter Time"

Song: "Easter! Easter!"

Prayer
Thank God for Easter time, when we remember how God's Son died for our sin and lives again.

Song: "On the Cross"

Memory verse
Review I Corinthians 15:3b–4. Review the meaning of "the gospel" and "good news" as you have the children recite the verse several times.

Song: "Christ Arose"

Bible lesson

Introduction
➤ Why did God send His Son down from heaven into the world to be born as a baby in a manger? *(to grow up and die on the cross)* Why did God's Son have to die? *(to take the punishment for our sin)* For whom did Christ obey and suffer? *(Catechism 38: Christ obeyed and suffered for sinners.)*

Lesson

God's Son, Jesus Christ, never did anything wrong. He could not sin because He is God. When He lived here on Earth, He helped so many people by healing the sick, feeding the many people, quieting the storms, and making the dead live again. He worked so hard to tell everyone of God's love and God's way.

Wouldn't you think everyone would love Him and want to obey Him? Well, some people did not love the Son of God. They did not believe He was God. They hated Him. Why did they hate Him?

Do you remember our lesson when we learned about Satan? Who is Satan? *(Catechism 27: Satan is an evil spirit who is the enemy of God and all Christians.)* Satan was an angel called Lucifer who once lived in heaven with God. But Lucifer became jealous of God and wanted to be as great as God. God had to make him leave heaven. Now Lucifer is called Satan or the Devil. Satan does not want anyone to love and obey God. He tries to get everyone to disobey God's Word. Some people believe Satan. They do not listen to God's Word.

When God's Son was working all the wonderful miracles that only God could do, some people did not believe in Him. One day, these people who hated Jesus took Him to one of the leaders of the land. The leader's name was Pilate. They told Pilate that Jesus was bad, that He said He was God, and that He wanted to be the king. They asked Pilate to crucify God's Son. "Crucify" means to kill someone by nailing him to a cross.

Since Pilate did not believe that Jesus had done anything wrong, he was afraid to hurt Him. Pilate wanted to let Him go, but he was also afraid of the Jewish leaders. Pilate told the people they could do what they wanted with Jesus.

And these people—God's own special chosen people, the Jews—did crucify our Lord. (Display "Christ on the Cross" picture.) They nailed Him to a cross and let Him hang there until He died. It was a sad, sad time.

But because we know Jesus is God, we know it was good for him to die. We know Jesus was taking the punishment for our sin because He loved us so much. God's Son died so that we could live, and we live when we believe and trust in Him.

Application

➤ Do you believe Jesus is God? Did Satan want God's Son to die on the cross? *(Allow discussion.)* Does Satan want God's will to be done? *(Catechism 29: No, Satan always wants people to do the opposite of what God wants them to do.)* Do you believe that God's Son took the punishment for your sin when He died for you on the cross? Let's thank God for His great love for us. (BAT: 7c Praise)

Song: "Praise Him, Praise Him"

Catechism

Review Catechism 45–46.

■ Did Christ remain in the tomb after His crucifixion? *(No, Christ rose bodily from the tomb on the third day after His death.)*

■ Will Christ come again? *(Yes, Christ has promised to return to take us to be with Him.)*

Lesson 126: Jesus Lives

Bible texts: Matthew 27:57–66; 28:1–8; Mark 15:43–47; 16:1–6; Luke 23:50–24:10; John 19:38–20:18

Doctrinal truths: God the Son; Man

Character traits: Trust; Thankfulness; Love

Memory verse: Review I Corinthians 15:3*b*–4.

Catechism: Review Catechism 38, 45, and 46.

Materials
• "The Open Tomb" (Picture Packet)

Opening chorus: "Easter Time"

Song: "Easter! Easter!"

Song: "On the Cross"

Prayer

Thank God for His Son who died and rose again for us.

Song: "How Do We Know?" stanzas 2–4

Memory verse

Review I Corinthians 15:3*b*–4.

Song: "Christ Arose"

➤ *Hallelujah* means "praise ye Jehovah" or "praise ye the Lord." Why do we praise our God? *(Answers may vary.)*

Bible lesson

Introduction

➤ When Jesus died on the cross, was it a bad time or a good time? Yes, it is sad when we think how much it hurt Him to be nailed to the cross, but it is a good time when we believe He died for us because He loved us so much. This is why *gospel* means "good news"—it tells us of God's plan to save us from our sin. For whom did Christ obey and suffer? *(Catechism 38: Christ obeyed and suffered for sinners.)*

Lesson

After the people who hated Jesus nailed Him to the cross, He died. Jesus' disciples and His other friends were very sad. Many of them had watched while Jesus was crucified. One of His friends who loved Him took His body down and buried it in a tomb. The tomb was a cave in the side of a rock. He rolled a big stone in front of the entrance to the tomb. The enemies of Jesus put some soldiers there to guard the tomb so that no one could take the Lord's body away.

All of Jesus' friends went home. Everyone had left the tomb, except for the soldiers.

Three days later, it was Sunday, the first day of the week. On this day very early in the morning, some of Jesus' friends came to the tomb. They were women who were bringing sweet-smelling spices to put in the tomb.

Suddenly there was a great earthquake; the whole earth shook. (Display "The Open Tomb" picture.) God the Father sent an angel down from heaven to roll back the stone from the entrance of the tomb. Then the angel sat on the stone. The angel was all white and shining. The soldiers fainted because they were so afraid.

The angel said to the women who had come to the tomb, "Don't be afraid; I know you came to see your crucified Lord, but He is not here: for He is risen, just as He said He would. Come and see for yourselves—the tomb is empty."

The women who had come to see the Lord looked into the tomb.

It was empty. Then the angel of the Lord told them to hurry to tell the disciples that God's Son had risen from the dead.

The women hurried away. They were so happy to be able to tell the good news to the disciples and to all the people who loved the Lord Jesus.

Application

➤ The women were happy to hear the good news that Christ was risen from the tomb. They were happy to be able to tell others the good news.

Jesus came to die for sinners. He had to die to fulfill God's plan for our salvation. We can believe all God has promised. (BATs: 1a Understanding Jesus Christ; 8b Faith in the power of the Word of God)

Are you happy to hear the good news "that Christ died for our sins according to the scriptures; And that he was buried, and that he rose again the third day according to the scriptures" (I Cor. 15:3b–4)?

Are you happy to tell this good news to others? There are many, many people today who do not believe God's Word. They believe Satan's lies. The Lord wants each of us to tell the gospel to members of our family and friends who have not trusted in God's Son as their Savior from sin. (BAT: 5c Evangelism and missions)

Song: "Be Ye Doers of the Word," stanza 10

Catechism

Review Catechism 45–46.

- Did Christ remain in the tomb after His crucifixion? *(No, Christ rose bodily from the tomb on the third day after His death.)*

- Will Christ come again? *(Yes, Christ has promised to return to take us to be with Him.)*

Lesson 127: On the Road to Emmaus

Bible text: Luke 24:13–35

Doctrinal truth: God

Character traits: Trust; Thankfulness

Memory verse: Review I Corinthians 15:3b–4.

Catechism: Review Catechism 38, 45, and 46.

Opening chorus: "Easter Time"

Song: "Easter! Easter!"

Song: "Christ Arose"

Prayer

Thank God that our Savior arose from the grave.

Memory verse

Review I Corinthians 15:3b–4.

Song: "How Do We Know?" stanzas 2–4

Bible lesson

Introduction: "He Bore the Punishment"

One time, a little boy made mud pies. When he was very dirty, he went into the house. He climbed up on Mother's clean bed. He got the bedspread very dirty. Mother had said that no one should get her bedspread dirty. The little boy disobeyed his mother. In a little while, Mother returned from the store. She saw what her bad boy had done. She said, "I must punish my boy. He disobeyed me."

Big brother heard the little boy crying. He came in, and saw the dirty bed. He knew that Mother was going to punish the little boy. He felt very sorry for the little boy. He said, "Mother, let me take my little brother's place. Let me bear his whipping." So Mother gave the punishment to big brother, and the little boy went free. How much the little boy loved his big brother. How he thanked his big brother for taking his punishment.

The Lord Jesus was punished on the cross for our sins. How we love Him! How we thank Him for "taking our punishment!" *(1,001 Stories for Children and Children's Workers)*

➤ God's Son paid for our sin. He took all the blame for our sin. He did it because He loves us. For whom did Christ obey and suffer? *(Catechism 38: Christ obeyed and suffered for sinners.)* (BAT: 1a Understanding Jesus Christ)

Lesson

In the afternoon after Jesus had risen from the tomb, there were two men walking along the road on their way home to Emmaus. They had been in Jerusalem and now they were talking together about everything that had happened in the past three days.

As they talked, Jesus Himself came and walked along with them. But the two men did not know it was the Lord. They thought it was just some stranger they did not know.

The Lord asked them what they were talking about and why they looked so sad. One of them, named Cleopas, answered, "Are you a stranger around there? Don't you know what has happened in Jerusalem these past few days?"

The Lord asked, "Who are you talking about?"

And they said, "About Jesus, who lived in Nazareth, who was a man of God, and who preached and worked miracles by God's power. The religious leaders in the temple had him crucified three days ago. We had hoped that Jesus was to be the Messiah whom God promised would come to be our Savior and the Savior of the world.

"And today some women who are our friends went to the tomb and said they saw an angel who said, 'He is risen'; the angel said that Jesus is alive. And some of our other friends also went to the tomb and found the same thing. They saw that the tomb was empty, and the Lord was not there. We don't know what has happened."

Then the Lord Jesus began to teach them what God's Word said about the promised Messiah who was to be the Savior of the world. He began to tell these two men about Himself and God's plan.

When they came to their little town of Emmaus, they asked Jesus to come and stay at their house since it was almost night. And He did.

When they sat down to eat, the Lord took some bread and thanked God the Father for it and then gave them each a piece. Then their eyes were opened so that they recognized their Lord. They knew what they had heard was true—that Jesus Christ had risen from the grave. Then the Lord disappeared from the room.

The two men were so happy about this good news of Jesus' Resurrection that they got up immediately and went back to Jerusalem to tell their friends that "the Lord is risen."

Application

➤ What a happy time! What good news this was to those who loved the Lord! And it is still the good news of the gospel "that Christ died for our sins according to the scriptures."

Jesus Christ came to die for sinners. He had to die to fulfill what God had said He would do to save us. He obeyed His heavenly Father. And Jesus blessed the bread. Even God's only Son gave thanks before eating. We should always give thanks to God for the food and all things that we have. (BATs: 1a Understanding Jesus Christ; 7c Praise)

Catechism
Review Catechism 45–46.

- ◼ Did Christ remain in the tomb after His crucifixion? *(No, Christ rose bodily from the tomb on the third day after His death.)*

- ◼ Will Christ come again? *(Yes, Christ has promised to return to take us to be with Him.)*

Lesson 128: In the Room at Jerusalem

Bible texts: Mark 16:14; Luke 24:36–48; John 20:19–31
Doctrinal truth: God the Son
Character trait: Trust
Memory verse: Review I Corinthians 15:3*b*–4.
Catechism: Review Catechism 38, 45, and 46.

Opening chorus: "Easter Time"

Song: "Christ Arose"

Prayer
Thank God for His power.

Memory verse
Review I Corinthians 15:3*b*–4.

Catechism
Review Catechism 38, 45, and 46.

- ◼ For whom did Christ obey and suffer? *(Christ obeyed and suffered for sinners.)*

- ◼ Did Christ remain in the tomb after His crucifixion? *(No, Christ rose bodily from the tomb on the third day after His death.)*

- ◼ Will Christ come again? *(Yes, Christ has promised to return to take us to be with Him.)*

Bible lesson

Introduction
Briefly review the last Bible lesson.

➤ Where were the two men in our last Bible lesson going? *(Emmaus, their home)*

Where had they been? *(Jerusalem)*

What were they talking about as they walked along the road? *(Jesus' death and Resurrection)*

Who walked along with them? *(the Lord Jesus)*

What happened? *(Answers may vary.)*

Lesson

Now the two men who had walked and talked with the Lord on the road to Emmaus hurried back to Jerusalem after the Lord went away from them. They came to where the disciples and some of their friends were talking together. They went into the room and closed the door. They wanted their meeting to be a secret. They closed the door because they were afraid the religious leaders and people who did not believe that Jesus is God's Son would see them and punish them for talking about the Lord Jesus. Then the two men told the others how they had walked and talked with the risen Lord.

While they were talking together, the Lord Jesus suddenly appeared and was in the room with them. The Lord said, "Peace be unto you."

All the people were afraid. They didn't know what had happened. The door had not opened and shut. How could the Lord have come in? They thought they were seeing a spirit.

Jesus said, "Don't be afraid; don't doubt God's power. Look at my hands and my feet. See for yourselves that I am not a spirit, but I am here in my body."

The disciples looked at the nail marks on his hands and his feet. Remember that the soldiers drove nails through our Lord's hands and feet when they nailed Him to the cross. It really was their Lord! They were so amazed and happy that they didn't know what to do.

Then Jesus asked them, "Do you have anything to eat?" They gave him some fish and honey, and He took the food and ate it there in front of His disciples so that they could see that He was not just a spirit. They knew that a spirit could not eat food.

Then Jesus preached to them what the Old Testament Scriptures long, long ago had told would happen—that Christ had to suffer by dying on the cross and then He would rise again. Now it had happened, just as God said it would long ago.

The Lord told His disciples to go and tell everyone everywhere to be sorry for their sin and accept Him. Jesus Christ was the Savior who took the punishment for our sin and the sin of all who will believe in Him.

Application

➤ How happy the disciples were to hear the gospel preached to them by the Lord Himself who had died and risen again! They went everywhere telling others about their Savior. The Lord wants each of you to trust His Son as your Savior and then go and tell others the good news of the gospel. (BATs: 1a Understanding Jesus Christ; 5c Evangelism and missions)

Song: "How Do We Know?" stanzas 2–4

Lesson 129: Jesus Prepares Our Heavenly Home

Bible texts: John 14:1–6; Revelation 21–22:7

Doctrinal truth: End Times (heaven)

Character trait: Contentment

Memory verse: Review I Corinthians 15:3*b*–4.

Catechism: Review Catechism 38, 45, and 46.

Materials
- Student pages 40–41 and cutouts
- Scissors
- Glue

Opening chorus: "Easter Time"

Song: "Christ Arose"

Song: "Growing, Knowing, Showing"

Prayer
Thank God for heaven, His happy home.

Song: "Heaven Is a Happy Place"

Doctrinal emphasis: Heaven

➤ God has given us many good gifts. We have good food to eat, clothes to wear, friends to play with, and toys to share. One of the best gifts He has given us is our homes, where our families live. God planned all of this for us. He planned for mothers and fathers to live in their homes with their children and teach them God's way.

But God has another special gift for us—a heavenly home. We don't know where heaven is, but we do know heaven is where God is. Remember, our God is one God who is three persons. And Jesus is God.

Before Jesus, God's Son, went back to live in heaven, He told His disciples that He was getting a home ready in heaven for everyone who trusts and believes in Him. He said that He is the only way to heaven. When we tell God we are sorry for our sin and believe that Jesus, God's Son, was punished for our sin when He died on the cross, that means we trust and believe God's Son is the way to heaven.

The Bible tells us that heaven is a beautiful place with precious jewels, such as pearls, and gold. There will be no darkness in heaven. God will shine so brightly there that we won't need to turn on lights. God's brightness will show us His glory.

There will be no sickness in heaven. There will be no sin in heaven. Everyone will be kind and thoughtful. Heaven will someday be our happy home forever if we believe in Jesus, God's Son.

There will be angels in heaven: Gabriel, God's special messenger; Michael; and many, many more. All the mothers and fathers, brothers and sisters, and grandmothers and grandfathers who believed God's Word and trusted in Jesus Christ will be in heaven. Heaven is God's home where we can live forever, and heaven will always be His home. We may move from one home to another here in this world. But when we go to live with God in heaven, we won't ever have to move again.

It's fun to go on a vacation to visit grandmother and grandfather or to go to a cottage at a lake. But it's always good to be back home with our family. God is good to give us homes to live in here on this Earth. But God has an even better home waiting for us in heaven.

Student pages 40–41

Instruct the children to cut out the pictures depicting the meaning of Easter. Read the sentence at the top of page 40. Lead a review discussion while guiding the children in sequencing and gluing the pictures. (Use the angel symbols to aid sequencing.) Read the sentence at the bottom of the page. Lead the children in reciting I Corinthians 15:3*b*–4.

Review "Five-Finger Salvation Reminder" on page 41. Encourage the children to use this method to share the Gospel with unsaved friends. Staple this page to the Easter sequence page before sending both pages home with the children.

Song: "John 3:16"

Catechism

Review Catechism 38, 45, and 46.

- For whom did Christ obey and suffer? *(Christ obeyed and suffered for sinners.)*

- Did Christ remain in the tomb after His crucifixion? *(No, Christ rose bodily from the tomb on the third day after His death.)*

- Will Christ come again? *(Yes, Christ has promised to return to take us to be with Him.)*

God's Workers

The Disciples: I Will Work for Jesus

Lesson 130: A Lame Man

Bible text: Acts 3; 4:4
Doctrinal truths: God (omnipotence); Salvation (repentance)
Character trait: Trust
Memory verse: Introduce Ephesians 4:32.
Catechism: Introduce Catechism 39–40.

Opening song: "All for Jesus," stanza 1

Song: "Oh, Be Careful"

Memory verse
Read Ephesians 4:32 aloud.

Ask the following questions, one at a time, and recite the memory verse after a few children respond to each question.

➤ How can you be kind to a friend here in kindergarten? *(share, take turns)*

How can you be kind to your teacher? *(follow directions, obey, listen quietly)*

Song: "Be Ye Doers of the Word," stanzas 6–7

Prayer
Ask God to help us show love and be kind to others.

Bible lesson

Introduction
➤ Have you ever hurt your leg or foot so that you could not walk? Some people are sometimes hurt so badly in an accident that they can never walk again.

Lesson

Peter and John were disciples of the Lord Jesus Christ. And after the Lord died on the cross, was buried, and arose from the dead, they went everywhere preaching and teaching this good news about our Lord.

One afternoon when they went together to the temple, they saw a crippled man who had been lame all of his life. He was born crippled, so he could not walk and run and play like other boys and girls when he was growing up. Now that he was older, he couldn't work to get food to eat, so

every day his friends carried him to an entrance gate at the temple. He would lie there and ask people who went in and out of the temple for money. Many of the people who saw him felt sorry for him and gave him money.

When this lame man saw Peter and John going into the temple, he asked them for money. Peter and John looked at him, and Peter said, "Look at us." So the lame man did what Peter said; he looked at them, expecting them to give him something.

But instead, Peter said, "I do not have silver and gold, but I do have something I can give you. In the name of Jesus Christ of Nazareth, rise up and walk."

And Peter took the man by the right hand and lifted him up, and immediately he was healed. He jumped up and walked into the temple with them, jumping for joy and praising and thanking the Lord.

When the people in the temple saw him, they recognized who he was—the lame man who had sat at the temple gate. They were so amazed that he could walk. When the man threw his arms around Peter and John to thank them, the people came to ask what had happened.

When Peter saw the people coming toward them, he began to preach. He told the people that he and John did not heal the man. He said, "The God of Abraham, Isaac, and Jacob has healed this man that you might see His power. You do not believe Jesus Christ is God's Son who came to die for the sin of the world. Some of you were there when God's Son was put on the cross and you said, 'Crucify him; crucify him.' But if you will tell God that you are sorry for your sin and will accept Jesus as your Savior, God will forgive you."

The Bible tells us that many people who heard the gospel preached that day by the Lord's workers believed and were saved.

Application
➤ That was a happy day for the lame man when God healed him. But it was an even happier day for all of the people who accepted God's Son as their Savior from sin. Then they knew that someday they could live in heaven forever and ever with God. Our God is a loving and all-powerful God. (BAT: 1b Repentance and faith)

Song: "God's Son," stanza 3

Catechism

Introduce Catechism 39–40.

- Who will be saved? *(Whoever repents and believes on the Lord Jesus Christ shall be saved.)*

- What is faith in Christ? *(Faith in Christ is trusting in Him alone for salvation.)*

➤ Many of the people who heard Peter and John preach that day in the temple repented and were sorry for their sin and trusted Jesus to save them from their sin.

Lesson 131: Peter and John in Prison

Bible texts: Acts 4:1–31; Acts 5:12, 42

Doctrinal truth: Church

Character trait: Courage

Memory verses: Review Ephesians 4:32, Hebrews 13:6, and Joshua 1:9.

Catechism: Review Catechism 36, 39, and 40.

Opening song: "All for Jesus," stanzas 1–2

Memory verse

Review Ephesians 4:32, explaining the phrase "forgiving one another."

➤ In the Bible lesson yesterday, we heard that many people repented—that means they were sorry for their sin and turned away from their sin—and God forgave them. God is a loving and merciful God. Remembering that God forgives us of our sin, we should also forgive others when they do unkind things to us.

Song: "Be Ye Doers of the Word," stanzas 6–7

Bible lesson

Introduction
Briefly review the previous Bible lesson.

➤ Who went to the temple? *(Peter and John)* Whom did they see there? *(a lame man)*

What was he doing? *(begging)*

Why? *(He needed money for food because he could not work.)* What happened to the lame man? *(He was healed.)*

What did the people think about this? *(Many believed in God's Son and were saved.)*

Lesson

After the lame man was healed in the temple, many people were saved. They believed in God's Son as their Savior from sin. Can anyone be saved by his own works? *(Catechism 36: No one can be saved by his own works.)* Who will be saved? *(Catechism 39: Whoever repents and believes on the Lord Jesus Christ shall be saved.)* What is faith in Christ? *(Catechism 40: Faith in Christ is trusting in Him alone for salvation.)*

Now the temple leaders did not believe in God's Son—that He died and arose again from the tomb. They thought Jesus was a man like themselves. And they did not want others to believe in God's Son. So when these temple leaders saw how many people trusted God's Son after God had healed the lame man, they were not happy. They said, "We must think of a way to stop Peter and John from preaching." So they put the two disciples in jail.

The next day the temple leaders had Peter and John brought to them. They asked them, "By what power did you heal the lame man?"

Boldly, Peter preached to them. He said, "This man has been healed in the name and by the power of Jesus Christ, God's Son, whom you crucified and God raised from the dead. Only by believing in Jesus Christ can you be saved."

The religious leaders tried to get Peter and John to promise not to preach about Jesus, but Peter and John said, "We must obey God rather than you. We must tell what great things God has done."

When the temple leaders saw how brave Peter and John were, they didn't know what to do. Many people believed what Peter and John had preached, so the temple leaders let them out of jail. The leaders warned Peter and John that if they preached the gospel again, they would be punished.

When Peter and John were released from jail, they went to a group of friends who believed in the Lord Jesus. They told their friends everything that had happened.

Then they all prayed together, "Lord, You are God, Who has made heaven, and earth, and the sea, and everything and everyone. Give us courage. Help us to be brave in preaching Your Word, and help us to do great miracles in Your name and by Your power."

The Bible tells us that they were able to preach and do God's work every day. And God helped them. He protected them and gave them strength and courage to teach and preach about Jesus Christ. Many believed God and trusted His Son as their Savior from sin.

Application

➤ Peter and John were faithful servants for God. Who helped these disciples to be strong and brave? *(Answers may vary.)* Yes, God's Holy Spirit. God will help you be strong and brave to do His work. God will always take care of you. (BAT: 8d Courage)

Memory verses

Review Hebrews 13:6 and Joshua 1:9.

Prayer

Ask God to help us be strong and brave to do this work.

Song: "I Will Trust in Thee"

Catechism

Review Catechism 36, 39, and 40.

- Can anyone be saved by his own works? *(No one can be saved by his own works.)*

- Who will be saved? *(Whoever repents and believes on the Lord Jesus Christ shall be saved.)*

- What is faith in Christ? *(Faith in Christ is trusting in Him alone for salvation.)*

Lesson 132: Saul Learned God's Way

Bible text: Acts 8:1–4; 9:1–25

Doctrinal truth: Salvation (sanctification)

Character trait: Courage

Catechism: Review Catechism 38–40.

Opening song: "All for Jesus," stanzas 1–3

Song: "Growing, Knowing, Showing"

Song: "How Do We Know?" stanzas 1–6

Prayer

Thank God for preachers and missionaries who preach His Word.

Song: "Where He Leads Me"

Bible lesson

Introduction

➤ In our lesson about Peter and John, we learned that many of the Jewish leaders did not believe that Jesus was the promised Savior. Some of these leaders did bad things to the preachers of the gospel. One of these Jewish leaders was named Saul. Saul believed in the God of heaven, but he did not believe Jesus was God. Saul hated the preachers who preached about God's Son. He wanted to stop them. He tried to hurt them and have them put into prison.

Lesson

One day Saul was going on a long trip from Jerusalem to Damascus. He was going there to find all of the people who believed in Jesus Christ. He was going to tie them up and bring them back to Jerusalem to put them all in prison there.

Suddenly, as they came very near the city of Damascus, something strange happened. A great light shone down from heaven. The light shone all around Saul. Saul fell down on the ground. Then he heard a voice from heaven saying, "Saul, Saul, why do you fight me?"

Saul answered, "Who are you, Lord?" And the Lord said, "I am Jesus of Nazareth whom you are trying to fight."

Oh, Saul was afraid. He began to shake all over. What had he done? He said, "Oh, Lord, what do you want me to do?"

When Saul got up from the ground, he opened his eyes, but he couldn't see anyone or anything. He was blind. The men who were with him took him by the hand and led him into the city of Damascus. Now Saul knew how wrong he had been to hurt those who believed in God's Son. He began to believe that Jesus was God.

In the city of Damascus, the Lord told a man named Ananias to find Saul. When he came to Saul, Ananias touched him, and God gave Saul's sight back to him. Saul met with the others in Damascus who believed in Jesus Christ. Immediately he began to study God's Word, pray, and preach about Jesus, God's Son—the promised Savior from sin. Saul was brave to do this. It takes courage to admit you have been wrong. He knew someone could also try to put him in prison and hurt or kill him for preaching the gospel.

And sure enough, when the Jewish leaders in Damascus heard how Saul's life had changed and saw that he was living God's way, they sent someone to kill him. Saul heard what they were trying to do. He hid with some friends until it was night and the sky was dark. Then his friends took him to a room on top of the wall that went all around the city like a big fence.

Saul climbed into a large basket, and his friends carefully lowered him down to the ground on the outside of the wall. So the Lord helped Saul escape from Damascus without being killed.

Saul was in danger many, many times, but God always took care of Saul and helped him to be brave. God changed Saul's name to Paul, and Paul became a great missionary preacher for God. God had Paul write many of the books we have in our Bible.

Application
➤ Just as God helped Paul to be brave, God has also promised to help us to be brave and to do hard things for Him. (BAT: 8d Courage)

Song: "When I Am Afraid"

Catechism
Review Catechism 38–40 and relate them to Saul's conversion.

■ For whom did Christ obey and suffer? *(Christ obeyed and suffered for sinners.)*

■ Who will be saved? *(Whoever repents and believes on the Lord Jesus Christ shall be saved.)*

■ What is faith in Christ? *(Faith in Christ is trusting in Him alone for salvation.)*

➤ Was Saul saved? *(yes)* Did he repent? *(yes)* Did he have faith in Christ? *(yes)*

Lesson 133: Dorcas

Bible text: Acts 9:36–43
Doctrinal truth: God (omnipotence)
Character trait: Love
Memory verse: Review Ephesians 4:32.
Catechism: Review Catechism 41.

Opening song: "All for Jesus"

Song: "Be Ye Doers of the Word," stanzas 6–7

Prayer
Ask God to help us to be kind to our friends.

Song: "My Bible Book," stanza 4

Memory verse
Review Ephesians 4:32.

Song: "Jesus Loves the Little Children"

Catechism
Review Catechism 41.

■ Does Christ care for little children? *(Yes, for He says in Mark 10:14, "Suffer the little children to come unto me, and forbid them not: for of such is the kingdom of God.")*

Bible lesson

Introduction
➤ Where is the Lord Jesus? *(in heaven and in our hearts when we accept Him as our Savior from sin)*

Lesson

Long ago after the Lord Jesus had gone back to heaven to live with God the Father, there was a lady named Dorcas who lived in a city called Joppa. Dorcas loved the Lord Jesus, and she had accepted Him as her Savior from sin. She went to church in Joppa where the gospel was preached. The gospel is the good news that Jesus Christ died, was buried, and rose again to be the Savior of all who believe and trust in Him.

Dorcas was so thankful that God loved her so much and sent His Son to die for her that she wanted her friends and everyone she met to love and obey her loving Lord. She asked the Lord to help her to obey and serve Him. She wanted to glorify God by the way she lived.

The Lord showed her how to live a loving life and be kind to others. She was always busy taking care of people who were sick and making clothes for people who needed them. Everyone who knew her loved her.

The Apostle Peter was preaching near the city of Joppa where Dorcas and her friends lived. While he was there, Dorcas became very sick. She was so ill that she died.

Oh, how sad her friends were. They knew that Dorcas had accepted Jesus as her Savior from sin and would go to heaven to live with Him forever, but they would miss her very much. She was so kind and helpful to everyone.

So when Dorcas's friends heard that Peter was not far away, they sent someone to tell him to come to Joppa at once. Peter came quickly and was taken to the room where they had laid the body of Dorcas. Many of her friends were there crying and talking about what a kind woman Dorcas had been. Some of them were even showing coats and other clothes that she had made for them.

When Peter came and saw how sorry all the people were, he asked all of them to leave the room. Then Peter kneeled down and prayed for God's will to be done. Then turning toward the body of Dorcas, he said, "Dorcas, arise." And she opened her eyes; when she saw Peter, she sat up. Peter gave her his hand and helped her get up.

Then he called her friends to come and see what God had done. How happy Dorcas's friends were to see her alive again!

Everyone who saw what God had done for Dorcas told others about it. And many people came to see Dorcas and to hear Peter preach about the Lord.

Application

➤ Dorcas glorified God by being kind to others. The Bible tells us to "be kind to one another." We can please God and show others what a loving God we serve by being kind and helpful. (BATs: 5b Giving; 5e Friendliness)

Song: "Even a Child Is Known"
Replace "do your work with all of your might" with "so be ye kind; obey God's Word."

Lesson 134: Peter's Friends Prayed

Bible texts: Acts 12:1–17; John 14:13–14; 16:23; Philippians 2:9–11
Doctrinal truth: Salvation (prayer)
Character trait: Trust
Catechism: Review Catechism 46 and introduce 42.

Opening song: "All for Jesus," stanzas 1–4

Song: "Growing, Knowing, Showing"

Song: "Thank God," stanzas 1–3

Song: "Learning God's Way," stanza 1

Catechism

Introduce Catechism 42.

■ What is prayer? *(Prayer is thanking God for what He has done and asking Him for things which He has promised to you.)*

➤ Isn't it good that we can ask God for anything? We can talk to Him about everything. We can thank Him for all the things He has given to us. We can ask Him for all the things we need. We can ask Him to help us to obey. We can ask Him to help those who are sick. We can ask Him to help others who do not believe He is God.

Song: "How Do We Know?" stanza 7

Bible lesson

Introduction

➤ Before He went to heaven, the Lord told His disciples and friends that He would go and make a beautiful home for all of them in heaven.

He said He would prepare a home in heaven for everyone who believes and trusts in the one true God who created all things and sent His Son to be our Savior from sin.

Will Christ come again? *(Catechism 46: Yes, Christ has promised to return to take me to be with Him.)*

Lesson

King Herod was the leader in the land where the Jews—God's special people—lived. Peter and John were two of God's faithful preachers. Peter and John preached the gospel of Christ's death and resurrection—that He died and lives again—to God's special people.

But many of the people did not believe the good news of the gospel. They did not believe that God had sent His Son to be the way to heaven. They wanted to stop the apostles from preaching. King Herod wanted the people to like him. When King Herod found out that they did not want the Christians to preach God's way, he had his soldiers kill the disciple James, the brother of John. Then Herod had his soldiers put Peter into prison.

While Peter was in prison, the Christians prayed for him in their homes. They needed Peter to preach the Word of God. Each day they met together at someone's home to pray for Peter. They asked God to help Peter get out of prison so that he could preach again. They knew that Herod would probably have Peter killed very soon.

One night Peter was sleeping in the prison. The guards had chained his hands together. Two soldiers were with Peter, and there were even guards at the door to keep Peter from escaping. Everything was dark and quiet.

Suddenly, the angel of the Lord came to Peter. There was a shining light in the dark prison room. The angel woke Peter.

"Get up quickly," he said.

The chains just fell off Peter's hands.

The angel said to Peter, "Put on your shoes and your coat and come with me."

Peter did what the angel told him, even though he thought he was dreaming. As they came to the iron gate of the prison, the door opened for them, and they were out of the prison and walking on the streets. Peter was free. Then the angel went away.

Peter knew then that he was not dreaming. He knew God had sent His angel to deliver him. He hurried to the house where the Christians had come together to pray for him.

Peter knocked on the door of the house. (Knock.) A young girl named Rhoda answered the door.

She called out, "Who is there?"

Peter answered, "It is I—Peter."

When she heard Peter's voice outside the door, she was so excited that she forgot to unlock the door to let him in. Instead she ran back to tell the other Christians, who were still praying, that Peter was at the door.

The Christians did not believe her at first. They said, "You must be wrong. Peter is in prison. That is why we are praying for him."

Peter kept on knocking, so everyone in the house went to see who it was. They were surprised to find Peter standing there at the door. Peter told the Christians what God had done for him. The people had asked the Lord to help Peter get out of prison, and the Lord answered their prayers.

Application

➤ God answers our prayers today. He says, "Ask, and it shall be given you" (Matthew 7:7). We can ask God for anything. He always hears us when we pray. (BAT: 6b Prayer)

Review Catechism 42.

■ What is prayer? (*Prayer is thanking God for what He has done and asking Him for things which He has promised to give.*)

Prayer

Take prayer requests today and call on two or three children to pray. Then close the prayer time "in Jesus' name. Amen."

Song: "Praise Him, Praise Him," stanzas 1 and 4

Lesson 135: John's Vision

Bible text: Revelation

Doctrinal truth: End Times

Character trait: Trust

Memory verse: Review Psalm 100.

Catechism: Introduce Catechism 47 and 50.

Materials
• Teacher's copy of "Our Thanksgiving Psalm" booklet (from Student Packet; used in Lesson 70)
• Student page 42 and cutouts
• Scissors
• Glue

Opening song: "All for Jesus," stanzas 1–4

Prayer

Thank God for heaven, His happy home.

Bible lesson

Introduction

➤ After God's Son went back to heaven, His disciples told His words to people everywhere. We've heard stories about how God helped His disciples work miracles and how some of them were put into jail because they preached God's Word. Today we will hear about what happened to the disciple, John, and about the work God gave him to do.

Lesson

John bravely preached God's Word; he told people everywhere that they were sinners and needed to trust God's Son to be their Savior. People do not like to be told that they have sinned. People like to think about how good they are instead of how perfectly good and holy God is. The Roman ruler of the land sent John away where he couldn't preach to those around him. He sent John to a little island called Patmos. An island is land that has water all around it. John had no church to go to and no other Christians for fellowship on the island.

John had more time to talk to God and think about His Son. And God had very special work for John to do while he was a prisoner on that small island.

On the Lord's Day, God spoke to John in a voice from heaven. God told John to write in a book all the things that He was going to tell him and send it to the Christians in the churches across the sea to read. When John heard God's voice, he turned around, looked up, and saw the Son of God, all bright and shining. Remember our lesson about God showing His glory to Moses? John also tells us in his book that the face of the Son of God was as bright as the sun. It was so bright that John had to cover his face and look away.

John fell down with fear when he saw the Lord. But the Bible tells us that the Lord Jesus laid his hand upon John and told him not to be afraid.

Then the Lord showed John many wonderful things that were going to happen in the years to come. You see, God knows all things even before they happen. We don't know exactly what will happen tomorrow, or the next day, or the next. But God does.

God showed John the new heaven and the new Earth. He told John all about Heaven. John wrote all the things God showed him in the book called *Revelation*, which is the last book in our Bible. (Open your Bible to show the book of Revelation.)

We don't know where heaven is, but we do know that heaven is where God is. Remember, our God is one God who is three persons. And Jesus is God.

Before Jesus, God's Son, went back to live in heaven, He told His disciples that He was getting a home ready in heaven for everyone who trusts and believes in Him. He said that He is the only way to heaven. When we tell God we are sorry for our sin and believe that Jesus, God's Son, was punished for our sin when He died on the cross, that means we trust and believe God's Son is the way to heaven.

Review other information about heaven included in the doctrinal emphasis about heaven in Lesson 129.

Application
➤ Let's thank God for the promise of the wonderful heavenly home He has prepared for us. (BAT: 7c Praise)

Memory verse
Review Psalm 100 with "Our Thanksgiving Psalm" booklet.

Song: "Heaven Is a Happy Place"

Catechism
Introduce Catechism 47 and 50.

■ What becomes of man at death? *(The body returns to dust, and the soul goes either to heaven or hell.)*

■ What is heaven? *(Heaven is a glorious and happy place, where the saved shall be forever with the Lord.)*

Student page 42

➤ God had many workers who shared the Gospel message with others. These workers were also good examples. They trusted God and did the work God had given to them.

Instruct the children to cut out the pictures of God's helpers and glue them in place by matching the shapes.

Read the sentences at the top of the page. Point to the picture of Saul. Ask the children, "Who do you see in this picture?" Briefly review how Saul served God. Ask the children to identify the other helpers and review how each one served God. Lead them in reciting Ephesians 4:32. Allow volunteers to tell how these "helpers" showed kindness to others and whether they obeyed God's command.

Lesson 136: Review—God's Workers

Bible text: Review.
Doctrinal truth: Church
Character trait: Work
Memory verse: Review Ephesians 4:32.
Catechism: Review Catechism 39–40.
Materials
• Student page 43 and cutouts
• Scissors
• Glue

Opening song: "All for Jesus," stanzas 1–4

Catechism
Review Catechism 39–40.

■ Who will be saved? *(Whoever repents and believes on the Lord Jesus Christ shall be saved.)*

■ What is faith in Christ? *(Faith in Christ is trusting in Him alone for salvation.)*

Song: "Even a Child Is Known"

Song: "Be Ye Doers of the Word," stanzas 1 and 10

Prayer
Ask God to help us be good workers for Him.

Student page 43
Instruct the children to cut out the pictures of children who are being helpers and glue them in the circles on the page (any order is acceptable). Ask volunteers to tell how each child is being helpful. Read the sentences and lead the children in reciting Ephesians 4:32. Allow the children to share ways that they can be helpers.

Song: "A Helper I Will Be"

God Hears Me

Prayer: I Talk to God

Lesson 137: What It Means to Pray

Bible texts: Matthew 6:9–13; Philippians 4:6–7

Doctrinal truth: Salvation (prayer)

Character trait: Trust

Memory verses: Review Romans 3:23 and introduce Psalm 55:17.

Catechism: Review Catechism 42.

Opening chorus: "Whisper a Prayer"
Explain that the phrase "to keep your heart in tune" means that praying will help us to remember to love and obey God.

Song: "The Doxology"

Song: "Learning God's Way," stanza 1

Memory verse
Read Psalm 55:17 to the children.

Prayer
Thank God that He lets us talk to Him in prayer.

Bible lesson

Introduction
Review Catechism 42.

■ What is prayer? *(Prayer is thanking God for what He has done and asking Him for things He has promised to give.)*

Lesson

When we pray, we talk to God. When do you talk to God? *(possible answers: mealtime, bedtime, in the morning; family devotions, on Sunday)* (Quote Psalm 55:17.)

Where do you talk to God? *(possible answers: at home, school, church, playground, in a car on vacation)* Anytime, anywhere, we can talk to God. God is always with us, and He always hears us when we pray.

What do you talk to God about? *(possible answers: ask Him to make sick people well; ask Him to keep us safe when we travel in a car)*

God is always pleased to hear us thank Him for all the things He gives to us. Remember the Bible stories about the ten lepers and Jacob. How many lepers remembered to thank God for healing them? *(only one)* What did Jacob thank God for? *(for His special promise to be with him wherever he went)*

What can we thank God for? *(Allow discussion.)* We can thank God for mothers and fathers who take care of us and teach us Bible ways. We can thank God for brothers and sisters to love and play with. We can thank God for churches and Christian schools that teach us God's way. We can thank God for the Bible that tells us His ways. We can thank God for food to eat and for strong bodies to work and play. We can thank God for the many beautiful things in His world.

What is the best gift God has given to us? *(His Son, Jesus Christ)* Why did Jesus come down from heaven to be born as a baby in this world? He came to grow up and die on the cross. He took the punishment for our sin. God says sin must be punished. "There is none that doeth good, no, not one" (Romans 3:12). "For all have sinned and come short of the glory of God" (Romans 3:23). God sent His Son to be our Savior from sin. We should thank God for His Son.

Application
➤ Let's always remember to praise God for all His gifts to us. (BAT: 7c Praise)

Song: "Thank God"

Lesson 138: The Lord's Prayer

Bible texts: Matthew 6:9–13; John 1:12

Doctrinal truth: Salvation (prayer)

Character trait: Trust

Memory verses: Review Psalm 55:17; Psalm 95:6; I Thessalonians 5:18; I John 1:9; Psalm 37:27; and Hebrews 13:6.

Catechism: Review Catechism 3, 28, and 42 and introduce Catechism 43–44.

Materials
• I Thessalonians 5:18 visuals 1 and 2 (optional; used in Unit 5)

Opening chorus: "Whisper a Prayer"
Review Psalm 55:17.

Catechism

Introduce Catechism 43–44.

- ■ Which guide did Christ give us to teach us how to pray? *(Christ has given us the Lord's Prayer.)*

- ■ Repeat the Lord's Prayer. *(Our Father which art in heaven, hallowed be thy name. Thy kingdom come. Thy will be done in earth, as it is in heaven. Give us this day our daily bread. And forgive us our debts, as we forgive our debtors. And lead us not into temptation, but deliver us from evil: for thine is the kingdom, and the power, and the glory, for ever. Amen.)*

Bible lesson

> This entire lesson is centered on the Lord's Prayer. You may wish to display the Lord's Prayer (Matthew 6:9–13) on a chart to refer to as you talk about the various phrases.

❶ We should pray to God our Father in heaven: "Our Father which art in heaven, hallowed by thy name."

➤ *Our Father:* We must remember God is not our Father until we become His child by asking Jesus to be our Savior from sin.

Read or quote John 1:12.

➤ *Hallowed be thy name:* This means we should think of God first when we pray. We should show that we love and honor God because He alone is holy. Only God can never sin. He made us and can save us from sin.

Sing "One God."

Recite Psalm 95:6 together.

❷ We should pray with thanksgiving. When we pray, we should always remember to thank God for all His gifts to us.

Recite I Thessalonians 5:18. You may use I Thessalonians 5:18 visuals 1 and 2 to review things to be thankful for.

Sing "Thank You, God."

Review Catechism 42.

- ■ What is prayer? *(Prayer is thanking God for what He has done and asking Him for things He has promised to give.)*

➤ What is the most important thing we can thank God for? *(Allow discussion.)* Yes, Jesus our Savior, God's only Son.

❸ We should pray for others. We call this "intercession." Jesus is in heaven praying for us.

➤ *Thy will be done in earth:* We can use our hands to remind us for whom we should pray. (Show the appropriate finger as you discuss the following.) Our *thumb* reminds us to pray for those closest to us—our family and friends. Our *pointer finger* reminds us to pray for those who point to or show us more about God's Word, the Bible—our pastors, preachers, teachers, and missionaries. Our *tall finger* reminds us to pray for the leaders of our country—our president and governor, policemen, and others. Our *ring finger* is weak; we have to help it stand up. It reminds us to pray for those we know who are sick and weak.

❹ We should pray for ourselves. Our *little finger* reminds us to pray for ourselves.

➤ *Give us this day our daily bread:* We pray that God will give us food, clothes, a home, and everything we need to live our lives for God's glory.

Forgive us our debts as we forgive our debtors: Debts means "sin." God has promised to forgive our sin if we confess it to Him.

Recite I John 1:9 together.

➤ We should be kind to and forgiving of others when they do mean things to us.

➤ *Deliver us from evil:* God will help us to depart from evil and do good.

Recite Psalm 37:27 together.

❺ We should praise God for who He is.

➤ *For thine is the kingdom:* This reminds us that God is all-powerful and He will give us the courage to do what He wants us to.

Recite Hebrews 13:6 together.

Review Catechism 28.

- ■ Who is stronger, God or Satan? *(God is stronger.)*

➤ *And the glory:* All things were made for God's glory.

Review Catechism 3.

- ■ Why did God make you and all things? *(God made me and all things for His own glory.)*

❻ We should pray for God's will to be done.

➤ *Amen:* This means "let it be so."

Prayer

Stand and pray together the Lord's Prayer (Catechism 44).

Song: "How Do We Know?" stanzas 1 and 7

Lesson 139: Praying in Jesus' Name

Bible texts: John 14:13–14; John 16:23; Philippians 2:9–11

Doctrinal truth: Salvation (prayer)

Character trait: Trust

Memory verse: Review Psalm 55:17.

Catechism: Review Catechism 3, 7, 8, and 42–44.

Materials
- Student page 44

Opening chorus: "Whisper a Prayer"
Review Psalm 55:17 and Catechism 42–43.

Song: "Thank God"

Prayer
Pray together the Lord's Prayer (Catechism 44).

Review the explanations of the phrases given in Lesson 138.

Song: "Father, We Thank Thee for the Night"

Doctrinal emphasis: Prayer

➤ Do you know why we end our prayers with the words *in Jesus' name*? The Lord Jesus tells us many times in the Bible that we should pray in His name. (Read John 14:13–14 and John 16:23 from your Bible.)

We are not good enough to pray to God. God is a holy God without sin. We have sinned. God does not answer our prayers because we deserve for Him to answer them or because we are good. We all have sinned and deserve nothing from God. God answers our prayers because of what Jesus has done for us. This is why we say, "in Jesus' name." When we pray in Jesus' name, we are showing that we believe Jesus died for us and that He took the punishment for our sin. We are showing that we remember that the Lord Jesus is the only way to God and heaven. God tells us in the Bible that He gave His Son a name "which is above every name." He says that everyone should worship His Son as God.

When we ask God for things that we need, for courage and for help, let's try to remember always to pray in Jesus' name. We pray in Jesus' name because of what Jesus has done for us. (BAT: la Understanding Jesus Christ)

> Review this doctrinal emphasis about prayer from time to time as your schedule permits.

Catechism
Review Catechism 3, 7, and 8.

◾ Why did God make you and all things? *(God made me and all things for His own glory.)*

◾ How can you glorify God? *(I can glorify God by loving Him and doing what He commands.)*

◾ Why ought you to glorify God? *(I ought to glorify God because He made me and takes care of me.)*

➤ Prayer is talking to God. Does God want us to talk to Him? *(Yes, He tells us to many times in the Bible.)*

Student page 44
Allow the children to connect the dots to finish the picture. Read the page, reciting Psalm 55:17 together before reading the last sentence.

Song: "How Do We Know?" stanza 7

Song: "Trust and Obey" chorus
Remind the children that "trusting" God is believing He will do what He says He will do and that He says He will hear us when we pray.

Lesson 140: Anytime, Anywhere

Bible texts: Psalm 5:3; Psalm 55:17; I Thessalonians 5:17

Doctrinal truth: Salvation (prayer)

Character trait: Trust

Memory verses: Introduce Psalm 66:18 and review Psalm 95:6 and Psalm 55:17.

Catechism: Review Catechism 26 and 42–44.

Materials
- Pictures of children in church, in a car, in bed, eating in a restaurant, at play (optional)
- Student page 45

Opening chorus: "Whisper a Prayer," stanzas 1–2

Song: "Growing, Knowing, Showing"

Song: "Thank You, God"

Doctrinal emphasis: Prayer

➤ When can we talk to God? *(possible answers: when we get up, before we eat, before we go to bed at night)* We can talk to God anytime. The Bible tells us we should pray in the morning (Psalm 5:3). It tells us we should pray at noon and at night (Psalm 55:17). The Bible also tells us we can pray anytime (I Thessalonians 5:17).

Where should we be when we talk to God? *(Answers may vary.)* We can be anywhere when we talk to God. We talk to God when we are in Sunday school and church. We talk to God during Bible time and chapel. We can talk to God anywhere.

You may show pictures of children in various situations as you continue this discussion.

➤ Have you ever prayed in a car before you went on a trip with your family? Did you ask the Lord to keep you safe?

Have you ever been afraid when you were in your bed at night? Did you ask the Lord to help you to be brave?

Have you ever eaten in a restaurant and bowed your head to pray as you thanked God for your food? Have you seen other families do this? Does it make you happy to know that they love and obey God too?

Have you ever been unkind when you were playing with a friend? Did you stop right then and whisper a prayer, asking God to forgive you?

God is happy when we remember to pray to Him anytime and anywhere. We can talk to Him when we are happy. We can talk to Him when we are sad. We can talk to Him when we are afraid, and God promises to hear and answer our prayers.

Song: "How Do We Know?" stanza 7

Memory verse
Read Psalm 66:18 to the children.

➤ What does *iniquity* mean? *(sin, disobeying God)* What is sin? *(Catechism 26: Sin is the transgression of the law of God.)*

"If I regard iniquity in my heart" means that if I know I have sinned and have not asked Jesus to forgive my sin, then the Lord will not answer my prayers.

Lead the children in repeating the verse with you several times.

Song: "Father, We Thank Thee for the Night"

Catechism
Review Catechism 42–44.

◼ What is prayer? *(Prayer is thanking God for what He has done and asking Him for things which He has promised to give.)*

◼ What guide has Christ given us to teach us how to pray? *(Christ has given us the Lord's Prayer.)*

◼ Repeat the Lord's Prayer. *(Our Father which art in heaven, hallowed be thy name. Thy kingdom come. Thy will be done in earth, as it is in heaven. Give us this day our daily bread. And forgive us our debts, as we forgive our debtors. And lead us not into temptation, but deliver us from evil: for thine is the kingdom, and the power, and the glory, for ever. Amen.)*

➤ Do you remember what the verse, Psalm 95:6, teaches us about worshiping God? Let's say it together. (Lead the children in reciting the verse.)

We are going to show God in a special way how great and good He is by kneeling for our prayer time today.

Direct the children to kneel next to their chairs quietly, to avoid touching anything else, and to close their eyes so that they will not see anything else while they talk to God.

Prayer
Kneel and pray together the Lord's Prayer.

Student page 45
Discuss the prayer reminder. Recite Psalm 55:17 and read the page with the children.

God's Plan

Paul the Missionary: I Can Be a Missionary Helper

You may wish to contact a missionary to send a letter or a recording to the class in which he introduces himself and tells about his missionary work. You could also invite a missionary who is home on furlough to visit and speak to the children. These activities may be included in Lesson 152, the last lesson of this unit.

You also may want to provide a missionary prayer card or picture to be sent home with each child's Student page completed in Lesson 152.

Lesson 141: God Called Paul

Bible texts: Acts 13:1–3; Acts 9:10–21

Doctrinal truth: Church

Character trait: Love

Memory verse: Introduce Proverbs 11:30*b*.

Catechism: Review Catechism 47.

Opening chorus: "Even a Child Is Known"

Song: "Jesus Saves"
Explain *Jesus saves*—Jesus died on the cross and took the punishment for our sin so that we could be saved from punishment if we believe on Him as our Savior; *tidings*—"good news"; *bear*—"take"; *steeps*—"hard places like mountains"; *waves*—"oceans."

Song: "Growing, Knowing, Showing"

Song: "Obedience Is," stanzas 8–9

Prayer
Ask God to help us remember to pray for missionaries.

➤ Do you know a missionary who has gone far away to tell about our Savior? *(Allow discussion.)*

Encourage the children to bring missionary prayer cards from home. Lead in a special prayer time each day for at least one missionary family. If you have a class or school missionary(ies), remember him (them) at this time.

Memory verse
Read Proverbs 11:30*b* from the Bible.

➤ What does it mean to "win souls"? *(Answers may vary.)* It means to tell others about Jesus and to help change lives by sharing God's Truth—to be a missionary.

What does the Bible mean when it says we are wise if we win souls? If we are wise, that means we will want to do what God says about something. We want to obey God, don't we? Then we will want to tell other people about His Son. (BAT: 5c Evangelism and missions)

Bible lesson

Introduction

➤ We are going to learn about mission work and missionaries in the next few lessons. What is a missionary? *(Answers may vary.)* Yes, someone who tells someone else about Jesus, God's Son—that He alone can save us from our sin. This is God's plan for all of His children.

Some of you have said that you know a missionary. Do we have to go far away across the ocean to be a missionary? *(Answers may vary.)* No, we can be home missionaries right here in (name your city). If we love Jesus and want to serve Him, we will want to tell others about our Savior, too. That means we can be missionary helpers. (BAT: 5c Evangelism and missions)

Review Saul's conversion from Lesson 132.

Lesson

After the Lord Jesus had gone back to heaven, His workers preached His Word. Many people asked Jesus to be their Savior from sin. Those who had become Christians by accepting Jesus as their Savior met together to worship the Lord. They were called a church, just as Christians who worship the Lord together today are called a church.

One day in the first church at Antioch, when the Christians were praying and asking the Lord to guide them in His way, the Lord spoke to them. He told them to send Paul and Barnabas to preach to people far away across the sea about God's Son, the Savior.

Application

➤ So Paul and his friend Barnabas became the first foreign missionaries. A foreign missionary is a person who goes to another land to preach the good news. This is God's plan—that His children tell others about Him. (BAT: 5c Evangelism and missions)

Catechism

Review Catechism 47.

■ What becomes of man at death? *(The body returns to dust, and the soul goes either to heaven or hell.)*

➤ This is why it is important that we be missionaries. Everyone's soul will live somewhere forever. We want everyone to hear about the home God has prepared in heaven for those who accept Jesus as their Savior from sin.

Lesson 142: The Lame Man at Lystra

Bible text: Acts 14:8–15

Doctrinal truth: Church

Character trait: Love

Memory verse: Review Proverbs 11:30*b*.

Catechism: Review Catechism 47.

Materials
• World globe, with a marker indicating where the class missionary is serving the Lord

Opening chorus: "Even a Child Is Known"

Song: "Jesus Saves"
Review the meanings of some of the words and phrases of the song. (See Lesson 141.) Explain *Spread the tidings all around*—tell everyone the good news that Jesus saves. Review the simple plan of salvation each time you sing this song throughout this unit.

Song: "A Missionary Helper"

➤ In our last lesson we learned that a missionary is someone who tells others the good news that Jesus can be their Savior from sin. Where do missionaries go to do this? *(Answers may vary.)* Yes, some go to foreign places like Africa, Spain, and South America. (Point to these places on a globe or map as you mention them. Point out the marker on the globe to indicate where your class missionary is serving the Lord.) Some are home missionaries here in the United States. We can be missionaries in our own town (city) and in the neighborhood in which we live. We can be missionary helpers. (BAT: 5c Evangelism and missions)

Memory verse
Review Proverbs 11:30*b*.

Bible lesson

Introduction
➤ In our last lesson we learned that Paul and Barnabas went out from the church in Antioch and sailed across the ocean to preach God's Word. They were the first missionaries the church sent out.

Lesson

While Paul and Barnabas were far away from their homes preaching in a city called Lystra, a lame man heard Paul preaching. He had been crippled since he was born. When he was growing up, he could not run and play like other children.

This crippled man listened carefully to Paul, who told him how the Lord Jesus had made blind men see, deaf people hear, and crippled people walk again.

While he was preaching, Paul noticed the lame man. He could see that the man believed what Paul was saying. Paul could tell that the man believed in God's Son and wanted the God of heaven to heal him and make him walk.

Paul stopped his preaching and said in a loud voice to the crippled man, "Stand up on your feet." And the man trusted God; he believed God could work a miracle. He jumped right up. He looked down at his feet—they were straight! God had healed him.

When the people heard what Paul had done, they said, "Paul and Barnabas are gods."

But Paul and Barnabas said, "No, we ourselves are not gods. But we have come to tell you about the one true God of heaven and His Son, Jesus Christ."

Application
➤ God helped Paul and Barnabas to be good missionaries. Did Paul or Barnabas have the power to heal the lame man? *(No, only God can work a miracle.)* (BAT: 8b Faith in the power of the Word of God) Our lesson tells us that some of the people believed on Jesus. Paul and Barnabas were winning souls, weren't they? (BAT: 5c Evangelism and missions)

Review Proverbs 11:30*b* again.

Prayer
Ask God to help us to be missionary helpers.

Catechism
Review Catechism 47.

■ What becomes of man at death? *(The body returns to dust, and the soul goes either to heaven or hell.)*

➤ What is our soul? *(Allow discussion.)* Our soul is the part of us that will live forever. Every person's soul will go to either heaven or hell when he or she dies.

Lesson 143: Paul and Silas at Philippi

Bible text: Acts 16:9–15; Mark 16:15

Doctrinal truth: Church

Character trait: Love

Memory verses: Review Proverbs 11:30*b* and introduce Proverbs 20:11.

Catechism: Review Catechism 47 and introduce Catechism 48.

Opening chorus: "Even a Child Is Known"

Song: "Jesus Saves"
Review that *bear* (not an animal) means to "take" the news, the good news, to every land—to go and tell others of our Savior.

Read Mark 16:15 from your Bible.

Song: "Be Ye Doers of the Word," stanza 10

Bible lesson

Introduction
Encourage a few of your children to share experiences that they have had with missionaries they know.

Lesson

What was the name of Paul's missionary helper in our last lesson? *(Barnabas)* In our lesson today, Paul was traveling with another helper, named Silas, to Macedonia, a country God called them to. God led Paul and Silas to the big city of Philippi in Macedonia. The people who lived in Philippi did not have a church or a preacher to tell them about God's Son.

On the Lord's Day, Paul and Silas went outside the city walls to a river, where they found some women praying together. These women were praying to God the Father, but they had not heard that God had sent His Son to die on the cross for their sin. So Paul and Silas sat down and told these women the good news of the gospel. They told them that they each had a soul that would live somewhere forever.

One of these women was Lydia. Lydia listened carefully to the missionaries as they told of God's love and His Son. She loved God and was so happy to hear that Jesus Christ wanted to be her Savior. So Lydia believed in Jesus, God's Son, and trusted Him as Her Savior from sin.

After Lydia trusted God's Son and was saved, Paul baptized her in the river outside the city. Paul baptized Lydia to show to others that she had turned away from her own way and wanted to live God's

way. Lydia then invited Paul and Silas to stay at her house while they preached in Philippi.

While Paul and Silas preached in that city, many people became Christians, and soon they were able to meet together as a church.

Application
➤ Every day Paul and Silas told the story of Jesus to the people of Philippi, and many people believed on Jesus. (BAT: 5c Evangelism and missions)

Paul and Silas were wise Christians: they were obeying God's Word, "Go ye into all the world and preach the gospel." Have you boys and girls ever told a friend about Jesus, God's Son? You can, you know, for "even a child is known by his doings." (Proverbs 20:11)

What was the name of the lady in our Bible lesson today who loved the Lord Jesus and accepted Him as her Savior from sin? *(Lydia)* What did Lydia do after she became a Christian? *(She took care of the missionaries, Paul and Silas, by letting them stay at her house.)* Lydia pleased the Lord, didn't she? Lydia was a missionary helper.

How can we help missionaries in this special way? *(Allow discussion.)* Yes, we can invite them to our homes to sleep and to eat. We can give money to help them buy food and clothes or airplane tickets to get to the faraway country where they serve the Lord. We can pray for them too.

Song: "Be Ye Doers of the Word," stanzas 6–7

Memory verses
Read Proverbs 20:11 from your Bible.

➤ Have you remembered to do good things for missionaries? Let's remember to pray for our missionary friends. That is a good thing we can do now. We want to do good things for Jesus because we love Him.

Review Proverbs 11:30*b*.

Prayer
Continue to pray for specific missionaries by name during this unit.

Catechism
Review Catechism 47.

▪ What becomes of man at death? *(The body returns to dust, and the soul goes either to heaven or hell.)*

Introduce Catechism 48.

▪ What is hell? *(Hell is a place of dreadful and endless torment.)*

➤ Hell is where those who have never asked Jesus to be their Savior from sin must go when they die. When we ask Jesus to be our Savior from sin, God forgives us our sin. He makes us His children. Even though we sometimes sin and disobey God, we are no longer wicked children of Satan. When God looks at us, He sees His Son's righteousness and goodness instead of our sin.

Lesson 144: Paul and Silas in Jail

Bible text: Acts 16:25–40

Doctrinal truth: Church

Character trait: Love

Memory verses: Review Proverbs 11:30*b* and Proverbs 20:11.

Catechism: Review Catechism 3 and 7.

Opening chorus: "Even a Child Is Known"

Song: "God's Way"

Prayer

Thank God for missionaries who serve Him in hard places.

Memory verses

Read Proverbs 20:11 to the children. Explain that people can tell if we love the Lord Jesus by seeing what we do.

➤ If someone sees us disobeying our mother or father, what might he think? *(Allow discussion.)* If someone hears us saying unkind words to our brother or sister or our friends, what might he think? *(Allow discussion.)* We want others to see us obeying God, which glorifies Him.

Review Proverbs 11:30*b*.

Catechism

Review Catechism 3 and 7.

■ Why did God make you and all things? *(God made me and all things for His own glory.)*

■ How can you glorify God? *(I can glorify God by loving Him and doing what He commands.)*

Bible lesson

Lesson

Paul and Silas had faithfully preached the gospel in the city of Philippi. They were happy to have a nice place to rest at night in the home of Lydia. Sick people had been healed by the miracles that God had worked there, and many people had been saved when Paul and Silas preached God's Word.

But some people did not like what Paul and Silas were doing. They didn't want to hear about their sin. They didn't want to stop living in their sinful ways. Some of them got so angry at Paul and Silas that they took them to the leader of the city. Paul and Silas were beaten with whips and even put into jail, not because they had done anything

wrong, but because they had preached the good news of the gospel. The leaders told the jailer not to let them escape, so he took them into a dark room far inside the jail, placed their feet between boards called stocks, and chained them so they couldn't get up and escape.

Don't you think it would have made Paul and Silas sad to be in a dark, damp jail when they really had done nothing wrong? Instead the Bible tells us that at midnight Paul and Silas were praying and even singing praises to God. They knew that God had put them there for a purpose. And when they sang, the other prisoners heard them. The other prisoners knew that there was something different about Paul and Silas.

Suddenly there was a great earthquake which caused the prison to begin to shake. It shook so hard that the boards and chains fell off the prisoners, and the prison doors even opened.

All of this noise and shaking woke the keeper of the prison, and he went to see what had happened. When he saw the prison doors had opened, he was afraid that the prisoners he was supposed to watch so carefully had escaped. He was so afraid that he took out his sword and was about to kill himself.

But Paul saw what the jailer was about to do, and he shouted, "Don't hurt yourself; we are all here."

Then the jailer called for his servant to bring a light, and when he saw that all the prisoners were there, he kneeled down in front of Paul and Silas and asked, "Sirs, what must I do to be saved?"

Paul and Silas answered him, "Believe on the Lord Jesus Christ, and you shall be saved." And then Paul and Silas told the jailer all about the God of heaven and His Son, the Savior. The jailer believed and trusted in Jesus Christ.

After the jailer was saved, he took Paul and Silas out of the prison to his house and washed their wounds from the beatings they had been given, and then he fed them. Paul and Silas continued to preach, and the Bible tells us that all of the jailer's family came to believe in God's Son.

So Paul baptized the jailer and his family to show that they had repented and turned from living their own way and were now living God's way.

Application

➤ Paul and Silas were missionaries wherever God put them. They were faithful and obedient to God because they loved Him. God wants us to tell others about Him. We can use our five fingers to witness to others about Jesus. We want to serve God because we love Him. (BATs: 1b Repentance and faith; 5c Evangelism and missions)

Refer to "Leading a Child to the Lord" in the Introduction to this teacher's edition.

Song: "Oh, How I Love Jesus"

Lesson 145: Paul in Troas

Bible text: Acts 20:7–13, 17–38

Doctrinal truth: Church

Character trait: Love

Memory verses: Review Proverbs 20:11; I Corinthians 15:3*b*–4; and Psalm 55:17.

Catechism: Review Catechism 47–48.

Materials
- Several missionary prayer cards (optional)
- Student page 46 and cutouts
- Scissors
- Glue

Opening chorus: "Even a Child Is Known"

Memory verse

Review Proverbs 20:11.

Song: "Jesus Saves"

Song: "Be Ye Doers of the Word," stanza 10

Song: "Learning God's Way," stanza 1

➤ God hears our prayers for missionaries. We need to pray for them to be healthy and strong so that they can do their work for Jesus. We can pray that God will help them to say what He wants them to say. We can pray for the people who hear about God's Son—that they will believe in Him so that their souls will go to heaven when they die.

Prayer

If you have several different prayer cards, let several children come to the front and hold a card. Each child may pray for that particular missionary.

Bible lesson

Introduction

➤ Paul continued to travel from one city to another to preach the good news about Jesus' death on the cross and His rising from the tomb.

Recite I Corinthians 15:3*b*–4.

Lesson

On Sunday, the day before Paul and his friends, Silas and Luke, were supposed to travel to another city, Paul preached in Troas to the believers there. He preached a long time. Paul preached so long that it grew dark, and lamps had to be brought to light the room. Some of the people were becoming very tired.

There was a young man named Eutychus who had come to hear Paul preach. Since it was so crowded in the room, Eutychus was sitting on the windowsill. After Paul had preached a long time, Eutychus became so sleepy that his head began to nod. Soon he was sound asleep, and he fell out of the upstairs window all the way down to the ground.

Paul rushed downstairs and out of the house to where Eutychus lay on the ground. Other people gathered around the young man. Eutychus did not move; he was dead.

As Paul bent over the boy, he said, "Don't worry; he will live." Then Paul lay down on the boy and put his arms around him, and the boy opened his eyes and lived again.

Everyone was so happy. God had worked another miracle. A miracle is something that only God can do. It shows us His power.

Application

➤ Paul and Silas and Luke told people about Jesus, God's Son, everywhere they went. Many people believed and trusted Christ. (BATs: 1a Understanding Jesus Christ; 1b Repentance and faith) God worked miracles such as bringing Eutychus back to life to show people that Paul was a missionary sent from God. Our God is omnipotent. What does *omnipotent* mean? *(Allow discussion.)* Yes, *omnipotent* means "all powerful." (BAT: 8b Faith in the power of the Word of God)

Before Paul and his friends left Ephesus to go to Jerusalem, God's people knelt down by the seashore to pray together. This reminds us again of how important it is that we pray for our missionaries. (BATs: 5c Evangelism and missions; 6b Prayer) We can pray for our missionaries at any time. Remember Psalm 55:17 tells us that God will hear us whenever we pray. Recite Psalm 55:17.

Catechism

Review Catechism 47–48.

- What becomes of man at death? *(The body returns to dust, and the soul goes either to heaven or hell.)*

- What is hell? *(Hell is a place of dreadful and endless torment.)*

Student page 46

Instruct the children to cut out the pictures of Paul. Guide them in gluing the pictures in the appropriate spaces. Read the sentences, allowing volunteers to tell what happened to Eutychus.

Lesson 146: Paul in Jerusalem

Bible text: Acts 21:17–20; 22:1–24

Doctrinal truth: Church

Character trait: Love

Memory verses: Review Proverbs 20:11; Proverbs 11:30b; and Hebrews 13:6.

Opening chorus: "Even a Child Is Known"

Memory verses
Review Proverbs 20:11 and Proverbs 11:30b.

Song: "Jesus Saves"

Prayer
Thank God that He is always with us to help us not be afraid.

Song: "Be Ye Doers of the Word," stanzas 1, 4, 9, and 10

Bible lesson

Introduction
➤ When Paul and his friends came to Jerusalem, the Christians there were eager to hear about their missionary journey. Paul told them how God took care of them and how many people in the places they visited had trusted in God's Son to be their Savior from sin.

Lesson

But some people in Jerusalem were not happy to see Paul and his friends. These people were the Jews, God's special people, whom we learned about in our lessons earlier this year. The Jews did not believe that Jesus was the Son of God, the promised Messiah. Even though God had told them He would send His Son to a Jewish family to be born in a special way in the town of Bethlehem, they did not believe Jesus was the Son of God.

So they did not like what Paul was doing. They did not like Paul preaching about how Jesus is the promised Savior who died for all people everywhere. They said Paul was causing trouble.

One day when Paul went to the temple to worship the Lord, many of these men who did not believe that Jesus was the Savior, and who hated Paul for preaching the gospel, came to Paul and dragged him out of the temple. They began beating Paul and would have killed him, but someone ran to tell the captain of the Roman soldiers.

The captain and his soldiers ran through the crowd of people. They took Paul and bound him with chains. Then the captain asked the people why they wanted to kill him. They all began shouting at once so that the captain couldn't understand what they were saying. The captain had his soldiers carry Paul into the castle. As the soldiers took him up the stairs, Paul said to the captain, "May I speak to you?"

The captain answered, "Can you speak my language?" Then Paul asked to speak to the crowd of people. So the captain let Paul stand on the stairs. He held up his hand to tell them to be quiet and listen. And then Paul told the crowd of people about how God had changed his life.

He told them that he had once hated the Christians and their Savior. He told them about the day he was on the road to Damascus to put some Christians in jail, when the Lord came to him in a bright light. He told them about his blindness and how he believed in God's Son and now wanted to go everywhere telling people about the Savior.

The mob of angry people listened for a while to Paul's preaching. But when Paul said that he wanted to preach the gospel to everyone—not just to the Jews—that made them even angrier.

So the captain had his soldiers lead Paul away from the mob and into the castle prison.

Application
➤ It seems sad that Paul had to go to prison again. But remember our Bible story about Joseph? We learned that God always knows what is best for us. God promised to take care of Joseph and Paul, and He promises to take care of us. (BAT: 8a Faith in God's promises)

We can boldly say, "The Lord is my helper, and I will not fear what man shall do unto me" (Hebrews 13:6). Do you think Paul was afraid? He remembered that God was with him, taking care of him. (BAT: 8d Courage)

Song: "When I Am Afraid"

Lesson 147: God's Plan for Paul

Bible text: Acts 23:10–35

Doctrinal truth: God (sovereignty)

Character traits: Trust; Self-concept

Materials:
• World globe or map

Opening chorus: "Even a Child Is Known"

Song: "Jesus Saves"

Prayer

Pray for missionary requests.

As each missionary is mentioned, have a child (with your help) point to the section of the globe or map that shows where the missionary is serving the Lord.

Song: "Be Ye Doers of the Word," stanzas 1, 4, 9, and 10

Song: "God Made Me"

Bible lesson

Introduction

➤ In our last Bible lesson, we heard that Paul was put into jail again. Why? (Briefly review.) He must have wondered how God would use him there. And during the night, God came to him and said, "Be of good cheer, Paul; don't be sad. I have a plan for you. Just as you have preached the gospel in Jerusalem, I plan for you to preach it also in the big city of Rome."

Lesson

But the Jews had another plan for Paul. They went to the chief priest and leaders of the Jews. They asked them to send a message to the captain of the Roman soldiers to ask him to bring Paul to them. The soldiers were to say that the Jewish leaders wanted to ask Paul some questions. But the Jewish leaders really planned to hide and then kill Paul.

But Paul's nephew overheard their plan and went to the prison to tell Paul. Paul sent his nephew to tell the captain what the Jews were planning. The captain listened to what the young man had to say. He told him not to tell anyone else what he had heard.

Then the captain ordered two hundred soldiers to take Paul safely to Felix, the governor of Caesarea. Felix also put Paul in prison there. But Paul remembered that God had a plan for his life. He knew God had told him he would someday be able to preach the gospel in Rome—one of the biggest cities in the world at that time.

Application

➤ After Paul accepted Jesus as His Savior, Paul's life was changed, wasn't it? Paul knew God had a plan and purpose for his life. He listened to God and obeyed Him. Paul knew that God works out all His plans.

God always kept His promises to Paul. God always keeps His promises to us. (BAT: 8a Faith in God's promises)

Did you know that God has a special plan for each of you? (BAT: 3a Self-concept) If you have asked Jesus to save you from your sin, then you know that you are a child of God. God has a special job for each of His children to do. God wants some of us to be preachers and some to be teachers. God plans for some people to be missionaries, some to be mommies and daddies to tell their children about God, and some to work at jobs where they can tell others about their Savior.

Each day, as we listen to God's Word and pray to Him, God will show us His plan for us. Do you want to serve God in His plan and His way? Oh, I hope so! That is the only way to be happy. We want to serve God because we love Him. (BAT: 7d Contentment)

Song: "Trust and Obey"

Lesson 148: Paul Spoke to a King and Queen

Bible texts: Acts 24:24–25; 25:13–27; 26:1–32
Doctrinal truth: God (sovereignty)
Character trait: Self-concept
Memory verses: Review Proverbs 3:5–6 and I Thessalonians 5:18.
Catechism: Introduce Catechism 49 and review Catechism 50.

Opening chorus: "Even a Child Is Known"

Song: "Jesus Saves"

Prayer

Thank God that He always does what is best for us.

Song: "How Do We Know?" stanzas 1–7

Memory verses

Review Proverbs 3:5–6 and I Thessalonians 5:18, relating these truths to Paul's life.

Bible lesson

Introduction

➤ While Paul was in prison in Caesarea, Felix, the governor, was kind to him. He let Paul's friends come to visit him. Paul told Felix about God and His Son. But Felix did not like to hear about his sin.

Lesson

One day the king and queen came to visit Festus, the new governor of Caesarea. Festus told King Agrippa about Paul. The king asked to see Paul. So Paul stood before the king and queen and bravely told them about the Lord.

The king listened carefully as Paul told him about the Lord Jesus dying on the cross and rising from the dead. He said, "Paul, you have almost persuaded me to believe in Jesus Christ and become a Christian."

The Jewish leaders asked the king to let them have Paul so they could kill him. But the king said, "No, Paul has asked to speak before the chief leader of the world—Caesar."

King Agrippa knew Paul had not done anything that he should be killed for. But Paul had asked to go to Rome to speak to Caesar; so Agrippa kept him in jail.

Application

➤ God was working out His plan for Paul. (BAT: 3a Self-concept) If Paul had not been in prison, he would not have been there to tell the king and queen about Jesus, God's Son. God always knows what is best for His children. Sometimes when things happen in our lives that we do not like, we fuss and grumble. (BAT: 7d Contentment) We should not do that because God will work everything out in our lives for His glory and for our good.

Song: "Trust and Obey"

Catechism

Introduce Catechism 49.

■ What will become of the righteous? *(The righteous shall be taken to heaven.)*

Review Catechism 50.

■ What is heaven? *(Heaven is a glorious and happy place, where the saved shall be forever with the Lord.)*

➤ Who are the righteous? *(those who have asked Jesus to be their Savior from sin)*

Lesson 149: Paul's Journey

Bible texts: Acts 27:1–28:16; Philippians 4:11

Doctrinal truths: God; Salvation (sanctification)

Character trait: Contentment

Memory verses: Review.

Catechism: Review.

Materials
• Small construction-paper ship
• Flannel board
• A long piece of blue yarn, placed across the flannel board to represent waves
• Student page 47 and cutouts
• Scissors
• Glue

Opening chorus: "Even a Child Is Known"

Song: "Growing, Knowing, Showing"

Song: "Where He Leads Me"

Song: "Obedience Is"

Prayer

Ask God to help us be happy always, even when things do not go our way.

Song: "Praise Him, Praise Him"
Replace "God is love" with "God knows best."

Bible lesson

Introduction

➤ After Paul believed in God's Son, he became a great missionary for God. Missionaries are people who tell others about Jesus. Paul was a missionary who traveled to many cities and countries to tell others about God's Son, our Savior from sin.

The people who heard Paul preach about God's way were not always kind to him. In many places where Paul preached, the people threw stones at him and beat him and put him into jail. Sometimes Paul was tied with chains to the soldiers who guarded him. These chains were used like the handcuffs that policemen use today.

Lesson

One day Paul was on a ship sailing to Rome, a big city in a faraway country. He was a prisoner. Some soldiers were taking him to the king in another country. Before the captain of the ship had set sail, Paul had told him that it would be best to wait. Paul told him that it would be a dangerous trip. But the captain did not listen to Paul. He ordered his sailors to sail the ship out into the ocean.

While they were sailing on their trip, they got caught in a big storm. The captain and his crew remembered that Paul had warned them not to go. They were afraid, but Paul told them not to be afraid. He told them God had sent an angel who told him that no one would die in the storm. He told the captain to have everyone stay on the ship. So no one left the ship. When daylight came, they saw they were near land. The sailors tried to get their ship to the land, but it crashed on big rocks. Everyone swam safely to shore. They were on an island called Melita. The people who lived on the island were kind to everyone from the ship.

Later Paul was gathering a bundle of sticks. He was helping to keep a big fire burning so everyone could get warm. After he had placed the sticks in the fire, a snake bit him on the hand.

The people who lived on the island knew that Paul was a prisoner. They thought that since Paul was a prisoner, he must have done something terrible—like murder. So when they saw the snake bite Paul, they thought God must be punishing him. They thought Paul would surely die.

They watched and they waited. But nothing happened. They wondered how this could be. They thought Paul must have some special power. They didn't know it was God's power that kept Paul safe.

God showed His power in another special way while Paul was on the island. The father of the man who was leader of the island was very sick. Paul prayed for him. God heard his prayers and answered them. The old man was made well.

When the people of the island saw the great power that Paul's God had, they brought their sick friends to Paul. God helped Paul work many miracles to make the sick people well.

Paul had to stay on the island for many days, but he never grumbled or complained. He knew that he was doing what God wanted him to do in the place where God wanted him to do it. He was obeying God and showing God's way to others. Wherever he went, Paul preached the gospel of God's Son, the Savior. Paul wanted to glorify God by loving and obeying Him.

Application
➤ Paul was put into jail and later was shipwrecked, but he always served the Lord wherever he was.

God wants us to be happy wherever we are, even when things do not go the way we would like for them to go. (BAT: 7d Contentment)

Song: "Even a Child Is Known"

Student page 47
Instruct the children to cut out the pictures of Paul and lay them in a row. Direct them to hold up each picture as you describe the following: 1) Saul on the road to Damascus, 2) Paul preaching, 3) Paul and Silas in prison, and 4) Paul shipwrecked. Guide the children in gluing the pictures onto the page. Lead them in reciting Proverbs 11:30b. Read the sentences.

Memory verses and catechism
As time permits, review verses and catechism. After each child answers a question, have him move the construction-paper ship across the "sea" from one wave to the next on the flannel board. (You may wish to provide two ships and two yarn-wave courses for team competition.)

Lesson 150: Paul in Rome

Bible text: Acts 28:11–31

Doctrinal truth: Church

Character traits: Obedience; Contentment

Memory verses: Review.

Catechism: Review.

Materials
- Small construction-paper ship
- Flannel board
- A long piece of blue yarn, placed across the flannel board to represent waves

Opening chorus: "Even a Child Is Known"

Song: "Jesus Saves"

Prayer
Thank God for our lessons on Paul, God's faithful missionary.

Bible lesson

Introduction
➤ In our last lesson we learned that Paul trusted the Lord even when he was shipwrecked, and God brought him safely to the island of Melita.

Lesson
During the winter season after the shipwreck, God was with Paul and helped him work many miracles on the island.

In the spring, the soldiers took Paul on another ship and sailed toward Rome.

The Christians who lived in Rome had heard that Paul was coming, so they went to meet him and walked the rest of the way with him into the city.

Paul was not taken to the jail like other prisoners. Instead he was kept in a house with one soldier to guard him.

Many people came to visit Paul during the two years that he lived in the house in Rome. He was happy to tell everyone about God's love in sending His Son to be our Savior.

While Paul was a prisoner in the house, he wrote letters to Christians all over the world. Some of his letters are in the Bible. (Demonstrate by pointing to the books of Ephesians, Philippians, Colossians, and Philemon in your Bible as you say their names.)

Paul wrote many other New Testament books. (Demonstrate by pointing to Romans, I and II Corinthians, Galatians, I and II Thessalonians, I and II Timothy, and Titus in your Bible as you say their names.) Some of the memory verses we have learned in kindergarten are in the books that God told Paul to write down for Him. (Review Romans 3:23, I Thessalonians 5:18, I Corinthians 15:3b–4, and Ephesians 4:32.)

Who told Paul what to write in these letters? *(God)* The Bible is God's Word. Who wrote the Bible? *(Catechism 18: Holy men who were taught by the Holy Spirit wrote the Bible.)*

Application

➤ Paul was put into jail many times. Because he was ship-wrecked and moved as a prisoner from place to place, he was able to reach many more people for God. Paul spread the tidings of the gospel wherever he went. Paul won many souls to God. Let's recite Proverbs 11:30b together. (BAT: 5c Evangelism and missions)

Did Paul complain and grumble? No, he said he would be happy anywhere God wanted him to be as long as he could serve God. It is wonderful to be a child of God. Let's pray that we will be faithful, obedient servants for our Lord as Paul was. (BATs: 2b Servanthood; 2c Faithfulness; 7d Contentment)

Memory verses and catechism

Review verses and catechism questions as time permits, using the ship activity from Lesson 149.

Lesson 151: Philemon

Bible text: Philemon

Doctrinal truth: Salvation (sanctification)

Character trait: Forgiveness

Memory verse: Review Ephesians 4:32.

Catechism: Review Catechism 18.

Opening chorus: "Even a Child Is Known"

Song: "All for Jesus"

Prayer

Thank God for forgiving our sin and ask Him to help us be forgiving toward others.

Song: "God's Way"

Bible lesson

Introduction

Open your Bible to the book of Philemon and review Catechism 18.

■ Who wrote the Bible? *(Holy men who were taught by the Holy Spirit wrote the Bible.)*

➤ Do you remember who wrote the book called *Philemon* in the New Testament of our Bible? *(Paul)*

Lesson

Paul was a missionary preacher for the Lord. He went from city to city telling people about God's Son, Jesus Christ. God told Paul to write many of the books of the Bible. Many of the Bible books that Paul wrote were letters to Christian friends in churches where he had preached.

Philemon is one of these. It is a short letter that Paul wrote to a rich man named Philemon. Paul wrote to Philemon about a young man named Onesimus.

Onesimus had been a slave in Philemon's house, but Onesimus didn't like working there and had run away from his job. He went to a big city (Rome) and met Paul there. Paul told him about the Lord Jesus Christ. Onesimus asked Jesus Christ to be his Savior from sin.

Onesimus wanted to obey God's Word after he had become a Christian. He knew he must go back to live in Philemon's house and be his servant. But he was afraid Philemon would be angry with him.

Paul wrote Philemon a letter and told him what had happened to Onesimus since he had run away. He asked Philemon to forgive Onesimus and love him as a Christian brother. Do you think Philemon did what Paul asked him to? *(Answers may vary.)* I believe he did.

Application

➤ In his letter to Philemon, Paul said he thanked God for Philemon's faith in God and his love for other Christians. Philemon loved God and loved his Christian friends. When he forgave Onesimus, he showed that he loved God. When we forgive others who have been unkind to us, we are showing love. (BAT: 6e Forgiveness)

Song: "Be Ye Doers of the Word," stanza 11

Memory verse

Review Ephesians 4:32. Choose several children to pantomime ways to show kindness and direct the others to guess what they are doing. Follow each pantomime with one or more children reciting Ephesians 4:32.

Lesson 152: Review—Paul the Missionary

Bible text: Acts

Doctrinal truth: Salvation (sanctification)

Character trait: Love

Memory verses: Review.

Catechism: Review.

Materials
- Several missionary prayer cards
- Student page 48 and cutouts
- Scissors
- Glue
- Toy boat (for review activity)

This review lesson provides a good opportunity for a missionary to speak to the children, or for the children to listen to a letter or a recording from a missionary.

Opening chorus: "Even a Child Is Known"

Doctrinal emphasis: The Holy Spirit

➤ We all need help to think God's way and to know God's way. We learn how to think God's way as we hear and learn Bible verses. We all need to grow in God's way so that we can live God's way. We learn to do this as we obey God's Word. We cannot be good by ourselves. We need God's help. Everyone does.

We have heard many lessons from God's Word during our Bible time—stories about good men and women who loved God. But always these people needed God's help to live God's way. Many times they disobeyed and had to ask God to forgive them.

Even though we love God, we need to learn more about what He tells us in His Word so that we can obey. We need to ask God to forgive us and to help us obey. Obeying is a big job. It's a hard job. But God has given us someone very special to help us.

When Jesus got ready to go back to heaven to live with God the Father, He told His disciples that He would send someone to help them live God's way. Remember that we learned that God is one God who is three persons. Who are the three persons who are the one true God of heaven? *(God the Father, God the Son, and God the Holy Spirit)* Why do we believe God is three persons? *(because the Bible tells us so)* And the Bible is holy and true. After we ask Jesus to be our Savior from sin, the Holy Spirit helps us to remember God's Word and live God's way. The Holy Spirit helps us to remember to be loving and kind instead of selfish. He helps us to be helpful and giving instead of jealous. He helps us to be brave when we are afraid. He helps us to tell the truth. He helps us to be happy with all that God gives us each day.

Some of you are wondering what God wants you to be someday when you grow up. You may think, "Oh, it

would be exciting to be a fireman, or a pilot of an airplane, or an astronaut—and to do many other grown-up jobs." But God tells us to obey His Word right now by obeying our parents and teachers, and then His Holy Spirit will show us each day as we grow up what He wants us to do.

And, boys and girls, the most exciting thing in the world is to obey God and live for Him each day. To be happy, we need to find out what God wants us to do and then do it. The only way to be really happy is to think and act God's way.

Song: "Jesus Saves"

Prayer

Pray for the missionary(ies) on the prayer cards.

Student page 48

Read the sentences and discuss how we can be missionary helpers. Instruct the children to cut out the pictures. Guide them in gluing the pictures in place (girl praying; and boy writing letter in the top sections of the globe; boy with piggy bank, and girl sharing God's Word in the bottom sections of the globe). Lead the children in reciting Proverbs 11:30b.

Poem: "A Missionary Helper"

Recite the following poem.

➤ A missionary helper now
That's what I want to be.
A missionary helper
To our friends across the sea.
I can give my money
And remember now to pray.
I can write some missionary
In a kind and friendly way.
If someday God calls me
To lands across the sea,
I will listen to His Word;
His missionary, then, I'll be!

If you have obtained a missionary prayer card for each child, send it home with today's completed student page.

Song: "Be Ye Doers of the Word," stanzas 1 and 10

Review activity

Give a toy boat to the child who answers the first review question. He may hold it until the next question is answered. Use the following review questions.

1. What had Saul planned to do in Damascus? *(hurt the Christians)*

2. What happened to Saul on the way to Damascus? *(God spoke to him.)*

3. Who were the first missionaries who were sent out by the church? *(Paul and Barnabas)*

4. What is a missionary? *(someone who tells others about the Savior)*

5. What did Lydia do for Paul and Silas? *(She invited them to stay at her house.)*

6. What happened when Paul and Silas were in jail at Philippi? *(An earthquake opened the jail doors and loosened the prisoners' chains; the jailer believed on the Lord Jesus Christ.)*

7. What happened to a young man named Eutychus when Paul was preaching at Troas? *(He fell out of a window and died, and God used Paul to bring Eutychus back to life.)*

8. Why was Paul put into jail at Jerusalem? *(because he said he wanted to preach God's Word to everyone, not just to the Jews)*

9. Who warned Paul about the plan of some Jews to kill him? *(his nephew)*

10. How did Paul happen to come to the island of Melita? *(His ship was wrecked.)*

11. How did God use Paul at Melita? *(Paul healed the sick by God's power.)*

12. Where did Paul live when he was in Rome? *(in a house with a soldier to guard him)*

13. Who was Onesimus? *(a runaway slave)*

14. What happened to him? *(He trusted in God's Son.)*

15. Who was his master? *(Philemon)*

16. How did Paul help Onesimus? *(He gave him a letter to take back to Philemon.)*

Continue with a review of memory verses and catechism as time permits.

God's Children

Review: I Will Remember

Lesson 153: Timothy Listened to God's Word

Bible text: I and II Timothy; Revelation 4:11

Doctrinal truth: Bible

Character trait: Obedience

Memory verses: Review.

Catechism: Review.

Materials
- "Boy Timothy" (Picture Packet)
- A scroll, a picture of a scroll, or a completed copy of Student page 49 (for use as a visual)
- Student pages 49–50 and cutouts
- Scissors
- Glue
- Question Mark visual (See Lesson 80.)

> You may wish to prepare a second Question Mark visual. Catechism question numbers could be inserted in one visual, and memory verse references could be inserted in the other.

Opening song: "A Child of the King," stanza 1
In this final unit teach stanza 1 and, if you have time, stanza 2.

Song: "God Made Me"

Prayer
Stand and pray the Lord's Prayer together.

Bible lesson

Introduction
Display "Boy Timothy" picture.

> ➤ The Bible tells us about a young boy named Timothy who lived long ago. Timothy's mother was Eunice. She loved the Lord. His grandmother was Lois, and she loved God too. When Timothy was very young, his mother and grandmother taught him from God's Word. The Bible they had didn't look like ours. It was a scroll. (Show a scroll or picture of a scroll.) But it had words that meant the same thing as the words we have in our Bible.

Lesson

Timothy was a good listener. He listened and learned God's Word. He remembered the words he had been taught. He believed in the Lord Jesus Christ as His Savior from sin. He wanted to tell other people about His God. He wanted to serve Jesus, God's Son.

Timothy grew up to be a young man. Paul, the missionary, came to where Timothy lived. Paul told Timothy he needed a helper. This was just what Timothy wanted to do—serve Jesus! So he became Paul's missionary helper.

Timothy knew God's Word because when he was very young, he had faithfully listened as his mother and grandmother taught him. When he grew up, he remembered what he had learned. He spoke God's Word to others as he went around preaching the gospel.

Paul wrote two letters to Timothy when they were preaching in different places. These letters are two of our New Testament books that God told Paul to write. They are called I and II Timothy. (Show the children these books in the Bible.) These letters helped Timothy to love and serve God.

Application
> ➤ You have been listening to Bible lessons and learning verses from the Bible all year during Bible time. Who wrote the Bible? *(Catechism 18: Holy men who were taught by the Holy Spirit wrote the Bible.)* I hope you have been good listeners. You can grow up and remember God's Word as Timothy did. Reading God's Word is very important and will make you happy children of God. (BAT: 6a Bible study)

Memory verse
Review Ecclesiastes 12:13*b*. Refer to Lesson 51 to review the meaning of "fear."

Song: "Holy Bible, Book Divine"

Catechism

Review Catechism 9 and 10.

- How can you glorify God? *(I can glorify God by loving Him and doing what He commands.)*

- Why ought you to glorify God? *(I ought to glorify God because He made me and takes care of me.)*

➤ Timothy's name means "honoring God." We honor God when we show by our words and actions that we love Him and want to obey Him. When we glorify God, we are honoring Him as King of kings and Lord of lords.

Read Revelation 4:11 from your Bible.

Song: "Praise Him, Praise Him"

Student pages 49–50

Instruct the children to cut out the pictures. Direct them to glue the picture of young Timothy in place on page 49. Read the page, reviewing the story and the song "A Child of the King."

Guide the children in gluing the pictures in the appropriate spaces on page 50. Read the page. Remind the children that it is important to read God's Word (they can ask Mom and Dad to read to them), pray, and share God's Word every day. Challenge them to do all three.

Review activity: Question Mark visual(s)
Review all memory verses and catechism questions during this last unit.

Lesson 154: Mark Prays

Bible text: Proverbs 9:1

Character traits: Wisdom; Trust

Memory verses: Review Ecclesiastes 12:13b; Genesis 1:1; Psalm 95:6; Psalm 25:4; and Psalm 20:11.

Materials
• A completed copy of Student page 51 (for use as a visual)

Opening song: "A Child of the King," stanza 1

Song: "God Made Me"

Prayer
Ask God to help us know and live His way.

Song: "Growing, Knowing, Showing"

Character story: "Mark Prays"

Introduction
➤ Let's think of our lives as houses. Everyone who loves the Lord is building some kind of a character life-house for Him. Our character is how we live. What kind of life does the Lord want us to build? What kind of house does the Lord want us to build with our lives? We're not talking about a house that we can see with our eye or that our bodies can live in.

What materials do we usually use to build a house? *(wood, bricks, cement blocks, stone)* Some people in the world even live in huts made of mud or straw. But our life-houses are not built with those kinds of materials. God wants us to build our lives for eternity, so we should use Godlike character traits for our building materials. We have already talked about these during our school year.

Read Proverbs 9:1.

➤ What is wisdom? Wisdom is not a material like wood that you can see or feel. Wisdom means thinking and living God's way. How does God want us to live? Does the Lord want us to be selfish or kind and giving? Does He want us to be afraid and fearful or brave? He wants us to live in a way that will show that we love and obey Him. Then we will be building lives that will glorify our heavenly Father. What is our duty in life? What are we supposed to do? (Recite Ecclesiastes 12:13b.)

Some of the character traits that will show others that we love God are wisdom or thinking God's way, trust, obedience, love, kindness, forgiveness, honesty, courage, thankfulness, and contentment. Contentment is being happy with what we have and with where God wants us to be.

The Bible lessons we have had during the year can help remind us of some of these character life-building materials.

We listen to Bible words to find out what God wants us to know. (Recite Genesis 1:1.) This tells us that the Lord our God made us. (Recite Psalm 95:6.)

When we believe God's Word—that God created the world and everything in it for His glory—then we are beginning to think God's way. Thinking God's way is wisdom. So we need to ask God to show us His ways and teach us His paths.

With this wisdom from God we can begin building our life-houses for the Lord.

Lesson
Make the sound of an emergency vehicle siren to introduce the story.

"Whoop, whoop, whoop, whoop, whoop."

"What is that noise?" Mother asked from the kitchen.

"A fire truck?" Mark asked excitedly, running down the hall from his room.

"A police car?" asked Joy. Her eyes widened as she quickly closed her coloring book and looked up.

Father hurried up from the basement and looked out the front window. "It's an emergency vehicle stopping in front of Mrs. Babb's house. Why, there are several neighbors standing outside in her yard. I'd better go and see what has happened."

Paul was already over in Mrs. Babb's yard, standing as close to the emergency vehicle as he could without being in the way. Mr. Heath walked up behind Paul and asked if he knew what had happened. About that time he saw Mrs. Babb lying on the ground beside a ladder. She had fallen off the ladder while she was washing windows, and another neighbor had seen her and called for an ambulance.

Mr. Heath and Paul moved closer as the hospital medics lifted Mrs. Babb onto the stretcher. She was smiling and thanking them for taking care of her, and then she saw Mr. Heath and Paul.

"I'm afraid I wasn't very careful this time. It feels like I may have broken my ankle."

"Now, don't you worry about a thing, Mrs. Babb," Mr. Heath said. "Since you know the Lord as your Savior, you can trust Him to take care of you. He will be with you. And we will take care of closing your house while you're in the hospital."

"And I'll finish washing your windows," Paul added.

By this time, Mrs. Heath, Joy, and Mark had come over to find out what had happened.

"Would you like me to ride along to the hospital with you?" Mrs. Heath asked Mrs. Babb.

"Oh, that would be so nice," answered Mrs. Babb. "You are all being so helpful. I just thank the Lord every day for Christian neighbors."

"And I'll get your paper and mail for you every day," Joy said, wanting to help too.

Mrs. Babb smiled and waved thanks to all of them as she was lifted up into the ambulance.

That evening at the supper table, Mark quietly listened as they all talked about Mrs. Babb's accident. It seemed everybody was doing something to help her except him. "What can I do?" Mark wondered. "Show me a way to help too, Lord," he prayed in his heart. "Shew me thy ways, O Lord, teach me thy paths" (Psalm 25:4).

That evening when they had family prayer before bedtime, Father asked Mark to pray first. When Mark prayed, he asked the Lord to take care of Mrs. Babb and help her to get well soon.

After prayer time, Father looked at Mark and said, "Mark, it was good to hear you remember to pray for our neighbor. That's one of the best ways we

can help her. The Lord tells us to 'Pray one for another.' And Mrs. Babb especially needs our prayers right now."

Mark went to bed with a smile on his face. God had showed him a way to help, and he was happy.

Application

➤ God has a plan for each of our lives. Even when we are in kindergarten, we can serve the Lord. Just like Mark, we can ask the Lord to show us how to live His way. (Recite Proverbs 20:11.)

Wisdom is the foundation of our house. In our character story today, Mark learned wisdom. He knew God had a plan for his life, and he wanted to live God's way. And God showed him what to do. What did Mark do? (*He prayed for Mrs. Babb.*)

Wisdom is knowing God loves us and has a plan for our lives and asking Him to show us what He wants us to do each day.

Show the children the completed copy of "My Life-House for God" (Student page 51).

➤ Wisdom is the way we should begin building our life-houses. Just as a builder lays a foundation for each house he builds, we need to begin building our character house with a foundation of wisdom that knows and lives God's way. (Point to the foundation of the house.) Remember, Proverbs 9:1 tells us, "Wisdom hath builded her house."

Song: "God's Way"

> Each lesson in this final unit includes a story that illustrates a character trait that the children will place in their "houses" (Student page 51). You will also review some of these same character traits as exemplified in the lives of the Bible characters studied throughout the year.

Lesson 155: Joy and Paul Trust

Bible text: Review

Character trait: Thankfulness

Memory verses: Review Psalm 100; Luke 2:11; John 3:16; I John 4:19.

Materials
- Teacher's copy of "Our Thanksgiving Psalm" booklet (from Student Packet; used in Lesson 70)
- A completed copy of Student page 24 (for use as a visual; used in Lesson 80)
- A completed copy of Student page 51 (for use as a visual; used in Lesson 154)

Opening song: "A Child of the King," stanza 1

Song: "Father, We Thank Thee for the Night"

Prayer

Thank God for our beautiful world.

Song: "Growing, Knowing, Showing"

Character story: "Joy and Paul Trust"

Introduction

➤ When we think of all that the Lord God has given to us—this beautiful world we live in, our parents, our homes, our churches, our schools, and our friends—we should thank God for all His gifts to us. (Recite Psalm 100, displaying "Our Thanksgiving Psalm" booklet pages.)

(Recite Luke 2:11 and John 3:16.) When we remember that God loves us so much that He sent His only Son, the Lord Jesus Christ, to be our Savior from sin, we can praise God for the *best* gift—His Son, the Lord Jesus Christ. (Display the completed copy of Student page 24.) (Recite I John 4:19.) Thankfulness is another character-building material that we should use to build our life-houses for the Lord.

Lesson

The Heaths were spending a vacation week at a cabin by a lake in the mountains. The children were having a good time fishing, hiking, and exploring around the lake. There was a boat dock in front of their cabin, and tied to the dock was a raft.

Since both Paul and Joy knew how to swim, their parents gave them permission to sit on the raft while it was tied to the dock with a long rope. Paul liked to push the raft with a long pole along the shore in the shallow water.

One afternoon, when Paul was pushing the raft along the shore and Joy was lying down looking over the side of the raft into the water, Joy noticed something dark swimming in the water below. She looked more closely and then yelled for Paul to come see. Paul laid his pole on the raft and knelt down beside Joy to see what she was pointing to.

"Oh, it's a catfish, a big one! Wow, a really big one!" Paul whispered, trying not to make any noise that might scare the fish away.

"Look at the long whiskers on his head," Joy said.

"I know; that's why they call it a catfish—because it has whiskers like a cat," Paul explained. "I'd say that catfish must be two feet long. It's the biggest one I've ever seen." Paul lay down on his stomach on the raft to look at the fish more closely.

"Me too," sighed Joy. "Oh, I'm so glad we came to the cabin this week."

"Look, Joy, there's a boat anchor stuck into the sand and a turtle resting on top of it."

Joy shifted her position to get a better look. When she did, her foot accidentally kicked the pole, and it fell over the side of the raft into the water.

When Paul heard the splash, he looked up. They had not noticed, but the rope that had attached the raft to the dock was now broken. And while they were both lying on the raft looking into the water, the wind had blown their raft away from the shore. Paul quickly tried to reach for the pole as it floated away from the raft, but he couldn't quite reach it.

Joy looked scared. "What are we going to do, Paul?"

As Paul looked around, he realized that the wind was beginning to blow harder. He tried to move the boat, using his arm as a paddle. But the wind was blowing too hard from the other way.

"I think we'd better yell for help and hope Mother and Daddy hear us," Paul said.

"But Daddy took Mark for a hike and may not be back yet," Joy said. She felt like crying.

"Well, let's just pray that Mother hears us, O.K.? Now, don't be afraid, Joy. Just trust in the Lord to take care of us. And, while we're both praying in our hearts to the Lord, let's both yell for help from someone on shore."

Joy began thinking the words of the chorus she had learned at kindergarten, "I will trust and not be afraid."

It seemed as though they had been yelling for a long time, and the raft was floating out even farther into the lake, when suddenly they saw Father and Mark walking back from their hike. They began to run when they heard the shouts for help. Both Paul and Joy were very happy to see their father.

Father called back. "Don't worry, children; I'll drive down the road and borrow the neighbor's boat and pull you back to shore."

While Paul and Joy were waiting, they prayed together and thanked the Lord for taking care of them. They thanked the Lord that they had both trusted in His Son as their Savior from sin. Now they were able to have the wisdom that God gives to build character houses for Him.

Application

Show the children the "Thankfulness" page of the "My Life-House for God" booklet (Student page 51). Remind them that we should always thank God and others for their kindnesses to us.

Song: "When I Am Afraid"

Song: "God's Way"

Lesson 156: Joy's Witness

Bible text: Review.

Character trait: Trust

Memory verses: Review Proverbs 3:5–6; I Thessalonians 5:18; Romans 3:23; John 14:6; John 10:30; I Corinthians 15:3b–4; and Psalm 23.

Materials
- A completed copy of Student pages 8, 12, and 15 (for use as visuals; used in Lessons 32, 47, and 56)
- A completed copy of Student page 51 (for use as a visual)

Opening song: "A Child of the King," stanza 1

Song: "Be Ye Doers of the Word," stanza 4

Prayer
Ask God to help us remember His promises and trust Him.

Song: "Growing, Knowing, Showing"

Character story: "Joy's Witness"

Introduction

➤ The stories about Abraham, Joseph, and Moses remind us how important it is to trust the Lord, no matter where we are and no matter what happens to us. God has promised to be with us always and take care of us. (Recite Proverbs 3:5–6 and sing "Trust in the Lord.") We know that God does all things well in our lives. (Recite I Thessalonians 5:18.) Trust is the most important building material for our lives.

We need to trust in or believe in Jesus Christ, God's Son, as our Savior from sin. (Recite Romans 3:23; John 14:6; John 10:30; and I Corinthians 15:3b–4.) Only then can we "fear God and keep His commandments." Only then can we have wisdom to build our life-houses for God.

Briefly review one or more of the lessons about Abraham, Joseph, or Moses, using the completed Student pages 8, 12, and 15 as visuals.

➤ When we believe in Jesus to save us from our sin, He will be our Shepherd. (Recite Psalm 23.)

Lesson

Every afternoon when Joy came home from kindergarten, it was her job to bring in the mail. Sometimes when the mailman was late, Joy would wait outside by their mailbox until he got there. Then, instead of putting the mail inside the box, the carrier would hand it to Joy. Joy liked Mr. Jackson, the mailman. He would always smile at her and ask if she was learning how to read in her kindergarten class.

For the past week, Joy and her whole family had anxiously waited for a letter from Grandmother Heath. Grandfather had been very ill. He had been so ill that he had to stay in the hospital for several days. Each day in family devotions, they had all prayed for him to get well. And during kindergarten Bible time, Joy had asked her teacher and the class to pray for her grandfather. Joy had told Mr. Jackson about her grandfather. She told him that her family and friends were praying for Grandfather Heath.

Mr. Jackson had smiled as he listened to his little friend. He hoped her grandfather would soon be well. But this thing about God answering prayer— he wasn't too sure about that. Oh, Mr. Jackson knew that there must be a God somewhere who made the world. But he had never thought about praying and believing that the God who had made him also loved him and cared about his problems.

So today, as Mr. Jackson walked up the sidewalk, he was glad that he had a letter for the Heaths from their grandmother. He hoped it was good news about their grandfather. He smiled as he handed the letter to Joy. When Joy saw the pink envelope, she recognized Grandmother's stationery. She quickly thanked Mr. Jackson and then ran into the house as fast as she could, waving the letter in the air.

Mother opened the envelope quickly and began reading the news. Joy saw her mother's anxious look turn into a smile as she said, "Grandfather is much better. The doctor says he can go home from the hospital next week. Oh, the Lord is so good, Joy. God always answers prayers."

The next day, Joy could hardly wait to meet Mr. Jackson and tell him the good news. When she saw him coming down the street, she ran down the sidewalk to greet him.

As they walked along together, Joy told Mr. Jackson that God had answered their prayers. She recited one of her kindergarten memory verses about prayer. The Bible says, "Evening, and morning, and at noon, will I pray, and cry aloud: and he shall hear my voice." Joy told her friend that their grandfather was much better and would leave the hospital soon for home.

As Mr. Jackson looked at Joy's smiling, believing face, he began to wonder if there really was a God who heard and answered prayer. On several occasions, Joy's father had talked to Mr. Jackson about God's Son, the Savior, and had asked him to visit their church with them. "Maybe I should learn more about their God," he thought. "Joy," he said, "tell your father I'd like to go to church with your family this Sunday, if I may."

Joy was so surprised. She looked into Mr. Jackson's eyes and said, "Oh, I'm so glad. Father will be happy too. But most of all, the Lord God will be happy."

Application

Show the children the "Trust" page of the "My Life-House for God" booklet (Student page 51). Review how *trust* is believing God will do what He says He will do and that He will always do what is best for us.

Song: "God's Way"

Lesson 157: Joy and Mark Obey

Bible text: Review.

Character trait: Obedience

Memory verses: Review Psalm 38:18 and Psalm 37:27.

Materials
• A completed copy of Student page 51 (for use as a visual)

Opening song: "A Child of the King," stanzas 1–2

Song: "Obedience Is"

Prayer

Ask God to help us obey our parents and teachers.

Song: "Growing, Knowing, Showing"

Character story: "Joy and Mark Obey"

Introduction

➤ When we obey our parents and teachers, we are also obeying God's Word because He tells us in Ephesians 6:1, "Children, obey your parents in the Lord." Our stories about Adam and Eve's disobedience and about Jonah and the children of Israel remind us how important it is to obey God. (Briefly review one or more of these lessons to illustrate this character trait.)

Just like Adam and Jonah, we must declare our "iniquity and be sorry for our sin." Just like the children of Israel, we need to "depart from evil and do good." (Recite Psalm 38:18 and Psalm 37:27.) Obedience is an important building material for our "life-houses."

Lesson

"Now remember, Joy, to watch Mark for me. I don't want him to play near the street. I'm afraid he might run out into the street," Mother warned.

"Yes, ma'am," Joy replied. Joy opened the back door and disappeared around the corner of the house.

"Come, on, Markie, follow me," she ordered as she hurried down the sidewalk. Mark hopped on his tricycle and followed Joy. Several children from the neighborhood were playing softball together in the vacant lot next door.

Mark rode his tricycle up and down the sidewalk as he watched the game. One of the older boys was up to bat. Whamm! The boy hit the ball hard, and it soared through the air. The second baseman jumped to catch it and missed, and the center fielder tripped as he ran backwards to try to stop the flying ball. The ball hit the ground and rolled toward the street.

Mark had seen the whole thing. He jumped off his trike to hurry after the runaway ball.

"Stop, Mark. Don't go into the street," Joy shouted just as Mark was about to step off the curb.

Mark looked up and stopped. Just then a car passed by and barely missed the rolling ball. Mark's eyes opened wide with surprise. In all the excitement he had not seen or heard the car coming.

But Joy's eyes closed as she whispered a thank-you prayer to the Lord for helping her to see Mark and stop him just in time.

Application

Show the "Obedience" page of "My Life-House for God" booklet (Student page 51). Discuss the importance of both Joy and Mark obeying in the story.

Song: "Trust and Obey"

Lesson 158: Paul Witnesses

Bible text: Review.

Character trait: Courage

Memory verses: Review Joshua 1:9; Romans 3:23; and John 3:16.

Materials
• A completed copy of Student pages 26, 27, and 31 (for use as visuals; used in Lessons 84, 87, and 95)
• A completed copy of Student page 51 (for use as a visual)

Opening song: "A Child of the King," stanzas 1–2

Song: "When I Am Afraid"

Prayer

Ask God to help us to be brave.

Character story: "Paul Witnesses"

Introduction

➤ What is the name of a Bible person who showed great courage because he remembered the Lord God was with him? *(Joshua, David, Daniel)* (Recite Joshua 1:9.) God wants us to be brave and have courage.

Review these stories with the children, using the completed Student pages 26, 27, and 31 as visuals.

Lesson

Paul was sick. He had pneumonia. He had been so sick that his parents had to take him to the hospital. During the first few days when he was alone in his hospital bed, he often thought about the Lord. He wondered why the Lord had let him become ill. His father had always said, "The Lord knows what is best for us, and nothing can happen to us unless God allows it."

As he felt better and was awake more often, he would smile at the doctor and the nurses who came into his room to take care of him. Then one day he noticed that there was another bed in his room and that someone was in that bed too. He turned his head to see who it was. It was another boy who looked to be about his age. The boy had a frown on his face. He looked very unhappy. When the doctor and nurses came in to take care of him, he was not at all polite to them.

Paul decided he would try to make friends with his roommate. When he saw that the boy was awake, he said, "Hi, I'm Paul. What's your name?"

"None of your business," the boy answered angrily.

"You must really be sick," Paul said, still trying to be kind.

"Yeah, I broke my leg, but . . . just . . . mind your own business."

Paul tried not to notice how grumpy the other boy was. "I guess it will be a while before you can play ball and other sports, huh? That's too bad. I missed my championship soccer game because I was here." Paul tried to be a good testimony to this unhappy boy.

The boy muttered back, "Who cares?"

"Oh, I know someone who cares," Paul said.

"Yeah, you mean your family. A big help that is!"

"Well, yes, they do care, and they've been praying for me. But I mean someone else."

"Who, your soccer coach? Or your teacher?"

"No, I mean the Lord God of heaven who made me and takes care of me."

"Takes care of you! If He takes care of you, why did He let you get sick?" the boy said as he looked at Paul with surprise.

"Well," Paul answered, "You know, I have wondered about that while lying here in bed. And I know there has to be a reason. God always does what's best for us when we're His children."

"What do you mean, when we're His children? I thought everyone was a child of God."

Paul knew then that God was giving him an opportunity to witness to the boy in the bed next to him. He breathed a prayer for God to give him courage to say the right words, and then he went on talking.

"By the way, what did you say your name is?"

"Joe," the boy answered softly.

"Well, Joe, the Bible tells us that only the people who are sorry for their sin and accept God's Son, Jesus Christ, as their Savior can become God's children."

"I thought God made everyone," Joe answered softly.

"He did. He made the world and everything in it, but He made us to love Him and obey Him." Paul spoke slowly and clearly. He wanted to make sure that Joe understood God's plan for his life.

After Paul finished, Joe raised his head and looked at him seriously.

"Do you really believe all you've just told me? Do you really believe there is a God in heaven who knows all about us and cares about what happens to us?"

"I surely do," Paul answered. "And I believe I know why God let me get sick and put me here in this hospital room."

"You do?" Joe asked, amazed. "Why?"

"I believe He wanted me to tell you about Him, Joe," Paul answered bravely. "God wants you to believe in Him and ask His Son to be your Savior from sin."

Joe lay back on his pillow and was very quiet for several minutes. Paul was quiet too; he was praying for Joe and also thanking the Lord for giving him the courage to witness to Joe.

Before long, Joe looked over at Paul and said, "I believe you really mean what you have told me. I'd like to have God's Son be my Savior." Paul reached over and picked up his Bible from the stand by his bed. He found Romans 3:23 and read it: "For all have sinned, and come short of the glory of God." And he read John 3:16: "For God so loved the world, that he gave his only begotten Son, that whosoever believeth in him should not perish, but have everlasting life."

And then right there in their hospital room, Paul asked Joe to close his eyes to pray and ask Jesus, God's Son, to be his Savior from sin.

Application

Show the picture of Paul sharing God's Word with Joe in the "My Life-House for God" booklet (Student page 51). Remind the children that God is always with them to help them do hard things. (BAT: 8d Courage)

Song: "Be Ye Doers of the Word," stanzas 9–10

Lesson 159: Mark's Surprise

Bible text: Review.
Character trait: Love
Memory verse: Review Ephesians 4:32.
Materials
• A completed copy of Student page 51 (for use as a visual)

Opening song: "A Child of the King," stanzas 1–2

Song: "Be Ye Doers of the Word," stanzas 6–7

Prayer
Ask God to help us be kind and friendly to others.

Song: "Even a Child Is Known"

Character story: "Mark's Surprise"

Introduction

➤ What is the name of a Bible person who was friendly and helpful to others? (*David, Jonathan, Lydia*) (Review any of these as time permits. Recite Ephesians 4:32.) This teaches us that kindness is another character-building trait. And the story of Onesimus and Philemon reminds us that being forgiving toward others is Christlike.

Honesty will help us be strong in the Lord. The story of Joseph's brothers reminds us how sinful it is to be jealous and to tell lies. God tells us that we should always tell the truth and be content or happy with what we have.

Lesson

Joy walked to the breakfast table with a big, broad smile on her face. Everyone knew why. "Happy birthday, Joy," they all called out together. Mother had stuck six candles on a big pancake, and she set it down in front of Joy. Joy made a wish as she blew out the candles. Then the Heath family all sang "Happy Birthday" to her.

Joy grinned her biggest grin. She could hardly wait to get to kindergarten today. This was her special day to sit in the birthday chair and wear the birthday crown. It was kind of like having a birthday party at school. And her mother had baked thirty cupcakes for her class.

Mark looked at the smile on Joy's face. He wished it were his birthday. He wished he had some lighted candles to blow out. He began to feel a little upset. There was nothing special for him to look forward to today. Mark was jealous. He wanted this to be his special day instead of Joy's.

After Joy and Paul had gone to school, and Daddy had gone to work, Mother said, "Mark, I really need you to help me today. I have planned a surprise birthday party for your sister. I have so many things to do. Can I count on you to be a good helper?"

Mark thought, "Not another special time for Joy! She gets everything." Mark was so jealous that his face showed it. He frowned and looked very gloomy.

Mother thought she knew what Mark was thinking, and she wanted him to learn a good lesson that day. Before Mark could answer her question about helping, she began to tell him all the jobs he could help her with.

"While I bake Joy's birthday cake, I want you to fold the party napkins for me. Here, I'll show you how to do them."

At first Mark didn't think he'd like folding the napkins, but he liked the picture of the clown holding the birthday balloons. He folded each napkin as his mother had shown him so that the balloons were hidden in the fold. He knew that seeing the balloons pop out when the napkins were unfolded would be a nice surprise for Joy and her guests.

By the time he had finished his job, Mother had mixed the cake, poured the batter into the pans, and put the pans into the oven. Then she gave Mark a warm hug as she thanked him for the good job he had done.

"Now, I want you to hide these candy kisses all around the den while I blow up the balloons," Mother said.

Mark tried to think of the best places to hide the candy. His mother had said not to make it too hard or too easy for the party guests to find them. By now, Mark was thinking about how much fun all the children would have at the party. Gradually, he forgot to be jealous of Joy. When he finished hiding the candy, he asked, "What else can I do to help, Mother?"

"What a good helper you are, Mark," Mother said. She smiled as she took the cake out of the oven and put it on the countertop to cool. "Now I am going to have to get up on a chair to hang these balloons, so I'll need you to bring them to me one by one, as I ask for them."

His mother put the chair into the right position, climbed up on it, and said, "Now please bring me the red one first, Mark." Next she asked for the yellow, then the green, the orange, and the blue ones.

Mark thought it was fun to hand his mother the balloon she asked for. He was happy that he had already learned his colors. Now he was wondering what his next job would be. Much to his surprise, the job turned out to be something for him instead of Joy. His mother let him lick the bowl after she had finished icing Joy's birthday cake, and yumm, it was good!

Then Mother said, "I believe if you will empty the trash now, Mark, we will be ready for Joy to come home from kindergarten. Mrs. White is driving the car pool this week and knows about our surprise. She is going to take her time driving home so that the other children have time to get here before Joy."

As Mark took the trash out and emptied it into the big trash can beside the garage, he was smiling and humming a song. When he came back in, his mother noticed and said, "What are you humming, Mark?"

Mark stopped and thought. What a surprise! Why, he was singing "Happy Birthday" to Joy. He was really happy that it was her special day.

Later, when all the children had gone home, Joy gave her mother a big hug as she thanked her for the nice surprise.

Her mother said, "I'm glad you liked it, Joy, but you really should thank your brother. I couldn't have had everything ready in time without his help today."

Joy smiled at her little brother and thanked him with a big hug too.

Mark was so surprised. Why, he felt good all over. He had learned a lesson. It had been a special day for him, too, because he had learned that loving and giving to help someone else could make him happy. And most of all, he knew the Lord was pleased with what he had learned.

Application
Show the picture of Mark helping Mother in the "My Life-House for God" booklet (Student page 51). Review how showing kindness helped Mark.

Song: "All for Jesus," stanzas 2 and 4

Lesson 160: The Special Night

Bible text: Review.

Doctrinal truth: End Times

Character trait: Diligence

Memory verses: Review Psalm 55:17; Hebrews 13:6; Psalm 66:18; I John 1:9; and Proverbs 11:30*b*.

Materials
- A completed copy of Student page 51 (for use as a visual)
- Student page 51 and cutouts
- Scissors
- Stapler

> This lesson may be taught over two days. Discuss the Lord's return and tell the story about the Heaths the first day. Review the character traits and guide the children in assembling "My Life-House for God" booklets the next day.

Opening song: "A Child of the King," stanzas 1–2

Song: "God's Way"

Prayer
Ask God to help us be good workers and witnesses for Him.

Song: "Even a Child Is Known"

Doctrinal emphasis: The Lord's Return

➤ The Lord Jesus has promised to prepare us a heavenly home. He has promised to send us the Holy Spirit to show us His way. He has also promised that His Son will come back someday to take all of those who love Him to live with Him in heaven forever.

When it is time for the Lord to return, the Bible tells us that God will send His angels from heaven to blow a loud trumpet sound. There will be a loud shout, and the Lord Jesus Himself will come in a cloud in the sky. The Lord will come suddenly and very quickly to take all of us who love Him back to heaven with Him. Even the dead people who trusted in God's Son will rise up to go meet the Lord in the sky.

The Bible says that no one knows when the Lord will return for those who love Him. But we are all to watch and wait and be ready for His coming. Before Jesus went up in a cloud to heaven, He told all of us who love Him that He had work for us to do. We are to tell people that God loves them. We are to tell everyone about God's Word and the way to heaven. What are some ways we can keep busy while we wait for the Lord Jesus to come back? *(possible answers: obey God's Word, obey our parents, be kind)* (BAT: 2e Work)

While we are doing all of these things, we can be happy as we remember God's promise to come again someday. (BATs: 7d Contentment; 8a Faith in God's promises)

Character story: "The Special Night"

Introduction

➤ Can you name a person in the Bible who faithfully worked hard for our Lord? *(Answers may vary.)* There are many, aren't there? Do you remember the lessons about the Lord's disciples and about Paul, the missionary? (Review some of these lessons.) We must pray and ask the Lord to show us how we can serve Him. (Recite Psalm 55:17; Hebrews 13:6; Psalm 66:18; and I John 1:9.) Faithful service is work that will strengthen the house we are building for the Lord.

Lesson

Everyone in the Heath family was working hard to get his job done. Father was trimming the hedge while Paul was mowing the lawn. Mark was upstairs in his room putting toys away and straightening up. Joy was in the kitchen helping Mother get ready for their picnic supper on the patio. This was the night they had invited the new people for dinner. The name of their guests was Bortolozzo. They were from Brazil, a country very far away.

Father had sat by Mr. Bortolozzo on an airplane when he was returning from a business trip a few weeks ago. As they talked together on the airplane, Mr. Bortolozzo told Father that he had moved here from a big city in Brazil about a year ago to work as an engineer for a big business. After they had talked a while, Father started talking about the Lord Jesus, and he asked Mr. Bortolozzo whether he was a Christian.

Mr. Bortolozzo quickly answered that he had attended a church in Brazil when he lived there. Then Father asked him a very important question. He asked, "Mr. Bortolozzo, if you were to die, do you know that you would go to heaven to be with the Lord?"

Mr. Bortolozzo paused and looked very serious. He answered, "Well, when I lived in Brazil, I tried to be kind to my friends and neighbors, and I gave money to my church."

He admitted to Mr. Heath that since they had moved to the United States, he and his wife had not found a church to go to, so Father invited him and his wife and family to come to church. Father asked him to write his name and address and phone number on a card just before the plane landed at the airport.

The Heaths had been praying in family devotions for Mr. and Mrs. Bortolozzo every day since Father had returned home from his airplane trip. Father had told his family all about the Bortolozzos. He told them that he was sure that they were not Christians who were trusting in God's Son as their

Savior from sin. He was afraid they believed that, if they went to their church, did everything that their church leader said to do, and tried to do more good things than bad, then they would go to Heaven.

When Father told his family this, Joy asked, "But didn't their pastor read the Bible verses to them that say Jesus, God's Son, is the only way to Heaven? Christ says, 'I am the way, the truth, and the life: no man cometh unto the Father, but by me.' Didn't he tell them that no one can do enough good things to be saved from their sin?"

Father answered sadly, "I'm afraid there are many leaders in many churches who do not really preach God's Word and God's way from the Bible. Many churches make up their own rules and ways to get to heaven."

That's why this night was to be very special. That's why everyone was busily working to get the house and yard cleaned up. And the harder everyone worked, the more they prayed—each one silently talked to God about the Bortolozzos, praying that they would be a good testimony to them and that they would show by the way they lived that they loved the God of the Bible; that they would be friendly and kind; that the Bortolozzos would visit their church with them to hear God's Word preached; and most of all, that the Bortolozzos would be sorry for their sin and accept God's only Son as their Savior.

Application

➤ The Heath family were living God's way, weren't they? They were using their lives and their home to work and witness to others about God. (Recite Proverbs 11:30*b*.) They were missionaries in the neighborhood and in the city where they lived. (BATs: 5a Love; 5c Evangelism and missions)

Can you think of someone you know who does not know Jesus as his Savior? Ask God to help you be a good testimony to him by the things you do and the words you say.

Show the picture of the family working in the "My Life-House for God" booklet (Student page 51). Review how the family worked and witnessed.

Student page 51

Instruct the children to cut out the character trait pages for "My Life-House for God" booklets. Assist them in putting the pages in numerical order and stapling the pages in place.

Review the story pictures and remind the children to build their "life-houses" with God's wisdom and character. Remind them that living God's way will please Him.

Song: "God's Way"

Appendix

Bible Action Truths

The quality and consistency of a man's decisions reflect his character. Christian character begins with justification, but it grows throughout the lifelong process of sanctification. God's grace is sufficient for the task, and a major part of God's gracious provision is His Word. The Bible provides the very "words of life" that instruct us in salvation and Christian living. By obeying God's commands and making godly decisions based on His Word, Christians can strengthen their character.

Too often Christians live by only vague guidance—for instance, that we should "do good" to all men. While doing good is desirable, more specific guidance will lead to more consistent decisions.

Consistent decisions are made when man acts on Bible principles—or Bible Action Truths. The thirty-seven Bible Action Truths (listed under eight general principles) provide Christians with specific goals for their actions and attitudes. Study the Scriptures indicated for a fuller understanding of the principles in Bible Action Truths.

Thousands have found this format helpful in identifying and applying principles of behavior. Yet, there is no "magic" in this formula. As you study the Word, you likely will find other truths that speak to you. The key is for you to study the Scriptures, look for Bible Action Truths, and be sensitive to the leading of the Holy Spirit.

1. Salvation-Separation Principle

Salvation results from God's direct action. Although man is unable to work for this "gift of God," the Christian's reaction to salvation should be to separate himself from the world unto God.

a. Understanding Jesus Christ (Matthew 3:17; 16:16; I Corinthians 15:3–4; Philippians 2:9–11) Jesus is the Son of God. He was sent to earth to die on the cross for our sins. He was buried but rose from the dead after three days.

b. Repentance and faith (Luke 13:3; Isaiah 55:7; Acts 5:30–31; Hebrews 11:6; Acts 16:31) If we believe that Jesus died for our sins, we can accept Him as our Savior. We must be sorry for our sins, turn from them, confess them to God, and believe that He will forgive us.

c. Separation from the world (John 17:6, 11, 14, 18; II Corinthians 6:14–18; I John 2:15–16; James 4:4; Romans 16:17–18; II John 10–11) After we are saved, we should live a different life. We should try to be like Christ and not live like those who are unsaved.

2. Sonship-Servant Principle

Only by an act of God the Father could sinful man become a son of God. As a son of God, however, the Christian must realize that he has been "bought with a price"; he is now Christ's servant.

a. Authority (Romans 13:1–7; I Peter 2:13–19; I Timothy 6:1–5; Hebrews 13:17; Matthew 22:21; I Thessalonians 5:12–13) We should respect, honor, and obey those in authority over us. (attentiveness, obedience)

b. Servanthood (Philippians 2:7–8; Ephesians 6:5–8) Just as Christ was a humble servant while He was on earth, we should also be humble and obedient. (attentiveness, helpfulness, promptness, teamwork)

c. Faithfulness (I Corinthians 4:2; Matthew 25:23; Luke 9:62) We should do our work so that God and others can depend on us. (endurance, responsibility)

d. Goal setting (Proverbs 13:12, 19; Philippians 3:13; Colossians 3:2; I Corinthians 9:24) To be faithful servants, we must set goals for our work. We should look forward to finishing a job and going on to something more. (dedication, determination, perseverance)

e. Work (Ephesians 4:28; II Thessalonians 3:10–12) God never honors a lazy servant. He wants us to be busy and dependable workers. (cooperativeness, diligence, initiative, industriousness, thoroughness)

f. Enthusiasm (Colossians 3:23; Romans 12:11) We should do all tasks with energy and with a happy, willing spirit. (cheerfulness)

3. Uniqueness-Unity Principle

No one is a mere person; God has created each individual a unique being. But because God has an overall plan for His creation, each unique member must contribute to the unity of the entire body.

a. Self-concept (Psalm 8:3–8; 139; II Corinthians 5:17; Ephesians 2:10; 4:1–3, 11–13; II Peter 1:10) We are special creatures in God's plan. He has given each of us special abilities to use in our lives for Him.

b. Mind (Philippians 2:5; 4:8; II Corinthians 10:5; Proverbs 23:7; Luke 6:45; Proverbs 4:23; Romans 7:23, 25; Daniel 1:8; James 1:8) We should give our hearts and minds to God. What we do and say really begins in our minds. We should try to think of ourselves humbly as Christ did when He lived on earth. (orderliness)

c. Emotional control (Galatians 5:24; Proverbs 16:32; 25:28; II Timothy 1:7; Acts 20:24) With the help of God and the power of the Holy Spirit, we should have control over our feelings. We must be careful not to act out of anger. (flexibility, self-control)

d. Body as a temple (I Corinthians 3:16–17; 6:19–20) We should remember that our bodies are the dwelling place of God's Holy Spirit. We should keep ourselves pure, honest, and dedicated to God's will.

e. Unity of Christ and the church (John 17:21; Ephesians 2:19–22; 5:23–32; II Thessalonians 3:6, 14–15) Since we are saved, we are now part of God's family and should unite ourselves with others to worship and grow as Christians. Christ is the head of His church, which includes all believers. He wants us to work together as His church in carrying out His plans, but He forbids us to work in fellowship with disobedient brethren.

4. Holiness-Habit Principle

Believers are declared holy as a result of Christ's finished action on the cross. Daily holiness of life, however, comes from forming godly habits. A Christian must consciously establish godly patterns of action; he must develop habits of holiness.

a. Sowing and reaping (Galatians 6:7–8; Hosea 8:7; Matthew 6:1–8) We must remember that we will be rewarded according to the kind of work we have done. If we are faithful, we will be rewarded. If we are unfaithful, we will not be rewarded. We cannot fool God. (thriftiness)

b. Purity (I Thessalonians 4:1–7; I Peter 1:22) We should try to live lives that are free from sin. We should keep our minds, words, and deeds clean and pure.

c. Honesty (II Corinthians 8:21; Romans 12:17; Proverbs 16:8; Ephesians 4:25) We should not lie. We should be honest in every way. Even if we could gain more by being dishonest, we should still be honest. God sees all things. (fairness)

d. Victory (I Corinthians 10:13; Romans 8:37; I John 5:4; John 16:33; I Corinthians 15:57–58) If we constantly try to be pure, honest, and Christlike, with God's help we will be able to overcome temptations.

5. Love-Life Principle

We love God because He first loved us. God's action of manifesting His love to us through His Son demonstrates the truth that love must be exercised. Since God acted in love toward us, believers must act likewise by showing godly love to others.

a. Love (I John 3:11, 16–18; 4:7–21; Ephesians 5:2; I Corinthians 13; John 15:17) God's love to us was the greatest love possible. We should, in turn, show our love for others by our words and actions. (courtesy, compassion, hospitality, kindness, thankfulness to men, thoughtfulness)

b. Giving (II Corinthians 9:6–8; Proverbs 3:9–10; Luke 6:38) We should give cheerfully to God the first part of all we earn. We should also give to others unselfishly. (hospitality, generosity, sharing, unselfishness)

c. Evangelism and missions (Psalm 126:5–6; Matthew 28:18–20; Romans 1:16–17; II Corinthians 5:11–21) We should be busy telling others about the love of God and His plan of salvation. We should share in the work of foreign missionaries by our giving and prayers.

d. Communication (Ephesians 4:22–29; Colossians 4:6; James 3:2–13; Isaiah 50:4) We should have control of our tongues so that we will not say things displeasing to God. We should encourage others and be kind and helpful in what we say.

e. Friendliness (Proverbs 18:24; 17:17; Psalm 119:63) We should be friendly to others, and we should be loyal to those who love and serve God. (loyalty)

6. Communion-Consecration Principle

Because sin separates man from God, any communion between man and God must be achieved by God's direct action of removing sin. Once communion is established, the believer's reaction should be to maintain a consciousness of this fellowship by living a consecrated life.

a. Bible study (I Peter 2:2–3; II Timothy 2:15; Psalm 119) To grow as Christians, we must spend time with God daily by reading His Word. (reverence for the Bible)

b. Prayer (I Chronicles 16:11; I Thessalonians 5:17; John 15:7, 16; 16:24; Psalm 145:18; Romans 8:26–27) We should bring all our requests to God, trusting Him to answer them in His own way.

c. Spirit-filled (Ephesians 5:18–19; Galatians 5:16, 22–23; Romans 8:13–14; I John 1:7–9) We should let the Holy Spirit rule in our hearts and show us what to say and do. We should not say and do just what we want to, for those things are often wrong and harmful to others. (gentleness, joyfulness, patience)

d. Clear conscience (I Timothy 1:19; Acts 24:16) To be good Christians, we cannot have wrong acts or thoughts or words bothering our consciences. We must confess them to God and to those people against whom we have sinned. We cannot live lives close to God if we have guilty consciences.

e. Forgiveness (Ephesians 4:30–32; Luke 17:3-4; Colossians 3:13; Matthew 18:15–17; Mark 11:25–26) We must ask forgiveness of God when we have done wrong. Just as God forgives our sins freely, we should forgive others when they do wrong things to us.

7. Grace-Gratitude Principle

Grace is unmerited favor. Man does not deserve God's grace. However, after God bestows His grace, believers should react with an overflow of gratitude.

a. Grace (I Corinthians 15:10; Ephesians 2:8–9) Without God's grace we would be sinners on our way to hell. He loved us when we did not deserve His love and provided for us a way to escape sin's punishment by the death of His Son on the cross.

b. Exaltation of Christ (Colossians 1:12–21; Ephesians 1:17–23; Philippians 2:9–11; Galatians 6:14; Hebrews 1:2–3; John 1:1–4, 14; 5:23) We should realize and remember at all times the power, holiness, majesty, and perfection of Christ, and we should give Him the praise and glory for everything that is accomplished through us.

c. Praise (Psalm 107:8; Hebrews 13:15; I Peter 2:9; Ephesians 1:6; I Chronicles 16:23–36; 29:11–13) Remembering God's great love and goodness toward us, we should continually praise His name. (thankfulness to God)

d. Contentment (Philippians 4:11; I Timothy 6:6–8; Psalm 77:3; Proverbs 15:16; Hebrews 13:5) Money, houses, cars, and all things on earth will last only for a little while. God has given us just what He meant for us to have. We should be happy and content with what we have, knowing that God will provide for us all that we need. We should also be happy wherever God places us.

e. Humility (I Peter 5:5–6; Philippians 2:3–4) We should not be proud and boastful but should be willing to be quiet and in the background. Our reward will come from God on Judgment Day, and men's praise to us here on earth will not matter at all. Christ was humble when He lived on earth, and we should be like Him.

8. Power-Prevailing Principle

Believers can prevail only as God gives the power. "I can do all things through Christ." God is the source of our power used in fighting the good fight of faith.

a. Faith in God's promises (II Peter 1:4; Philippians 4:6; Romans 4:16–21; I Thessalonians 5:18; Romans 8:28; I Peter 5:7; Hebrews 3:18; 4:11) God always remains true to His promises. Believing that He will keep all the promises in His Word, we should be determined fighters for Him.

b. Faith in the power of the Word of God (Hebrews 4:12; Jeremiah 23:29; Psalm 119; I Peter 1:23–25) God's Word is powerful and endures forever. All other things will pass away, but God's Word shall never pass away because it is written to us from God, and God is eternal.

c. Fight (Ephesians 6:11–17; II Timothy 4:7–8; I Timothy 6:12; I Peter 5:8–9) God does not have any use for lazy or cowardly fighters. We must work and fight against sin, using the Word of God as our weapon against the Devil. What we do for God now will determine how much He will reward us in heaven.

d. Courage (I Chronicles 28:20; Joshua 1:9; Hebrews 13:6; Ephesians 3:11–12; Acts 4:13, 31) God has promised us that He will not forsake us; therefore, we should not be afraid to speak out against sin. We should remember that we are armed with God's strength.

Memory Verses

Psalm 25:4

Genesis 1:1

Psalm 95:6

Romans 3:23

Psalm 37:27

Proverbs 3:5–6

I Thessalonians 5:18

Ecclesiastes 12:13b

Psalm 38:18

Psalm 100

John 3:16

Luke 2:11

Joshua 1:9

Psalm 23

John 10:30

Hebrews 13:6

John 14:6

I John 1:9

I John 4:19

I Corinthians 15:3b–4

Ephesians 4:32

Psalm 55:17

Psalm 66:18

Proverbs 11:30b

Proverbs 20:11

Catechism

1. **Who made you?**
   God made me. (Genesis 1:27; Job 33:4)

2. **What else did God make?**
   God made all things. (Genesis 1:1–31; Deuteronomy 10:14; Nehemiah 9:6; John 1:3)

3. **Why did God make you and all things?**
   God made me and all things for His own glory. (I Chronicles 16:28; Romans 11:36; I Corinthians 6:20; 10:31)

4. **Who made God?**
   Nobody made God. (Psalm 90:2)

5. **Has God ever had a beginning?**
   No, God has always been. (Psalm 90:2; 93:2; Revelation 4:8)

6. **Will God ever die?**
   No, God lives forever. (Psalm 90:2)

7. **How can you glorify God?**
   I can glorify God by loving Him and doing what He commands. (Micah 6:8; John 15:8; I John 5:3)

8. **Why ought you to glorify God?**
   I ought to glorify God because He made me and takes care of me. (Psalms 117:1–2; 146:5–10)

9. **Are there more gods than one?**
   No, there is only one God. (Isaiah 45:6, 18, 21–22; I Timothy 2:5)

10. **In how many persons does this one God exist?**
    God exists in three persons. (Matthew 3:16–17; 28:19; II Corinthians 13:14)

11. **Who are the three persons of God?**
    The three persons of God are the Father, the Son, and the Holy Spirit. (Matthew 28:19)

12. **Who is God?**
    God is a spirit and does not have a body like man. (John 4:24)

13. **Where is God?**
    God is everywhere. (II Chronicles 2:6; Psalm 139:7–12; Proverbs 15:3)

14. **Can you see God?**
    No, I cannot see God, but He always sees me. (Jeremiah 23:23–24; John 1:18)

15. **Does God know all things?**
    Yes, nothing can be hidden from God. (Job 34:21; Ezekiel 11:1)

16. **Can God do all things?**
    Yes, God can do all His holy will. (Matthew 19:26)

17. **Where do you learn how to love and obey God?**
    I learn how to love and obey God in the Bible alone. (Deuteronomy 30:11–16; Joshua 1:8)

18. **Who wrote the Bible?**
    Holy men who were taught by the Holy Spirit wrote the Bible. (II Peter 1:21)

19. **Who were our first parents?**
    Adam and Eve were our first parents. (Genesis 2:7, 18–22; 3:20)

20. **Of what were our first parents made?**

God made the body of Adam out of the dust of the ground and formed Eve from the body of Adam. (Genesis 2:7, 21–22)

21. **What did God give Adam and Eve besides bodies?**

God gave them souls that could never die. (Genesis 2:7)

22. **Do you have a soul as well as a body?**

Yes, I have a soul that can never die. (Ecclesiastes 12:7; Mark 8:36; I Thessalonians 5:23)

23. **In what condition did God make Adam and Eve?**

God made them holy and happy. (Genesis 1:27–31)

24. **Did Adam obey God?**

No, Adam chose to disobey God. (Genesis 3:6)

25. **How did God punish Adam's disobedience?**

Adam's punishment was death and separation from God. (Genesis 3:17–24; Romans 5:12)

26. **What is sin?**

Sin is the transgression of the law of God. (I John 3:4)

27. **Who is Satan?**

Satan is an evil spirit who is the enemy of God and all Christians. (Matthew 13:39; Luke 22:3; John 8:44; I Peter 5:8)

28. **Who is stronger, God or Satan?**

God is stronger. (I John 3:8; 4:4)

29. **Does Satan want God's will to be done?**

No, Satan always wants people to do the opposite of what God wants them to do. (I Chronicles 21:1; John 8:44; Ephesians 6:11–12, 16)

30. **What was the sin of our first parents?**

Adam and Eve disobeyed God and ate the fruit that God told them not to eat. (Genesis 2:17; 3:6)

31. **Who tempted Adam and Eve to sin?**

Satan tempted Eve, and she gave the fruit to Adam. (Genesis 3:1–6)

32. **What does every sin deserve?**

Every sin deserves the wrath and curse of God. (Genesis 2:17; Psalm 89:30–32; Galatians 3:10)

33. **What does God require of man before he can go to heaven?**

No one can enter heaven unless his heart is changed. (John 3:3, 16; 5:24; 14:6; Acts 4:12)

34. **Who can change a sinner's heart?**

The Holy Spirit can change a sinner's heart. (Titus 3:5)

35. **What is grace?**

Grace is God's kindness to us when we deserve punishment. (Deuteronomy 7:6–9; Romans 3:22–24; 5:1–8, 19–21; Ephesians 2:8–9)

36. **Can anyone be saved by his own works?**

No one can be saved by his own works. (Galatians 2:16; Ephesians 2:8–9; Titus 3:4–7)

37. **Did Christ ever sin?**

No, Christ was holy, sinless, and undefiled. (Isaiah 53:9; II Corinthians 5:21; Hebrews 4:15; 7:26; I Peter 2:21–23)

38. **For whom did Christ obey and suffer?**
Christ obeyed and suffered for sinners. (Romans 5:8)

39. **Who will be saved?**
Whoever repents and believes on the Lord Jesus Christ shall be saved. (Isaiah 55:7; Luke 13:3; 24:47; John 3:16; 6:47)

40. **What is faith in Christ?**
Faith in Christ is trusting in Him alone for salvation. (Romans 3:22–25; Galatians 2:16; Philippians 3:9; Hebrews 12:2)

41. **Does Christ care for little children?**
Yes, for He says in Mark 10:14, "Suffer the little children to come unto me, and forbid them not: for of such is the kingdom of God." (Mark 10:14)

42. **What is prayer?**
Prayer is thanking God for what He has done and asking Him for things which He has promised to give. (Psalm 10:17; John 16:23; Philippians 4:6; I John 5:14)

43. **What guide has Christ given us to teach us how to pray?**
Christ has given us the Lord's Prayer. (Matthew 6:9–13)

44. **Repeat the Lord's Prayer.**
"Our Father which art in heaven, hallowed be thy name. Thy kingdom come. Thy will be done in earth, as it is in heaven. Give us this day our daily bread. And forgive us our debts, as we forgive our debtors. And lead us not into temptation, but deliver us from evil: for thine is the kingdom, and the power, and the glory, for ever. Amen."
(Matthew 6:9–13)

45. **Did Christ remain in the tomb after His crucifixion?**
No, Christ arose bodily from the tomb on the third day after His death. (Matthew 16:21; 28:1–6; Romans 6:4; I Corinthians 15:3–4)

46. **Will Christ come again?**
Yes, Christ has promised to return to take us to be with Him. (John 14:1–3; Acts 1:11)

47. **What becomes of man at death?**
The body returns to dust, and the soul goes either to heaven or hell. (Genesis 3:19; Romans 6:23)

48. **What is hell?**
Hell is a place of dreadful and endless torment. (Matthew 25:41, 46; Mark 9:43; Luke 16:19–26; Revelation 20:10, 13–15)

49. **What will become of the righteous?**
The righteous shall be taken to heaven. (Matthew 5:11–12; 25:46; John 10:28; 14:1–3; Colossians 3:4)

50. **What is heaven?**
Heaven is a glorious and happy place, where the saved shall be forever with the Lord. (John 14:1–3; I Thessalonians 4:17; Revelation 7:15–17; 21:3–4, 22–27; 22:1–5)

Songs

A Blind Man

(Tune: "Did You Ever See a Lassie?")

Elementary Authors

German Folksong

Let us sing a-bout a man,— a man,— a man.— Let us sing a-bout a man,— a man who was blind. He heard Je-sus com-ing. He called out, "Have
(Cover eyes with hands.) *(Cup hands to ears.)* *(Cup hands to mouth.)*
mer - cy." Let us sing a - bout a blind man— a man God's Son healed.

Abraham

(Tune: "London Bridge")

Elementary Authors

English Folksong

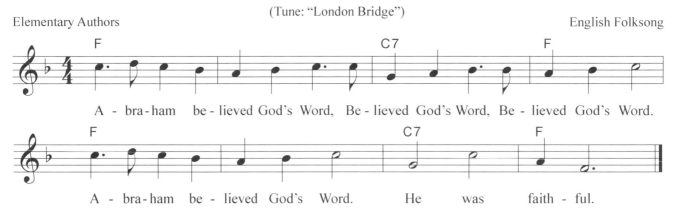

A - bra-ham be - lieved God's Word, Be - lieved God's Word, Be - lieved God's Word.
A - bra-ham be - lieved God's Word. He was faith - ful.

A Child of the King

Hattie E. Buell

John B. Sumner

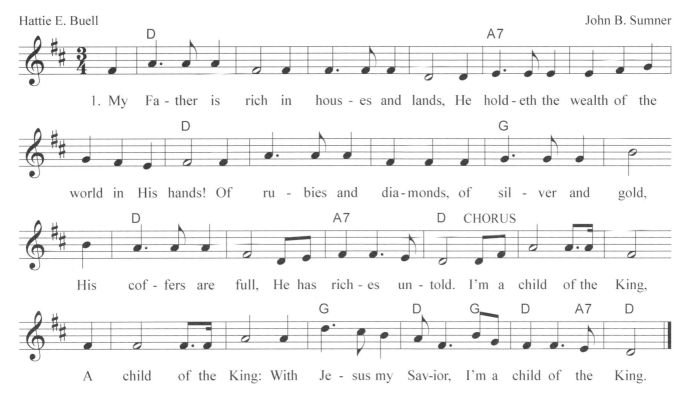

1. My Fa-ther is rich in hous-es and lands, He hold-eth the wealth of the world in His hands! Of ru-bies and dia-monds, of sil-ver and gold, His cof-fers are full, He has rich-es un-told. I'm a child of the King, A child of the King: With Je-sus my Sav-ior, I'm a child of the King.

2. My Father's own Son, the Savior of men,
   Once wandered on earth as the poorest of them;
   But now He is reigning forever on high,
   And will give me a home in heaven by and by.
   CHORUS

3. I once was an outcast stranger on earth,
   A sinner by choice, and an alien by birth;
   But I've been adopted, my name's written down,
   An heir to a mansion, a robe, and a crown.
   CHORUS

A Helper I Will Be

(Tune: "The Farmer in the Dell")

Elementary Authors

English Folksong

A help-er I will be._____ A help-er I will be._____
There's work to do for Je-sus; So a help-er I will be._____

All for Jesus

E. E. Hewitt

William J. Kirkpatrick

1. Lit - tle hands to work for Je - sus, Lit-tle feet to walk His ways,
Lit - tle ears to hear His mes-sage, Lit-tle lips to sing His praise.

CHORUS

All for Je - sus, all for Je - sus, True and faith - ful may I be;

All for Je - sus, all for Je - sus, All for Him who died for me.

2. Little hands to help each other,
   Little lips His grace to tell,
   Little songs to raise to heaven,
   Little hearts to love Him well.
   CHORUS

3. Little eyes to read the story
   Of His love in all around,
   Little minds to learn the lessons
   In the Holy Bible found.
   CHORUS

4. Little lips to speak so gently,
   Little knees to bow in pray'r,
   Little feet to do His errands,
   Little hearts to trust His care.
   CHORUS

All Things Were Made by God

John 1:3

Muriel Murr

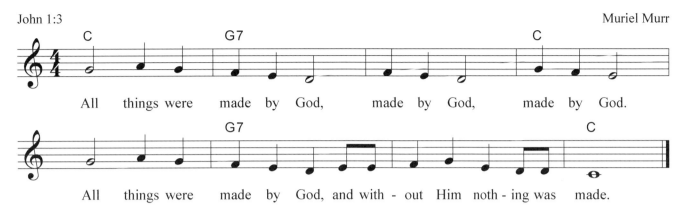

All things were made by God, made by God, made by God.

All things were made by God, and with-out Him noth-ing was made.

A Missionary Helper

(Tune: "The Farmer in the Dell")

Elementary Authors

English Folksong

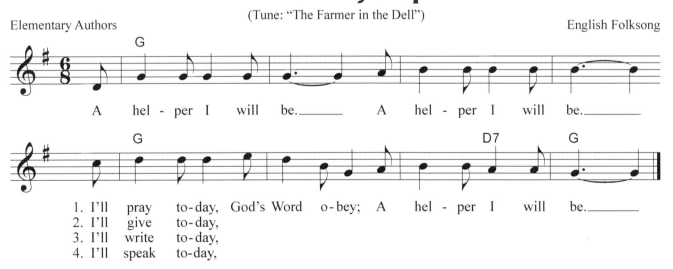

A hel-per I will be._____ A hel-per I will be._____

1. I'll pray to-day, God's Word o-bey; A hel-per I will be._____
2. I'll give to-day,
3. I'll write to-day,
4. I'll speak to-day,

Away in a Manger

Unknown
Stanza 3: John T. McFarland

James R. Murray

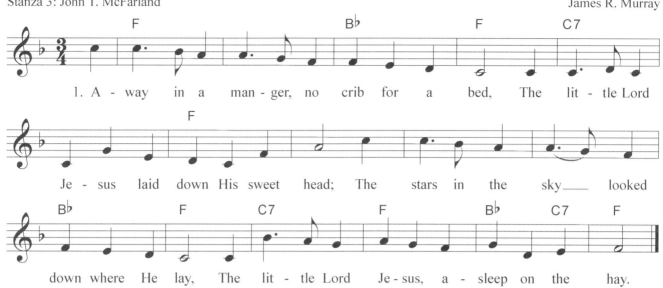

1. A - way in a man - ger, no crib for a bed, The lit - tle Lord
Je - sus laid down His sweet head; The stars in the sky____ looked
down where He lay, The lit - tle Lord Je - sus, a - sleep on the hay.

2. The cattle are lowing, the Baby awakes,
   But little Lord Jesus, no crying He makes;
   I love Thee, Lord Jesus, look down from the sky,
   And stay by my cradle, till morning is nigh.

3. Be near me, Lord Jesus, I ask Thee to stay
   Close by me forever, and love me, I pray;
   Bless all the dear children in Thy tender care.
   And fit us for heaven, to live with Thee there.

A14

Songs

Be Ye Doers of the Word

James 1:22

Tim Fisher

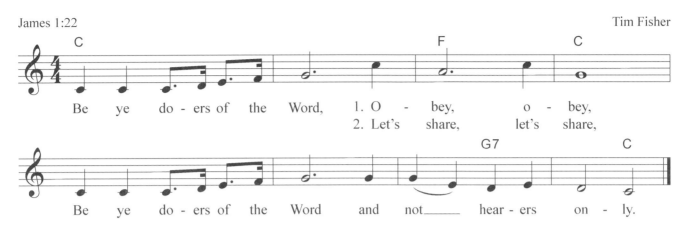

Be ye do-ers of the Word,
1. O - bey, o - bey,
2. Let's share, let's share,

Be ye do-ers of the Word and not_____ hear-ers on - ly.

3. Work well, work well,
4. Trust God, trust God,
5. Thank God, thank God,
6. Show love, show love,
7. Be kind, be kind,
8. Speak truth, speak truth,
9. Fear not, fear not,
10. Go tell, go tell,
11. Forgive, forgive,

May be sung antiphonally, one group singing the first part of each line, followed by the second group completing the line.

Books of Moses

Unknown

Adapted from a French Folksong

Let us sing the books of Mos - es called the Law;____ Let us sing the books of Mos - es called the Law. Gen - e - sis and Ex - o - dus, Le - vit - i - cus and Num - bers, Deu - ter - on - o - my, Deu - ter - on - o - my.

Books of the New Testament

(Tune: "Bring Them In")

Unknown

William A. Ogden

Mat - thew,__ Mark,__ Luke, and John, Acts, Ro - mans, I and II__ Cor - in - thi - ans, Ga - la - tians, E - phe - sians, Phil - lip - pi - ans, Co - los - sians, I and__ II__ Thes - sa - lo - ni - ans, I Tim - o - thy, II__ Tim - o - thy, Ti - tus, Phi - le - mon,__ He - brews, James, I Pe - ter, II__ Pe - ter, Three Johns, Jude, and Rev - e - la - tion.

Christ Arose

Robert Lowry

Robert Lowry

1. Low in the grave He lay— Je - sus, my Sav - ior!

Wait - ing the com - ing day— Je - sus, my Lord!

CHORUS
Up from the grave He a - rose, With a might - y tri - umph o'er His foes; He a -

rose a Vic - tor from the dark do - main, And He lives for - ev - er with His

saints to reign. He a - rose! He a - rose! Hal - le - lu - jah! Christ a - rose!

2. Vainly they watch His bed—
   Jesus, my Savior!
   Vainly they seal the dead—
   Jesus, my Lord!
   CHORUS

3. Death cannot keep his prey—
   Jesus, my Savior!
   He tore the bars away—
   Jesus, my Lord!
   CHORUS

Christmas Is a Happy Time

(Tune: "Oats, Peas, Beans")

Elementary Authors

English Folksong

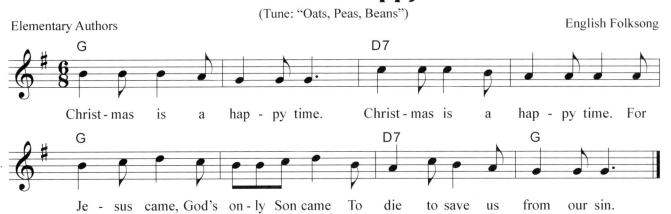

Christ - mas is a hap - py time. Christ - mas is a hap - py time. For Je - sus came, God's on - ly Son came To die to save us from our sin.

Creation Song

Lucille Fisher

Muriel Murr

1. God made the world. God made the world. God made the world. He's so good to me.

CHORUS

Our God is great. Our God is great. Our God is great. He's so good to me.

2. God made the light.
God made the dark.
God made them both.
He's so good to me.
CHORUS

3. God made the sky.
God made the clouds.
God made the air.
He's so good to me.
CHORUS

4. God made the land.
God made the trees.
God made the flowers.
He's so good to me.
CHORUS

5. God made the sun.
God made the moon.
God made the stars.
He's so good to me.
CHORUS

6. God made the fish.
God made the birds.
God made them all.
He's so good to me.
CHORUS

7. God made the animals.
God made the man.
God made them all.
He's so good to me.
CHORUS

Easter! Easter!

(Tune: "Praise Him, Praise Him")

Elementary Authors

Anonymous

1. Eas - ter! Eas - ter! Now it's time for Eas - ter; Je - sus came, Je - sus came.

(Display a manger visual.)

Eas - ter! Eas - ter! Now it's time for Eas - ter; Je - sus came, Je - sus came.

2. Easter! Easter!
Now it's time for Easter;
Jesus died, Jesus died.
(Display a cross visual.)
Easter! Easter!
Now it's time for Easter,
Jesus died, Jesus died.

3. Easter! Easter!
Now it's time for Easter;
Jesus lives, Jesus lives.
(Display open tomb visual.)
Easter! Easter!
Now it's time for Easter,
Jesus lives, Jesus lives.

Easter Time

(Tune: "London Bridge")

Elementary Authors

English Folksong

Eas - ter time is com - ing soon, com - ing soon, com - ing soon.

Eas - ter time is com - ing soon. Christ is ri - sen!

Even a Child Is Known

Proverbs 20:11

Muriel Murr

E-ven a child is known by his do-ings, wheth-er his work be pure___ or right.

E-ven a child is known by his do-ings; so do your work with all of your might.

Father, We Thank Thee for the Night

Rebecca J. Weston

Daniel Batchellor

1. Fa - ther, we thank Thee for the___ night, And for the pleas-ant morn - ing___ light;
2. Help us to do the things we___ should, To be to oth-ers kind___ and___ good;

For rest and food and lov-ing___ care, And all that makes the___ world so___ fair.
In all we do in work and___ play, To love Thee bet-ter___ day by___ day.

A20

Fishers of Men

Harry D. Clarke

Harry D. Clarke

I will make you fish-ers of men, Fish-ers of men, fish-ers of men;

I will make you fish-ers of men, If you fol-low me,

If you fol-low me, If you fol-low me.

I will make you fish-ers of men, If you fol-low me.

Fixing God's House

(Tune: "The Mulberry Bush")

Elementary Authors

English Folksong

This is the way we fix God's house, Fix God's house, fix God's house.

This is the way we fix God's house, As King Jo-si-ah com-mands.

Gabriel Told

(Tune: "London Bridge")

Elementary Authors

English Folksong

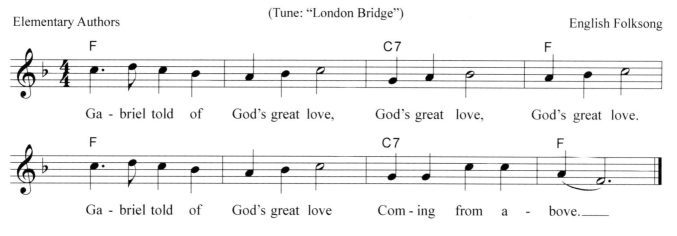

Ga - briel told of God's great love, God's great love, God's great love.

Ga - briel told of God's great love Com - ing from a - bove.___

God Is with Me

Unknown

Unknown

He sees all I do, He hears all I say, My Lord is with me all the time, time, time;

He sees all I do, He hears all I say, My Lord is with me all the time.

God Made Me

(Tune: "London Bridge")

Elementary Authors

English Folksong

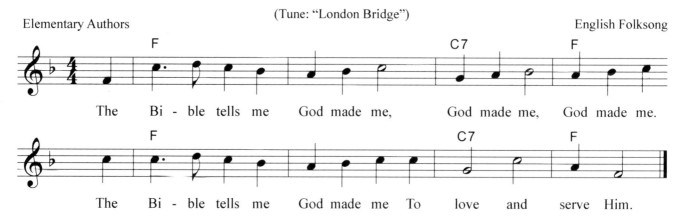

The Bi - ble tells me God made me, God made me, God made me.

The Bi - ble tells me God made me To love and serve Him.

God Made the World

(Tune: "Jesus Loves Me")

Elementary Authors

William B. Bradbury

1. God has made the world, I know, For the Bi - ble tells me so.

Night and day and sky and seas, Earth and seeds and flowers and trees.

CHORUS

Yes, God has made them. Yes, God has made them.

Yes, God has made them. The Bi - ble tells me so.

2. God has made the world, I know,
   For the Bible tells me so.
   Sun and moon and stars above,
   Tell us all of God's great love.
   CHORUS

3. God has made the world, I know,
   For the Bible tells me so.
   Birds to fly and fish to swim,
   All of these were made by Him.
   CHORUS

4. God has made the world, I know,
   For the Bible tells me so.
   All the animals on land,
   Were created by His hand.
   CHORUS

5. God has made the world, I know,
   For the Bible tells me so.
   Adam, Eve, first man and wife,
   It was God who gave them life.
   CHORUS

God's Son

Muriel Murr   Muriel Murr

Je - sus was kind.   Je - sus was good. 1. He made the deaf to hear. For He is God.

2. He made the blind to see.
3. He made the lame to walk.
4. He helped four fishermen.
5. He fed the hungry crowd.
6. He walked upon the waves.
7. He made ten lepers well.
8. He made the dead to live.

God's Special Day

(Tune: "London Bridge")

Elementary Authors   English Folksong

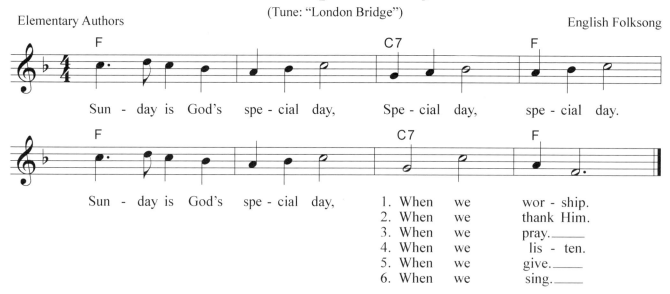

Sun - day is God's spe - cial day,   Spe - cial day,   spe - cial day.

Sun - day is God's spe - cial day,

1. When we wor - ship.
2. When we thank Him.
3. When we pray.____
4. When we lis - ten.
5. When we give.____
6. When we sing.____

God's Way

Muriel Murr

Muriel Murr

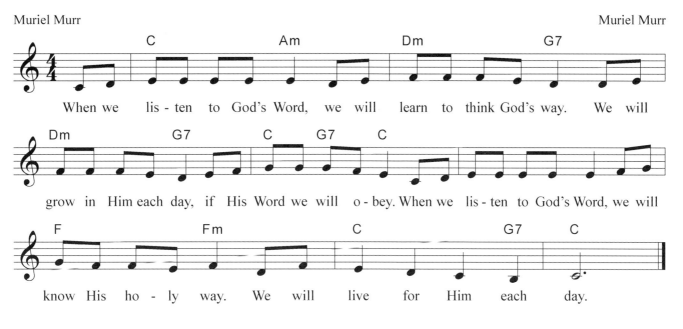

When we lis - ten to God's Word, we will learn to think God's way. We will grow in Him each day, if His Word we will o - bey. When we lis - ten to God's Word, we will know His ho - ly way. We will live for Him each day.

God's Word

Stella B. Daleburn

Stella B. Daleburn

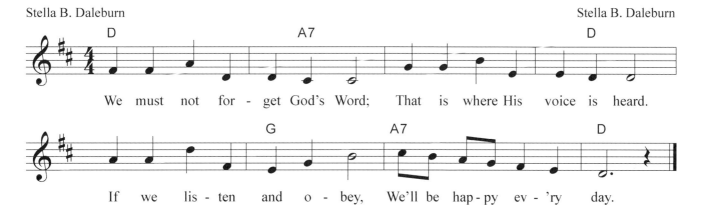

We must not for - get God's Word; That is where His voice is heard. If we lis - ten and o - bey, We'll be hap - py ev - 'ry day.

Growing, Knowing, Showing

Muriel Murr   Muriel Murr

Grow-ing, grow-ing as God wants us to; Know-ing, know-ing that His Word is true.

Show-ing, show-ing cour-age, love, and joy; Grow-ing, know-ing, show-ing for each girl and boy.

Heaven Is a Happy Place

(Tune: "London Bridge")

Elementary Authors   English Folksong

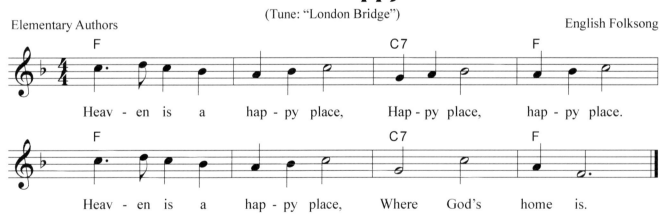

Heav - en is a hap - py place, Hap - py place, hap - py place.

Heav - en is a hap - py place, Where God's home is.

Holy Bible, Book Divine

John Burton

William B. Bradbury

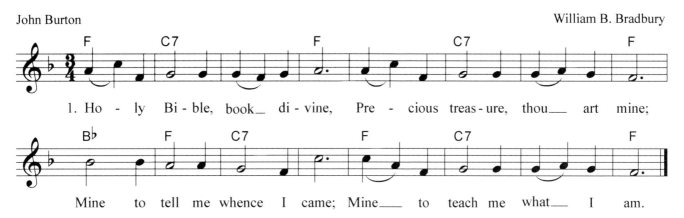

1. Ho - ly Bi - ble, book__ di - vine, Pre - cious treas - ure, thou__ art mine;

Mine to tell me whence I came; Mine__ to teach me what__ I am.

2. Mine to chide me when I rove;
   Mine to show a Savior's love;
   Mine thou art to guide and guard;
   Mine to punish or reward.

3. Mine to comfort in distress,
   Suff'ring in this wilderness;
   Mine to show, by living faith,
   Man can triumph over death.

4. Mine to tell of joys to come,
   And the rebel sinner's doom;
   O thou Holy Book divine,
   Precious treasure, thou art mine.

Holy, Holy, Holy

Reginald Heber

John B. Dykes

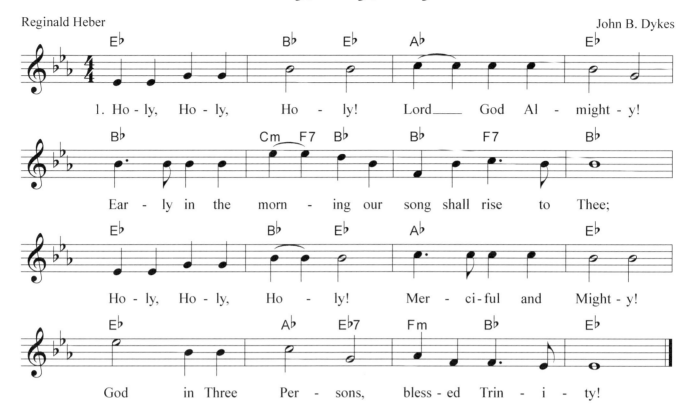

1. Ho-ly, Ho-ly, Ho - ly! Lord___ God Al - might-y!

Ear - ly in the morn - ing our song shall rise to Thee;

Ho - ly, Ho-ly, Ho - ly! Mer - ci-ful and Might-y!

God in Three Per - sons, bless-ed Trin - i - ty!

2. Holy, Holy, Holy! All the saints adore Thee,
   Casting down their golden crowns around the glassy sea;
   Cherubim and seraphim falling down before Thee,
   Which wert and art, and evermore shalt be.

3. Holy, Holy, Holy! Tho' the darkness hide Thee,
   Tho' the eye of sinful man Thy glory may not see,
   Only Thou art holy; there is none beside Thee,
   Perfect in pow'r, in love, and purity.

4. Holy, Holy, Holy! Lord God Almighty!
   All Thy works shall praise Thy name, in earth, and sky, and sea;
   Holy, Holy, Holy! Merciful and Mighty!
   God in Three Persons, blessed Trinity!

How Do We Know?

Muriel Murr

Muriel Murr

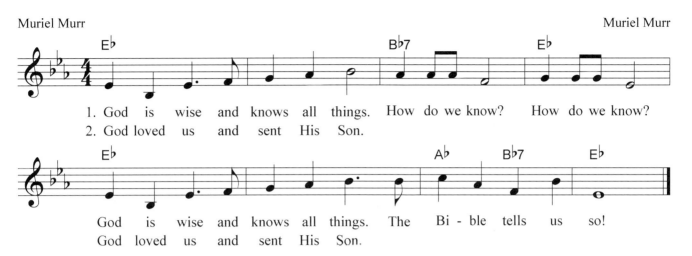

1. God is wise and knows all things. How do we know? How do we know?
2. God loved us and sent His Son.

God is wise and knows all things. The Bi - ble tells us so!
God loved us and sent His Son.

3. Jesus died upon the cross.
4. Jesus rose up from the grave.
5. Jesus went back up to heav'n.
6. Soon He's coming back again.
7. God is good and answers prayer.

I'm His Little Child

Muriel Murr

Traditional

1. God___ made___ me. God___ made___ me. God___ made___ me. I'm His lit-tle child.
2. God___ loves___ me.
3. God___ speaks to me.
4. God___ cares for me.
5. Je - sus died for me.
6. God___ hears___ me.

In Everything Give Thanks

(Tune: "The Farmer in the Dell")

I Thessalonians 5:18

English Folksong

In ev - 'ry-thing give thanks,____ In ev - 'ry-thing give thanks,____

For this is the will of God for you. In ev - 'ry-thing give thanks.____

In the Beginning

(Tune: "Oh, Be Careful")

Elementary Authors

Old Melody

In the be - gin - ning God cre - a - ted heav'n and earth. In the be -

gin - ning God cre - a - ted heav'n and earth. God just spoke and it was so. By His

Word and pow'r we know, In the be - gin - ning God cre - a - ted heav'n and earth.

I Obey

(Tune: "Are You Sleeping?")

Elementary Authors

French Folksong

Where is Sam-uel? Where is Sam-uel? Here I am. Here I am.
I will quick-ly an-swer; I will quick-ly an-swer. I o-bey. I o-bey.

I Trust in God

(Tune: "The Farmer in the Dell")

Elementary Authors

English Folksong

I trust in God my Lord.____ I trust in God my Lord.____
He knows what's best; He'll care for me. I trust in God my Lord.____

I Will Obey

(Tune: "The Farmer in the Dell")

Elementary Authors

English Folksong

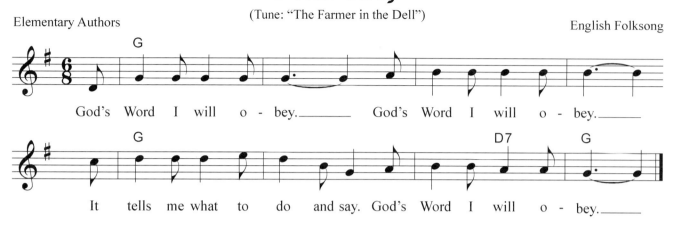

God's Word I will o - bey._____ God's Word I will o - bey._____

It tells me what to do and say. God's Word I will o - bey._____

I Will Trust in Thee

Psalm 56:3

Muriel Murr

What time I am a - fraid, I will trust in Thee.

Jesus, Born in Bethlehem

Elementary Authors

American Folksong

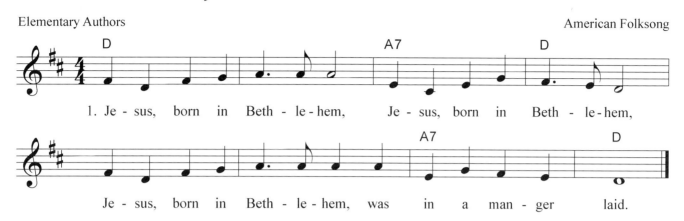

1. Je - sus, born in Beth - le - hem, Je - sus, born in Beth - le - hem,

Je - sus, born in Beth - le - hem, was in a man - ger laid.

2. Shepherds watched their flocks by night,
   Shepherds watched their flocks by night,
   Shepherds watched their flocks by night,
   And saw a shining star.

3. Wise men traveled from afar,
   Wise men traveled from afar,
   Wise men traveled from afar,
   And followed God's bright star.

Jesus Christ Is Born

Muriel Murr

Finnish Folksong

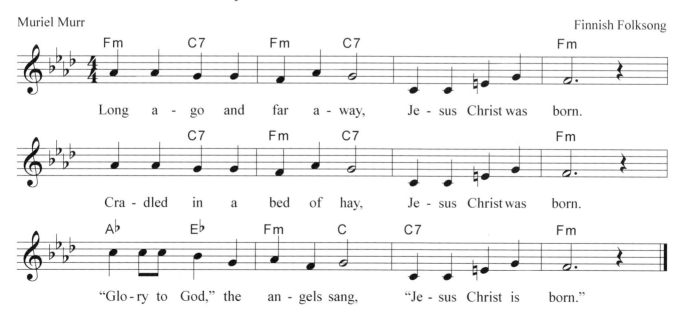

Long a - go and far a - way, Je - sus Christ was born.

Cra - dled in a bed of hay, Je - sus Christ was born.

"Glo - ry to God," the an - gels sang, "Je - sus Christ is born."

Jesus Loves Even Me

Philip P. Bliss

Philip P. Bliss

1. I am so glad that our Fa-ther in heav'n Tells of His love in the Book He has giv'n;

Won-der-ful things in the Bi-ble I see — This is the dear-est, That Je-sus loves me.

CHORUS

I am so glad that Je-sus loves me, Je-sus loves me, Je-sus loves me;

I am so glad that Je-sus loves me, Je-sus loves e - ven me.

2. Though I forget Him and wander away,
   Still He doth love me wherever I stray;
   Back to His dear loving arms would I flee.
   When I remember that Jesus loves me.
   CHORUS

3. O if there's only one song I can sing,
   When in His beauty I see the great King,
   This shall my song in eternity be:
   "O what a wonder that Jesus loves me."
   CHORUS

Jesus Loves Me

Anna B. Warner
Stanza 4: Unknown

William B. Bradbury

1. Je - sus loves me! this I know, For the Bi - ble tells me so; Lit - tle ones to Him be - long; They are weak, but He is strong.

CHORUS

Yes, Je - sus loves me, Yes, Je - sus loves me, Yes, Je - sus loves me, The Bi - ble tells me so.

2. Jesus loves me! He Who died,
   Heaven's gate to open wide;
   He will wash away my sin,
   Let His little child come in.
   CHORUS

3. Jesus loves me! Loves me still,
   Though I'm very weak and ill;
   From His shining throne on high,
   Comes to watch me where I lie.
   CHORUS

4. Jesus loves me when I'm good,
   When I do the things I should;
   Jesus loves me when I'm bad,
   But it makes Him very sad.
   CHORUS

Jesus Loves the Little Children

C. Herbert Woolston

George F. Root

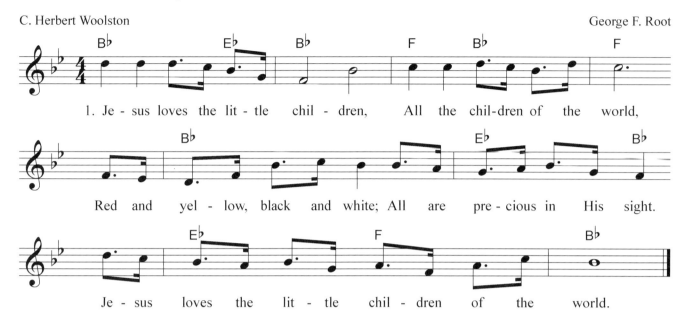

1. Je - sus loves the lit - tle chil - dren, All the chil-dren of the world,

Red and yel - low, black and white; All are pre - cious in His sight.

Je - sus loves the lit - tle chil - dren of the world.

2. Jesus came for all the children,
   All the children of the world,
   Red and yellow, black and white;
   All are precious in His sight.
   Jesus came for all the children of the world.

3. Jesus died for all the children,
   All the children of the world,
   Red and yellow, black and white;
   All are precious in His sight.
   Jesus died for all the children of the world.

4. Jesus rose for all the children,
   All the children of the world,
   Red and yellow, black and white;
   All are precious in His sight.
   Jesus rose for all the children of the world.

Jesus Saves

Priscilla J. Owens

William J. Kirkpatrick

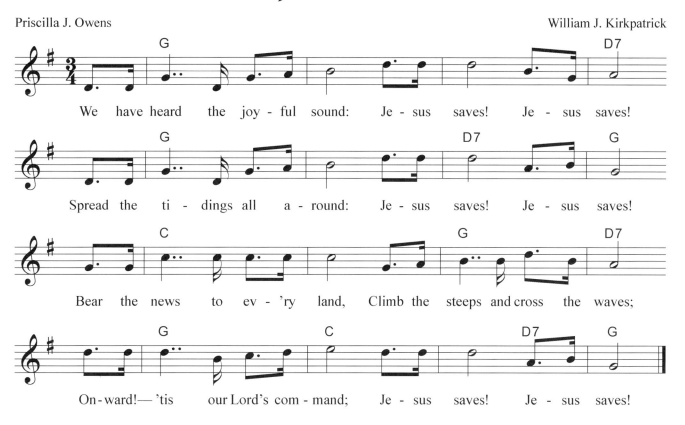

We have heard the joy - ful sound: Je - sus saves! Je - sus saves!

Spread the ti - dings all a - round: Je - sus saves! Je - sus saves!

Bear the news to ev - 'ry land, Climb the steeps and cross the waves;

On - ward!— 'tis our Lord's com - mand; Je - sus saves! Je - sus saves!

John 3:16

(Tune: "Silent Night")

John 3:16

Franz Gruber

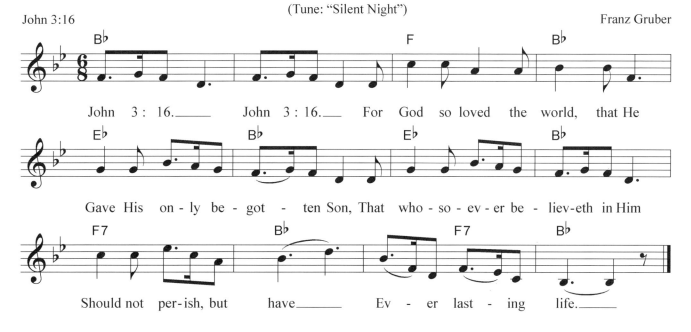

John 3 : 16.___ John 3 : 16.___ For God so loved the world, that He

Gave His on - ly be - got - ten Son, That who - so - ev - er be - liev - eth in Him

Should not per - ish, but have___ Ev - er last - ing life.___

Learning God's Way

Muriel Murr

Muriel Murr

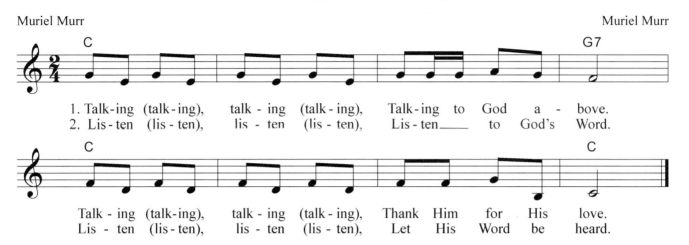

1. Talk-ing (talk-ing), talk-ing (talk-ing), Talk-ing to God a - bove.
2. Lis-ten (lis-ten), lis-ten (lis-ten), Lis-ten___ to God's Word.

Talk-ing (talk-ing), talk-ing (talk-ing), Thank Him for His love.
Lis-ten (lis-ten), lis-ten (lis-ten), Let His Word be heard.

My Bible Book

Johnie B. Wood
Stanzas 4 & 5: Elementary Authors

Johnie B. Wood

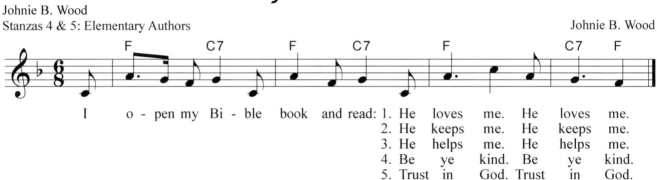

I o - pen my Bi - ble book and read:
1. He loves me. He loves me.
2. He keeps me. He keeps me.
3. He helps me. He helps me.
4. Be ye kind. Be ye kind.
5. Trust in God. Trust in God.

My Eyes Can See a Flower

(Tune: "Did You Ever See a Lassie?")

Elementary Authors

German Folksong

My___ eyes can see a flo - wer, A flo - wer, a flo - wer.

My___ eyes can see a flo - wer, A flo - wer that's red.

My Gift

Christina Rossetti

Muriel Murr

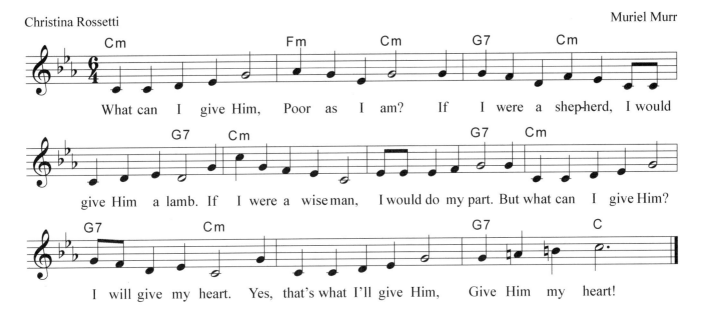

What can I give Him, Poor as I am? If I were a shep-herd, I would give Him a lamb. If I were a wise man, I would do my part. But what can I give Him? I will give my heart. Yes, that's what I'll give Him, Give Him my heart!

Nothing but the Blood

Robert Lowry

Robert Lowry

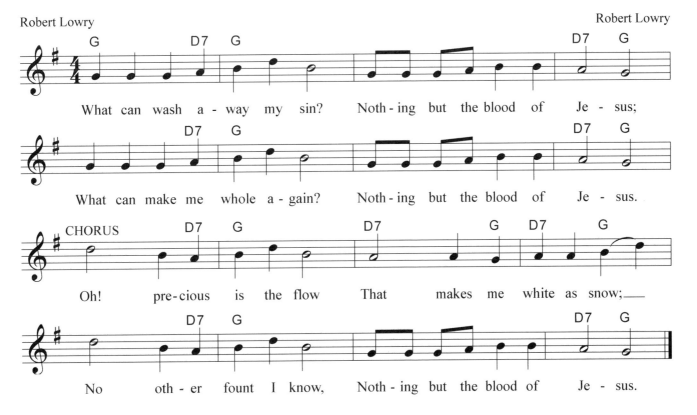

What can wash a - way my sin? Noth - ing but the blood of Je - sus;

What can make me whole a - gain? Noth - ing but the blood of Je - sus.

CHORUS

Oh! pre - cious is the flow That makes me white as snow;___

No oth - er fount I know, Noth - ing but the blood of Je - sus.

Obedience Is

Muriel Murr

Muriel Murr

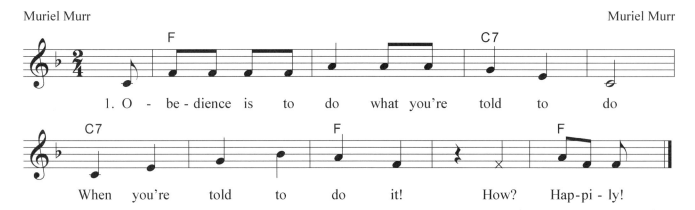

1. O - be - dience is to do what you're told to do

When you're told to do it! How? Hap-pi - ly!

2. Sharing is to take your turn;
That's a lesson we all must learn.
How? Patiently (Cheerfully)!

3. Faith is to believe that God will do
Everything He has promised to.
How? Faithfully!

4. Praise is to thank the Lord
In song and prayer and service.
How? Joyfully!

5. Enthusiasm is to do everything
With a happy, willing spirit.
How? Energetically!

6. Thoughtfulness is to think of others
Before you think of yourself.
How? Thoughtfully!

7. Neatness is a place for everything
And everything in its place.
How? Neatly!

8. Joyfulness is to have a cheerful face
Even when you've lost the race.
How? Joyfully!

9. Gratefulness is to thank the Lord alway
Even when all things don't go your way.
How? Gratefully!

O Come and Let Us Worship

(Tune: "O Come, All Ye Faithful" [Chorus])

Elementary Authors

John F. Wade's *Cantus Diversi*

O come and let us wor - ship, O come and let us wor - ship,

O come and let us wor - ship,____ Christ,_____ the Lord.

O Give Thanks

Psalm 106:1

Muriel Murr

O give thanks un - to the Lord; for He is good: For His mer - cy en - dur - eth for - ev - er.

Oh, Be Careful

Anonymous

Old Melody

2. Oh, be careful, little ears, what you hear.
3. Oh, be careful, little hands, what you do.
4. Oh, be careful, little heart, whom you trust.
5. Oh, be careful, little mind, what you think.
6. Oh, be careful, little tongue, what you say.
7. Oh, be careful, little feet, where you go.

Oh, How I Love Jesus

Frederick Whitfield

American Melody

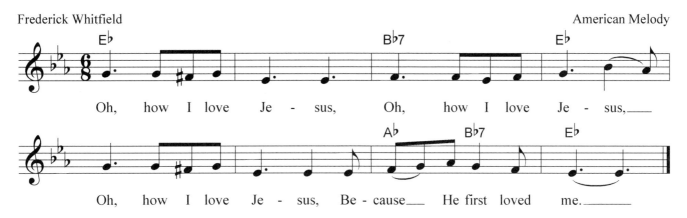

Oh, how I love Je - sus, Oh, how I love Je - sus,___

Oh, how I love Je - sus, Be - cause___ He first loved me.___

One God

(Tune: "One Door")

Elementary Authors

Arr. by A. T. Hardy

One God, and on - ly one, Oh, yes, I know it's true. One God in hea - ven Who

made me and you. One God, and on - ly one, Oh, yes, I know it's true.

One God in hea - ven Who made me and you.

Songs

A43

On the Cross

(Tune: "Near the Cross" [Chorus])

Elementary Authors

William H. Doane

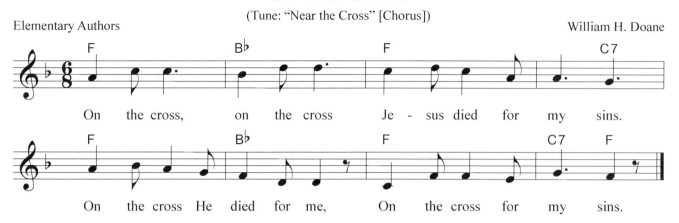

On the cross, on the cross Je - sus died for my sins.

On the cross He died for me, On the cross for my sins.

Our Bible Time's Begun

(Tune: "The Farmer in the Dell")

Elementary Authors

English Folksong

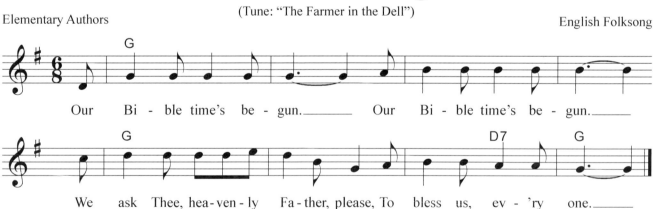

Our Bi - ble time's be - gun._____ Our Bi - ble time's be - gun._____

We ask Thee, hea - ven - ly Fa - ther, please, To bless us, ev - 'ry one._____

Politeness Is

Muriel Murr

Muriel Murr

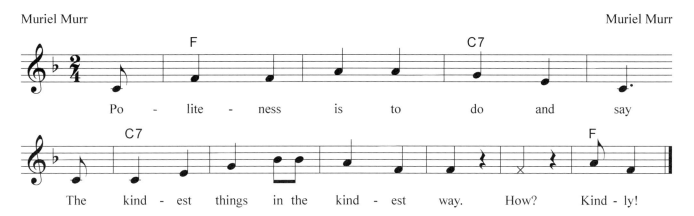

Po - lite - ness is to do and say
The kind - est things in the kind - est way. How? Kind - ly!

Praise Him, Praise Him

Anonymous

Anonymous

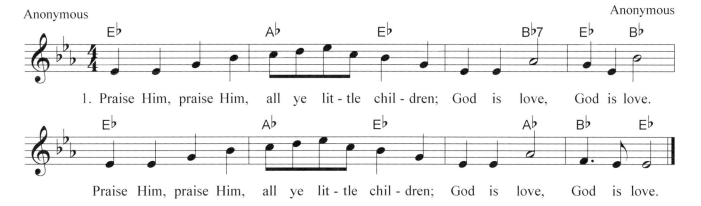

1. Praise Him, praise Him, all ye lit - tle chil - dren; God is love, God is love.
Praise Him, praise Him, all ye lit - tle chil - dren; God is love, God is love.

2. Love Him, love Him, all ye little children;
   God is love, God is love.
   Love Him, love Him, all ye little children;
   God is love, God is love.

3. Thank Him, thank Him, all ye little children:
   God is love, God is love.
   Thank Him, thank Him, all ye little children;
   God is love, God is love.

4. Serve Him, serve Him, all ye little children;
   God is love, God is love.
   Serve Him, serve Him, all ye little children;
   God is love, God is love.

5. Crown Him, crown Him, all ye little children;
   God is love, God is love.
   Crown Him, crown Him, all ye little children;
   God is love, God is love.

Pray with Me

American Folksong
Adapted by Muriel Murr

Muriel Murr

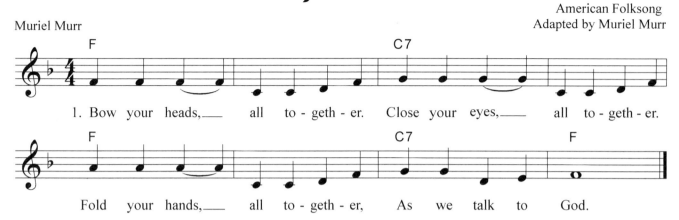

1. Bow your heads,___ all to - geth - er. Close your eyes,___ all to - geth - er.

Fold your hands,___ all to - geth - er, As we talk to God.

2. Pray with me, all together.
   Pray with me, all together.
   Pray with me, all together,
   As we talk to God.

3. We give thanks for our mothers.
   We give thanks for our fathers.
   For our sisters and our brothers,
   We give thanks to God.

4. Clap with me, all together.
   Clap with me, all together.
   Clap with me, all together.
   Thank God for our hands.

5. Walk with me, all together.
   Walk with me, all together.
   Walk with me, all together.
   Thank God for our feet.

6. Listen with me, all together.
   Listen with me, all together.
   Listen with me, all together.
   Thank God for our ears.

Rejoice, Ye Pure in Heart

Edward H. Plumptre

Arthur H. Messiter

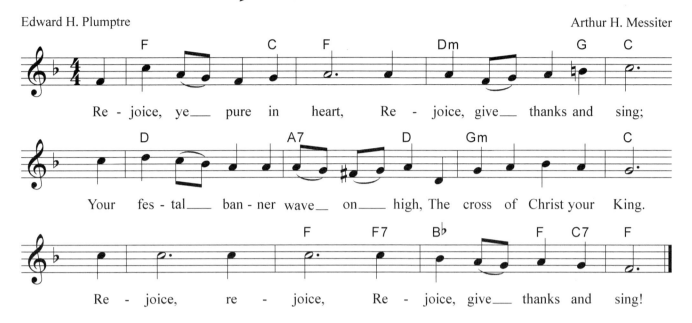

Re - joice, ye__ pure in heart, Re - joice, give__ thanks and sing;

Your fes - tal__ ban - ner wave__ on__ high, The cross of Christ your King.

Re - joice, re - joice, Re - joice, give__ thanks and sing!

Ring the Bells

(Tune: "Row, Row, Row Your Boat")

Elementary Authors

Traditional

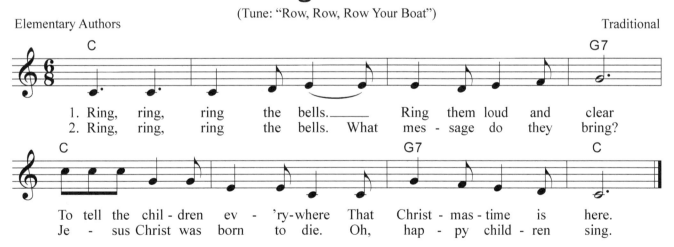

1. Ring, ring, ring the bells.____ Ring them loud and clear
2. Ring, ring, ring the bells. What mes - sage do they bring?

To tell the chil - dren ev - 'ry-where That Christ - mas - time is here.
Je - sus Christ was born to die. Oh, hap - py chil - dren sing.

Savior, Like a Shepherd Lead Us

Dorothy Ann Thrupp

William B. Bradbury

1. Sav-ior, like a shep-herd lead___ us,___ Much we need Thy ten-der care;

In Thy pleas-ant pas-tures feed___ us,___ For our use Thy folds pre-pare:

Bless-ed Je-sus, Bless-ed Je-sus, Thou hast bought us, Thine we are;

Bless-ed Je-sus, Bless-ed Je-sus, Thou hast bought us, Thine we are.

2. We are Thine; do thou befriend us,
Be the Guardian of our way;
Keep Thy flock, from sin defend us,
Seek us when we go astray:
Blessed Jesus, Blessed Jesus,
Hear, O hear us when we pray;
Blessed Jesus, Blessed Jesus,
Hear, O hear us when we pray.

3. Thou hast promised to receive us,
Poor and sinful though we be;
Thou hast mercy to relieve us,
Grace to cleanse, and pow'r to free:
Blessed Jesus, Blessed Jesus,
Early let us turn to Thee;
Blessed Jesus, Blessed Jesus,
Early let us turn to Thee.

4. Early let us seek Thy favor;
Early let us do Thy will;
Blessed Lord and only Savior,
With Thy love our bosoms fill:
Blessed Jesus, Blessed Jesus,
Thou hast loved us, love us still;
Blessed Jesus, Blessed Jesus,
Thou hast loved us, love us still.

Shepherds Came

(Tune: "London Bridge")

Elementary Authors

English Folksong

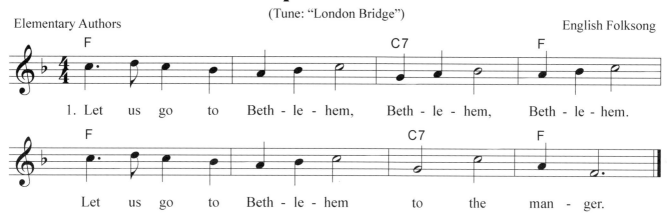

1. Let us go to Beth - le - hem, Beth - le - hem, Beth - le - hem.

Let us go to Beth - le - hem to the man - ger.

2. Let us see the Baby there, Baby there, Baby there.
   Let us see the Baby there, in the manger.

3. Let us tell to all our friends, all our friends, all our friends.
   Let us tell to all our friends, Jesus Christ is born.

4. Let us tell to everyone, everyone, everyone.
   Let us tell to everyone, Jesus Christ is born.

Words © 1987 BJU Press. All rights reserved.

Show Me Thy Ways

Psalm 25:4

Karen Wilson

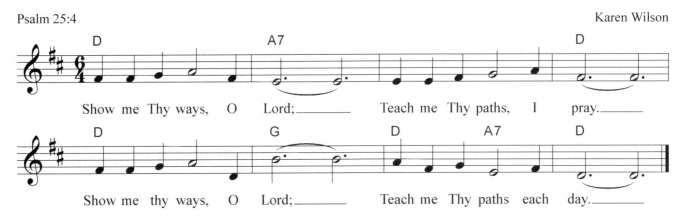

Show me Thy ways, O Lord;_____ Teach me Thy paths, I pray._____

Show me thy ways, O Lord;_____ Teach me Thy paths each day._____

Story Review Song

Karen Wilson

Karen Wilson

1. Trust God, lit - tle Jo - seph, God is watch - ing you.
2. Fear not, ba - by Mos - es, God is watch - ing you.

He will keep you, keep you safe, For His Word is true.
He will keep you, keep you safe, For His Word is true.

Songs

Tell Me the Stories of Jesus

William H. Parker

Frederic A. Challinor

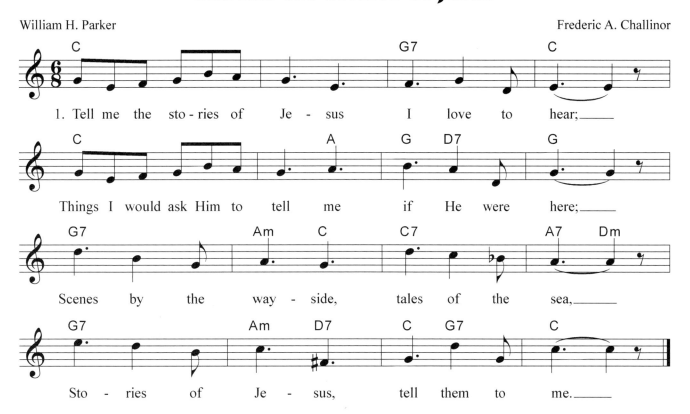

1. Tell me the sto-ries of Je - sus I love to hear;
Things I would ask Him to tell me if He were here;
Scenes by the way - side, tales of the sea,
Sto - ries of Je - sus, tell them to me.

2. First let me hear how the children stood 'round His knee;
   And I shall fancy His blessing resting on me:
   Words full of kindness, deeds full of grace,
   All in the lovelight of Jesus' face.

3. Into the city I'd follow the children's band,
   Waving a branch of the palm-tree high in my hand;
   One of His heralds, yes, I would sing
   Loudest hosannas! Jesus is King.

4. Tell me in accents of wonder how rolled the sea,
   Tossing the boat in a tempest on Galilee!
   And how the Master, ready and kind,
   Chided the billows, and hushed the wind.

Music © NCEC. Reproduced with the permission of Christian Education.

Thank God

Muriel Murr

Muriel Murr

1. For our school and toys to share, We thank God for His dai-ly care.
2. For our food and clothes to wear,
3. For the rain and sun-shine fair,

Thank You, God

Muriel Murr

Muriel Murr

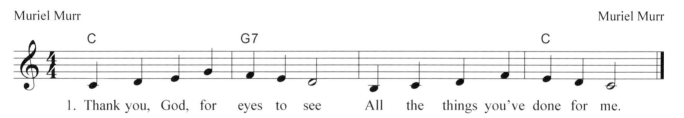

1. Thank you, God, for eyes to see All the things you've done for me.

2. Thank you, God, for ears to hear
   Many sounds both far and near.

3. Thank you, God, for legs to walk,
   Hands to clap, a voice to talk.

The Children's Friend

Gordon E. Hooker

Gordon E. Hooker

1. Je - sus is___ the chil - dren's Sav - ior; Je - sus is the chil - dren's Friend;

For He lived and died to save them, And___ His love___ will nev - er end.

2. Day by day He marks their footsteps;
Dangerous ways are known to Him.
Guardian angels soon deliver
When the way is dark and grim.

3. Satan works to keep them idle,
And would lead them into wrong.
But the prayer of faith to Jesus
Turns defeat to vict'ry's song.

4. Jesus wants to make them useful
In His whitened harvest field;
Wants each one to tell the story,
And a fruitful harvest yield.

The Doxology

Thomas Ken

Louis Bourgeois

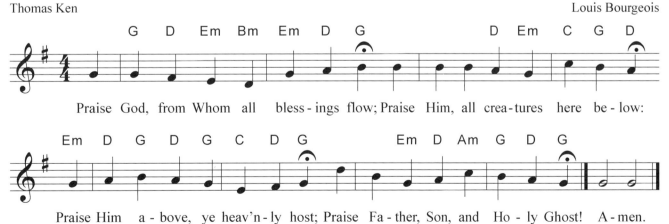

Praise God, from Whom all bless - ings flow; Praise Him, all crea - tures here be - low:

Praise Him a - bove, ye heav'n - ly host; Praise Fa - ther, Son, and Ho - ly Ghost! A - men.

The Gospels

(Tune: "Oats, Peas, Beans")

Elementary Authors

English Folksong

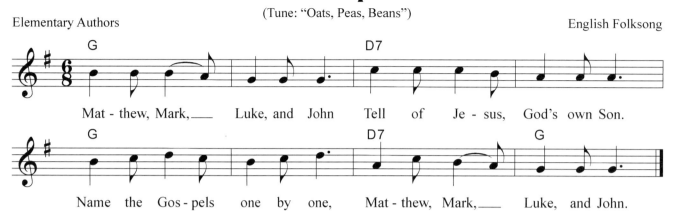

Mat - thew, Mark,___ Luke, and John Tell of Je - sus, God's own Son.

Name the Gos - pels one by one, Mat - thew, Mark,___ Luke, and John.

The Lord Is My Shepherd

Psalm 23:1–2

Anonymous

The Lord is my___ shep-herd; I'll walk with Him al - way. He leads by still___

wa - ters; I'll walk with Him al - way. Al - way, al - way, I'll

walk with Him al - way. Al - way, al - way, I'll walk with Him al - way.

The Patriarchs

(Tune: "Ten Little Indians")

Elementary Authors

American Folksong

A-bra-ham had a son, And his name was I-saac.
I-saac had a son, And his name was Ja-cob. Ja-cob had a son, And his
name was Jo-seph. And God blessed them all.

Words © 1987 BJU Press. All rights reserved.

The Rain Was Coming Down

(Tune: "The Farmer in the Dell")

Elementary Authors

English Folksong

1. The rain was com - ing down.___ The rain was com - ing down.
(Hold hands high and move downward to imitate rain.)

Down, down,___ down,___ down, The rain was com - ing down.___

2. The water was coming up.
   (Hold hands low and move
      upward to imitate flood.)
   The water was coming up.
   Up, up, up, up,
   The water was coming up.

4. God must punish sin.
   (Open hands like a Bible.)
   God must punish sin.
   The Bible tells me, so I know
   That God must punish sin.

3. Noah was safe in the ark.
   (Rock body as if in a boat.)
   Noah was safe in the ark.
   God took care of Noah,
   And Noah was safe in the ark.

5. God takes care of me.
   (Open hands like a Bible.)
   God takes care of me.
   The Bible tells me, so I know
   That God takes care of me.

There Is None that Doeth Good
(Tune: "Oh, Be Careful")

Romans 3:12b

Old Melody

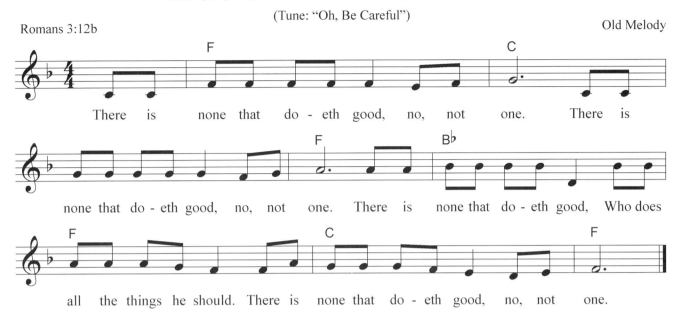

There is none that do - eth good, no, not one. There is

none that do - eth good, no, not one. There is none that do - eth good, Who does

all the things he should. There is none that do - eth good, no, not one.

There Were Twelve Disciples
(Tune: "Bringing in the Sheaves")

George A. Minor

George A. Minor

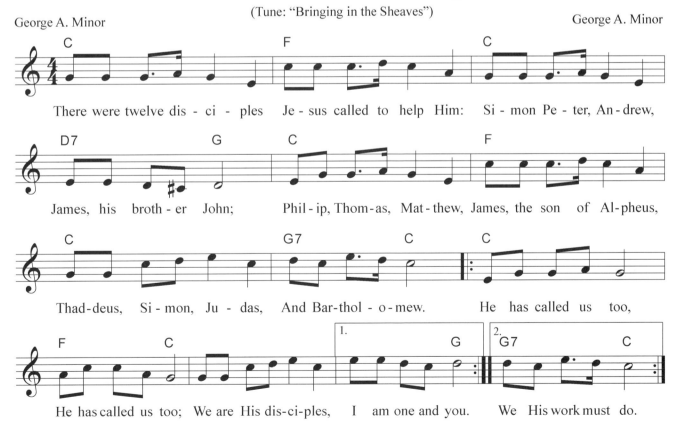

There were twelve dis - ci - ples Je - sus called to help Him: Si - mon Pe - ter, An - drew,

James, his broth - er John; Phil - ip, Thom - as, Mat - thew, James, the son of Al - pheus,

Thad - deus, Si - mon, Ju - das, And Bar - thol - o - mew. He has called us too,

He has called us too; We are His dis - ci - ples, I am one and you. We His work must do.

The Tossing Boat

(Tune: "London Bridge")

Elementary Authors

English Folksong

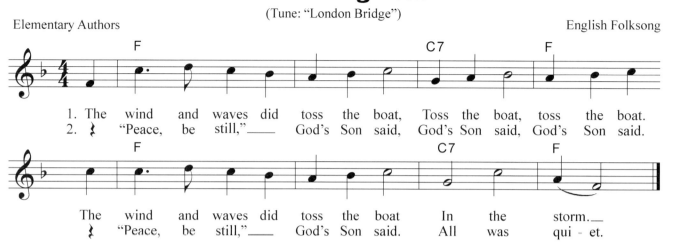

1. The wind and waves did toss the boat, Toss the boat, toss the boat.
2. "Peace, be still," ___ God's Son said, God's Son said, God's Son said.

The wind and waves did toss the boat In the storm. ___
"Peace, be still," ___ God's Son said. All was qui - et.

The Trinity

Lucille Fisher

Lucille Fisher

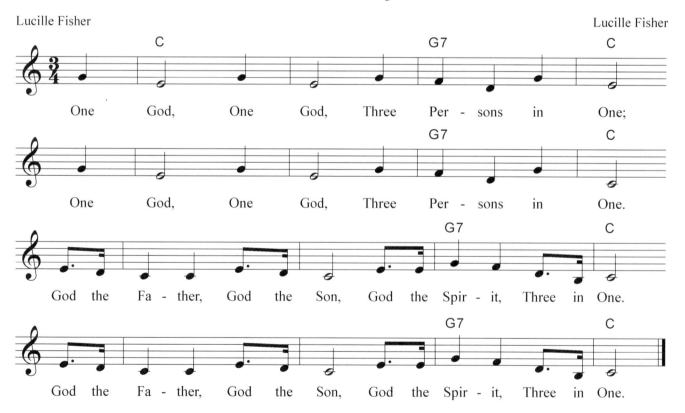

One God, One God, Three Per - sons in One;

One God, One God, Three Per - sons in One.

God the Fa - ther, God the Son, God the Spir - it, Three in One.

God the Fa - ther, God the Son, God the Spir - it, Three in One.

Songs

The Wonder Song

Grace W. Owens

Clara Lee Parker

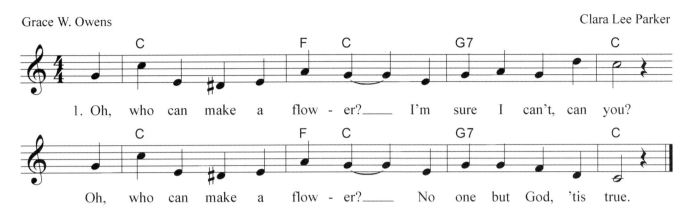

1. Oh, who can make a flow - er?___ I'm sure I can't, can you?

Oh, who can make a flow - er?___ No one but God, 'tis true.

2. Oh, who can make the raindrops?
   I'm sure I can't, can you?
   Oh, who can make the raindrops?
   No one but God, 'tis true.

3. Oh, who can make the sunshine?
   I'm sure I can't, can you?
   Oh, who can make the sunshine?
   No one but God, 'tis true.

4. Oh, who can make a butterfly?
   I'm sure I can't, can you?
   Oh, who can make a butterfly?
   No one but God, 'tis true.

5. Oh, who can make the wind blow?
   I'm sure I can't, can you?
   Oh, who can make the wind blow?
   No one but God, 'tis true.

This Is the Way We Row Our Boat

(Tune: "The Mulberry Bush")

Elementary Authors

English Folksong

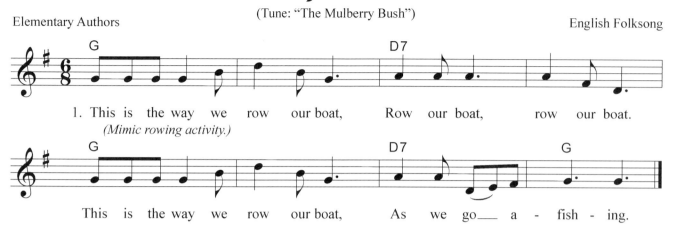

1. This is the way we row our boat,
Row our boat, row our boat.
(Mimic rowing activity.)

This is the way we row our boat,
As we go a-fish-ing.

2. This is the way we drop our net,
(Mimic throwing a net.)
Drop our net, drop our net.
This is the way we drop our net,
Over the side of the boat.

3. Let us listen to Jesus speak,
(Cup hands to ears.)
Jesus speak, Jesus speak.
Let us listen to Jesus speak;
He will help us grow.

4. We'll obey Jesus; yes, we will;
(Nod head up and down.)
Yes, we will; yes, we will.
We'll obey Jesus; yes, we will;
For He knows what is best.

Tiptoe Quietly

Muriel Murr

Muriel Murr

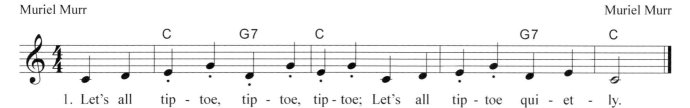

1. Let's all tip - toe, tip - toe, tip - toe; Let's all tip - toe qui - et - ly.

2. Let's go marching, marching, marching;
   Let's go marching 'round the room.

3. Let's go skipping, skipping, skipping;
   Let's go skipping 'round the room.

4. Let's go walking, walking, walking;
   Let's go walking 'round the room.

5. Let's go hopping, hopping, hopping;
   Let's go hopping 'round the room.

Alter the tempo, rhythmic pattern, and dynamic level to match the action of each stanza.

© 1984 BJU Press. All rights reserved.

Trust and Obey

John H. Sammis

Daniel B. Towner

1. When we walk with the Lord in the light of His Word, what a glo-ry He sheds on our way! While we do His good will He a-bides with us still, And with all who will trust and o-bey. Trust and o-bey, For there's no oth-er way to be hap-py in Je-sus, But to trust and o-bey.

2. Not a shadow can rise, not a cloud in the skies,
   But His smile quickly drives it away;
   Not a doubt nor a fear, not a sigh nor a tear
   Can abide while we trust and obey.

3. But we never can prove the delights of His love
   Until all on the altar we lay;
   For the favor He shows, and the joy He bestows,
   Are for them who will trust and obey.

4. Then in fellowship sweet we will sit at His feet,
   Or we'll walk by His side in the way;
   What He says we will do, where He sends we will go—
   Never fear, only trust and obey.

Trust in the Lord

Proverbs 3:5–6

Karen Wilson

Trust in the Lord with all thine heart: and lean not to thine own un-der-stand-ing.

In all thy ways ac-knowledge Him, and He shall di-rect thy paths.

What Does the Bible Say?

Muriel Murr

Muriel Murr

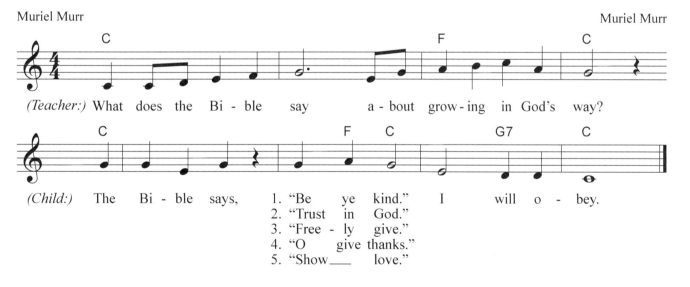

(Teacher:) What does the Bi-ble say a-bout grow-ing in God's way?

(Child:) The Bi-ble says,
1. "Be ye kind." I will o-bey.
2. "Trust in God."
3. "Free-ly give."
4. "O give thanks."
5. "Show love."

When I Am Afraid

Psalm 56:3

Muriel Murr

When I am a-fraid, I will trust in God. I will trust in God and not be a-fraid.

Where He Leads Me

Ernest W. Blandly

John S. Norris

Where He leads me I will fol-low. Where He leads me I will fol-low.

Where He leads me I will fol-low. I will fol-low, fol-low in God's way.

Where Is Jason?

(Tune: "Are You Sleeping?")

Elementary Authors

French Folksong

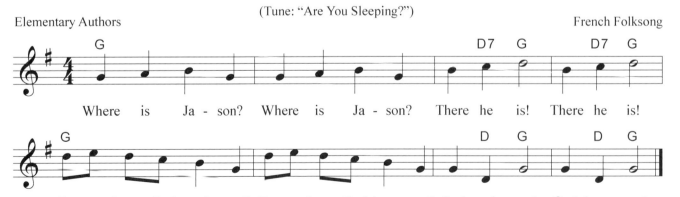

Where is Ja-son? Where is Ja-son? There he is! There he is!

Do you know God made you? Do you know God loves you? God made you! God loves you!

Whisper a Prayer

Harry Dixon Loes

Arr. by Harry Dixon Loes

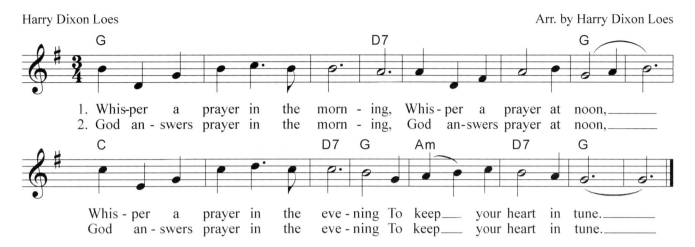

1. Whis-per a prayer in the morn - ing, Whis-per a prayer at noon,_____
2. God an - swers prayer in the morn - ing, God an-swers prayer at noon,_____

Whis - per a prayer in the eve - ning To keep___ your heart in tune._____
God an - swers prayer in the eve - ning To keep___ your heart in tune._____

Who God Is

(Tune: "London Bridge")

Elementary Authors

English Folksong

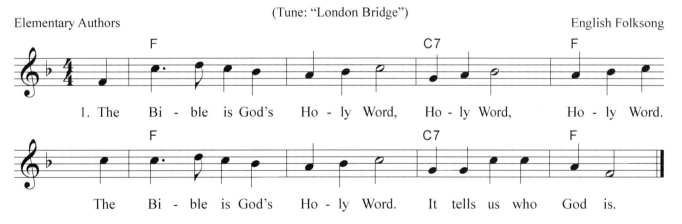

1. The Bi - ble is God's Ho - ly Word, Ho - ly Word, Ho - ly Word.

The Bi - ble is God's Ho - ly Word. It tells us who God is.

2. Jesus is God's Holy Son,
   Holy Son, Holy Son.
   Jesus is God's Holy Son.
   He shows us who God is.

3. Heav'n and earth were made by God,
   Made by God, made by God.
   Heav'n and earth were made by God.
   They show us who God is.

Words © 1987 BJU Press. All rights reserved.

Wise Men Came

(Tune: "London Bridge")

Elementary Authors

English Folksong

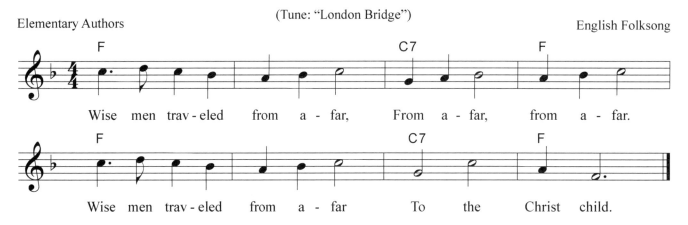

Wise men trav-eled from a-far, From a-far, from a-far.

Wise men trav-eled from a-far To the Christ child.

Zacchaeus

(Luke 19:1–10)

Anonymous

Anonymous

Zac-chae-us was a wee lit-tle man. A wee lit-tle man was

he. He climbed up in a sy-ca-more tree For the

Lord he want-ed to see; And as the Sav-ior passed that way, He

looked up in the tree, *(Spoken:)* And He said: "Zacchaeus, you come down, For I'm

go-ing to your house to-day, For I'm go-ing to your house to-day."

Index of Poetry

(listed alphabetically by title or first line)

Father, we thank Thee for the night,

"Father, We Thank Thee for the Night"
Introduced in Lesson 6

A77

And for the pleasant morning light;

"Father, We Thank Thee for the Night"
Introduced in Lesson 6

A79

For rest and food and loving care,

"Father, We Thank Thee for the Night"
Introduced in Lesson 6

A81

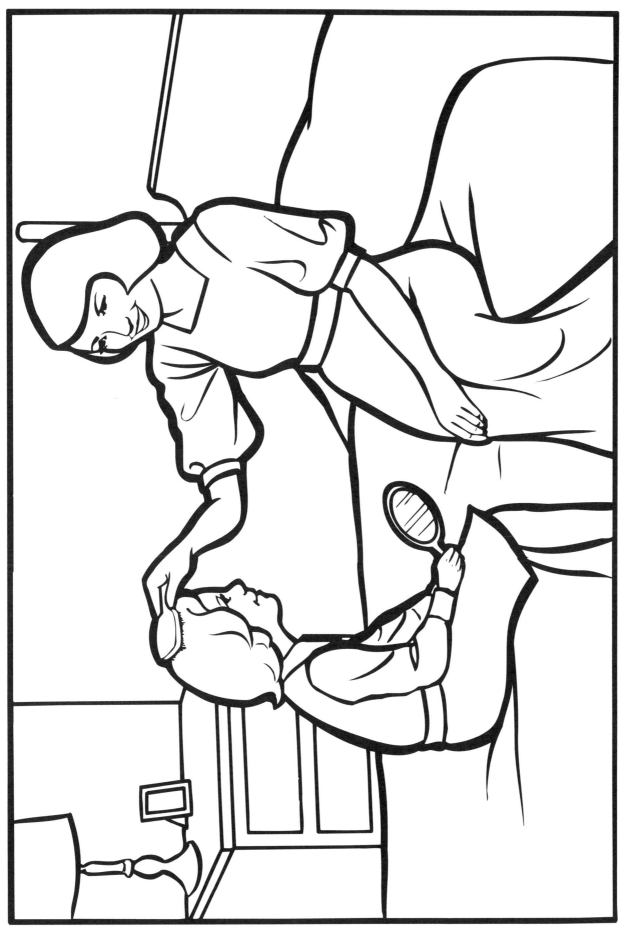

And all that makes the world so fair.

"Father, We Thank Thee for the Night"
Introduced in Lesson 6

A83

"The Wonder Song"
Introduced in Lesson 10

A85

"The Wonder Song"
Introduced in Lesson 10

A87

"The Wonder Song"
Introduced in Lesson 10

A89

"The Wonder Song"
Introduced in Lesson 10

"The Wonder Song"
Introduced in Lesson 10

A93

Seasonal Activity: Summer

Use with Lesson 10.

A95

Seasonal Activity: Fall
Use with Lesson 10.

A97

Seasonal Activity: Winter
Use with Lesson 10.

Seasonal Activity: Spring
Use with Lesson 10.

Write on an eight- or nine-inch paper plate the numerals one through six. Have the children take turns matching creation petals to corresponding creation-day numerals.

For God's Glory Visual, Day 1
Use with Lesson 14.

A103

For God's Glory Visual, Day 2
Use with Lesson 14.

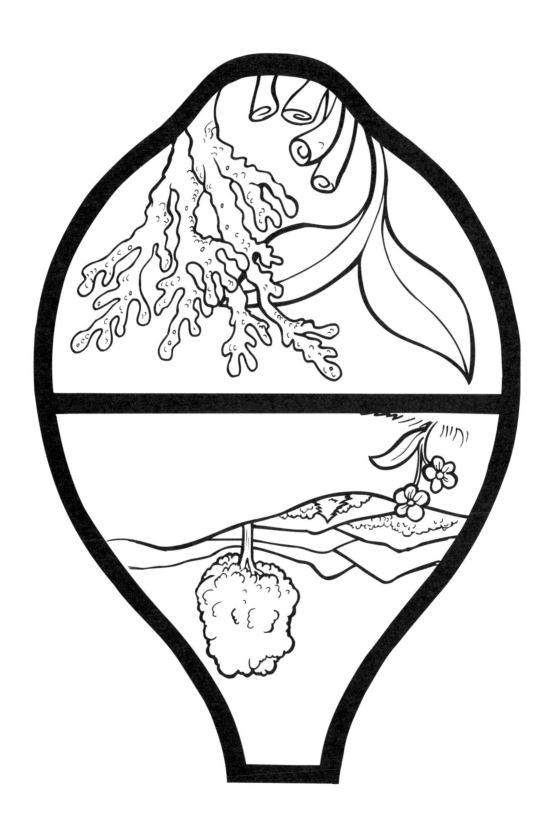

For God's Glory Visual, Day 3
Use with Lesson 14.

For God's Glory Visual, Day 4
Use with Lesson 14.

For God's Glory Visual, Day 5
Use with Lesson 14.

A111

For God's Glory Visual, Day 6
Use with Lesson 14.

A113

Trace the squirrel on cardboard or construction paper.
Cut a hole in the side of an oatmeal box. Cover the box
with burlap, brown construction paper, or wallpaper.

Squirrel Visual
Use with Lesson 18.

Back the Bible with lightweight cardboard and attach a gummed picture hook to the circle at the top of the Bible.

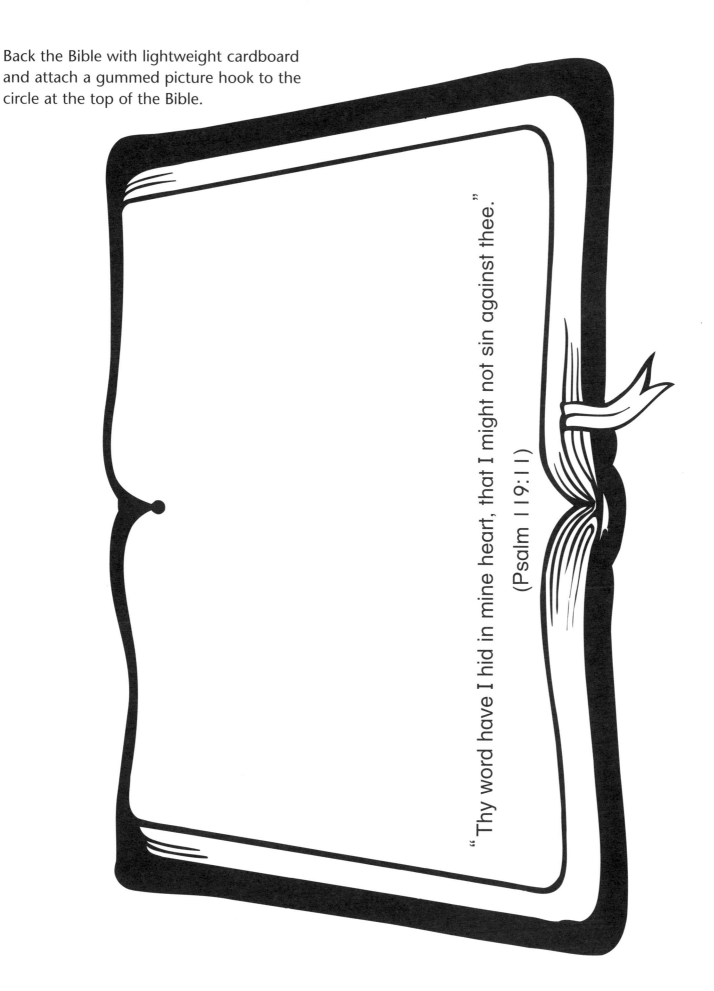

"Thy word have I hid in mine heart, that I might not sin against thee." (Psalm 119:11)

"Thy Word have I hid in mine heart" Visual
Use with Lesson 24.

A117

Copy, cut out, color, and attach to craft sticks for stick-puppet visuals, or use as flannel-board figures.

Sarai

Abram

Abram and Sarai Visuals
Use with Lesson 27.

A119

Jacob's Dream Visual, scene 1

Use with Lesson 37.

A121

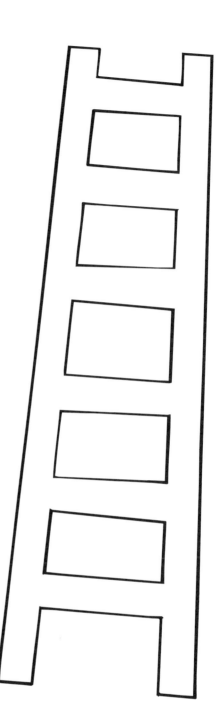

1. Color the background picture of Jacob (Appendix page A121), and mount it on lightweight cardboard.
2. Cut a piece of blue acetate (for the sky) to cover the picture from the top of the paper to the base of the mountains. Attach gummed stars to this sky flap.
3. Cut another piece of blue acetate the same size as the background picture. Add the ladder and angels (Jacob's dream) to this flap.
4. Punch holes at the top of the three pieces and hold together with book ring binders. When beginning the story, place the two top flaps behind the background picture. As you tell the story, bring forward to visualize the story action.

Jacob's Dream Visual, scenes 2 and 3

Use with Lesson 37.

HOLY BIBLE

I Thessalonians
5:18

Color and cut out pictures to make a picture wheel. Attach the pictures to the front of a large cardboard circle. Make a slightly smaller circle with one quarter cut out. Allow enough room at the center to insert a brad. See the diagram.

I Thessalonians 5:18 Visual 1
Introduced in Lesson 40

A125

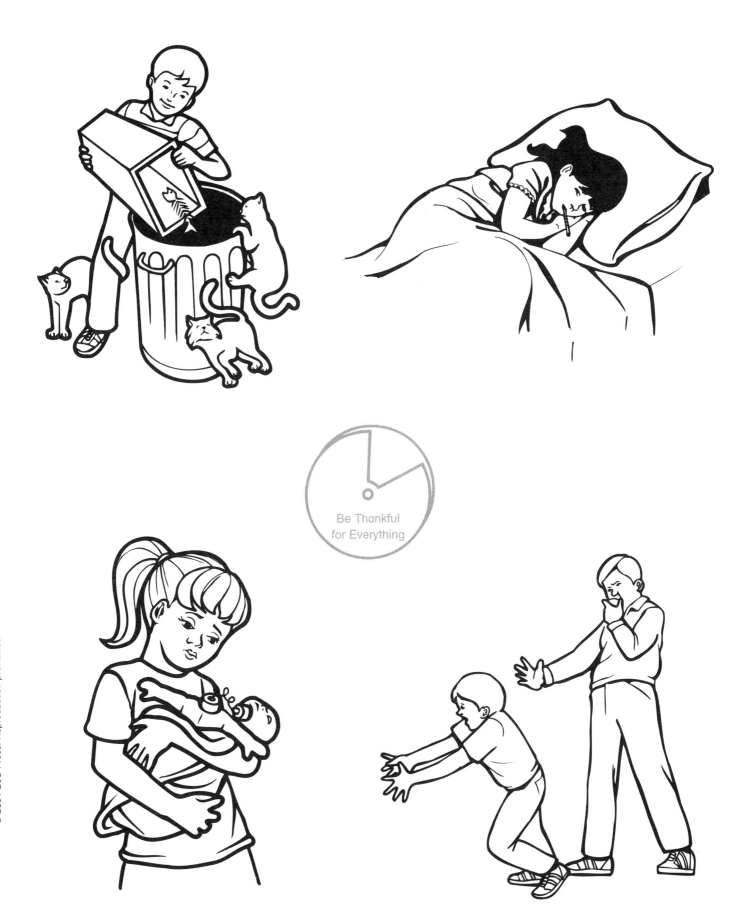

Be Thankful
for Everything

I Thessalonians 5:18 Visual 2
Introduced in Lesson 41

A127

Copy, cut out, color, and attach to craft sticks for stick-puppet visuals, or use as flannel-board figures.

Children of Israel

Moses

Aaron

Moses, Aaron, Children of Israel Visuals
Introduced in Lesson 59

Cloud

Pillar of Fire

Cloud and Pillar of Fire Visuals
Introduced in Lesson 60

A131

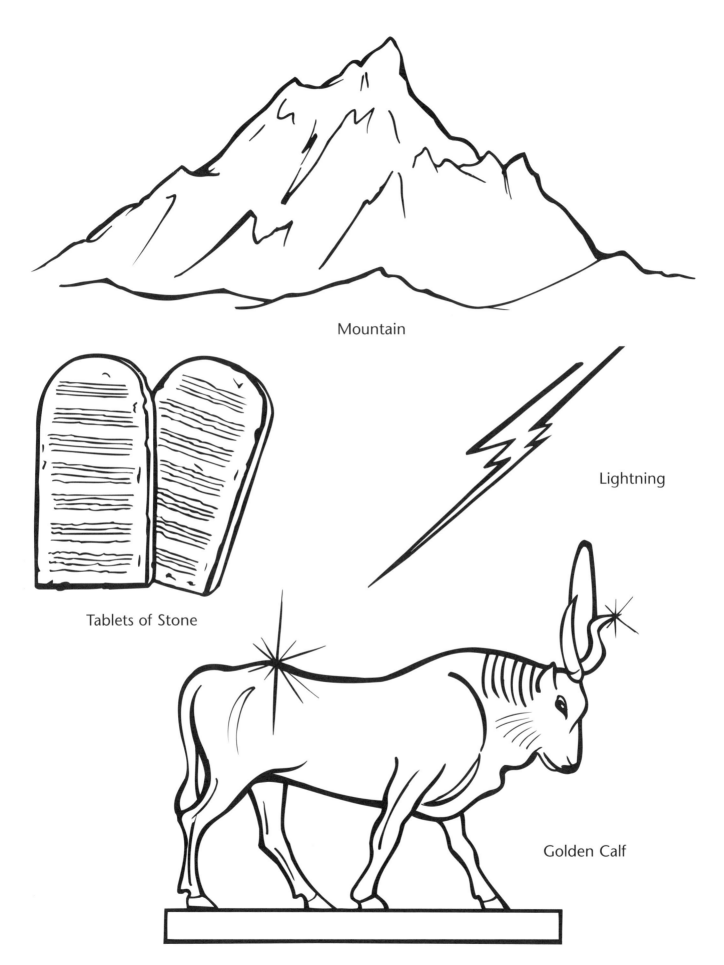

Mountain

Lightning

Tablets of Stone

Golden Calf

Mountain, Lightning, Tablets of Stone, Golden Calf Visuals
Introduced in Lesson 61

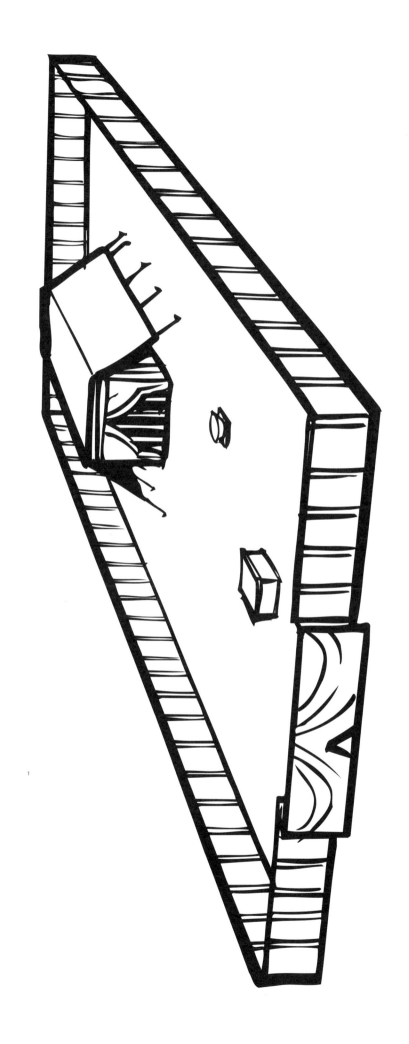

Tabernacle Visual
Use with Lesson 63.

A135

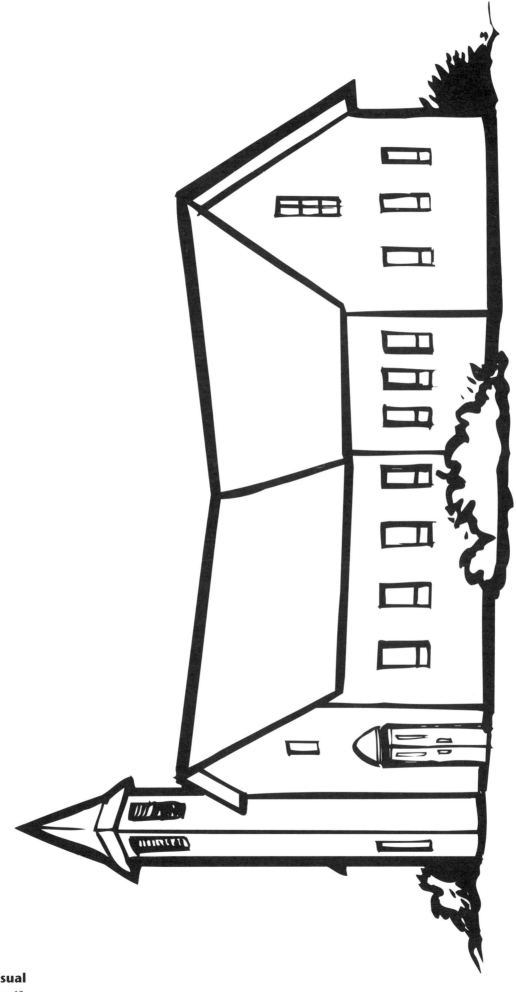

Church Visual
Use with Lesson 63.

A137

1. Trace the bell pattern four times on red construction paper.
2. Color the four pictures (See the following page.) and attach one to each bell.
3. Decorate with a colorful ribbon through the loop on the top of the bells.

John 3:16 Visual—Bell Pattern
Introduced in Lesson 74

A139

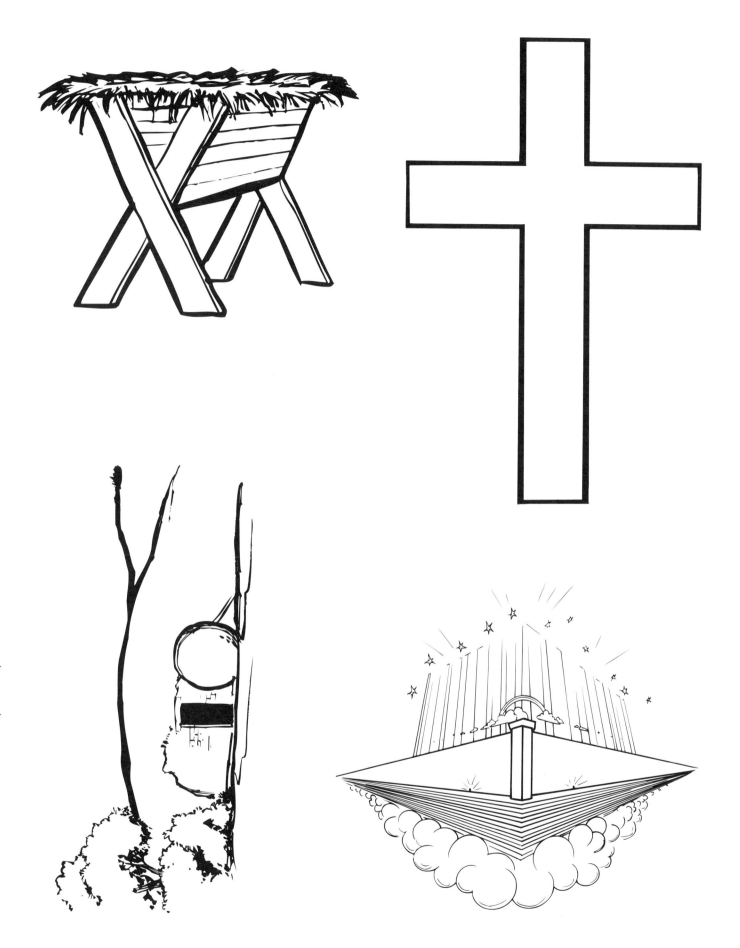

John 3:16 Visual—Manger, Cross, Open Tomb, Heaven
Introduced in Lesson 74

A141

large fish

small fish

1. Cover a shoe box inside and out with light blue construction paper (or spray the box with blue paint).

2. Place the box on its side with the uncovered top facing the children. Add a blue strip of construction paper to stand up on the front edge of the box (to represent waves in the water).

3. Cut a slit in the top (the side of the box) and in the front of the ship, large enough to slip the Jonah figure through. (See ship and Jonah figures on the following page.)

4. You may also add shells or construction-paper seaweed.

Jonah Diorama—Fish

Use with Lesson 96.

A143

Jonah

ship

Jonah Diorama—Jonah and Ship
Use with Lesson 96.

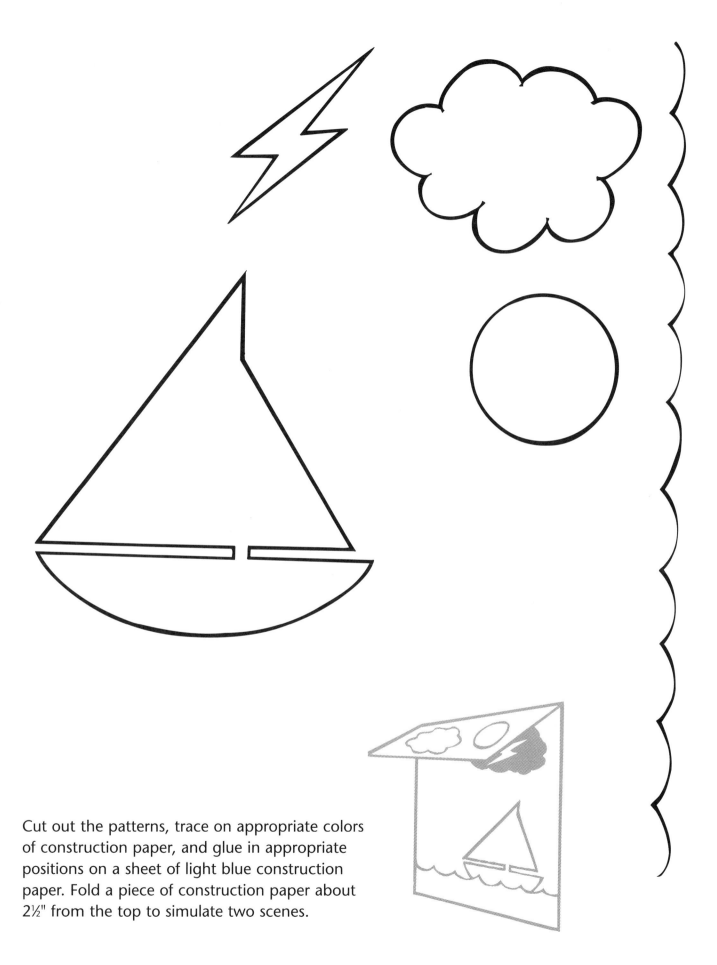

Cut out the patterns, trace on appropriate colors of construction paper, and glue in appropriate positions on a sheet of light blue construction paper. Fold a piece of construction paper about 2½" from the top to simulate two scenes.

Storm Visual
Use with Lesson 110.

A147

Bulletin Boards

Use with Unit 1.

Use with Unit 2.

God Loves Me

Use with Unit 3.

The Friend of God

Use with Unit 4.

Joseph's Dream

Use with Unit 5.

God's Leader

God Led His People

God Spoke to Moses

God Sent His Law

Use with Unit 6.

A151

God's Gifts

Use with Unit 7.

God's Best Gift

Use with Unit 8.

A152

God's Big Fish

Use with Unit 9.

God's Son

Use with Unit 10.

A153

God's Son Lives

Use with Unit 11.

God's Workers

Use with Unit 12.

God Hears Me

Use with Unit 13.

God's Plan

Use with Unit 14.

God's Children

Use with Unit 15.